REST DAYS

THE MACMILLAN COMPANY
NEW YORK · BOSTON · CHICAGO · DALLAS
ATLANTA · SAN FRANCISCO

MACMILLAN & CO., Limited
LONDON · BOMBAY · CALCUTTA
MELBOURNE

THE MACMILLAN CO. OF CANADA, Ltd.
TORONTO

REST DAYS

A Study in Early Law and Morality

BY

HUTTON WEBSTER, Ph.D.

PROFESSOR OF SOCIAL ANTHROPOLOGY IN THE UNIVERSITY OF NEBRASKA
AUTHOR OF "PRIMITIVE SECRET SOCIETIES"

"The study of their own species is doubtless the most interesting
and important that can claim the attention of mankind; and this
science, like all others, it is impossible to improve by abstract
speculation, merely. A regular series of authenticated facts is
what alone can enable us to rise towards a perfect knowledge in it."

— WILLIAM MARSDEN, *The History of Sumatra*, London, 1811, Preface.

New York

THE MACMILLAN COMPANY

1916

PREFACE

WHAT perhaps might be described as the first edition of this work appeared in 1911 in the *University Studies* of the University of Nebraska. The title of the original monograph has been retained for the present volume, in which the same line of argument is followed and the same conclusions are reached. After a lapse of nearly five years I have not felt the necessity of modifying, to any essential degree, the results of the earlier investigation. The book, then, differs from its predecessor chiefly in providing a more extensive collection of the relevant data.

Although much has been written on the Jewish Sabbath and the Christian Sunday, and on the assumed Babylonian prototype of these institutions, little inquiry has hitherto been made into the rest days so commonly observed outside the Semitic area in antiquity and later ages. The principal reason for this neglect of the comparative aspects of the subject must doubtless be found in the still imperfect appreciation of the fact that the great institutions of modern civilization have their roots in the beliefs and customs, and often in the superstitions, of savage and barbarian society. It will be the task of social anthropology, by an impressive accumulation of evidence, to make this truth a commonplace of popular knowledge.

Among the friends and correspondents who have aided me by criticisms and suggestions I wish particularly to mention Dr. Crawford H. Toy, now Professor Emeritus in Harvard University, and Dr. Louis H. Gray, now Assistant Editor of Hastings's *Encyclopædia of Religion and Ethics.* Mr. G. D. Swezey, Professor of Astronomy in the University of Nebraska, was good enough to help me in some troublesome details relating to the calendar. The late Walter Kendall Jewett, formerly University Librarian, and the kindest and most genial of men, put at my disposal many books which otherwise would have been difficult of access.   To my honoured colleague, Professor George Elliott Howard, I owe the inspiration, reaching back to undergraduate days, which comes from association with one whose devotion to scholarly ideals is matched only by his enthusiasm for social service.   Finally, I must acknowledge my obligation to Chancellor Samuel Avery, whose interest in the book has made possible its publication at this time.

HUTTON WEBSTER.

LINCOLN, NEBRASKA,
February, 1916.

CONTENTS

INTRODUCTION

CHAPTER I

TABOOED DAYS AT CRITICAL EPOCHS

CHAPTER II

Tabooed Days after a Death and on Related Occasions

CHAPTER III

Holy Days

CHAPTER VI

LUNAR CALENDARS AND THE WEEK

CHAPTER VII

THE BABYLONIAN "EVIL DAYS" AND THE SHABATTUM

CHAPTER VIII

THE HEBREW SABBATH

CHAPTER IX

UNLUCKY DAYS

CONCLUSION

REST DAYS

INTRODUCTION

THE custom of refraining from labour on certain occasions is by no means unknown to peoples in the lower stages of culture. Associated practices include the discontinuance of public gatherings, the closing of the house or of the village against all strangers, the extinguishing of lights, and fasting, either partial or complete. Bright and gay dresses may be laid aside, bathing and anointing given up, and songs, dances, and loud noises forbidden. Under these conditions the cessation of labour merges into a cessation of all the usual activities. The day of rest becomes a day of abstinence and quiescence.

It might be thought that such observances, especially those which impose a period of rest, have a rationalistic basis and arise from man's need of relaxation and idleness as a relief from daily toil and the harsh conditions of existence. Yet for the vast proportion of the rest days observed by primitive peoples it would be rash to assume an origin in considerations of practical utility. A survey of the evidence to be submitted indicates that the sabbatarian regulations have arisen chiefly, if not wholly, as pure superstitions, the product of an all-too-logical intellect or of a disordered fancy. In the last analysis they are based primarily on fear, that "fear of things invisible," which Hobbes, foreshadowing modern anthropological theories, regarded as "the natural seed of religion." [1] They find their clearest expression in the "taboos," or prohibitions, first noticed among the natives of the South Seas,

[1] *Leviathan*, chap. xi.

but now known to exist in many other regions of the aboriginal world.[1]

"Taboo," from the Polynesian *tabu*, is one of the few words which the languages of the Pacific have contributed to our English speech. *Tabu* appears to be, properly, the Tonga term, *tapu*, the word as found in Samoa, the Marquesas Islands, the Society Islands, and New Zealand, and *kapu*, the Hawaiian expression.[2] The etymology of *tapu* is uncertain, though an attempt has been made to derive it from *ta*, to mark, and *pu*, an adverb of intensity. The compound *tapu* would then mean "marked thoroughly," and would come to signify "sacred" in a secondary sense, since sacred things and places were commonly indicated in a particular manner.[3] The word *tapua'i* means "to abstain from all work, games, etc." [4] — a translation which indicates how intimately the idea of abstinence was associated with the notion of *tapu*.

In all the Polynesian languages *tapu* or *tabu* appears to have been employed with an adjectival meaning, referring to something holy, sacred, and inviolable, or to something polluted and accursed. The word, we learn, did not imply any moral quality, but expressed "a connection with the gods, or a separation from ordinary purposes, and exclusive appropriation to persons or things considered sacred; sometimes it means devoted as by a vow." [5] In a derivative sense

[1] For the leading facts relating to the institution of taboo see Sir J. G. Frazer, "Taboo," *Encyclopædia Britannica*,[9] xxiii, 15–18; *idem, Taboo and the Perils of the Soul*, London, 1911; N. W. Thomas, "Taboo," *Encyclopædia Britannica*,[11] xxvi, 337–341; L. Marillier, "Tabou," *La grande encyclopédie*, xxx, 848 *sq.*; A. Bros, *La religion des peuples non-civilisés*, Paris, 1907, pp. 185–213; C. H. Toy, *Introduction to the History of Religions*, Boston, 1913, pp. 239–264.

[2] A list of the equivalents of *tabu* in the languages of Polynesia and Melanesia will be found in William Churchill, *The Polynesian Wanderings*, Washington, 1911, pp. 263 *sq.*
[3] E. Shortland, *Traditions and Superstitions of the New Zealanders*,[2] London, 1856, p. 101.
[4] E. Tregear, *The Maori-Polynesian Comparative Dictionary*, Wellington (N.Z.), 1891, p. 472.
[5] William Ellis, *Polynesian Researches*, London, 1859, iv, 385.

tabu came naturally to signify "forbidden" or "prohibited";[1] and this is the most general meaning of the word in its anglicized form. But in anthropological usage the term "taboo" refers, not to all negative regulations or prohibitions, but to those only which are supported by a supernatural sanction and the violation of which is visited with a supernatural punishment.

The progress of comparative research has shown that conceptions very similar to the Polynesian *tabu* have a wide prevalence in the lower culture and even among peoples of archaic civilization. The Melanesian *tambu*, though never signifying any inherent holiness or awfulness, does refer to the sacred and unapproachable character which things may possess when solemnly cursed in the name of a powerful ghost or spirit.[2] Among the natives of the Gabun colony of French Equatorial Africa *orunda* meant, originally, "prohibited from human use." Under missionary hands the word developed into its related sense of "sacred to spiritual use," and in the Mpongwe Scriptures *orunda* serves as the translation of our word "holy."[3] The Malagasy equivalent of *tabu* is *fady*, which means, primarily, "dangerous," but which has the derivative meanings *sacré*, "prohibited," "ill-omened," "unlucky."[4] Anthropologically, it is no far cry from such expressions to the Greek ἅγιος or to the Latin *sacer*, since each of these terms conveys the twin ideas of sanctity and pollution.[5]

[1] The proper term for "prohibit" was *rahui* (*ibid.*, iv, 386).

[2] R. H. Codrington, *The Melanesians*, Oxford, 1891, p. 215. In the Banks Islands and in the New Hebrides the word *rongo* is employed to indicate the naturally holy character which certain objects may possess, quite independently of any human sanction or prohibition (*ibid.*, p. 181).

[3] R. H. Nassau, *Fetichism in West Africa*, London, 1904, p. 80.

[4] A. van Gennep, *Tabou et totémisme à Madagascar*, Paris, 1904, pp. 12 *sqq.*, 23.

[5] As Sir James Frazer has pointed out (*Encyclopædia Britannica*,[9] xxiii, 18), the Greeks usually discriminated the two ideas, ἅγιος being devoted to the sense of "sacred" and ἐναγής to that of "unclean" or "accursed." The two words, of course, have no connection, ἅγιος being related to Skt. *yaj-*, "sacrifice" and ἐναγής to

It is convenient to distinguish between taboos which are artificially imposed and those which follow inevitably as the consequence of particular acts or as the outcome of certain situations. Thus, a chief may set a taboo over the common crops until harvest time, or a private individual may protect his own property through the use of the same supernatural machinery: these are prohibitions analogous to the laws of an advanced society, though supported by sanctions both human and divine. On the other hand, new-born children with their mothers, strangers, manslayers, and mourners are frequently subjected to taboos which exist in the social consciousness rather as well-defined customs of anonymous origin than as specific ordinances laid down by some superior authority. In both cases, however, it is legitimate to suppose that a reason has always existed for the ascription of the *tabu* character to persons and things — although an explanation may not now be forthcoming and although the ideas on which the practice was once based may have become obscure or meaningless with the lapse of time.

A comparative study of the taboos observed by primitive peoples indicates that originally things or persons are tabooed because they are considered dangerous, mysterious, abnormal, uncanny, "awful" — because they are felt to be potent for weal or woe in the life of man. Primitive psychology, refining these ideas and applying them to different classes of phenomena, produces the cognate notions of pollution and sanctity. The corpse is unclean; the shedder of human blood is likewise unclean; but the chief or king, who belongs

---

Skt. *āgas-*, "sin" (E. Boisacq, *Dictionnaire étymologique de la langue grecque*, Heidelberg and Paris, 1907, pt. i, 7, 9). Among the Romans *sacer* always continued to retain the double meaning; it may be closely rendered by *tabu*. Compare Servius on Vergil, *Æneis*, iii, 75. The late W. Robertson Smith referred to the fact that the Hebrew *ṭāmē* "is not the ordinary word for things physically foul; it is a ritual term and corresponds exactly to the idea of taboo" (*Kinship and Marriage in Early Arabia*, London, 1903, p. 309). For a list of Biblical passages containing *ṭāmē* see Brown, Driver, and Briggs, *A Hebrew and English Lexicon of the Old Testament*, Boston, 1906, p. 379.

to a superior order of beings, is sacrosanct or holy. These characteristics are easily regarded as infectious, as capable of transmission, not alone by physical contact, but also by sight and mere proximity. It is probably true that, in using such expressions as "contagion" and "infection," we are resorting to a refined terminology to express what must be really simpler in the thought of the savage. Living in a mental stage where distinctions of cause and effect are not clearly drawn, where a rigid distinction of the natural and the supernatural can scarcely be said to exist at all, he finds no difficulty in imagining an universe in which all things have power, after their kind, a power for good or a power for ill — in other words, have *mana*. This now-familiar Melanesian term, like the Algonkin *manitou*, the Iroquoian *orenda*, and the Siouan *wakanda*, may be said to express early man's sense of those ever-present, though vague and impersonal, forces immanent in nature.[1]

At the same time the fact must be recognized that the majority of taboos are now supported by animistic beliefs of a much more precise character. The penalty for the infraction of a taboo is generally death or some physical ailment supposed to be inflicted by the offended spirits or demons.[2] The Polynesian *atua*, by entering the body of any impious person, caused disease or "intestinal embarrassment": the culprit forthwith swelled up and died. The same demonic beings, if angered, might visit entire tribes with an epidemic, or send down lightning and fire from heaven, or bring about the unsuccessful issue of a war.[3] Among the

---

[1] The notion of transmissibility has been especially developed by such writers as A. E. Crawley, *The Mystic Rose*, London, 1902, *passim*, Hubert and Mauss, "Esquisse d'une théorie générale de la magie," *L'année sociologique*, 1904, vii, 108 *sqq.*; F. B. Jevons, *An Introduction to the History of Religion*,[4] London, 1908, pp. 59–68, and R. Marett, *The Threshold of Religion*,[2] London, 1914, pp. 99–121.

[2] On the general belief in the omnipresence of demons and their action in causing human ills see Sir J. G. Frazer, *The Scapegoat*, London, 1913, pp. 72–108.

[3] J. S. Polack, *Manners and Customs of the New Zealanders*, London, 1840, i, 234.

Kayan and other pagan tribes of Borneo the minor
spirits, or *toh*, play a considerable part in the regulation of conduct. They are the powers that bring
misfortunes upon an entire house or village when any
member of it ignores taboos or otherwise violates
tribal customs, without performing the propitiatory
rites demanded by the occasion. "Thus on them,
rather than on the gods, are founded the effective
sanctions of prohibitive rules of conduct."[1] Among
the Akikuyu of British East Africa, who possess a most
elaborate system of taboos, it is a general belief that
any one in the condition of *thahu* becomes emaciated
and ill or breaks out in eruptions and boils. If the
thahu is not removed, the patient will die. "In many
cases this undoubtedly happens by the process of auto-
suggestion, as it never occurs to the Kikuyu mind to be
skeptical in a matter of this kind. It is said that the
thahu condition is caused by the *ngoma*, or spirits of
departed ancestors, but the process does not seem to
have been analyzed any further."[2] The Babylonians,
again, appear to have entertained very definite conceptions of taboo, and conceptions, equally definite,
of the evil spirits which vexed the soul and body of
one who had infringed a *mamit*, or prohibition with a
supernatural penalty.[3] With the progress of religious
conceptions the punishment of the taboo-breaker
may come to be regarded as an important function
of the tribal or national god, whose chief concern is the
maintenance of the customary moral rules.

Since persons, objects, and even actions are all
liable to infection, prudence dictates a variety of precautions: the dangerous individual or thing is removed
to a safe distance; or is carefully isolated; or is subjected to a series of insulating regulations. The en-

[1] Hose and McDougall, *The Pagan Tribes of Borneo*, London, 1912, i, 26.

[2] C. W. Hobley, "Kikuyu Customs and Beliefs. *Thahu* and its Connection with Circumcision Rites," *Journal of the Royal Anthropological Institute*, 1910, xl, 428.

[3] R. C. Thompson, *The Devils and Evil Spirits of Babylonia*, London, 1904, ii, pp. xxxix *sqq*.

tire community is interested in such proceedings, and on certain occasions may itself be placed under a rigid quarantine. When this happens, a period of abstinence and quiescence is regarded as the surest means of avoiding dangers felt to threaten each and every member of the social group. Nor will the procedure greatly differ where distinctly animistic ideas prevail, and when the impending danger is specifically attributed to the action of spiritual beings or of gods. In the latter case, it is true, the idea of propitiation becomes increasingly prominent, since it is often felt to be necessary to appease by various rites and ceremonies the supernatural powers responsible for the visitation. The two conceptions of abstinence and propitiation are not, indeed, always sharply distinguishable in concrete cases, and with advancing culture they tend to become more and more closely conjoined.

It is highly probable that the origin of some of the communal regulations is to be sought in the taboos observed by persons at such great and critical seasons as birth, puberty, marriage, and death.[1] Comparative studies have indicated how numerous are the prohibitions which attach to these times of high solemnity and significance; and it is reasonable to suppose that, with the deepening sense of social solidarity, observances once confined to the individual alone, or to his immediate connections, would often pass over into rites performed by the community at large. Some evidence tending to substantiate this opinion will be presented incidentally as the investigation proceeds.

[1] For an extensive presentation of the ethnographic evidence see Sir J. G. Frazer, *Taboo and the Perils of the Soul*, London, 1911, pp. 131–223; *idem, Balder the Beautiful*, London, 1913, i, 22–100, ii, 225–278. The whole subject is most suggestively treated by Professor A. van Gennep, *Les rites de passage*, Paris, 1909.

CHAPTER I

OUR knowledge of taboo within the Polynesian area rests chiefly on the vague and unsatisfactory accounts by early missionaries, who were unable to describe much more than its exterior aspects, its origin and inner significance having quite escaped their consideration. Fundamentally, the system of taboos formed a religious institution, if religion be understood in its broadest sense as a recognition of the supernatural. The Polynesian belief that the violator of a taboo would be punished by the offended *atua*, or spirits, readily lent itself to priestcraft and statecraft and so became in the hands of the ruling classes an *instrumentum regni*, a powerful engine of social and political control. In Hawaii, where the superstitions in question reached their most elaborate and grotesque development, communal taboos could be imposed only by the priests, although this action was often taken at the instance of the civil authorities. Police officers were even appointed to make sure that all prohibitions were strictly observed. For every breach of the rules the death penalty was inflicted, unless the delinquent had some very powerful friends who themselves were either priests or chiefs.

The range of these Hawaiian taboos, as extended for reasons of state or religion, was very wide. We are told that idols, temples, the persons and names of the king and his family, the persons of the priests, and the houses and clothes of the king and priests were always *tabu*. Certain much-prized articles of food, besides almost everything offered in sacrifice, were reserved

8

by taboos for gods and men; hence women, except in cases of particular indulgence, were restricted from using them. Sometimes an entire island or district was tabooed and no one was allowed to approach it.[1]

The institution of taboo also included regulations for the special observance of certain times and seasons. Their duration was various, and apparently much longer in remote ages than in the period immediately preceding the arrival of the missionaries. In Hawaii, before the reign of Kamehameha II, forty days was the usual length of time. There were also periods of ten days and of five days, and sometimes of only one day. Tradition declares, however, that once a taboo was in force for thirty years and that during this time the men were not allowed to trim their beards. A tabooed period kept for five years is also mentioned. Elsewhere in the South Seas less extensive periods prevailed, the longest known being at Huahine, one of the Society Islands, where a season of abstinence is said to have lasted for ten or twelve years.[2]

The observance of such taboos varied according as they were common or strict. When a common season prevailed, the men were required only to abstain from their usual duties and to attend at the *heiau*, or temple, where prayers were offered every morning and evening. During a period strictly tabooed the regulations had a sterner character, and in consequence a general gloom and silence pervaded the whole district or island. Every fire and light was extinguished; canoes were not launched; no person bathed; and no one was to be seen out of doors, save those whose presence was required at the temple. Even the lower creation felt the force of the law: "no dog must bark, no pig must grunt, no cock must crow — or the *tabu* would be broken, and fail to accomplish the object designed. On these occasions they tied up the mouths

[1] Ellis, *Polynesian Researches,* iv, 387 *sqq.*
[2] *Idem, Narrative of a Tour through Hawaii or Owhyhee,* London, 1826, p. 366; *idem, Polynesian Researches,* iv, 387 *sq.*; J. J. Jarves, *History of the Hawaiian or Sandwich Islands,*[2] Boston, 1843, p. 57.

of the dogs and pigs, and put the fowls under a cala-
bash, or fastened a piece of cloth over their eyes."[1]
From another account we learn that any one found in
a canoe on a *tabu* day incurred the death penalty, and
that the same Draconian punishment was meted out
to the individual who indulged in carnal pleasures
or made only a noise at such a time.[2]

The sabbatarian regulations introduced by Christian missionaries among their Hawaiian adherents
presented no sharp contrast to the rigours of the old dis-
pensation. The natives even called Sunday *la tabu*,
"the tabooed day." No food was cooked on that
day, the meals being all prepared on the previous
Saturday; no fires were kindled; and no canoes
were paddled. The people neither fished nor tilled the
soil and, if on a journey, they halted until the sacred
day was over.[3] In Tahiti, also, the Sunday rest was
rigidly maintained. On that day no canoes were
launched, and no person was seen abroad except on the
road to church or when returning from divine service.
The success of the missionaries in introducing this
strict observance of Sunday was, we learn, "ascribed
by themselves in a great degree to its analogy to the
taboo days of heathen times."[4]

[1] Ellis, *Narrative*, pp. 366 *sq.*; compare *idem*, *Polynesian Researches*, iv, 388.

[2] H. T. Cheever, *The Island World of the Pacific*, Glasgow [1851], p. 63.

[3] Ellis, *Narrative*, p. 368; Hiram Bingham, *A Residence of Twenty-one Years in the Sandwich Islands*, Hartford, 1849, pp. 177 *sq.* Describing his experiences at Kihoro, the missionary Ellis could not restrain his admiration of the conduct of the native converts on Sunday: "No athletic sports were seen on the beach; no noise of playful children shouting as they gambolled in the surf, nor distant sound of the cloth-beating mallet was heard through the day; no persons were seen carrying burdens in or out of the village, nor any canoes passing across the bay. It could not but be viewed as the dawn of a bright sabbatic day for the dark shores of Hawaii" (*Polynesian Researches*, iv, 408). For similar statements see C. S. Stewart, *A Visit to the South Seas*, London, 1832, pp. 277 *sqq.*, 302 *sq.*

[4] Charles Wilkes, *Narrative of the U.S. Exploring Expedition*, Philadelphia, 1845, ii, 13. "The *tabu* system," wrote an early missionary, "making sacred certain times, persons, and places, and containing many restrictions and prohibitions, may easily be interpreted

Communal taboos were observed by the Hawaiian Islanders generally in connection with important religious ceremonies. Of these, one of the most elaborate was the consecration of a *luakini*, or chief temple. The rites, which were often performed just before a war in order to insure victory, occupied ten or more days. After a solemn purification of the island or district all the people were summoned to divine service, during which a priest sprinkled them with holy water, *i.e.*, salt water mixed with a little turmeric, some moss, and a bunch of a sacred fern. "The next thing in order was to bring down the principal idol, called the *hakuohia*, from the forest. A great procession was formed, consisting of the king, the *hakuohia* priest, and a crowd of attendants carrying idols and various offerings, and leading a human victim. The tree had been selected and the axe consecrated the day before. On arriving at the tree, the priest recited the appropriate *aha* [prayer] amid dead silence, after which the king pronounced the *amama* [spell], and killed the hog with a single blow. The priest inquired whether any sound of man or beast or bird or cricket had been heard during the *aha*, and if not, it was a good omen. The doomed man was then brought forward, and offered to the god by the king, after which his body was buried at the foot of the tree. The consecrated hog was baked in an oven on the spot, while the tree was cut down, trimmed, and covered with *ieie* vines. After the company had feasted, a procession was formed with the feather-gods in front, followed by the chiefs and people

as a relic, much changed and corrupted, from the ancient ceremonial observances of the Jews" (Sheldon Dibble, *History of the Sandwich Islands*, Lahainaluna, 1843, p. 27). The resemblances between the Polynesian institution and certain customs recorded in the Old Testament impressed another early writer, who refers to taboo as "ce singulier usage, en partie politique, au moins dans quelques-uns de ses effets, mais éminemment religieux dans son origine, non moins que l'interdit des Hébreux, avec lequel il avait des rapports frappans, qui n'ont point encore été signalés, quoique méritant assurément toute l'attention du philosophe . et du moraliste" (J. A. Moerenhout, *Voyages aux îles du grand océan*, Paris, 1837, ii, 6).

with *pala* fern, *ohia*-branches, etc., and others carrying the new idol. . . . The inhabitants remained indoors, for it was death to meet the procession, and all fires were strictly forbidden. The images were finally carried to the *heiau*, where they were deposited with shoutings and beating of drums." [1] Following this rite came a long series of services at the *heiau*. The night of the great *aha* "was the most solemn and critical of all. The omens were carefully observed, and prayers were offered in every house for the success of the coming· *aha*, and for auspicious weather, that there might be no wind or rain, no thunder or lightning, no high surf, and no sound of man or beast to mar the ceremonies. If the sky was clear and everything favourable, between midnight and morning the king and high-priest entered the small house, called *waiea*, to perform the great *aha* (*hulahula*), while the congregation sat in front of the *mana* house, listening and watching in profound silence. The king stood listening intently and holding a pig, while the high-priest, clad in white *kapa*, and holding a *lama* rod wound with *aloa* (white *kapa*), recited the long prayer. At its close the king killed the pig with a single blow, and offered it up with a short prayer to the four great gods. The priests then asked the king whether the *aha* was perfect, and whether he had heard the voice of man or dog or mouse or fowl, or anything else during the prayer. If not, he tapped the large drum as a signal that it was over, and they both went out to question the assembly outside. If no one had heard a sound during the ceremony, the high-priest congratulated the king, and predicted for him victory and long life. The people then raised loud shouts of *Lele wale ka aha e!* which were repeated by all who heard them, and so the news travelled far and wide." [2] Such were

---

[1] W. D. Alexander, *A Brief History of the Hawaiian People*, New York, 1899, p. 55. The author's work is based largely on unpublished Hawaiian manuscripts and the early archives of the government.

[2] Alexander, *op. cit.*, pp. 56 *sq.* Elsewhere this excellent authority describes the Hawaiian prayers as

some of the ceremonies at the dedication of an important temple.[1]

Communal taboos also marked the celebration by the Hawaiians of the great *makahiki*, or New Year's festival, sacred to the god Lono. On the twenty-third of the month Welehu, which nearly corresponded to November, Lono's image was decorated and, when night came on, all the people went to bathe in the sea. This rite of purification having been accomplished, men and women donned new clothing in preparation for the festival which began at sunrise on the morrow. During the four days of its continuance no fishing, no bathing, no pounding of *kapa*, and no beating of drums or blowing of conchs was permitted. Land and sky and sea were *tabu* to Lono, and only feasting and games were allowed. The high-priest was blindfolded and remained in seclusion. On the fifth day the bandage was removed from his eyes and canoes were allowed to put to sea. On the sixth day the *tabu* season began again and continued for about twenty days longer. The festivities at length drew to a close, the ornaments of Lono's image were packed up and deposited in the temple for use another year, and all restrictions on fishing and farming were taken off — *noa ka makahiki.*[2]

in some measure magical incantations, which, to secure the desired effect, required to be repeated without the slightest mistake. "During the most important class of prayers, called *aha*, it was necessary that absolute silence should be preserved, as the least noise would break the spell and destroy the whole effect of the charm" (*ibid.*, p. 50). A similar precaution, as is well known, characterized the ritual of a Roman sacrifice.

[1] For additional data on this subject see Jarves, *op. cit.*, pp. 51 *sq.*, and David Malo, *Hawaiian Antiquities*, Honolulu, 1903, pp. 210–248. The latter work,

translated from the Hawaiian by N. B. Emerson, is an exceptionally valuable repository of native lore.

[2] Alexander, *op. cit.*, pp. 59 *sqq.*; Malo, *op. cit.*, pp. 186–210. This New Year's festival with its accompanying taboo is also referred to in an early work entitled *Voyage of H.M.S. Blonde to the Sandwich Islands in the Years 1824–1825*, London, 1826, pp. 11 *sq.* According to A. Fornander (*An Account of the Polynesian Race*, London, 1878, i, 119 *sq.*) the Hawaiian year consisted of twelve 30-day months with five additional *tabu* days intercalated at the end of Welehu.

In old Hawaii, as in the other Polynesian islands, fishing formed one of the chief means of livelihood and ranked next to agriculture in importance. The fishermen, who composed almost a distinct class, observed many religious rites peculiar to themselves. For instance, a man would not venture to use a new net or to build and launch a new canoe, without prayer and sacrifice to his gods. Communal regulations relating to fishing were imposed twice a year in connection with two sacred fish, the *aku*, or bonito, and the *opelu*. Each was *tabu* by turns for six months. In Hinaiaelee (July) the taboo began on the first night of the month, at which time no fire might be kindled, and no sound of man or beast or fowl might break the profound silence. The following morning the high-priest repaired to the house of Ku-ula, the god of fishermen, to offer a pig and to recite the great *aha*, as during a dedication. Meanwhile a man was sent to the woods to gather *pala* fern. All that day a solemn rest was observed on shore. Next morning the head fisherman, wearing a white *malo*, or girdle, took the sacred fern and a new net in his canoe and put to sea. After prayers to his tutelary deities and to Ku the fisherman proceeded to cast the net. If he and his crew made a haul of *opelu*, they paddled joyfully for the shore and presented the fish to the high-priest, who sent some to the king and placed the rest on the altar in the temple. Next day the *opelu* became *noa*, or free to all, but the *aku* in its turn was prohibited to human use for six months, and was not to be eaten on pain of death.[1]

The Hawaiian religious system included a remarkable approximation to the institution of a weekly Sabbath. In every lunar month there were four *tabu* periods, dedicated severally to the four great gods of

If this statement be correct, the Hawaiian epagomenal days would furnish a remarkable parallel to those of the ancient Mexicans and Egyptians (below, pp. 279 *sqq.*). But the best authorities agree that the Hawaiian year was strictly lunar, with months of 29 and 30 days in alternation and an occasional intercalary month.

[1] Alexander, *op. cit.*, pp. 52 *sq.*, 62 *sq.*

the native pantheon. The first was that of Ku, from the third to the sixth night; the second, that of Hua, at full moon, including the fourteenth and fifteenth nights; the third, that of Kaloa, on the twenty-fourth and twenty-fifth nights; and the fourth, that of Kane, on the twenty-seventh and twenty-eighth nights. During these *tabu* periods a devout king generally remained in the *heiau*, busy with prayer and sacrifice. Women at such times were forbidden to enter canoes, and sexual intercourse was also prohibited.[1]

The occasions when seasons of communal abstinence and quiescence were enforced in the Society Islands, the Marquesas Islands, Samoa, and New Zealand were not always the same as in the Hawaiian group. Divergencies of custom might well be expected among the widely scattered divisions of the Polynesian race. But, if such rites as those for the dedication of a temple or for the observance of four *tabu* periods in every month were confined to the Hawaiians, some other ceremonies, notably those connected with fishing, were much alike throughout the entire Pacific area.

In the Society and the Marquesas islands the bonito fishing in November or December opened with a ceremony removing the prohibition which had previously rested on the capture of that fish. A strict taboo of all activity marked the first day of the proceedings: no one could approach the seashore, or make a fire, or cook food, or even eat before the going-down of the sun. The customary employments of the men in canoe-building and house-building, of the women in the preparation of cloths, mats, and thread, were aban-

---

[1] *Ibid.*, pp. 50 *sqq.*; Dibble, *op. cit.*, 25 *sq.*; Malo, *op. cit.*, p. 56. The latter authority, a native writer intimately versed in Hawaiian antiquities, declares that the seasons of taboo were not observed during the four *makahiki* months of the year, when the regular religious services were suspended for games and ceremonies in honour of the god Lono. The same point is made by Judge Fornander (*op. cit.*, i, 123 *n.*[5]), whose information was derived from the Hon. S. M. Kamakau, an intelligent Hawaiian, born and brought up under the heathen *régime*. On these Hawaiian Sabbaths see below, pp. 88, 188, 233, 258, 303.

doned; "in a word, all work was forbidden; it was a
day of silence and of devotion." Meanwhile the priests
remained in the *marai*, or temple, engaged in prayer;
and their assistants prepared an altar to receive the
first-fruits of the fishing. At nightfall the single canoe
which had gone forth to the fishing returned with the
catch of bonito. Several of the largest fish were
placed on the altar, and the others were entirely con-
sumed in a blazing fire before the altar. The fish
caught on this day belonged to the gods and those on
the following day to the high-priest; but on the third
day fishing was opened to all.[1] Among the Maori
of New Zealand the preparations for mackerel fishing included the observance of various taboos. Every
one concerned in making or mending nets, the ground
where the nets were made, and the river, on the banks
of which the work went on, were in a state of sacredness.
Nobody might walk over the ground, no canoe might
pass up and down the river, no fire might be made
within a prescribed distance, and no food might be
prepared, until the holy season came to an end.[2] In
this instance only fishermen and their assistants appear
to have been subject to the restrictions. The Maori,
however, observed communal taboos in connection
with the planting of the *kumara*, or sweet potato,
formerly the most important agricultural product of
New Zealand and the chief reliance of the natives for
food. An old chief of Mokoia Island, Lake Rotorua,
has described how, when the time to plant *kumara*
arrived, the priests went forth to the woods for branches
of the sacred *mapau* tree. "On that day and the day
following, everything was *tapu*. The people fasted and
did no cooking. The waters of the lake were *tapu*;
no canoes were allowed to put out and no fishing was

[1] J. A. Moerenhout, *Voyages aux îles du grand océan*, Paris, 1837, i, 516 *sq*. See further Mathias G— [Garcia] (*Lettres sur les îles Marquises*, Paris, 1843, p. 210), who refers to the first day of fish-ing as "un jour de silence et de repos, *tapu* pour ceux qui restent à la maison."

[2] William Yate, *An Account of New Zealand*, London, 1835, p. 85.

done." The priests took the *mapau* twigs to the stone image of the *kumara*-god (still kept on the island), and laying them on the idol, prayed for an abundant harvest. In the evening they went to the gardens and stuck the branches in the earth. The skull of a tribal chief of *ariki* rank was disinterred and placed beside the *mapau* sticks, in order that the *mana*, or magical power of the dead chieftain, might guard the plantation and assist in securing a bountiful harvest.[1]

Still another critical epoch when the Maori subjected themselves to communal taboos occurred at the beginning of a war. Hostilities having been decided on, the first thing necessary was to take the auspices by casting the *niu*. One of the leading priests procured a quantity of fern-stalks, some of which represented spears, and the remainder, warriors. The warrior-sticks were stuck in a mat and a fern-stalk was hurled at each one. If the missile fell on the left side of the warrior-stick, this was a sign that the person whom it represented would fall in battle, if on the right side, that he would live. A similar procedure was enacted with sticks named for enemies, and for the men, women, and children who were to be left at home. On the completion of the *niu* ceremony, the priests lifted the taboo which had rested over the settlement, a taboo imposing abstinence from food, but not, apparently, from work.[2]

[1] James Cowan, *The Maoris of New Zealand*, Melbourne and London, 1910, pp. 116 *sq.* The *kumara* crop was sacred, all persons engaged in its cultivation were temporarily tabooed, and the offering of the first-fruits of the *kumara* formed a very solemn religious ceremony (E. Tregear, in *Journal of the Anthropological Institute*, 1890, xix, 110). Compare Richard Taylor, *Te Ika A Maui*, London, 1855, p. 57.

[2] E. Tregear, in *Journal of the Anthropological Institute*, 1890, xix, 110. No food might be cooked on the day before a war-party set out (*ibid.*, p. 108). Mr. Tregear, an excellent authority, declares that in New Zealand "there were no long periods of silence such as the kings of Hawaii laid on their people by proclaiming *tapu*" (*ibid.*, p. 122). Another writer assures us that the Maori "had no days more sacred than others" (Taylor, *op. cit.*, p. 92). Yet in one part of New Zealand it was customary to celebrate the new year with a *karakia*, or magical incantation and prayer;

c

The sacrifice of first-fruits seems to have formed a regular part of the religious system of the Polynesian peoples, for we possess specific references to it among the Hawaiians, the Samoans, the New Zealanders, the natives of the Society Islands, and those of the Tonga Islands. In the latter group the ceremony, called *inachi*, generally took place about October. It was observed with scrupulous care, since the people believed that to neglect it would bring upon them the vengeance of the gods. We are fortunate in possessing a detailed description of the ceremony by an eye-witness of it.[1] According to William Mariner the word *inachi* referred to that portion of the fruits of the earth and of other eatables which was offered to the god in the person of the divine chief Tooitonga, an allotment made once a year, just before the yam crop had arrived at maturity. On the day before the ceremony the first-fruits of the yam season were dug up, ornamented with ribbons, and dyed red, in preparation for the procession on the morrow. "The sun has scarcely set when the sound of the conch begins again to echo through the island, increasing as the night advances. At the *mooa* [capital] and all the plantations the voices of men and women are heard singing *Nófo, óooa tegger gnaoóe, óooa gnaoóe,* 'Rest thou, doing no work; thou shalt not work.'"[2] This

in another place there was a *karakia* when the new moon appeared; and in still another place "the most sacred day of the year was that appointed for hair-cutting; the people assembled from all the neighbouring parts, often more than a thousand in number; the operation being commenced with *karakia*, the operator and his obsidian (substitute for scissors) being thus rendered peculiarly sacred" (*ibid.*, p. 93).

[1] John Martin, *An Account of the Natives of the Tonga Islands . . . from the Extensive Communications of Mr. William Mariner*, Boston, 1820, pp. 381-385. Mariner passed four years among the Tonga Islanders as the adopted son of the king Finow. His picturesque, but apparently reliable, narrative describes the natives in their aboriginal state before the arrival of Christian missionaries.

[2] Not only was all work prohibited at the time of the *inachi*, but even any one's appearance abroad, unless for the purposes of the ceremony, was interdicted (Martin-Mariner, *op. cit.*, p. 383 n.[2]). The Tongans observed a

increases till midnight, men generally singing the first part of the sentence, and the women the last, to produce a more pleasing effect: it then subsides for three or four hours, and again increases as the sun rises. Nobody, however, is seen stirring out in the public roads till about eight o'clock, when the people from all quarters of the island are seen advancing towards the *mooa*, and canoes from all the other islands landing their men; so that all the inhabitants of Tonga seem approaching by sea and land, singing and sounding the conch. At the *mooa* itself the universal bustle of preparation is seen and heard; and the different processions entering from various quarters, of men and women, all dressed up in new *gnatoos*, ornamented with red ribbons and wreaths of flowers, and the men armed with spears and clubs, betoken the importance of the ceremony about to be performed." The proceedings consisted in the solemn presentation of the first-fruits to the divine chief at the grave of his predecessor, and closed with a feast and dance. Then the people returned to their homes, perfectly assured of the protection of the gods.

The natives of Samoa possessed a remarkably complex pantheon of household and village gods, the recipients of prayer and sacrifice, and, in the case of the village gods, honoured with temples, priests, and annual festivals. The Samoans had also war-gods, who in character resembled the other deities, since they were supposed to be incarnate in animals or embodied in inanimate objects.[1] One of these militant divinities was the cuttle-fish (*fe'e*), said to have been imported

---

like restriction after a death. When a corpse was being taken to the burying-ground, all persons in the roadway or the adjacent fields were obliged to keep out of sight, under pain of becoming tabooed. Those who showed themselves at such a time were generally killed on the spot (*ibid.*, pp. 243 *sq.*, 394).

[1] This Samoan religious system has been fully described by Sir J. G. Frazer, who believes that it exhibits "what seems to be the passage of pure totemism into a religion of anthropomorphic gods with animal and vegetable attributes, like the deities of ancient Greece" (*Totemism and Exogamy*, London, 1910, ii, 152).

from Fiji. In one place Fe'e was a general village
god whose province was not confined to war. "The
month of May was sacred to his worship. No traveller
was then allowed to pass through the village by the
public road; nor was any canoe allowed in the lagoon
off that part of the settlement. There was great
feasting, too, on these occasions, and also games, club
exercise, spear-throwing, wrestling, etc. . . . In another district three months were sacred to the worship
of Fe'e. During that time any one passing along the
road, or in the lagoon, would be beaten, if not killed,
for insulting the god. For the first month torches and
all other lights were forbidden, as the god was about
and did not wish to be seen. White turbans were
also forbidden during the festivities, and confined to
war. At this time, also, all unsightly burdens — such
as a log of firewood on the shoulder — were forbidden,
lest it should be considered by the god as a mockery of
his *tentacula*." [1] Another village god, who rejoiced
in the name of Titi Usi, or Glittering Leaf Girdle,
received worship at the new moon. "At that time
all work was suspended for a day or two. The cocoa-
nut-leaf blinds were kept down, and the people sat
still in their houses. Any one walking in front of the
house risked a beating. After prayer and feasting
a man went about and blew a shell-trumpet as a sign
to all that the ceremonies were over, and that the usual
routine of village and family life might be resumed." [2]
The festivals of the other village deities of Samoa seem
not to have been marked by compulsory cessation of
activity.[3]

The observance of regular periods consecrated to
the gods has been noticed in some other parts of Polynesia. At Fakaofo, or Bowditch Island, in the Union
group, the month of May was devoted to the worship
of the great god Tui Tokelau. All work was then

[1] George Turner, *Samoa*, London, 1884. pp. 29 *sq.*
[2] *Ibid.*, p. 60.
[3] *Ibid.*, pp. 26 *sq.*, 41, 44, 47, 49,
53, 57.

laid aside. The people assembled from the three islands of the group to enjoy feasting and dancing. They
prayed to their divinity for life, health, and a plentiful
supply of fish and cocoanuts.[1] In tiny Manahiki,
or Humphrey Island, the natives had special days for
worship, every three or four months. At such times
heaps of food were collected in the place of public
assembly, and the king, who was high-priest as well,
prayed for food and life and health in behalf of his
people.[2] We are told, also, that when the god Ratu-
mai-Mbulu visited the Fiji Islands, the inhabitants
lived very quietly for an entire month, lest they should
disturb the deity in his task of making the fruit-trees
blossom and bear fruit. During this Lenten season
the natives did not plant or build or sail on the ocean
or go to war. The priests announced the time of the
god's advent and departure.[3] According to a later
account Ratu-mai-Mbulu (Lord from Hades) was
probably a deity of foreign extraction. "Through
him the earth gives her increase. In December he
comes forth from Mbulu, and pours sap into the fruit-
trees, and pushes the young yam shoots through the
soil. Throughout that moon it is *tabu* to beat the drum,
to sound the conch-shell, to dance, to plant, to fight, ·
or to sing at sea, lest Ratu-mai-Mbulu be disturbed,
and quit the earth before his work is completed. At
the end of the month the priest sounds the consecrated
shell; the people raise a great shout, carrying the good
news from village to village; and pleasure and toil
are again free to all." [4]

The descriptions of Polynesian customs by early
observers, though frequently the only accounts we
possess, are sometimes very brief and obscure. These
remarks apply to a curious ceremony annually performed by some Fijian tribes. The time of its cele-

[1] Turner, *Samoa*, p. 269.
[2] *Ibid.*, p. 279.
[3] J. E. Erskine, *Journal of a Cruise among the Islands of the Western Pacific*, London, 1853, pp. 245 *sq.*
[4] Basil Thomson, *The Fijians*, London, 1908, p. 114.

bration was determined by the appearance of a certain sea-slug, which swarms out in dense shoals from the coral reefs on a single day of the year, usually in November during the last quarter of the moon. The arrival of the sea-slugs furnished the signal for a general feast at those places where they were taken. Hostilities were suspended between rival communities for four days, and a taboo was laid to prevent noise or disturbance during this period. No labour might be done and no person might be seen outside his house. "In Ovolau the ceremony begins by a man ascending a tree and praying for fine weather and winds throughout the year. Thereupon a tremendous clatter, with drumming and shouting, is raised by all the people inside of the houses for about half an hour, and then a dead quiet ensues for four days, during which they are feasting on the *mbalolo*. If in any dwelling a noise is made, as by a child crying, a forfeit (*ori*) is immediately exacted by the chief."[1] According to another account the rule requiring quiescence was so strictly observed that not even a leaf might be plucked or the offal removed from the houses. During these four days the men lived in their special club-house (*mbure*), and the women and children remained shut up in the family abodes. At daylight, on the expiry of the fourth night, the whole town was in an uproar; and men and boys scampered about, knocking with sticks at the doors of the dwellings and crying *Sinariba*. This concluded the ceremony.[2] It would seem that these accounts refer to a Fijian New Year's festival, which, like that of the Hawaiians, was held in November for a period of four days, and was marked by communal taboos imposing abstinence and quiescence.[3]

[1] *U.S. Exploring Expedition*, Philadelphia, 1846, vi, 67 *sq.* (*Ethnography and Philology*, by H. Hale).

[2] Charles Wilkes, *Narrative of the U.S. Exploring Expedition*, Philadelphia, 1845, iii, 90 *sq.*

This festival bore the name of *tambo nalanga* (*ibid.*, iii, 342).

[3] In Samoa the second half of the year was called the *palolo* season, from the appearance of this singular worm for three days in the course of a year. If the last

The western tribes of Viti Levu, largest of the Fiji Islands, in traditions, language, and physical type are recognized as distinctly Melanesian. In former days these tribes possessed a secret association known as *nanga*, or *mbaki*, which closely resembled the secret societies so common in the Melanesian Archipelago. It is highly probably, therefore, that, at least in its known form, the *nanga* was a late importation into the island of Viti Levu. Initiation into the *nanga* was supposed to bring the youth of the tribe into relations with the ancestral spirits, who were represented, at the time of the ceremonies, by the elders and by some of the middle-aged men. The sanctuary and lodge of the association formed the earthly dwelling-place of the spirits; it was a tabernacle as holy to these Fijians as was the structure in the Wilderness to the Israelites; there the first-fruits of the yam harvest were solemnly presented to the ancestors; and there the young men of Viti Levu were introduced to the mysteries of the tribe. When the *nanga* enclosure was being raised for the initiatory performances, the people suspended all other work. Not even food-planting might be done at such a time. "If any impious person transgressed this law, 'he would only plant evil to himself and to his kinsfolk.'" [1]

quarter of the moon is late in October, the *palolo* is found the day before, the day of, and the day after that quarter. Should the last quarter of the moon be early in October, the worm does not come till the last quarter of the November moon (Turner, *Samoa*, p. 207). The *palolo*, it may be noted, is not an entire animal, but only the "propagation-body" of a sea-annelid (apparently *Eunice Viridis* Gray), which lives in holes in the coral stone and comes to the surface for the act of fertilization. It is found in various parts of Polynesia, including Samoa, Fiji, and Tonga, and also in Melanesia (New Hebri-des and Banks Islands). See A. Krämer, *Die Samoa-Inseln*, Stuttgart, 1903, ii, 399–406, and B. Friedländer, "Notes on the *palolo*," *Journal of the Polynesian Society*, 1898, vii, 44–46.

[1] L. Fison, "The *nanga*, or Sacred Stone Enclosure, of Wainimala, Fiji," *Journal of the Anthropological Institute*, 1885, xiv, 18. The solemn rite of initiation into the *nanga* was always celebrated at the time of the New Year's festival, late in October or early in November. This Fijian festival, called *solevu ni vilavou*, corresponded to the Tahitian and Hawaiian *makahiki* (A. B. Joske, "The

In this instance there was no attribution of the sacred period to any particular divinity, though all the ceremonies connected with the *nanga* were supposed to be directed by the ancestral spirits.

The scanty records of aboriginal Polynesian society also contain some passing references to the observance of communal rest days on certain occasions when the social consciousness had been deeply moved by untoward and disastrous events. In Futuna, or Erronan, an island which lies close to the dividing line between Polynesia and Melanesia, the custom of taboo is said to be very common. "They go so far as to *tapu* the day — *e.g.*, to interdict all work in order to please the gods, or to avert the hurricanes." [1] In Hawaii a *tabu* period was declared during the sickness of chiefs. [2] In Samoa the death of a chief of high rank was followed by the suspension of all work in the settlement for from ten to thirty days, until the funeral ceremonies were performed. During this time no stranger might approach the stricken village; a luckless wayfarer, pushing in by accident, would have been promptly clubbed. [3] This Samoan regulation, as we shall see, is only a particular instance of a widespread primitive custom. Communal rest days are still observed in some parts of Micronesia, as on the island of Yap, one of the Carolines. Here two aged "wizards," before whom all important questions come for decision, have the power of imposing taboos on an entire village. The periods of seclusion have been known to last for six months. The critical epochs, when such interdicts are enforced, occur during a

nanga of Viti Levu," *Internationales Archiv für Ethnographie*, 1889, ii, 259). On the *nanga* see further H. Webster, "Totem Clans and Secret Associations in Australia and Melanesia," *Journal of the Royal Anthropological Institute*, 1911, xli, 506 *sq.*

[1] S. P. Smith, in *Journal of the Polynesian Society*, 1892, i, 40.

[2] Ellis, *Polynesian Researches*, iv, 387.

[3] W. T. Pritchard, *Polynesian Reminiscences*, London, 1866, pp. 149 *sq.*; George Turner, *Nineteen Years in Polynesia*, London, 1861, p. 229; *idem, Samoa*, p. 146. See also A. Bastian, *Inselgruppen in Oceanien*, Berlin, 1883, p. 55.

time of drought, famine, or sickness, after a death of a chief or famous man, and before a fishing expedition.[1] "In short, any great public event is thus celebrated, and, in fact, there is always a *tabu* in full swing somewhere or other, to the great disgust of the traders, who only see in these enforced holidays an excuse for idling, drunkenness and debauchery."[2]

The accounts preserved in the older literature relating to Polynesia thus make it evident that communal taboos occurred at critical, or especially important, seasons. The prohibitions were negative in character, required a period of abstinence sometimes verging upon complete quiescence, and were closely connected with the aristocratic and theocratic organization of Polynesian society. At the same time the communal regulations, artificially created, are to be assimilated to those which rested upon individuals alone and arose spontaneously as a result of various circumstances. Every description of aboriginal culture, from Hawaii to New Zealand, contains numerous references to the network of taboos which invested private life. All persons dangerously ill, all mothers at childbirth, together with their infants, all persons who handled a corpse or assisted at a funeral, were deemed unclean and hence were subjected to a rigid quarantine, a protective measure necessary for the safety of the social group. If we assume that the individual taboos represent the earlier phase of the institution, then the communal taboos may be regarded as merely an extension to the body politic of these simpler and more rudimentary customs. The probability of such a transition will be strengthened by a consideration of the tabooed days found among some other primitive peoples.

[1] For an interesting description of the regulations imposed on the fishermen themselves see W. H. Furness, 3d., *The Island of Stone Money*, Philadelphia, 1910, pp. 38 *sq.* On taboos observed by hunters and fishers, generally, see Frazer, *Taboo and the Perils of the Soul*, pp. 190–223.

[2] F. W. Christian, *The Caroline Islands*, London, 1899, p. 290.

Seasons of communal abstinence are not found in Australia, and only faint indications of them exist within the Melanesian area, that great island group which extends from New Guinea to the Fiji Archipelago. In New Guinea itself a few instances of the custom under consideration have been noted, all within the British possessions there.[1] Among the Roro-speaking tribes, inhabiting the strip of coast from Cape Possession in the west to Kabadi in the east, it is said that an entire village will mourn for a chief or influential man "by abstaining from fishing, hunting, and pot-making, and by reducing garden-work to a minimum." The period of mourning lasts from six to ten days.[2] In the neighbourhood of Port Moresby are the Motu and Koita tribes, some of whose customs were described, many years ago, by a native missionary who long laboured in New Guinea. Among these tribes, we are told, "fishing work lays the people under a number of restrictions. There must be no talking; any one causing another to speak prevents his getting any fish. If the fishermen are going on a turtle expedition, all must be still throughout the village. None go about among the houses, or on the public road. All go up to their houses and sit still. No sound of a voice, or chopping firewood, or any movement is allowed, until it is supposed that the fishing party is clear of the lagoon, and out into the deep ocean, and then the villagers resume their usual occupation."[3] These taboos in connection with fishing closely resemble the regulations so common in Polynesia.

The Indonesian inhabitants of Borneo are divided into a large number of tribes, among which the Kayan,

---

[1] A close observer, G. A. J. van der Sande, did not notice any special rest days among the natives with whom he came in contact, and whose customs he has so fully described (*Nova Guinea*, Leiden, 1907, iii, 270).

[2] C. G. Seligmann, *The Melanesians of British New Guinea*, Cambridge, 1910, p. 275.

[3] Quoted in Turner, *Samoa*, p. 349. The custom mentioned in the text must now be obsolete. It is not referred to in Dr. Seligmann's exhaustive account of the Koita and Motu tribes.

the Sea Dyak, and the Land Dyak are perhaps the best known. All these peoples till the soil and live in long communal houses situated on the banks of the rivers. Though now spread over a wide area in Borneo, the different tribes possess in common many social and religious customs, notably the cult of omen animals, together with the observance of numerous taboos which are regularly enforced at the time of rice (*padi*) plant-ing and harvesting, sometimes also at mid-harvest.[1] The taboos found among the Kayan on the Baram River, Sarawak, have been well described by a recent traveller, whose picturesque narrative deserves an extended notice.[2] "During the days devoted to search for omens in reference to the sites of the rice-fields, and also again in reference to the planting, the Kayan refrain from their usual daily occupations, and neither leave their houses themselves nor allow strangers to enter. These days of seclusion are termed *permantong padi*, or *lali padi*, and correspond very closely to taboo elsewhere."[3]

The rude agricultural methods of the Kayan start with the preliminary process of clearing a site in the

---

[1] It would seem that among the Bornean tribes, generally, the chief is responsible for the proper obser-vation of the omens and for the regulation of taboos affecting an entire community. Compare Hose and McDougall, *The Pagan Tribes of Borneo*, London, 1912, i, 65.

[2] W. H. Furness, 3d., *The Home-life of Borneo Head-hunters*, Philadelphia, 1902, pp. 160–169.

[3] *Permantong* is the term used by the Kayan of the Baram Dis-trict; among the Kayan in the valley of the Kapuas River, Dutch Borneo, the word is *pantang*, the regular Malay equivalent of *tabu*. Both these forms are possibly de-rived from the Malay *hantu*, a word meaning demon or evil spirit, with the prefix *per* and the affix *an*.

The Malay word in full would thus be *per-hantu-an*, meaning "possessed by spirits" or "be-witched." *Lali* is probably a pure Kayan word and means both "prohibited" and "sacred" (Fur-ness, *op. cit.*, p. 160; A. W. Nieuwenhuis, *Quer durch Borneo*, Leiden, 1904–1907, i, 109). Ac-cording to Messrs. Hose and McDougall *malan* and *parit* are the proper Kayan words for taboo, though *lali* and *tulak* are used as their *lingua franca* equivalents. *Malan* applies to acts involving risks to the entire community, *parit* to those involving risk to the individual committing the for-bidden act (*Pagan Tribes of Borneo*, i, 14 n.[1]).

dense jungle. The work is extremely tedious and if, after all the heavy labour, the crops should fail or be destroyed by monkeys, birds, or beetles, the entire household feels that some act has been committed whereby the displeasure of the spirits is aroused. Accordingly, before beginning so arduous a task, it is essential to take omens from the actions of certain birds, mammals, and reptiles, called *amau*, which are supposed to be in the confidence of the spirits.[1] A patch of jungle having been tentatively selected, the work begins with the removal of the dense undergrowth. During this preliminary stage, while the labour is less heavy than it will be later, when trees must be felled, the household is not as yet under a taboo. Each person, nevertheless, keeps a sharp eye for evil omens. Should a native on the way to the clearing see any one of four ominous animals, a certain species of snake, a deer, a civet cat, or a rain-bird, the site will be at once abandoned, regardless of the work already done there. Wilfully to ignore such a warning "not only compromises the abundance and quality of the crops, but also the health, or even the life, of the whole household." [2]

If no evil omens are observed for three days, the Kayan workers feel sufficiently encouraged to proceed to the next stage of felling the heavy timber on the site, which has now been stripped of its underbrush. Then ensues an elaborate series of auguries. While the various families making up the household of a communal dwelling remain secluded on the long ve-

[1] On these omen animals see further Sir Spenser St. John, *Life in the Forests of the Far East*, London, 1862, i, 191 *sqq.;* J. Perham, in H. L. Roth, *The Natives of Sarawak and British North Borneo*, London, 1896, i, 191–201; A. C. Haddon, *Head-hunters*, London, 1901, pp. 384 *sqq.;* E. H. Gomes, *Seventeen Years among the Sea Dyaks of Borneo*, London, 1911, pp. 47 *sq.,* 152 *sqq.,* 298; Hose and McDougall, *op. cit.*, ii, 51–114 (with some interesting parallels between the modern Kayan and the Roman auspices). Compare W. D. Wallis, "Divination and Omens in Borneo and in Ancient Rome," *Classical Journal*, 1914, ix, 272–274.

[2] Furness, *op. cit.*, p. 161.

randa, or in their small private rooms, sitting very still all day and smoking and talking, two hawk-men are off in the forest looking for a hawk, called *niko*. Three days must be devoted to this search : if the hawk is seen on the first day, but not on the two days following, the omen is unfavourable. The people will continue the preparation of the soil, but they expect poor crops, a result pretty certain to follow their half-hearted and discouraged labours. On the second day the search is continued, and if the hawk is seen, the omen is favourable, but not completely so. If the third day's search again reveals a hawk, the two men return at once to the house and spread the good news. Every one now watches the actions of the hawk. "Should he sail away out of sight without once flapping his wings all are delighted; it means that the clearing of the jungle may now continue prosperously, and that neither attack of enemies nor accident to the workers need be feared. Should the hawk flap his wings, it follows that some men, in felling the jungle, will be badly cut by their axes or perhaps crushed under falling trees. All instantly avert their eyes from the flapping hawk, lest the bird should recognize them in the fields and select them as victims." [1]

There now occurs a brief respite of the *lali* observance, and the people may leave their houses. But the same formalities must be observed by the natives while search is made for four other ominous animals. In each case there is a period of seclusion and abstinence lasting for three days. These are all the omens that must be consulted before the heavy timber may be felled, the ground burned over, and the rice planted.

Such are the various taboos which affect the inmates of a communal house or village, before the crop is started. Other regulations concern outsiders. From the hour when the real labour of felling the jungle begins and until the seed-planting is completed, no stranger may enter house or field. Should a neighbour,

---

[1] Furness, *op. cit.*, pp. 162 *sq.*

by accident or necessity, come within the tabooed
district, he must atone for the trespass by making a
small payment, called *usut*. It consists, ordinarily,
of a few beads or an iron implement. These objects
are placed in a basket and hung up in the rice-field
till they rust away or disappear. It is a special duty
of the women to see that this *usut* is paid.

The *lali* ordinances of the Kayan are not confined to
the time of seed-planting. Once more, when the crop
is all harvested, the house is closed to strangers. For
eight days no one may go away on an expedition or
return to the village from abroad. Another season
of restriction follows during the period when the rice
is being stored in the granaries. "But as soon as this
harvesting is over, a general feast is prepared, and merri-
ment of all sorts makes up for the weariness of the
long day's work. The women don every stitch of
their finery and every bead to their name; some even
assume men's clothes, and carry shield, spear, and
parang. In the evening all join in a long procession
round the house; guests are invited to participate in
the festivities, and 'jest and youthful jollity' rule the
hour; the brimming cup passes freely, and to the
harmonious strains of the *kaluri* the women 'trip it as
they go,' or leap in war-dances in imitation of the
men." After this festival there follows yet another
period of taboo, ten days in length, when no one is
allowed to do a stroke of any work that resembles the
cultivation of rice: "should any restless creature
express a desire for active work, he is scoffed at and
scorned as a spoil-sport and kill-joy." [1]

These customs of the Kayan of Sarawak are significant as showing how for a Bornean community the
whole period of farming, from the initial task of select-
ing a site to the final storing of the rice in the granaries,
is supposed to be subject to supernatural influences.
Planting and harvesting are critical times, when every
precaution must be taken to win the approval, and to

---

[1] Furness, *op. cit.*, pp. 164 *sq.*

thwart the ill will, of the spirits which affect the tribal life. If we turn, now, to the Kayan on the Mendalam River in Dutch Borneo, we shall find here also a community of primitive farmers who depend mainly on the rice crop for subsistence, and by whom all agricultural operations have been invested with a religious significance. Without the consent of the spirits no farm work may be undertaken; without a strict regimen of sacrifices and taboos their aid cannot be secured for the growth and maturity of the crops. A traveller, who has described in detail the agricultural rites of the Kayan, tells us that the sowing festival lasts several weeks and that during this period certain communal regulations are enforced. On the first day of the festival every one, save the very old and the very young, must refrain from bathing; then for eight successive days no work may be done and no intercourse may be held with neighbouring communities. The custom of excluding strangers at this time has a purely religious meaning: the presence of strangers, so the Kayan believe, would frighten or annoy the spirits and consequently endanger the welfare of the crops.[1] Following the rites at sowing come those which inaugurate the hoeing of the fields, and finally the New Year's festival, eight days in duration, when the harvest has been safely garnered and the long period of labour and anxiety is at an end.[2]

But the critical occasions demanding the observance of taboos are not confined by the Kayan to agricultural occupations. Every important undertaking may be commenced only when favourable omens have been

[1] This period of seclusion is employed by the Kayan in various games and masquerades, which, if they have a recreative value, possess as well a religious or magical meaning in the minds of the people. During the sowing festival the men play at spinning tops, the youths engage in athletic sports, and maskers, disguised by wooden helmets and bandages of banana leaves, simulate the actions of evil spirits. On the magical significance of games in primitive agriculture, see Sir J. G. Frazer, *Spirits of the Corn and of the Wild*, London, 1912, i, 92-112.

[2] A. W. Nieuwenhuis, *Quer durch Borneo*, Leiden, 1904-1907, i, 166 sqq.

vouchsafed by the good spirits, and when the spirits
of evil intent have been pacified by many acts of
abstinence. These aborigines, for example, entertain
the belief that house-building, which necessarily in-
volves the cutting-down of many trees, is a dangerous
occupation, because it arouses the animosity of the
tree-spirits. Hence some Kayan villages, after the
erection of a communal house, observe a period of
penance for an entire year. The Ulu-Ayar Dyak
on the Mandai River, when they use the valuable
ironwood as timber, feel it necessary, in consequence,
to deny themselves various dainties for three years.[1]
To the Kayan on the Mahakam River in Dutch Borneo,
the building of a chief's house, in which task all take
part by contributing either materials or labour, forms
a matter of great moment. Dr. Nieuwenhuis, who
witnessed the ceremonies on such an occasion, tells us
that the regulations enforced begin with the collection
of materials for the new dwelling. Nothing may be
done at full moon, a time when important business is
always suspended.[2] During the search for satisfactory
trees and while these are being turned into piles, planks,
and shingles, watch is kept for spirit-warnings as
revealed by the flight and cries of the ominous birds.
Work on the house always terminates at nightfall,
when birds are silent. Important stages in the construction of the house, such as the sinking of the piles
and the placing of the finely carved wooden figure-
heads at the two ends of the ridgepole, are signalized
by appropriate sacrifices to the spirits. When a sufficient quantity of shingles has been prepared for covering the roof, another offering, consisting of a fat pig
and two chickens, is made to the spirits. Then follows a rest period, called *melo*,[3] two days in length.
During this time a strip of rattan is stretched around

[1] Nieuwenhuis, *op. cit.*, i, 107.
[2] The Kayan call the full moon the "evil moon" and at this time build neither houses nor boats, and do not go forth on the search for omens (*ibid.*, i, 415).
[3] Translated by Dr. Nieuwenhuis as "sitzen, nicht arbeiten."

the house to indicate that no one may enter it.   While the house is being shingled, any untoward event will interrupt the progress of the work.   For instance, should a man tumble off the roof, it would be necessary to perform another sacrifice and to declare a *melo* lasting eight days.   Thus anxiously and seriously does the Kayan conduct himself in all the crises of his tribal life.[1]

Among the most numerous and powerful of the Bornean tribes are the Iban, or Sea Dyak, who occupy much of the country between the Baram River in Sarawak and the Kapuas River in Dutch Borneo. Throughout this extensive district the Iban use the same language and possess substantially uniform customs.   A Christianized native, who has given to us a remarkably intimate description of the religious observances of his people, thus sets forth the omens and incidents which require abstention from work.

"When at night the Iban dreams of insult, anger, or that he has been bitten by a snake, crushed by a falling tree, waylaid by a ghost, chased by a crocodile, the following day he rests from all work : to go abroad or about his work after such dreams would cause him to be wounded, hurt by falling wood, or shot by an arrow from the evil spirits' blowpipe.   On the frequent recurrence of such dreams the medicine-man is called in, who rubs the patient's body with a charm which makes him invisible to the evil spirits.   This ceremony is called *bedinding, i.e.,* the shielding. . . . To dream of being enveloped by a swarm of bees, of being overwhelmed by falling earth, that the waistcloth has rotted away, or of eating rice from a winnowing-fan, will deter the Iban from going on the warpath, for they tell of defeat and of being overpowered by the enemy.

[1] A. W. Nieuwenhuis, "Religiöse Zeremonien beim Häuserbau der Bahau-Dajak am obern Mahakam in Borneo," *Verhandlungen des II internationalen Kongresses für allgemeine Religionsgeschichte,* Basel, 1905, pp. 107-119; compare *idem, Quer durch Borneo,* ii, 174.

D

"To hear the cry of a bird of evil omen on first waking in the morning, or on rising up from the morning meal, prevents the Iban from going to his work on that day. . . . When the Iban is setting out to his work and has descended the ladder leading from his house, if the note of a bird of any kind is heard at the same time as his foot first touches the ground, he must turn back. The cry of the *kikeh senabong*, gazelle, or deer, heard on the path, will cause him to give up work for that day. The same happens if these omens are heard as he enters the field; arrives at the *pankalan*, *i.e.*, 'resting place'; when commencing his work; whilst sharpening his chopper, or after the midday meal.

"The news of a death occurring in the neighbourhood or at a distance, the time of full moon,[1] the performance of ceremonies over the sick by the medicine-man, a sacrifice to the spirits, are incidents that require all the villagers to rest from work. Likewise, if some of the villagers attend a feast in a neighbouring village, those that remain behind must rest from work lest they should incur the anger of the guardian spirits of those attending the feast."[2]

But these are not all the circumstances under which an Iban community subjects itself to the rule of abstinence. Rice-planting here, as among the Kayan, necessitates certain rest periods, each of three days' duration.[3] While a village is under construction, weaving the native cloth, settling quarrels, and going on the warpath are forbidden; to break this taboo would cause a death in the village.[4] When rumours are abroad of cholera, smallpox, or fever, another season of seclusion is imposed. The entrance to the village

---

[1] "At certain seasons of the moon, just before and just after the full, the [Sea] Dyaks do not work at their farms; and what with bad omens, sounds, signs, adverse dreams, and deaths, two-thirds of their time is not spent in farm labour" (Charles Brooke, *Ten Years in Sarawak*, London, 1866, i, 149).

[2] Leo Nyuak, "Religious Rites and Customs of the Iban or Dyaks of Sarawak," translated from the Dyak by the Very Rev. Edm. Dunn, *Anthropos*, 1906, i, 410 *sq.*

[3] *Ibid.*, i, 176.   [4] *Ibid.*, i, 181.

is railed off, and no one is allowed either ingress or egress for three days, during which time all rest from work. Meanwhile the village elders have prepared an offering to the evil spirit of the epidemic. This sacrifice, together with a winnowing-fan on which is the figure of man drawn in chalk, is placed in a shed near the village. The evil spirit, it is thought, will stop to observe the chalk-drawing and thus will be led to discover the food which has been left in the shed. Having satisfied his hunger, he will not seek to enter the village.[1] The general character of these taboos as propitiatory rites is further illustrated by some of the customs relating to agriculture. When the forest land has been fully cleared and left to dry, sun and wind become of vital consequence to the Iban, for, if the people are unable to burn the immense mass of timber and brush-wood in the jungle, famine stares them in the face during the year to come. "If it pour with rain day after day and week after week, and there is no promise of continued fine weather, they are apt to imagine that some impurity has defiled the tribe and that the face of the Great Spirit is hid from them. So the elders of the people get to work to find it out, and adjudicate on all cases of incest and bigamy, and purify the earth with the blood of pigs. Prayers are offered to Betara [2] from one end of the country to the other; for the space of three days the villages are tabooed, and all labour is discontinued; the inhabitants remain at home and strangers are not admitted. But if the weather is warm and dry, the farms are ready in a very few days for the burning." [3]

[1] *Ibid.*, i, 416 *sq.*

[2] Betara, otherwise *petara*, is the ordinary Sea Dyak name for deity. The word is incorrectly translated as "Great Spirit"; in general belief there are many *petara*. These gods, it may be noted, are separated by no distinct line of demarcation from the thousands of *antu*, or spirits, with which the Dyak has peopled his universe. See J. Perham, "*Petara*, or Sea Dyak Gods," *Journal of the Straits Branch of the Royal Asiatic Society*, 1881, no. 8; H. L. Roth, *The Natives of Sarawak and British North Borneo*, London, 1896, i, 168–182.

[3] Brooke Low, in Roth, *op. cit.*, i, 401. See also *idem*, in *Journal*

The seasons of communal abstinence found among the Land Dyak, who dwell in the southwestern part of Sarawak, differ only in minor details from those of other Bornean tribes. There are three principal occasions when the Land Dyak subject themselves to *pamali*, or taboo:

"The first, *pamali mati*, is on a house, and on everything in it for twelve days after the decease of any person belonging to it: during this time, no one who is not an inhabitant of the dwelling can enter it, nor are the persons usually residing in it allowed to speak to such, nor can anything, on any pretence whatever, be removed from it, until the twelve days of the prohibition be expired: its conclusion is marked by the death of a fowl or pig, according to the circumstances of the family.

"The *pamali peniakit* is undertaken by a whole village during any sickness which prevails generally amongst the members of the tribe; it is marked by a pig slain, and a feast being made in order to propitiate the divinity who has sent the malady among them; in its severest form it is of eight days' continuance, and during this period everything in the village is at a standstill, the inhabitants shutting themselves up from all intercourse with strangers. . . . The *pamali peniakit* is also undertaken by individuals when any member of the family is sick; thus parents often put themselves under its regulations, fondly hoping that by denying themselves for a time the pleasures of intercourse with their fellow creatures, they will prevail upon the malignant spirit, which is supposed to have shed its withering influence over their offspring, to restore it to its wonted health and strength.

of the Anthropological Institute, 1893, xxii, 24. Many primitive peoples are accustomed to trace a direct connection between sexual sins and the welfare of the crops. As Sir James Frazer has shown, this superstition has undoubtedly contributed to a stricter observance of the rules of sexual morality, both among the married and the unmarried. See *The Magic Art and the Evolution of Kings*, London, 1911, ii, 104–119.

"The *pamali omar*, or taboo on the farms, occurs immediately after the whole of the seed is sown: it lasts four days, and during that period, no person of the tribe enters any of the plantations on any account; a pig and feast are, according to their practice, also necessary. The proper observance of these various forms of *pamali* is probably amongst the most ancient of their customs, and was practised by their tribes previously to the introduction of the Hindu religion."[1] From another authority we learn that the Land Dyak recognize a variety of incidents, more or less inimical to the operations of farming, which suffice to impose taboos. "If the basket in which the paddy is put as it is cut during harvesting be upset, that farm must rest for a day, and a fowl must be killed, or all their paddy will go rotten. If a tree falls across the farm-path, a fowl must be killed on the spot, and the path be disused for one day, or some one will meet with an accident on it. . . . At full moon, and on the third day after it (called *bubuk*), no farm work may be done, unless it is wished that the paddy should be devoured by blight and mildew. In some tribes the unlucky days are those of the new and full moon, and its first and third quarters."[2]

In the course of an excellent study of the Land Dyak festivals,[3] Mrs. S. B. Scott argues that they are far more effective as social observances when accompanied by the various taboos. The change of occupations heightens the sacredness of the feast, and also enables all the inhabitants of a village to join in the long, elaborate ritual. At the same time the closed house prevents intrusion and secures the presence of every member of the community. Furthermore, the

[1] Sir Hugh Low, *Sarawak*, London, 1848, pp. 260–262. See also Sir Spenser St. John, *Life in the Forests of the Far East*, London, 1862, i, 175 *sqq*. According to this writer *porikh* is the Land Dyak expression equivalent to *pamali*.

[2] William Chalmers, in Roth, *op. cit.*, i, 401.

[3] Mrs. S. B. Scott, "Harvest Festivals of the Land Dyaks," *Journal of the American Oriental Society*, 1908, xxix, 236–280.

prospect of feasting, drinking, and general excitement gives an added zest to the labours of the Dyak farmers. The mid-harvest festival, when this is celebrated, affords a much needed rest from the heavy work of harvesting; and the last and greatest of the festivals comes as a natural period of relaxation after the long strain of toil and frugality is suddenly relaxed.[1]

That in actual practice the Land Dyak observances have this outcome, it is impossible to deny. Yet it must be noticed that similar regulations are in force on other and quite different occasions. As we have just seen, the Land Dyak place an interdict, twelve days in length, upon a house in which any one has died; the same event also causes a general banning of the village for one day only.[2] Childbirth imposes a taboo of eight days' duration on a Land Dyak family;[3] in this case the regulation does not appear to be extended to the community at large. Sickness is another event which puts a family under the ban;[4] when the sickness assumes an epidemic form and threatens the general well-being, the rule of abstinence must be observed by every one in the village. Such evidence from the Land Dyak customs, confirmed as it is by the facts relating to the customs of other Bornean tribes, clearly illustrates the passage of individual

[1] Mrs. S. B. Scott, "Harvest Festivals of the Land Dyaks," *Journal of the American Oriental Society*, 1908, xxix, 244 *sqq.*

[2] St. John, *op. cit.*, i, 163.

[3] *Ibid.*, i, 160. The Sea Dyak make an interesting distinction between *mali* and *penti*, the former absolutely forbidding certain kinds of work to a person under the ban, the latter allowing it to be undertaken, if started by some one not subject to the taboo. For instance, though both parents are *penti* during the wife's pregnancy, the expectant mother may engage in basket-making and mat-weaving, provided some other woman begins the work for her; and the husband may dig a trench or erect a post, if the hands of others are first set to the task. Taboos of this sort prevail until the child cuts its first teeth (F. W. Leggatt, in Roth, *op. cit.*, i, 98).

[4] Sir Hugh Low observes that among the Land Dyak the favourite remedies for the cure of internal diseases are turmeric and spices, taken in huge quantities; "but for anything at all serious, recourse is had to the *pamali*, both in medical and surgical cases" (*Sarawak*, p. 308).

taboos, based on gross superstition, into community ordinances which may sometimes have a real justification in their social usefulness.

These Bornean regulations disclose a fairly consistent effort to adjust the length of the communal taboo to the importance of the event which it commemorates. Thus, housebuilding imposes a shorter season of abstinence than does planting or sowing; a single death in the village may require the cessation of activity by the inhabitants for only one day; but an epidemic sickness may necessitate a three days' rest, as among the Iban, or even eight days' rest, as among the Land Dyak. The restrictions themselves appear to be substantially the same in all instances : the inhabitants "remain in their houses, in order to eat, drink, and sleep; but their eating must be moderate, and often consists of nothing but rice and salt. . . . People under interdict may not bathe, touch fire, or employ themselves about their ordinary occupations." [1] To these prohibitions should be added that of sexual intercourse, a taboo specifically mentioned for one Bornean tribe, and probably found among others.[2]

The close resemblances, even in details, between the communal taboos observed in different parts of Borneo must, unquestionably, be attributed to a long-continued process of diffusion among the various Indone-

---

[1] St. John, op. cit., i, 175 sq. (Land Dyak). Mr. Charles Hose declares that at such times the inhabitants of a Kayan communal house may taboo their private rooms to the other inmates. Small fines are imposed for infringing the rule, if the act is unintentional, but when a man forces his way into a tabooed house, a serious quarrel, ending in bloodshed, may result (Journal of the Anthropological Institute, 1894, xxiii, 170). "It is an old custom among the Iban for a stranger, before climbing the ladder of a house, to ask in a loud voice whether there is no taboo" (L. Nyuak, in Anthropos, 1906, i, 175).

[2] The Murik on the Baram River, a community of hardworking farmers, in addition to the communal taboos observed by them at sowing, also keep a lemalli of seven days, when the paddy crop is about to be harvested. "For the first three days of this no one stirs out of the house, no work is done, and no sexual intercourse is allowed" (R. S. Douglas, in Sarawak Museum Journal, 1911, i, 146 sqq.).

sian tribes. These taboos have not been found, at any rate have not been described, among the nomadic hunting tribes, which occupy the interior parts of Borneo and probably represent an aboriginal population. Though our knowledge of Bornean ethnography is still very imperfect, there seems to be no doubt that the present Indonesian inhabitants are descended from immigrants into the island at no very remote date. We are justified, therefore, in seeking a foreign source for various elements of the existing Bornean culture. In particular, the practice of observing communal taboos, in its rudiments, if not in its completely developed form, may reasonably be regarded as an importation into Borneo, if similar customs are found to prevail among other Indonesian peoples.

Between the Andaman Islands in the Bay of Bengal and the northern coast of Sumatra lies the archipelago of the Nicobars. The inhabitants appear to be of Indonesian type, but more or less intermixed with Malays and with the natives of Burma and Siam. In spite of the labours of numerous missionaries the Nicobarese are said to entertain no conception of a Supreme Being or of a future state. They have, however, a very lively belief in evil spirits, which seem to be chiefly the ghosts of the wicked. These malignant beings, the source of all misfortune and disease, are propitiated with offerings or driven out by exorcisms. On such occasions the Nicobarese hold lengthy festivals, some of which are accompanied by periods of communal abstinence. The native name for these enforced rest days or holidays is *anoiila*.[1] Every year the inhabitants of Kar Nicobar observe the ceremony of *kataphang*, at which time the group of buildings, called the *elpanam*,[2] is cleaned out and purified to the accom-

---

[1] See below, p. 165.

[2] The *elpanam* consists of several large structures, which serve as a guest-house for strangers and as a town-hall for feasts and public gatherings. The institution is found under different names in many of the East Indian islands, and even more widely. See H. Webster, *Primitive Secret Societies*, New York, 1908, pp. 8 *sqq.*

paniment of much singing and dancing. When this preliminary work is done and the rubbish has been cast into the sea, the doors of the houses in the *elpanam* are closed and the people return to their private abodes in the village. "Silence has now to be observed for a full month; no fire or light may be seen; no cheroot may be smoked. Women and children are interdicted from coming to the *elpanam*, and, if they have to come during the night on urgent affairs (to purchase things), they have to place a light at the entrance of the *elpanam* and then come without noise. . . . The chief sufferers by this festival are the Burmans, because the people cannot supply any nuts nor can they work in making *kopra*, for the reason that they cannot go into the jungle to fetch nuts nor can they come to the *elpanam*." The natives believe that during this time the evil spirits from the jungle visit the *elpanam*. When the month is up, a great feast is given to the spirits and they are sent back to the jungle.[1] Another Nicobar festival is that of *kiala*. The word means, properly, "to take food." The *kiala* is celebrated with much feasting, to which the inhabitants of neighbouring communities come as guests. At midday a cry of supplication is heard from each building: "Let our house be enriched with plenty of food. Let us have many eatable things from other villages. Let there come new women to our villages. Let us be happy." Then follow in regular sequence a day of rest — *anoiila* — a day of pig-hunting in the jungle, a second *anoiila*, and a second day of pig-hunting. One more rest day ends the festival.[2] The exact meaning of these observances is difficult to make out.

Very similar customs have been found among the

[1] V. Solomon, in *Journal of the Anthropological Institute*, 1902, xxxii, 215 *sq.* See also C. B. Kloss, *In the Andamans and Nicobars*, London, 1903, pp. 293 *sqq.*

[2] V. Solomon, in *Journal of the Anthropological Institute*, 1902, xxxii, 210; Kloss, *op. cit.*, pp. 297 *sq.* Another *kiala* festival, also followed by alternate periods of rest and work, appears to be observed in connection with fishing (Kloss, *op. cit.*, p. 295).

people of Bali, an island to the east of Java. When
the Balinese are confronted by some real or imaginary
danger, such as an epidemic, an earthquake, or a lunar
eclipse, they at once take measures to drive away the
evil spirits, or *buta*, which have caused the ominous
event. This praiseworthy object is supposed to be
accomplished partly by verbal commands "go away!
go away!" addressed to the *buta*, partly by means of
an unearthly uproar of shouting and knocking. Then
follow two days of absolute silence, the stillness of the
grave. During this period, known as *sepi*, no one
ventures out of doors and no strangers are admitted
to the village. Even the usual domestic work, including cooking, is discontinued. The interdict against
all activity is lifted on the third day, but even then
work in the rice-fields and buying and selling in the
market are forbidden. The evil spirits, it is believed,
would like to return at once to their old haunts, hence
they must be led to think that Bali is not Bali, but
some uninhabited island.[1] This period of quiescence
is clearly a means of avoiding contact with the ghostly
powers. The reason given for abstaining from activity — to make the spirits suppose that Bali is not Bali
— may be taken as a naïve effort to explain a custom
no longer understood. The Balinese have also a
New Year's festival, which shows the influence of
Buddhism in the date chosen for its observance, the
first five weeks of the Buddhist year. "At this time
the gods are supposed to dwell on the earth, and the
pitara especially return to the bosoms of their families;
hence the constant offerings and the incessant games
and amusements, which are regarded as necessary less
for the living generation than for the *pitara* and gods
sojourning among them; hence also the cessation
from work and the disinclination to intercourse with
foreigners during this period. Trade and foreigners

---

[1] R. van Eck, in *Tijdschrift voor
Nederlandsch-Indië*, 1879, n.s., viii,
58 *sqq.* Van Eck's account is
reproduced by J. Jacobs, *Eenigen
tijd onder de Baliërs*, Batavia,
1883, pp. 190 *sqq.*

are not agreeable to the *pitara*, who desire to see the old institutions and usages faithfully preserved."[1]

In the island of Nias, lying off the western coast of Sumatra, the news of an epidemic sickness will cause a quarantine to be established in every community, not only against the inhabitants of the infected village, but against all strangers without discrimination. The quarantine lasts for eight days.[2] Probably this taboo is observed on other occasions, as seems to be the case with the inhabitants of the Pagi Islands, which form the southern extension of the Mentawi group. These islanders are scarcely above the level of culture reached by Bornean tribes : they live in large communal houses, practise tattooing assiduously, and worship the evil spirits which manifest their power in thunder and lightning, earthquakes, tornadoes, and floods. The natives, at certain times, are said to remain in their villages and to exclude all strangers. During this period of separation from the world they may neither give nor receive anything, they must refrain from eating certain articles of food, and they may not engage in trade.[3] A very competent observer, who has made a special study of the taboo system in the Mentawi Islands, describes the seasons of restriction found there under the name of *punän*. The "great" *punän* arises from any circumstance which vitally affects the welfare of a community : when a chief erects a house for himself, when a village is visited by an epidemic, or when a cocoanut-palm is overthrown by some *force majeure*. Similarly, the inauguration of a superior chief or the choice of a priest requires the imposition of a "great" *punän*. The same propitiatory usage becomes necessary when a villager has been killed by a crocodile. The "little" *punän* relates

---

[1] R. Friederich, in *Journal of the Royal Asiatic Society*, 1877, n.s., ix, 77. On the *petara* see above, p. 35 *n.*[2]
[2] F. Krämer, "Der Götzendienst der Niasser," *Tijdschrift voor indische taal-land-en volkenkunde*, 1890, xxxiii, 486 *sqq.*
[3] Hinlopen and Severin, *ibid.*, 1855, iii, 329 *sq.*

rather to individuals and to families. Many are the
occasions when it is imposed — at house-building, at
the setting-out of a garden, at boat-making, and when
a native leaves his village to settle elsewhere. The
"little" *punän* is especially obligatory for women
during pregnancy, at birth, and for eight months
thereafter. It occurs also as an accompaniment of
marriage, when there is sickness in a family, and when
some member of the household has died. All crises
in the communal and individual life of the Mentawi
Islanders are thus kept as periods of restriction; in
some cases, however, these rest days have become to
all intents and purposes festivals and holidays.[1]

The wild and little-known aborigines of Formosa,
who are probably of Indonesian origin, appear to possess similar customs. Of them it is said, generally,
that "great fasts are held after a sickness or when any
of the tribe have been killed. At such times they will
be silent, and will only eat sufficient food to maintain
life."[2] Another traveller refers to these communal
fast days under the native name of *hiang*, and adds
the further fact that at such times strangers are excluded from the village.[3] A very intelligent observer,
describing the superstitions of the Peiwan, mentions
a curious custom according to which "one who has
unpleasant dreams must confine himself to his house
for the day."[4] This very scanty information will
doubtless be supplemented by much more evidence,
when the Formosan tribes have been scientifically
studied.

The Philippine Archipelago contains a great number

[1] A. Maass, "Ta-kä-käi-käi
tabu," *Zeitschrift für Ethnologie*,
1905, xxxvii, 155 *sq.* The greater
part of this valuable article is concerned with the analogies between
the taboo system in the Mentawi
Islands and related systems in
Indonesia and Polynesia.

[2] W. A. Pickering, *Pioneering in
Formosa*, London, 1898, p. 71.

[3] W. Joest, in *Verhandlungen der
Berliner Gesellschaft für Anthropologie, Ethnologie, und Urgeschichte*, 1882, p. (62) (bound with
Zeitschrift für Ethnologie, vol. xiv).

[4] G. Taylor, in *Proceedings of the
Royal Geographical Society*, 1889,
n.s., xi, 233; *idem*, "Folklore of
Aboriginal Formosa," *Folk-lore
Journal*, 1887, v, 150.

of Indonesian tribes, among which are the Subanu of
Mindanao, a mountain people occupying the interior
portions of the Zamboanga District, where they have
taken refuge from the raids of their hereditary enemies,
the Moros and Filipinos. The Subanu are described
as a suspicious and superstitious people with a pronounced belief in spirits — both good and evil. Ceremonies of propitiation accompany all important undertakings, such as the clearing of a new plantation,
the building of a house, the beginning of a journey,
hunting, and the harvesting of the crops. Festivals
are held to propitiate these spirits, or to celebrate some
event in which an entire settlement is interested.
From the following account it would seem that the
custom of communal abstinence is frequently observed
by the Subanu. "In contending against the difficulties
of their settlement life the Subanu have gradually
adopted an effective quarantine service against the
spread of infectious diseases like smallpox, measles,
and cholera. Upon the appearance of the first case
among any of the settlement families, the *timuai*
[communal chief] orders the establishment of the signals
of quarantine, and these are quickly provided. Fences
of poles and split bamboo, or *bejuco*, are erected across
the main trails leading to the houses of the settlement.
On these fences are placed, in fixed positions, carved
imitations of war weapons, such as spears, *kampilan*,
barong, and *pira*, pointed outward to warn the approaching stranger or visitor to remain away. It is a notice
that death will be visited upon the person who attempts
to enter the settlement while the scourge of disease
prevails. . . . Near the signal fences are erected
light wooden stands with offerings of various articles
of food to appease the wrath of the gods and cause
them to assist in extirpating the disease. Small sheds
are also sometimes erected near the stands, under
which guards may be stationed to prevent the food
from being taken by wild animals, birds, and mis-
chievous persons. But the guards go to sleep and th

food (cooked rice, boiled eggs, fruit, tobacco, betel-nut, cooked chicken, etc.) disappears, whereupon the guards report that *diuata* (god) has accepted the gifts and will drive away the disease. Superstition and good sense are strangely but effectively mingled in this scheme of practical and efficacious quarantine; and the Subanu stand alone among all the tribes and peoples of Mindanao in devising and operating such protective measures." [1]

Another Indonesian people of the Philippines are the Bontoc Igorot, a non-Christian folk dwelling in northern Luzon. They are mountain farmers and live in towns made up of political divisions, or *ato*, analogous to the wards of an American city. The business of each *ato* is conducted by a council of elders. These Bontoc Igorot observe a sacred rest day, called *tengao*.[2] It occurs, on an average, about every ten days during the year, though not with absolute regularity. Three men, belonging to what might be described as a hereditary priesthood, fix the time for the *tengao*, as for all other ceremonials of the pueblo. They then inform the elders of each *ato*, who, in turn, make a public announcement on the evening preceding the day. "The small boys, however, are the true 'criers.' They make more noise in the evening before the rest day, crying *Tĕng-aó! whi tĕng-aó!* ('Rest day! hurrah! rest day!') than I have heard from the pueblo at any other time." The *tengao* appears to be marked by the cessation of agricultural work, but not by abstinence from all activity. "If a person goes to labour in the fields on a sacred day — not having heard the announcement, or in disregard of it — he is fined for 'breaking the Sabbath.'" The lawbreaker has to surrender firewood or rice or a small

[1] J. P. Finley and William Churchill, *The Subanu*, Washington, 1913, pp. 31 *sq.*

[2] The word is also spelled *tengau* and translated "holiday." See W. C. Clapp, "A Vocabulary of the Igorot Language," *Bureau of Science, Division of Ethnology, Publications*, Manila, 1908, v, 198.

chicken to the value of about ten cents, or the wage of two days. The fines are then expended in buying chickens and pigs for certain religious ceremonies, known as *patay*. These rites are performed every new moon for the general well-being of the pueblo.[1] We are further told that the rest days are selected in order that "such intimate, important interests as agriculture and beneficial weather may be given the amount of attention they deserve. The people have no calendar for succeeding ceremonial observances, so a priesthood has developed to fix such days at the opportune time when needed. They are sacred because all petitions are made to Lumawig their god, a living spirit, hero, and benefactor."[2]

There seems to be every reason for supposing that this remarkable institution of an almost periodic Sabbath is of native origin. The Bontoc Igorot dwell in a remote and inaccessible region; and they are a fairly primitive people whose religious ideas have been unaffected by either Christianity or Mohammedanism. The *tengao* itself is apparently confined to this single tribe of northern Luzon. At the same time the sacred rest day does not stand without relation to the other observances of the Igorot. Like the Bornean tribes they have a number of agricultural ceremonies, religious in character, and designed to secure an abundant harvest. Some of these ceremonies are accompanied by periods of rest. Every year, on the occasion when *camotes* are planted, the pueblo priest kills a chicken or a pig, and petitions Lumawig for so many *camotes* "that the ground will crack and burst open." This rite takes place in the fifth period of the Igorot year, called *baliling*. A similar rite is performed when black beans are planted. The end of *baliling* (about

[1] A. E. Jenks, "The Bontoc Igorot," *Ethnological Survey Publications*, Manila, 1905, i, 205 *sqq*.

[2] From a letter to the author, dated December 10, 1910. In a second letter, under date March 8, 1911, Professor Jenks writes, "I believe the rest days are first for the purpose of having time for religious observances — this fact necessitated the rest. I never proved this point, however."

the first of September) is marked by a three days'
rest, known as *kopus*. At this time one of the priests
charged with the performance of the *patay* rite addresses
a short supplication to Lumawig and then solemnly
kills a chicken. It is a critical moment for the people
of the pueblo. Should the gall of the fowl be found
white or whitish, this means that disaster will overtake the community. But a gall with a dark green
colour implies that the spirit enemies of Bontoc are not
revengeful and that the pueblo will enjoy prosperity.
Another occasion when the Igorot rests from labour
comes at the *fakil* ceremony for rain. It occurs four
times each year, on four succeeding days, and is performed by four different priests. There is the usual
sacrifice of a pig by the priest, and each night, just
before this rite takes place, all the people cry *I-těng-aó
ta-ko nan fa-kil'!*, an expression meaning, "Rest
day! We observe the ceremony for rain!"[1] These
and other instances cited by Professor Jenks indicate
clearly that the Igorot festivals are intended to propitiate evil-minded spirits and to secure material
blessings from Lumawig, the supreme being.[2] The
evidence from Borneo and other regions suggests
that here in Luzon the rest accompanying some of the
festivals has likewise a propitiatory character, quite
as much as the prayers and sacrifices. The same
interpretation would accordingly apply to the *tengao*,
though that day seems now to be regarded in some
degree as a holiday. Furthermore, the conjecture is
plausible that the *tengao* in its earlier form was not a
periodic but an occasional observance, called forth
only by particular emergencies in the communal life.
The present form of this institution gives evidence of
a tendency, doubtless directed by the Igorot priesthood, to calendarize seasons of taboo at definite and
regular intervals. And the dedication of this "Sab-

[1] Jenks, *op. cit.*, p. 213.
[2] "It is safe to say that one feast is held daily in Bontoc by some family to appease or win the good will of some *anito* [ancestral spirit]" (Jenks, *op. cit.*, p. 198).

bath" to Lumawig may be only a natural outcome of the preëminence assigned to that supreme god, who stands out in such bold relief against the crowd of ancestral spirits, good and bad, investing the Igorot world.[1]

The foregoing examples suffice to show how numerous are the occasions on which the natives of Indonesia subject themselves to the rule of abstinence. Assuming, with modern ethnographers, that the Indonesian peoples represent an admixture in various proportions of primitive Indian and southern Mongolian stocks, we need not be surprised to discover that in certain parts of southeastern Asia, and notably among the Tibeto-Burman tribes of Assam and Burma, there flourishes a system of communal regulations strikingly similar to those which have just been described.

The Naga tribes, who are said to resemble more closely the natives of the Indian Archipelago than any of the other peoples occupying the hills of Assam, apply the name *genna*[2] to their system of taboos.[3] The following description refers particularly to the Naga of Manipur. Here, as in Borneo, the regular communal taboos are for the most part connected

[1] Some, if not all, of the Igorot peoples of northern Luzon are familiar with the idea of taboo as applied to individuals or to families at certain critical times. The Ibaloi Igorot equivalent of taboo is *pidiu*. A man, while in the peculiarly solemn condition of *pidiu*, "must not bathe, must not admit visitors into his house, and must not work, travel, etc.," under penalty of punishment by the *making*, or departed souls, for transgression of the regulations (O. Scheerer, "The Nabaloi Dialect," *Ethnological Survey Publications*, Manila, 1905, ii, 167). But these prohibitions do not seem to be socialized.

[2] T. C. Hodson, "The *genna* amongst the Tribes of Assam,"

Journal of the Anthropological Institute, 1906, xxxvi, 92–103; *idem*, "Some Naga Customs and Superstitions," *Folk-lore*, 1910, xxi, 296–312; *idem*, "Genna," *Encyclopædia Britannica*,[11] xi, 596; *idem*, *The Naga Tribes of Manipur*, London, 1911, pp. 164–186.

[3] "The word *genna* is used in two ways: (1) it may mean practically a holiday — i.e., a man will say, 'My village is doing *genna* to-day,' by which he means that, owing either to the occurrence of a village festival or some such unusual occurrence . . . his people are observing a holiday; (2) *genna* means anything forbidden" (A. W. Davis, in *Census of India, 1891, Assam*, i, 249).

with the crops. Every stage of the rice cultivation is marked by a village *genna*, the duration of which varies. Thus, among the Mao Naga the rice-sowing necessitates a ten days' *genna*, the transplanting of the rice calls for only one day of restriction, the beginning of the harvest for four days, and the harvest home for ten days. At such times the village gates are shut and neither egress nor ingress is allowed. "Among all these tribes from the day of the first crop *genna* to the final harvest home all other forms of industry and activity are forbidden. All hunting, fishing, tree- and grass-cutting, all weaving, pot-making, salt-working, games of all kinds, bugling, dancing, all trades are strictly forbidden — are *genna* — lest the grain in the ear be lost." [1]

It is obvious that some of these taboos tend, indirectly, to produce beneficial effects. The prohibition of all labour, except agricultural, during the season of rice-planting and harvesting permits the inhabitants of a village to devote their time and attention solely to the care of the crops. And the practical result of the taboo against hunting is to provide a much-needed close season for wild animals, "for these sportsmen spare not the game." It is equally obvious, however, that the regulations in question have had no utilitarian origin. Identical taboos are imposed on a great variety of other occasions. A rain-compelling ceremony, when the headman works magic for the benefit of the entire village, is accompanied by a *genna*. General *genna* are also proclaimed after the occurrence of unusual phenomena, such as earthquakes, eclipses

---

[1] Hodson, *Nāga Tribes*, pp. 167 *sq*. Among some of the Manipuri Naga the various *genna* are marked by rope-pulling contests, when the women and girls have a tug-of-war with the men. This is described as a means of taking omens for the future of the crops (*ibid*., p. 168). The Naga ceremonial is a serious business, but among the Meithei, the Hinduised neighbours of the Naga, the tug-of-war has dwindled into a mere pastime (Hodson, in *Folk-lore*, 1910, xxi, 300). On the magical significance of the games played by the Kayan of Borneo during their periods of seclusion, see above, p. 31 *n*.[1]

of the sun or moon, and the appearance of comets. These events are attributed to supernatural activity.[1] The destruction of a village by fire occasions a general *genna*, sometimes for three days, before any steps are taken to rebuild the houses. Such an event indicates that spirits inimical to the people are about and active; consequently the mere sight of the burning of a neighbouring village is enough to require the imposition of a *genna*.[2] The outbreak of epidemic sickness necessitates a *genna*, the purpose of which is clearly prophylactic. Animal sacrifices of a propitiatory nature are made at such times. Some of the Mao Naga even hold a regular village *genna*, as a means of preventing all sickness during the year, while the Kabui Naga observe an annual *genna* in order to protect themselves from being hurt by bamboos. The occurrence of mysterious cases of death requires a *genna*, for the purpose of separating the living as soon as possible from the dangerous dead; in the Mao group it is customary to hold a village *genna* when a villager dies, irrespective of the immediate cause of his decease.[3] All the Naga communities hold a *genna* devoted to the praiseworthy object of finally laying to rest the ghosts of those who have died during the preceding year. The rite takes place at the time of cold weather, after the crops have been reaped. At this annual festival, "they restore to the living those of their members who have been in jeopardy of the contagion of death."[4] Communal *genna* are also enforced in connection with the first death in the year of any domestic animals; on the return to the village of a party of warriors with human heads taken in a foray; when a python — a serpent closely associated with sickness — is killed and eaten; during the deliberations of the village council;

[1] Hodson, *Nāga Tribes*, pp. 166 *sq.*, 175.

[2] *Ibid.*, pp. 109, 167, 175.

[3] *Ibid.*, pp. 166 *sq.*, 173.

[4] *Ibid.*, pp. 151 *sq.*, 174. According to another account the festival occurs on the night of the December new moon. The shades of the dead are supposed to visit the living at this time (S. E. Peal, in *Zeitschrift für Ethnologie*, 1898, xxx, 355).

and also when a man rashly allows his private or secret name to be mentioned in public.[1] We may agree with an early writer, who, commenting on these practices among the Angami Naga, remarks that there is "no end to the reasons on which a *kennie* must or may be declared, and as it consists of a general holiday when no work is done, this Angami Sabbath appears to be rather a popular institution."[2]

A survey of these Naga ordinances indicates that here in Assam they have much the same purpose as in other regions: they are protective and conciliatory; to a certain extent they are even compelling, in so far as the observance of the taboos is supposed to prevent the evil spirits from inflicting further harm. The coercive quality of a *genna* is also illustrated by the idea that, while the ill effects of an interruption of a village ceremony are sometimes irremediable, there are other cases where a repetition of the rite is enough to avert all disastrous consequences.[3] It is to be observed, furthermore, that all *genna* are declared and supervised by the *khullakpa*, the secular and religious head of the village. He acts in a representative capacity, whenever a rite is to be performed which requires the whole force of the community behind it, a force which operates through him. "These village *genna*," declares Mr. Hodson, "seem in many cases to be inspired by the belief that man, *the man*, the *khullakpa*, when fortified by the whole strength and will of the village, is

---

[1] Hodson, *op. cit.*, pp. 109, 144, 173, 175 *sq*. The Naga west of the Doyang River are said to have a *genna* also at the annual ceremony of making new fire for the village. The fire, produced by friction, is first used in burning down the jungle before the sowing of the crops (W. Crooke, *Natives of Northern India*, London, 1907, p. 45; E. T. Dalton, *Descriptive Ethnology of Bengal*, Calcutta, 1872, p. 43). The Angami Naga mark by a three days' *genna* the first full moon of the lunar year (D. Prain, in *Revue coloniale internationale*, 1887, v, 489).

[2] John Butler, in *Journal of the Asiatic Society of Bengal*, 1875, n.s., xlv, i, 316. This observer describes the *kennie* as a system of taboo, "singularly similar to that in vogue among the savages inhabiting the Pacific islands."

[3] Hodson, *Nāga Tribes*, p. 167, citing C. A. Soppitt, *Account of the Kachcha Nāgas*, p. 10.

able to control and constrain forces which are beyond his control if unaided. He relies on coöperative strength." [1]

In addition to the village *genna* the Naga are subject to numerous regulations which affect individuals or families only, and do not extend to the community at large. Household *genna* are occasioned by such events as the birth of children or of domesticated animals, the first hair-cutting and ear-piercing, the naming of children, and finally the death of domesticated animals in the house. The restrictions apply to all who are normally inmates of the house, and to any others, such as midwives, who may be temporarily members of the family. The duration of these *genna* varies not only from tribe to tribe but also from village to village. The Mayang Khong Naga, in particular, have worked out an elaborate scale for *genna* following the birth of domestic animals. "When a cow calves, the *genna* lasts for five days; when a sow litters, three days' *genna* is necessary; while when a bitch has pups, or a cat has kittens, two days are ample. A hen hatching out a brood of chickens brings on a *genna* of one day." [2] Such observances may be said to mark the acme of the Naga taboo system, or, from another point of view, to reduce it to an absurdity.

The *genna* custom, which seems to have attained its most complicated and grotesque development

---

[1] Hodson, *op. cit.*, p. 141. The *khullakpa*, also called *gennabura*, or "authorizer of *genna*," is himself subject to a number of vexatious restrictions designed to prevent any impairment of the efficiency of his sacred office. On these taboos see below, pp. 233 *sq.* It is worthy of note that the *khullakpa* enjoys a good deal of indirect authority because of his power to close a village and declare a *genna*. An individual who violated any of the taboos imposed by him would be obliged to pay a fine, the proceeds being used to provide a substantial repast for the village elders (Hodson, in *Journal of the Anthropological Institute*, 1901, xxxi, 307).

[2] Hodson, *Nāga Tribes*, pp. 177, 180. The Naga of eastern Assam strictly taboo a house where tattooing is being done (W. H. Furness, 3d., in *Journal of the Anthropological Institute*, 1902, xxxii, 466).

among the Naga, prevails, or in the past has prevailed, throughout a wide area of Assam. The Hinduised Meithei of Manipur, whose affinity to the wild hill tribes such as the Naga and Kuki is admitted, no longer possess the custom itself, though preserving the memory of it in their word *namungba*, or taboo.[1] General seasons of restriction seem to be unknown among the Khasi, who inhabit the Khasi and Jaintia hills, except in a single instance.[2] Their neighbours on the west, the Garo, a people of Tibeto-Burman stock, have the equivalent of *genna* in the word *marang*, conveying the ideas of "unlucky" and "unlawful." But the Garo custom itself is scarcely socialized: the taboos relate to individuals, and in only one case extend to the community at large. This is the prohibition for any one in a village to labour in the fields on the day when a child is born. It is believed that should a farm be visited at such a time the crop would be cursed and blighted.[3] Another Tibeto-Burman people, the Mikir, who dwell in the Mikir Hills to the northwest of Manipur, have individual taboos of various kinds and, in addition, a compulsory village festival called *rongker*. It is held annually at the beginning of cultivation. At this time the gods are invoked for good crops, good health, and preservation from tigers. There is no music or dancing during the festival.[4] The *genna* exists among the Mishmi and Abor on the frontiers of northeastern Assam and Tibet.[5] The Lushei (sometimes called Kuki) of the Lushei Hills to the south of

[1] T. C. Hodson, *The Meitheis*, London, 1908, p. 118. It is significant that the Moirang, a more or less backward and isolated Meithei tribe, still keep up something like a system of communal *genna* connected with agricultural operations (*ibid.*, p. 119).

[2] P. R. T. Gurdon, *The Khasis*, London, 1907, p. 158.

[3] A. Playfair, *The Garos*, London, 1909, p. 114; see below, p. 57 n.[1]

[4] Edward Stack, *The Mikirs*, edited by Sir Charles Lyall, London, 1908, p. 43.

[5] Hodson, *Nāga Tribes*, p. 20. The Mishmi have household *genna* whenever the members of a family are visited by illness or misfortune of any kind. Possibly there are also village rites of the same nature. See R. Wilcox, in *Selections from the Records of the Bengal Government*, Calcutta, 1855, no. 23, p. 64.

Manipur have a well-developed system of taboo, here known as *hrilh*. Persons subject to *hrilh* "must do no work, except necessary household tasks, and must not leave a prescribed area." [1] These restrictions sometimes affect households only, sometimes entire villages. They are communally imposed in connection with the sacrifice performed before a large hunting party starts out, at the harvest festival, when an epidemic sickness rages, and on other occasions. [2] West of the Lushei dwell the Tippera and Mro tribes, among whom the communal taboo observed in consequence of an epidemic goes under the name of *khang*. "The quarantine is inaugurated and declared with a certain degree of ceremony. A sacrifice is offered, and the village is encircled with a fresh-spun white thread. The blood of the animal sacrificed is then sprinkled about the village, and a general sweeping and cleansing takes place, the houses and gates being decorated with green boughs. They attach great importance to the quarantine being kept unbroken. It generally lasts three days, and during that time no one is allowed to enter or leave the village. I have known several murders committed, owing to persons persisting in breaking the *khang*." [3] The same communal taboo is observed when a village is being built, and regularly in July, when the rice requires cultivation. [4] These tribes formerly lived in the Arakan Hills of Lower Burma, where identical regulations, known as *ya*, are also enforced. [5]

The *genna* custom may be traced in various parts of Burma. From the Naga, Lushei, and other tribes

[1] J. Shakespear, *The Lushei Kuki Clans*, London, 1912, p. 69.

[2] *Ibid.*, pp. 72 *sq.*, 75, 78, 80, 87; C. A. Soppitt, *A Short Account of the Kuki-Lushai Tribes*, Shillong, 1887, p. 19.

[3] T. H. Lewin, *The Hill Tracts of Chittagong*, Calcutta, 1869, p. 78. Captain Lewin's interesting work was republished under the title *Wild Races of South-eastern India* (London, 1870), where the reference to the *khang* will be found on pp. 196 *sq.*

[4] Lewin, *Hill Tracts*, p. 94; idem, *Wild Races*, p. 236 (Mro).

[5] R. F. St. Andrew St. John, in *Journal of the Anthropological Institute*, 1873, ii, 240.

of Assam the ethnical transition is unbroken to the
Chin, who occupy the Chindwin valley and the hills
to the west. Probably these aborigines are not un-
familiar with the *genna* as a device to avoid a visitation
by demonic powers identified with smallpox, cholera,
and other diseases. We are told that once, when
cholera broke out among some Chin on a visit to Rangoon, they spent the day hiding under the bushes so
that the cholera-spirit might not find them.[1] The
Kachin (Chingpaw) on the upper Irawadi River, a
people generally regarded as closely akin to the Chin
on the one hand and to the Karen on the other, recognize six occasions during the year, when no one is
supposed to do any work. The rest days, numbering sixteen in all, are known collectively as *na na ai*,
which may be translated "ceremonial holiday." They
all occur in connection with agriculture — when the
jungle is fired, before and after seed-planting, while
the crop is ripening, and at harvest — as a means of
securing the good will of the *nat*, or spirits.[2] Similar
customs are still observed by some of the Karen tribes.
Of the Tsawku Karen it is said that their religion consists entirely in attempts to appease various malignant
spirits. When the inhabitants of a village or the members of a household are engaged in ceremonies of propitiation, "they put up a bow with an arrow ready fitted
to the string, or some other sign to indicate that there
is 'no admittance,' or that 'trespassers will be prose-
cuted according to law,' and these insignia are scru-
pulously respected."[3] The Sawngtung Karen forbid
any one to leave the village on the day of the birth of
a child in it, and no eggs may be kept in the village
while the fields are being reaped. The Taungthu
Karen believe that giving away anything at all on

[1] B. S. Carey and H. N. Tuck, *The Chin Hills*, Rangoon, 1896, i, 198.

[2] *Gazetteer of Upper Burma and the Shan States*, edited by Scott and Hardiman, Rangoon, 1900, pt. i, vol. i, pp. 425 *sq.*

[3] A. R. McMahon, *The Karens of the Golden Chersonese*, London, 1876, p. 292.

sowing or planting days means blight for the crop.[1]
These superstitions no doubt represent decadent forms
of a once-extensive *genna* system among the Karen.
The *genna*, again, has been noticed among the Muhso,
or Lalu, a large tribe which has emigrated from China to
the Shan States. The Muhso close their villages
against strangers for five days during an annual festival, which begins on the Chinese New Year's Day.
Bamboo gateways and symbols are erected along the
paths approaching a settlement, in order to warn
possible intruders. If an outsider persists in entering
a village, he is kept a prisoner there till the festival is
over. All his possessions, even his clothes, are taken
away from him and he is returned naked to the world.
In explanation of this conduct the natives say that
the spirits, in whose honour the feast is held, are dis-
pleased at the presence of strangers.[2] The Wild Wa,
a head-hunting tribe on the northeastern frontier of
the Shan States, are said to have no regularly re-
current festivals, but hold them as often as they are
confronted by "particular dangers or necessities." [3]
The Miao (Miao-tse), one of the little-known tribes
of southwestern China, celebrate musical festivals
throughout the year. These seem now to be *fêtes*
pure and simple, though at one time possessing a
religious character. "If asked why they hold these
festivals, they say that if they failed to do so their
crops would be bad; and yet they do not profess

[1] Sir R. C. Temple, "Burma,"
Hastings's *Encyclopædia of Religion and Ethics*, iii, 37. Similarly,
the Yabim of German New Guinea
require all the inhabitants of a
village to remain at home on the
morning after the birth of a child.
This is regarded as a necessary
precaution, if the fruits of the fields
and gardens are not to be spoiled
by the noxious influences emanating
from a woman in childbed (K.
Vetter, in *Nachrichten über Kaiser*

*Wilhelms-Land und den Bismarck-
Archipel*, 1897, xiii, 87).
[2] R. G. Woodthorpe, in *Journal of the Anthropological Institute*,
1897, xxvi, 27 *sqq.*; Sir J. G. Scott,
"Buddhism in the Shan States,"
Journal of the Royal Asiatic Society,
1911, n.s., xliii, 931. On taboos
affecting intercourse with strangers
see, in general, Frazer, *Taboo and
the Perils of the Soul*, pp. 101–116.
[3] *Gazetteer of Upper Burma and
the Shan States*, pt. i, vol. i, p. 515.

to understand how the harvests are influenced by this custom." [1]

The *genna*, either in vigorous activity or in attenuated survival, has now been traced throughout a wide area in southeastern Asia, and particularly among the Tibeto-Burman tribes of Assam and Burma. Modern ethnographers recognize in the Indo-Chinese an immigrant population, probably from western China, which for many centuries has been gradually moving southward along the course of the great rivers emptying into the Bay of Bengal. The custom of the *genna* appears to be one of the most characteristic features of Indo-Chinese culture; its presence, therefore, throughout this area must be explained as the result of diffusion and not of independent origination. Furthermore, we have found that in the various Indonesian islands as far as New Guinea, and especially in Borneo, customs closely akin to that of the *genna* also belong to the native culture. It is likely that the ancestors of the Polynesians passed through these islands on their way to the Pacific; if this be so, we can understand why *tabu* in Polynesia should present so many obvious resemblances to *lali* in Borneo and to *genna* in Assam. The student whose primary concern is the wanderings of peoples cannot neglect such evidence of extensive diffusion, showing how for ages cultural elements have been drifting from the interior of Asia over the Indo-Chinese region and the Indian Archipelago, and thence into the island world of the Pacific.

What general conclusions may be drawn from a comparative survey of these communal taboos in the several areas under consideration? In the first place it seems clear that the various negative regulations, such as those imposing idleness, fasting, and continence, closely resemble some of the pains and penalties to which the savage subjects himself on other occasions. For instance, the well-known custom of the *couvade* imposes on the husband, during the pregnancy of his wife

[1] S. R. Clarke, *Among the Tribes in South-west China*, London, 1911, p. 63.

or after the birth of the child, a number of restrictions, which often include abstention from various sorts of work, and sometimes from all occupations whatsoever. The practice of the *couvade* appears to be an outgrowth of the idea that under special circumstances the close ties uniting husband and wife engender a mystic sympathy between them, so that the acts of the one affect the welfare of the other. Similar ideas underly the numerous rules of abstinence observed by hunters, fishers, and warriors when absent from home, and by the relatives and friends whom they have left behind.[1] We cannot always fathom the savage logic which has generated the numberless regulations observed at such critical seasons; but they would seem to be particular expressions of an ancient doctrine — "In quietness shall be your strength."

In the second place it is difficult to avoid the conclusion that, however vexatious and burdensome may be the restrictions resting on a primitive community, these are not without a definite psychological value. The consciousness that all the omens have been duly taken and that all taboos have been properly observed is itself invigorating; the community goes forward, henceforth, with renewed strength and confidence to the tasks which lie before it.[2]

Finally, it may be pointed out how directly these communal regulations make for social solidarity. Students of early society have long recognized the fact that the institution of taboo, in its individualistic

---

[1] For instances of "magical telepathy" in hunting, fishing, and warfare see Frazer, *The Magic Art and the Evolution of Kings*, i, 119-134.

[2] As Messrs. Hose and McDougall judiciously observe, the cult of omen-birds found among the Kayan of Borneo, though it hampers their undertakings at almost every turn and might seem to be wholly foolish and detrimental, has really "two great practical advantages: namely, it inspires confidence, and it promotes discipline and a strong sense of collective unity and responsibility. It is not improbable, then, that the advantages of this seemingly senseless cult outweigh its drawbacks, which, in the shape of endless delays and changes of plans, are by no means small" (*Pagan Tribes of Borneo*, i, 170 n.[1]).

aspects, has helped to nurse in man a sense of reverence and a power of self-restraint greatly needed under
primitive conditions.   Such beneficial results are even
more manifest in the case of communal taboos.   For,
when the restrictions are violated by any one, there is
always the feeling that misfortune will overtake the
entire social group, and hence a duty devolves on each
man to see that his neighbour obeys the law.   Altru-
ism becomes a coercive process, and social cohesion
is secured by each member of the group making himself his brother's keeper.   It is desirable to keep in
mind these positive benefits inherent in the taboo system, since perhaps excessive attention has been directed
to its hampering influence on society.

In the three regions which have been selected for
close examination — the Hawaiian Islands, Borneo,
and Assam — it thus appears that there are certain
occasions when the normal current of life is interrupted,
and when what may well be called a crisis presents
itself.[1]   In general any time of special significance, inaugurating a new era or marking the transition from
one state to another, any period of storm and stress,
any epoch when untoward events have occurred or
are expected to occur, may be invested with taboos
designed to meet the emergency in the communal life
and to ward off the threatened danger or disaster.
Periods of abstinence are imposed because of such
unusual, and therefore critical, events as a conflagra-
tion, an epidemic sickness, or an earthquake; after
a death; at the changes of the moon; at the end of
the old year and the beginning of the new year; during a time devoted to the banning of ghosts and demons ;
and in connection with such important undertakings
as the commencement of a war, seed-planting, and
harvest, and the celebration of a solemn religious or
magical ceremony.   The peoples whom we have just

[1] On the sociological conception
of crisis see W. I. Thomas, *Source
Book for Social Origins*, Chicago,
1909, pp. 16 *sqq.*; R. R. Marett,
The Threshold of Religion,[2] London,
1914, pp. 198 *sqq.*

studied have, so to speak, institutionalized their fears, working out thereby a protective procedure highly complex and elaborate. But the conceptions which generated the tabooed day in Polynesia, Indonesia, and southeastern Asia are not local and confined; on the contrary they underly a wide range of social phenomena.

CHAPTER II

TABOOED DAYS AFTER A DEATH AND ON RELATED OCCASIONS

AMONG the lower races perhaps the most common occasion for the suspension of ordinary occupations is after a death.[1] The prohibition of work at this time usually forms only one of a number of regulations, which also impose partial or complete abstinence from food and place a ban on loud talking, singing, and the wearing of ornaments and gay clothing. The taboos are often confined to the family or at most to the relatives of the deceased; in other cases they affect the entire community. The explanation of these rules must sometimes be sought in animistic conceptions. The soul of the dead man is supposed to remain for a time with the body in the grave or near the scenes of the earthly life. Until the funeral ceremonies are completed, when the ghost is finally "laid" or departs for the abode of the dead, prudence requires the survivors to avoid all conspicuous activity, if they would not attract the unwelcome attentions of the ghost. A similar period of quiescence may be considered

[1] On the primitive ideas of death see particularly R. Hertz, "Contribution à une étude sur la représentation collective de la morte," *L'année sociologique*, 1905-1906, x, 48-137; E. S. Hartland, "Death and Disposal of the Dead (Introductory)," Hastings's *Encyclopædia of Religion and Ethics*, iv, 411-444; W. H. R. Rivers, "The Primitive Conception of Death," *Hibbert Journal*, 1912, x, 393-407; Sir J. G. Frazer, *The Belief in Immortality and the Worship of the Dead*, London, 1913, i, 31-58; A. van Gennep, *Les rites de passage*, Paris, 1909, pp. 209-236; L. Lévy-Bruhl, *Les fonctions mentales dans les sociétés inférieures*, Paris, 1910, pp. 321-330, 352-396. For a useful collection of ethnographic evidence see E. Samter, *Geburt, Hochzeit, und Tod*, Leipzig, 1911.

necessary when the death is attributed to an evil spirit, which lurks about its quarry and seeks another victim.

But earlier, probably, in development, and certainly far more general, is the belief in the pollution of death.[1] Primitive peoples seldom recognize a death as due to what we should call natural causes. Sickness, and death following on sickness, when not attributed to the direct action of an evil spirit or of some malevolent person who has been practising nefarious magic, are thought to be due to the contaminating miasma of death. Death is a mysterious atmospherical poison which extends its defiling influence far and wide. Hence we have at least one motive for the very common custom of destroying the house and personal property of the deceased. Hence arise the taboos of the corpse, of persons who have anything to do with the corpse, of the relatives of the deceased, and of mourners, generally. An obvious application of such ideas requires that all activities should be abandoned by the survivors for some time after a death; and, where the sense of social solidarity is strong, the notion of abstinence at so critical a season may be extended to the entire community.[2]

Communal taboos following a death are not unknown in Polynesia, Micronesia, and New Guinea,[3] and may be traced elsewhere in the Oceanic area. In Timor, when a king dies, no work is done for seven days thereafter.[4] In Halmahera an entire village will

[1] A. E. Crawley, *The Mystic Rose*, London, 1902, pp. 95 *sqq.*; L. R. Farnell, *The Evolution of Religion*, London, 1905, pp. 96 *sqq.*; E. Westermarck, *The Origin and Development of the Moral Ideas*, London, 1906-1908, ii, 535 *sqq.*

[2] On the sociological aspects of these and other superstitions see H. Webster, "Influence of Superstition on the Evolution of Property Rights," *American Journal of Sociology*, 1910, xv, 794-805; H. Berkusky, "Der Einfluss abergläubischer Vorstellungen auf das wirtschaftliche und soziale Leben der Naturvölker," *Zeitschrift für Socialwissenschaft*, 1913, n.s., iv, 489-498, 567-584.

[3] Above, pp. 24, 25, 26.

[4] H. O. Forbes, in *Journal of the Anthropological Institute*, 1884, xiii, 420.

be tabooed in consequence of the death of one of its members. Violations of the taboo (*pomali*) are severely punished.[1] The practice of intermitting work in a village until a corpse is buried prevails in many of the Molucca Islands.[2] Among all the non-Christian tribes of northern Luzon, "there is no field work in an *ato* on the day when an adult person is buried."[3] The inhabitants of Kar Nicobar exhibit great fear of ghostly influence before the funeral ceremonies have been completed. The corpse of any one who has died in the village is conveyed at once to the "dead house," and the inhabitants proceed to barricade themselves in their houses and to keep fires burning before the doors. The houses, canoes, and ground about the village are covered with palm leaves to prevent the ghost from entering. Some of the dead man's pigs are killed, a few cocoa palms are cut down, and on rare occasions his house is burnt, or unroofed and left deserted. "Shaving the head is sometimes indulged in as a sign of mourning, together with frequent bathing and abstinence from work."[4] The Malay fishermen of the Patani States in the Malay Peninsula observe various restrictions and prohibitions, the transgression of which would bring sickness or misfortune. If a death occurs in a fishing village, no boat from that village must go to sea on the following day, and no one must set out on a land journey. The fisherman or the traveller who disregarded this injunction would have no luck and would probably meet with some disaster.[5]

[1] A. Maass, "Ta-kā-kāi-kāi tabu," Zeitschrift für Ethnologie, 1905, xxxvii, 155; J. G. F. Riedel, ibid., 1885, xvii, 69.
[2] J. G. F. Riedel, De sluik-en kroesharige rassen tusschen Selebes en Papua, The Hague, 1886, pp. 168 (Seranglao and Gorong archipelagoes), 197 (Watubela Islands), 223 (Kei Islands), 341 (Babar Archipelago), 414 (Keisar Island).

[3] D. C. Worcester, in Philippine Journal of Science, 1906, i, 844. Compare F. C. Cole, in American Anthropologist, 1909, n.s., xi, 337 (Tenguian).
[4] C. B. Kloss, In the Andamans and Nicobars, London, 1903, pp. 303 sqq.
[5] Annandale and Robinson, Fasciculi Malayensis, London, 1903–1904, i, 83.

Periods of abstinence after a death are observed by
many of the tribes of Borneo, in close connection with
the prevailing institution of taboo.   When a death
occurs in an Iban village, the inhabitants give up their
outdoor occupations and remain at home, seven days
in the case of a male, three days for a female, and one
day for an infant.   During this time the relatives
of the deceased lay aside their ornaments and bright
dresses, assume deep mourning, and abstain from music
and jollity.[1]   Another authority declares that after a
death "it is tabooed to work on the farm : at busy times
for three days ; at other times for seven days."[2]   In
the case of a chief's death the natives refrain from work
for a longer period than is usual when a commoner dies.[3]
Similar restrictions are found among the Land Dyak,[4]
the Dusun, or Sundyak, of British North Borneo,[5]
and some other tribes.   Members of a Kayan household
observe various mourning ceremonies, and in particular
avoid all music, feasts, and jollifications for a period
which varies in length according to the social standing
of the deceased.[6]

Among the Naga tribes of Manipur, with the notable
exception of the Mao people by whom a village *genna*
is held whenever a villager dies, it is not necessary or
usual to perform this communal rite in cases of regular
and non-mysterious death.   The *genna* is then confined
to the clan, that is, to the group of individuals who com-
prise the heirs of the deceased.[7]   But all cases of death
by sudden illness, by accident, by the hand of an enemy,

[1] Brooke Low, in *Journal of the Anthropological Institute*, 1892, xxi, 122; *idem*, in Roth, *Natives of Sarawak and British North Borneo*, i, 155.
[2] L. Nyuak, in *Anthropos*, 1906, i, 413.
[3] E. H. Gomes, *Seventeen Years among the Sea Dyaks of Borneo*, London, 1911, p. 139.
[4] Above, p. 36.
[5] De Crespigny, in *Proceedings* of the *Royal Geographical Society*, 1858, ii, 348.
[6] Hose and McDougall, *op. cit.*, ii, 37 *sq*. The Kayan on the Mahakam River require all those who have been polluted by taking part in burial ceremonies to undergo a two days' *melo*, or ceremonial abstention from work (Nieuwenhuis, *op. cit.*, ii, 119).
[7] Hodson, *Nāga Tribes*, pp. 99, 174, 177.

and by wild animals or snakes necessitate general or village *genna*.[1] The same rule prevails when a woman has died in childbirth.[2] The purpose of these regulations seems to be that of separating the living as soon as possible from the dangerous spirits of the dead, or of avoiding the contagion of death. Among the Khasi of Assam, who do not observe general seasons of restriction, clan *genna* are imposed after a death. The surviving clansmen are not allowed to work until three days have elapsed from the time of placing the bones of the deceased in the clan tomb.[3] In northern Arakan, Lower Burma, when any native has been killed by a tiger, crocodile, or other animal, when any woman resident in the village dies in childbed, or when the body of a person who died in such a manner is brought into the village, all intercourse with that village is cut off until the appearance of the next new moon.[4] Similar regulations exist among the Lao of northern Siam and among the savage inhabitants of Indo-China.[5]

Taboos following a death and imposing abstinence from work are found in various parts of India. Among the Muppan, a hill-tribe of Wynaad, Malabar, the relatives of the deceased do no work on the day after the funeral, and also partially abstain from food. At

[1] Hodson, *op. cit.*, pp. 100, 152, 166, 174. Compare *idem*, "Mortuary Ritual and Eschatological Beliefs among the Hill Tribes of Assam," *Archiv für Religionswissenschaft*, 1909, xii, 449.

[2] Hodson, *Nāga Tribes*, p. 88. "We find among the Naga tribes that, if a woman died in childbirth (an event of rare occurrence), the child was never allowed to live, because they believed it to be an evil spirit, a disembodied ghost, incarnated in the mother whose death it had caused" (*idem*, "Some Nāga Customs and Superstitions," *Folklore*, 1910, xxi, 301). Among the Kabui Naga not only does the death of a woman in childbirth necessitate a five days' village *genna*, but the same period of restriction is also imposed after the death of a child dying in infancy (J. Shakespear, "Customs at Death among the Manipuris and Cognate Clans," *Folk-lore*, 1912, xxiii, 466 *sqq.*).

[3] P. R. T. Gurdon, *The Khasis*, London, 1907, p. 143.

[4] R. F. St. Andrew St. John, in *Journal of the Anthropological Institute*, 1873, ii, 240.

[5] A. Coussot and H. Ruel, *Douze mois chez les sauvages du Laos*, Paris, 1898, p. 205; A. Cabaton, "Indo-China (Savage Races)," Hastings's *Encyclopædia of Religion and Ethics*, vii, 232.

a subsequent date they perform a final ceremony to remove every trace of the death pollution and to give peace to the departed spirit.[1] In former times the Kataharayan, a fisher folk living on the Malabar coast, intermitted their fishing for three days after the death of a prince of Malabar.[2] Among the Kasuba, a forest tribe inhabiting the Nilgiri Hills in the Madras Presidency, fear of pollution requires the relatives of the deceased to abstain from all kinds of work for an entire day.[3] Far away to the north, among the Paharia of British Sikkim, the same ideas of pollution prevail. All persons belonging to the household of the deceased must observe strict silence during the period of mourning, and they may eat only one meal a day and that "half a bellyful." Under such circumstances, we are told, work in the fields is impossible.[4] With these regulations may be compared those observed in Tibet, where rich and respectable men, when their parents die, abstain for a year from participating in marriage ceremonies and festivities, and undertake no lengthy journeys. Upon the demise' of the Dalai Lama or of the Tashi Lama, all work ceases for seven days, public offices are closed, and markets are suspended. The people refrain from amusements and festivities and from going into groves for pleasure, sport, and lovemaking. For thirty days women are forbidden to put on their jewellery, and neither men nor women may wear new clothes. Thus the land of Tibet goes into mourning for the loss of one of its great hierarchs.[5]

Very similar customs are found within the African area. They seem to be generally observed by the Bantu peoples of South Africa. Among all the Zulu tribes it is the rule that no one labours in the fields on the day following a death, and that after the death of a chief

[1] F. Fawcett, in *Folk-lore*, 1912, xxiii, 42.

[2] A. K. Iyer, *The Cochin Tribes and Castes*, Madras, 1909, i, 265.

[3] C. H. Rao, in *Anthropos*, 1909, iv, 181.

[4] H. Hosten, "Pahāria Burial Customs (British Sikkim)," *Anthropos*, 1909, iv, 673, 675.

[5] S. C. Das, *Journey to Lhasa and Central Tibet*, London, 1902, p. 256.

work of every sort is suspended for six months.[1] "If a person is struck by lightning, the whole kraal fast and do not even drink water, until the mediciner has performed his office."[2] The Basuto, who form the eastern branch of the widespread Bechuana people, abstain from all public work on the day when an influential person dies.[3] In Ussindja, a district of German East Africa, the Sultan Rwoma gave vent to his sorrow for the loss of a favourite son by forbidding all agricultural work for six years. Within a few months, however, famine stared his subjects in the face, and the grief-stricken father was compelled to rescind the prohibition.[4] Mourning regulations which impose abstinence from work have been described among various tribes of British East Africa occupying the territory to the east and north of Lake Victoria Nyanza. The Akikuyu, who observe many restrictions connected with the corpse, regard the day after a death as unlucky. "People will not travel, and goats and sheep will not bear, and all the inhabitants of the village shave their heads. The women will not go out for four days. On the next day the sons who have taken part in the burial do not work."[5] The taboos enforced by the Nandi present some curious resemblances to those which we have met among Indonesian peoples. The Nandi, probably in former days a hunting tribe, have now taken to agriculture and raise large crops of eleusine grain and millet. Their superstitions invest the process of farming with many restric-

[1] Dudley Kidd, *The Essential Kafir*, London, 1904, p. 253; Farewell, in W. F. W. Owen, *Narrative of Voyages to explore the Shores of Africa, Arabia, and Madagascar*, London, 1833, ii, 397. A Kafir chief, on succeeding to power, is said to have declared a taboo of all field work for an entire year and to have put to death every woman who became pregnant during this period (*Globus*, 1889, lvi, 62).

[2] Joseph Shooter, *The Kafirs of Natal and the Zulu Country*, London, 1857, p. 216.
[3] E. Casalis, *Les Bassoutos*, Paris, 1859, p. 275.
[4] P. Kollmann, *Der Nordwesten unserer ostafrikanischen Kolonie*, Berlin, 1898, p. 77.
[5] W. S. Routledge and Katherine Routledge, *With a Prehistoric People*, London, 1910, p. 172.

tions: no one while in a plantation may carry a spear or rest a spear on the earth; thigh-bells must not be worn; a hide must not be dragged along the ground; whistling is strictly forbidden. Work is prohibited for an entire day following an earthquake, a phenomenon which Nandi speculation, in common with other savage philosophies, attributes to the movement of underground spirits.[1] If a hailstorm occurs, if a hoe breaks, or if a beast of prey seizes a goat, no work must be done in the fields for the rest of the day and for twenty-four hours afterwards. It is believed that any sick person who eats the grain when harvested, or who drinks beer made from the grain, will die, and that pregnant women will abort. If the owner of a plantation dies while his crops are ripening, all the grain must be eaten and none reserved for sowing; otherwise the grain will rot in the ground.[2] The Nilotic Kavirondo do not cultivate their fields for three days after the death of any one of importance, and for ten days after the death of a chief.[3] Their neighbours, the

[1] R. Lasch, "Die Ursache und Bedeutung der Erdbeben im Volksglauben und Volksbrauch," *Archiv für Religionswissenschaft*, 1902, v, 236–257, 369–383; B. Struck, "African Ideas on the Subject of Earthquakes," *Journal of the African Society*, 1909, viii, 398–411.

[2] A. C. Hollis, *The Nandi*, Oxford, 1908, pp. 17, 20, 100. The rules imposed by Nandi custom on persons ceremonially unclean include abstinence from work. For instance, after Nandi girls have been operated upon at puberty, they must stay in their mothers' huts in complete seclusion for a month or more. After recovering from the effects of the operation, they may be married. But if no husbands appear, the girls continue to live in a secluded state for several weeks longer. If they go abroad, they must always wear long masks and veils; they must not stand near anybody or call a person by name; they may not enter a cornfield or a cattle-kraal; and they may do no work. Again, a Nandi bride, for an entire month after her marriage, is waited on by the bridegroom's mother, since it is unlawful for a bride during this period to perform labour. Similarly, a Nandi mother, after the birth of a child, is unclean and may not do any housework for a month (*ibid.*, pp. 59 *sq.*, 63 *sqq.*). Among the Habbe of the western Sudan a man, whose wife is menstruating, dares not undertake any journey, hunt, or sow (L. Desplagnes, *Le plateau central nigérien*, Paris, 1904, p. 227).

[3] C. W. Hobley, *Eastern Uganda*, London, 1902, p. 28 (*Occasional Papers of the Royal Anthropological Institute*, no. 1).

Basoga, sometimes extended the days of mourning for
a deceased chief to two months. It is said that the
crops not infrequently suffered because of the strict
abstention from work in the fields.[1] Certain Abyssinian tribes refrain from ploughing, sowing, and grind-
ing grain until a corpse is buried.[2] Among the Arabs
of Morocco, studied by Professor Westermarck, there is
a prohibition of all work in the village until the funeral
has taken place.[3]

The belief in the pollution of death is very strong
among the Malagasy. On the decease of a sovereign
many practices are tabooed (*fady*) to the common
people, such prohibitions extending to various periods
according to the will of the new ruler. Thus, to sing,
to play music, to clap hands, to laugh boisterously,
to dance, to wear ornaments or brightly coloured garments, to dress or anoint the hair, to wear a hat, to
cut the nails, to clean the teeth, to bathe, to gaze in a
mirror, and to carry the arms akimbo are all *fady*.
Such tasks as pottery-making, spinning and weaving,
plaiting of mats, carpentry, and metal-working are
often suspended. Furthermore, no one is allowed to
lie on a bedstead or to ride in a palanquin or on horse-
back, and every one is expected to shave the head and
uncover the shoulders. Many of these regulations, it
is to be noticed, are also enforced after the death of a
near relative.[4]

In the New World the funeral ceremonies of the rulers
of Mechoacan furnish another illustration of the superstition under discussion. We are told that when a king
was buried all who had participated in the obsequies
washed themselves and went to dinner in the yard of

[1] Sir H. H. Johnston, *The Uganda Protectorate*, London, 1902, ii, 176 *sqq.*
[2] W. Munzinger, *Ostafrikanische Studien*, Schaffhausen, 1864, p. 528 (Barea and Kunama).
[3] Westermarck, *Origin and Development of the Moral Ideas*, ii, 283.
[4] H. E. Standing, "Malagasy fady," *Antananarivo Annual*, 1883, no. 7, p. 74. Compare A. Grandidier, *ibid.*, 1891, no. 15, p. 316; A. van Gennep, *Tabou et totémisme à Madagascar*, Paris, 1904, pp. 100 *sqq.*, 203.

the king's house, "and having dined they wiped their hands upon certain locks of cotton-wool, hanging down their heads, and not speaking a word, except it were to ask for drink." These purificatory rites were accompanied by a season of communal abstinence which lasted five days, "and in all that time no fire was permitted to be kindled in the city, except in the king's house and temples, nor yet any corn was ground, or market kept, nor durst any go out of their houses."[1] Among the Seminoles of Florida on the day of a funeral, and for three days thereafter, the relatives of the deceased remained at home and abstained from work. During this time the dead man was supposed to remain in his grave. Subsequently he took his departure for an abode in the skies, and mourning then ceased.[2]

The restrictions following a death appear to be especially prominent among the Eskimo tribes, who possess a well-marked system of taboos. In Greenland we meet the practice of requiring not only the kindred of the deceased, but likewise all who have lived in the same house with him to abstain from certain articles of food and from work for some time after death.[3] Among the Eskimo of Baffin Land and Hudson Strait after the death of any person it is forbidden "to scrape the frost from the window, to shake the beds or to disturb the shrubs under the bed, to remove oil-drippings from under the lamp, to scrape hair from skins, to cut snow for the purpose of melting it, to work on iron, wood, stone, or ivory. Furthermore, women are forbidden to comb their hair, to wash their faces, and to dry their boots and stockings."[4] These Eskimo require the

[1] Thomas Gage, *A New Survey of the West-Indies,* London, 1699, p. 160.

[2] C. MacCauley, in *Fifth Annual Report of the Bureau of Ethnology,* p. 521.

[3] Hans Egede, *A Description of Greenland,* London, 1745, pp. 149 *sq.*

[4] F. Boas, in *Bulletin of the American Museum of Natural History,* 1901, xv, 121 *sq.* With these regulations may be compared the restrictions which, among the Kwakiutl of British Columbia, are imposed on a man who has eaten human flesh as a ceremonial rite and who, therefore, is considered unclean. He must not approach his wife for an entire year, nor is he allowed either to gamble or to work

relatives of the deceased to shut themselves up in his hut and mourn his loss for three days. During this time the inhabitants of a village must not use their dogs, but must walk to the hunting-ground. For one day at least they are not allowed to go hunting, and the women refrain from all work whatsoever. Dr. Boas notes how in the winter a long space of bad weather occasions privation, since hunters cannot leave their huts. "If by chance some one should happen to die during this time, famine is inevitable, for a strict law forbids the performance of any kind of work during the days of mourning." During these three days the soul of the deceased is supposed to be still with the body, not having yet gone to the home of the goddess Sedna in the underworld.[1] According to one account the Innuit, from the head of Bristol Bay to the Arctic, require the survivors to refrain from work for twenty days after a death in the family.[2] This is probably too broad a statement and does not allow for minor divergencies of custom throughout so extensive an area. On the lower Kuskokwim River the Alaskan villagers abstain from work on the day of a death, and, in many instances, on the day following such an event. None of the relatives of the deceased may perform any labour during the period, four or five days in length, when the shade is believed to remain with the body.[3] The rule requiring no work in a village on the day when a person dies prevails among the Bering Strait Eskimo. Relatives of the deceased must ab-

during this time (Boas, "The Social Organization and the Secret Societies of the Kwakiutl Indians," *Report of the U.S. National Museum for 1895*, pp. 537 *sq.*).

[1] F. Boas, in *Sixth Annual Report of the Bureau of Ethnology*, pp. 427, 613 *sq.;* compare *idem,* "Die Sagen der Baffin-Land Eskimos," *Verhandlungen der Berliner Gesellschaft für Anthropologie, Ethnologie, und Urgeschichte,* 1885, p. (164) (bound with *Zeitschrift für Ethnologie,* vol. xvii). These Eskimo observe like restrictions after the capture of whales, seals, and walruses, which form their principal food supply.

[2] H. W. Elliott, *Our Arctic Province,* New York, 1887, p. 389.

[3] E. W. Nelson, in *Eighteenth Annual Report of the Bureau of American Ethnology,* p. 319.

stain from activity during the three following days.[1] One observer tells of a Point Barrow woman who declined to sew on clothing, even at his house, because there was a dead man in the village who had not yet been carried to the cemetery. She feared that "he would see her." But after consultation with her husband she concluded that it was possible to protect herself from "him" by tracing with a snow-knife a circle about herself on the floor. Within this area she did the sewing required, being very careful to keep all her work inside it.[2]

Remarkably similar customs prevail among some of the Asiatic Eskimo, and incidentally reinforce the argument for the transmission of cultural elements between northwestern America and northeastern Asia. The Reindeer Chukchi forbid any kind of woman's work with needle and scraper during the period of the funeral ceremonies. This rule refers to all the houses of the camp or village, and even to other settlements in the vicinity.[3] The Koryak stopped all work in the

---

[1] *Ibid.*, p. 312. Similarly, a hunter who has participated in the capture of a whale is not allowed to do any work for the next four days, that being the time during which the ghost of the whale is supposed to stay with its body (*ibid.*, p. 438).

[2] J. Murdock, in *Ninth Annual Report of the Bureau of Ethnology*, p. 424. The Alaskan Eskimo are now being rapidly converted to Christianity or, rather, are accepting as many of the Christian teachings as can be assimilated by them to their old pagan observances. The missionary they regard as a shaman and his prohibitions, especially those relating to Sunday observance, they treat as so many new taboos to be added to their long catalogue of restrictions. "An Eskimo who is a great admirer of the white people (and some

Eskimo are not) said to me once that some Eskimo foolishly maintained that white men were less intelligent than Eskimo are. But he said that he had a crushing reply to those who made this statement. He would say to them: 'Our wise men have taboos on food and drink, they have taboos on clothing and methods of travel, on words and thoughts; but until the white man came did we ever hear of Sunday? Did the wisest of us ever think of the fact that a *day* might be taboo?'" (V. Stefánsson, "On Christianizing the Eskimo," *Harper's Magazine*, 1913, cxxvii, 674; idem, *My Life with the Eskimo*, New York, 1913, p. 412; compare pp. 36 *sq.*, 89 *sqq.*, 374 *sq.*, 416 *sqq.*

[3] W. Bogoras, in *Memoirs of the American Museum of Natural History*, xi, 521.

settlement before the last rites to the dead. No one
went hunting or sealing, no one went to fetch wood,
and the women did no sewing. At the present time
this rule is so far abrogated as to apply only to those
in the house where the body lies.[1] Among the Yakut,
when a man dies, the members of his household may
not execute any work until after the next full moon.[2]

Taboos of this nature are not confined to savage and
barbarous communities, since the fear of the death pollution has been felt by various civilized peoples and has
found expression in their funeral ceremonies. Thus,
we learn that in Rabbinical times and among some
modern Jews, during the *shib'a*, or seven days of
strict mourning, "the relatives abstain from work and
remain at home, sitting on the floor or on a low bench,
reading the *Book of Job*, and receiving visits of con-
dolence. Bereaved children should abstain for a
year from music and recreation."[3] Outcroppings of
the same belief occasionally manifest themselves among
the folk of Europe. German peasants abstain from all
work, except what is absolutely necessary, before the
funeral,[4] and the Scotch think that "it is not right to
spin if there be a corpse in the same township." [5]
This latter instance furnishes a close parallel to the
Eskimo superstition.

Feasts of the dead, the primitive All Souls' days, are
sometimes occasions for abstinence from work. The
same custom may be observed at times devoted to the
public and ceremonial expulsion of ghosts and demons
from the community.[6] Here, as elsewhere, we may

[1] W. Jochelson, *ibid.*, x, 104 *sq.*
[2] W. G. Sumner, "The Yakuts,"
abridged from the Russian of
Sieroshevski, *Journal of the Anthropological Institute*, 1901, xxxi, 107.
[3] W. H. Bennett, in Hastings's
Encyclopædia of Religion and Ethics,
iv, 499.
[4] A. Wuttke, *Der deutsche Volks-
aberglaube der Gegenwart*,[3] edited by
E. H. Meyer, Berlin, 1900, p. 461.

[5] George Henderson, *Survivals
in Belief among the Celts*, Glasgow,
1911, p. 296 (Isle of Iriskay).
[6] On feasts of All Souls, in
general, see Sir J. G. Frazer, *Adonis,
Attis, Osiris*,[3] London, 1914, ii,
51–83; on the public expulsion of
evils see *idem, The Scapegoat*, London, 1913, pp. 109–169. Compare
also P. Sartori, *Die Speisung der
Toten*, Dortmund, 1903, pp. 48–55.

well raise the query whether such proceedings have
always existed with the particular meaning now assigned
to them; or whether in many instances they may not
hark back to a "pre-animistic" epoch when the evil
influences, instead of being personified under the form
of spirits, were more vaguely regarded as some mysterious and infectious contamination.

Rites for commemorating kindly spirits or for expel-
ling those of evil intent were doubtless first performed
at irregular intervals, as the supposed need for them
arose. They tend, however, to be massed and assigned
to particular times, thus meeting a demand for order
and precision. Their celebration usually takes place
at a period which coincides with well-marked changes
of the seasons, or with one of the great epochs of the
agricultural year, as sowing or harvest. They have a
particular and appropriate association with the end of
the old year or with the beginning of the new year, a
time which, by many primitive peoples, is itself fixed
with reference to seasonal changes or to agricultural
operations.

Ceremonies of ghost-riddance and demon-riddance,
accompanied by communal abstinence, have already
been noted in Polynesia, Indonesia, and southeastern
Asia.[1] They are not unknown in Africa. The Basuto,
who do no work on the day when an influential man
dies, also observe as holidays the times of sacrifice or of
great purification. "Hence it is," writes a French
missionary, "that the law relative to the repose of the
seventh day, so far from finding any objection in the
minds of the natives, appears to them very natural,
and perhaps even more fundamental, than it seems to
certain Christians."[2] The Bahima, a Bantu-speaking

[1] Above, pp. 13, 21 sq., 31, 40
sqq., 51, 57.
[2] E. Casalis, Les Bassoutos, Paris,
1859, p. 275. The king of the
Matabele was obliged to abstain
from food and drink on the new
moon following the beginning of
the Matabele year. The late ruler,
Lobengula, compromised this self-
denying ordinance by drinking beer
only out of a bottle. During the
new-moon day "he was supposed
to have communication with the
spirits of his ancestors, and he

tribe of Ankole, a district which lies immediately to
the west of Lake Victoria Nyanza, set apart one day
each month for festival purposes.   It is then that the
Bahima seek to appease certain ghastly, shrivelled
demons who, though they expend most of their fury
on one another, frequent the kraals and occasionally
take a native by the arm and shake him mercilessly.
These demons are called *balubale*.   Their placation is
said to consist chiefly of drum-beating and beer-drink-
ing.   "There is no work on *balubale* day." [1]   On the
next-to-the-last day of the year the Swaheli of German
East Africa observe an ancient custom, which probably
antedates Mohammedan influence in this part of Africa.
They parch some millet and pour it, together with ashes,
on the corners of their houses as a prophylactic against
the evil spirits supposed to be particularly troublesome
at this time.   Swaheli school-children enjoy a holiday
on the last two days of the year and New Year's Day. [2]
The great national *fête* of the *fandroana*, marking the
commencement of the Malagasy year, occurs at the new
moon of the month Alahamady, and the first days of
this month are regarded as very unlucky for commoners,
who therefore abstain from all activity. [3]   We may
conjecture that this festival, though traditionally
established only about three centuries ago, in its present
form incorporates observances connected with the new
year as a critical season.   Some of the Gold Coast
tribes of west Africa hold a festival toward the end of
August, called *affirah-bi*, when there is a general remembrance of the dead.   No work may be done during this
festival, which lasts eight days. [4]   The Guinea negroes

abstained altogether from business" (L. Decle, *Three Years in
Savage Africa*, London, 1900,
p. 156).
    [1] J. F. Cunningham, *Uganda and
its Peoples*, London, 1905, pp. 12 *sq.*
The Bahima demons, a numerous
company, are mostly identified
with the various maladies from
which the natives suffer. See Sir

H. H. Johnston, *The Uganda
Protectorate*, London, 1902, ii, 631 *sq.*
    [2] C. Velten, *Sitten und Gebräuche
der Suaheli*, Göttingen, 1903, p. 342.
    [3] Soury-Lavergne and de la
Devèze, "La fête nationale du
fandroana en Imerina, Madagascar," *Anthropos*, 1913, viii, 308.
    [4] A. B. Ellis, *The Tshi-speaking
Peoples*, London, 1887, pp. 227 *sq.*

would seem also to perform annual rites for the expulsion of evil spirits. The ceremony of demon-riddance, formerly held at Cape Coast Castle, on the Gold Coast, was intended to drive the devil Abonsam out of the town by means of an unearthly uproar of shouts, screams, beating of sticks, rattling of pans, and firing of guns, in which all the inhabitants joined. "The custom is preceded by four weeks' dead silence; no gun is allowed to be fired, no drum to be beaten, no palaver to be made between man and man. If, during these weeks, two natives should disagree and make a noise in the town, they are immediately taken before the king and fined heavily. If a dog or pig, sheep or goat be found at large in the street, it may be killed, or taken by any one, the former owner not being allowed to demand any compensation. This silence is designed to deceive Abonsam, that, being off his guard, he may be taken by surprise and frightened out of the place. If any one die during the silence, his relatives are not allowed to weep until the four weeks have been completed." [1]

The Yoruba tribes of the Slave Coast celebrate every June an All Souls' festival lasting seven days. It resembles the *affirah-bi* rites, but the ceremony is held in honour of Egungun, who is supposed to have risen from the dead and after whom a powerful secret society has been named. [2] Since in west Africa, as in some other parts of the world, secret societies are intimately related to the cult of the dead, [3] it may be that the tabooed days, observed when these organizations hold their ceremonies, were once connected with feasts of the dead or expulsion of ghosts. The belief may also exist that the god of the secret society affects with his holiness the

[1] "Extracts from Diary of the late Rev. John Martin, Wesleyan Missionary in West Africa, 1843–1848," *Man*, 1912, xii, 138 *sq.* Compare A. J. N. Tremearne, *The Tailed Head-hunters of Nigeria*, London, 1912, pp. 202 *sq.*

[2] A. B. Ellis, *The Yoruba-speaking Peoples*, London, 1894, pp. 107 *sq.*
[3] See H. Webster, *Primitive Secret Societies*, New York, 1908, pp. 104 *sq.*

day of his public appearance, and so makes it unfit
for business. However, the taboos seem now to be
maintained chiefly as a means of securing the respectful
attention of non-initiates, particularly women. The
presence in Yoruba towns of the bugbear god Oro
compels women to seclude themselves from seven
o'clock in the evening until five o'clock in the morning.[1]
On the great feast days of Oro women must remain
indoors from daybreak till noon.[2] A native writer
points out that these Oro confinements, as they may
be called, are declared in times of political crisis, when
a new law or other measure of importance is under
consideration, and whenever a sacrifice is offered in
behalf of the community. The streets are then cleared
of all unseemly traffic and of women, in order to permit
the god and his followers to appear abroad without
danger of contamination.[3] Again, in Old Calabar,
when the great *egbo* society visits a community, all
business is suspended, all doors are shut, and absolute
silence prevails. On the departure of the god and his
attendant mummers, the town-bell is rung in a peculiar
way to indicate that normal occupations may be now
resumed. The cessation of business on the occasion
of these visits of *egbo* may last a day, but frequently
extends to two or three days. In the latter case,
however, the strict rule of seclusion is relaxed for an
hour or more to permit the holding of the daily market.[4]
During an *egbo* visitation it would be death for any one
not a member of the order to venture forth; even
members themselves, if their grade is lower than that
which controls the proceedings for the day, would be
severely whipped.[5]

[1] Mrs. R. B. Batty, in *Journal of the Anthropological Institute*, 1889, xix, 160.
[2] Ellis, *Yoruba-speaking Peoples*, pp. 110 *sq.* The Oro rites are attributed by Ellis to the *ogboni* society, but it is probable that the term "Oro" is also applied to other secret associations of Yorubaland.
[3] R. E. Dennett, *Nigerian Studies*, London, 1910, pp. 41 *sq.*, quoting Adesola in the *Nigerian Chronicle*.
[4] J. B. Walker, in *Journal of the Anthropological Institute*, 1877, vi, 121 *sq.*
[5] T. J. Hutchinson, *Impressions of Western Africa*, London, 1858, pp. 141 *sq.*

The festivals of the dead, observed in classical antiquity, were marked by taboos. Among the Greeks the rites took place on the so-called ἀποφράδες ἡμέραι, unlucky days accompanied by complete idleness and cessation of business. "At such times no one would address any one else, friends avoided all intercourse with one another, and even sanctuaries were not used." [1] Ancient authorities also refer to these days as times when magistrates suspended their functions, when courts were closed, when sacrifices were not offered and oracular responses were not delivered, and when people refrained from any business which it was hoped would have a prosperous outcome.[2] At Athens the festival of the Genesia, an annual commemoration of the dead, occurred on the fifth of Boëdromion, a day which was included among the ἀποφράδες ἡμέραι.[3] Three more unlucky days were the eleventh, twelfth, and thirteenth of Anthesterion, when the Athenians celebrated the festival of the Anthesteria. Though in outward semblance only a brilliant ceremony in honour of Dionysus, the Anthesteria had also a sombre significance as the time when the shades of the dead issued from the underworld and walked the streets.[4] Ropes were fastened round the temples to keep out the wandering ghosts, and the people smeared their houses with pitch

[1] Scholium on Lucian, *Timon*, 43.
[2] Plato, *Leges*, vii, 800; Lucian, *Pseudologistes*, 12; Plutarch, *De El apud Delphos*, 20; *idem*, *De defectu oraculorum*, 14; *idem*, *Vita Alexandri*, 14; Hesychius, *s.v.* ἀποφράδες ἡμέραι (ed. M. Schmidt, Jena, 1867, col. 211).
[3] E. Rhode, *Psyche*,⁴ Tübingen, 1910, p. 235; P. Stengel, *Die griechischen Sakralaltertümer*, Munich, 1890, p. 156 (with references to the classical authorities). The fifth day of every Athenian month was regarded as unpropitious, and hence was not dedicated to any divinity. A superstitious avoidance of the "fifths" of the month

can be traced back to Hesiod (*Opera et dies*, 802 *sqq.*).
[4] Compare Hesychius, *s.v.* μιαραί ἡμέραι (ed. Schmidt, col. 1045): "the polluted days of the month of Anthesterion, on which days they think that the souls of the departed are sent up from the nether world." Photius, *s.v.* μιαρὰ ἡμέρα (ed. S. A. Naber, Leiden, 1864–1865, i, 423), says that on the second day the people used to chew buckthorn and anoint their doors with pitch. See Frazer's note (*The Scapegoat*, p. 153 *n.*[1]) on the widespread use of buckthorn and pitch as prophylactics against ghosts and evil influences.

to catch any rash intruders into the dwellings of living men. For the entertainment of the unseen guests during their short stay pots of boiled food were everywhere placed in the streets; but at the end of the festival the souls were roughly bidden to depart. The Anthesteria, in substance, thus formed one of those numerous ceremonies for the riddance of ghosts by means of feasting and placation which have so wide a diffusion in the lower culture.[1]

Corresponding to the Greek ἀποφρᾶδες ἡμέραι were the Roman *dies religiosi*, true days of abstinence, when it was unlucky to begin a journey or to undertake any important business. During their continuance temples and law courts were, or ought to be, closed, magistrates laid aside the insignia of office, armies did not march, and no marriages took place.[2] Among the *dies religiosi* were those on which the Romans celebrated two festivals of the dead, the so-called Parentalia in February, the last month of the old Roman year, and the Lemuria

[1] On the Anthesteria, from an anthropological standpoint, see particularly Miss Jane E. Harrison, *Prolegomena to the Study of Greek Religion*, Cambridge, 1903, pp. 32 *sqq.*, 49 *sqq.* Dr. L. R. Farnell thinks that only in the ritual for the third and final day of the Anthesteria have we a genuine ceremony of ghost-riddance, this day falling so near the Dionysiac celebration as to become attached to the latter as a mournful finale (*The Cults of the Greek States*, Oxford, 1906–1910, v, 215 *sqq.*). But, on this view, it is difficult to see why the second day, the Choes, should have been expressly mentioned as "polluted" (μιαρά), and why the first day, the Pithoigia, should have been described as "totally unlucky" (ἐς τὸ πᾶν ἀποφράς).

[2] Festus, *De verborum significatione*, ed. C. O. Müller, Leipzig, 1839, p. iuMcsroq, Satuar-156;

nalia, i, 16, 24. The *dies religiosi* were sometimes confused, even by the ancients, with the *dies nefasti* (compare Gellius, *Noctes Atticæ*, iv, 9, 5), which were days marked in the calendar as occasions when the prætor's court was not open and assemblies (*comitia*) could not lawfully meet. But not all *dies religiosi* were observed as non-comitial and non-judicial days. It seems, indeed, that the priestly authorities who drew up the calendar did not wish to recognize these products of popular superstition by incorporating all of them, under the guise of *dies nefasti*, in the Roman state religion. On the *dies religiosi*, also described as *dies atri* or *dies vitiosi*, see G. Wissowa, *Religion und Kultus der Römer*, Munich, 1902, pp. 376 *sq.*; W. W. Fowler, *The Religious Experience of the Roman People*, London, 1911, pp. 38 *sqq.*; T. Mommsen, in *Corpus inscriptionum Latinarum*, i, pt. i,[2] 296.

in May. The February celebration, from the thirteenth
to the twenty-first of that month, has been taken to
embody all that was least superstitious and fearful in
the generally terrifying worship of the dead. The
Lemuria (May 9, 11, 13), had rather an opposite character and probably represents the more ancient rite
for the expulsion of the ghosts of the dead.[1] The three
days in the Roman year, August 24, October 5, and
November 8, when the door of the Lower World was
unclosed for the spirits of the dead to come forth —
quibus mundus patet — were also *religiosi*, or unlucky.
"When the *mundus* is open," said Varro, "the gate of
the doleful underworld gods is open; therefore, it is
not proper on those days for a battle to be fought,
troops to be levied, the army to march forth, a ship to
set sail, or a man to marry."[2]

To the Hebrews the Day of Atonement was a *shabbāth shabbāthôn*,[3] the holiest of rest days, "a Sabbath of
solemn rest," when "no manner of work" might be performed. The transgressor of this regulation was threatened with death: "Whoever doeth any work at all on
that same day, I will destroy from among his people."[4]
A similar punishment was prescribed for one who did
not fast on that day; the expression "to afflict your
souls" ('*innā nephesh*) was considered by late theologians to be a synonym for fasting, and as a matter of
fact the Atonement fast was the only one enjoined by
the Law. On the Day of Atonement a goat, laden
with the sins of the people, was sent forth into the wild-

---

[1] Gellius, *op. cit.*, iv, 9, 5;
Varro, *De lingua Latina*, vi, 29 *sq.*;
Ovid, *Fasti*, v, 419-486; W. W.
Fowler, *The Roman Festivals of the
Period of the Republic*, London,
1899, pp. 106 *sqq.*, 306 *sqq.* The
first eight days of the Parentalia
belonged only to the sphere of
family worship, but the ninth
day (Feb. 21) was also a public
celebration, known as the Feralia.
The Lemuria, at least in historic
times, was not a state festival, but
a purely domestic affair.

[2] Varro, *ap.* Macrobius, *op. cit.*,
i, 16, 18; Festus, *op. cit.*, p. 156.
Compare Fowler, "Mundus Patet,"
Journal of Roman Studies, 1912, ii,
25-33.

[3] Both expressions are commonly
derived from the Babylonian *shabattum;* see below, p. 235.

[4] *Leviticus*, xvi, 31, xxiii, 26-32;
compare *Numbers*, xxix, 7.

o

erness, where it was sacrificed to Azazel, a bad angel or demon. In the later centuries of Jewish history this rite took on a more spiritual character, as the ceremonial aspects of sin and atonement became increasingly prominent.

The Day of Atonement has been usually considered a very late institution, unknown in the time of Zechariah and even in the age of Nehemiah not employed for the special purpose of a national humiliation. What seems more probable is that the Day of Atonement was taken over and adopted into the Priestly Code of post-Exilic Judaism from a popular and primitive ceremony of sin-riddance, doubtless of high antiquity. It is to be observed that the fast was held on the tenth day of the seventh month, a day which appears to have marked, originally, the beginning of the new year.[1] This would have been an appropriate time for an annual ceremony of purification, since the new year is so frequently observed with ceremonies of a cathartic or apotropaic character. Even in late Old Testament ritual, New Year's Day, celebrated as the Feast of Trumpets on the first day of the seventh month, was also a *shabbāth shabbāthōn*, a time of "solemn rest" and of "holy convocation." No toilsome work might then be performed; trumpets were to be blown, perhaps to indicate its solemnity, and special sacrifices were to be offered.[2] Moreover, certain features of the Atonement ceremony, especially that of the sin-laden goat, which has so many parallels among the lower races,[3] strengthen the probability that the ritual for the day represents an elaboration of earlier and simpler customs familiar in pre-Exilic times. If this be true,

---

[1] *Leviticus*, xxv, 9; *Ezekiel*, xl, 1.

[2] *Leviticus*, xxiii, 23-25; *Numbers*, xxix, 1-7. It has been suggested that the first ten days of the seventh month were epagomenal, bridging the gap, as it were, between the old lunar year of 355 days and the solar year (J. Wellhausen, *Prolegomena zur Geschichte Israels*,[5] Berlin, 1905, p. 105 n.[2]; see below, p. 247 n.[2]). In the ritual of the Jewish church they are described as days of "penitence."

[3] See Sir J. G. Frazer, *The Scapegoat*, London, 1913, pp. 170 *sqq.*

it is not unreasonable to suppose that the "Sabbath of solemn rest" forms likewise a survival from a still ruder past, when sin was conceived so materially as a contaminating influence that common prudence dictated abstinence from work and other activities at a critical season devoted to the driving-out of evil.[1]

Ideas of this sort live long in the minds of men. The greatest of Mohammedan festivals, the so-called Feast of Sacrifices, is now celebrated as a means of securing moral purification and blessing. But the ceremony rests on a heathen basis, and its principal feature, an animal sacrifice, was borrowed by Islam from Arabian paganism. An eminent authority, who has noticed the striking prevalence of cathartic ceremonies at the Great Feast, suggests that its primary object may have been to expel evils which were supposed to threaten the people at the time of the year when the sacrifice occurred. "Throughout Morocco the first day of the feast is kept as a holiday, both by men and women, and so is generally the second day also, which in some places is regarded as a particularly dangerous time. I am told that anybody who should work on that day would have some grave misfortune — robbers would kill him at night, or some of his children or animals would die, or he would be struck with blindness — and travelling on that day is likewise supposed to be accompanied with danger. But labour is also suspended on other days of the feast, especially by the women." [2]

[1] On the relation of the Hebrew *kipper*, or atonement, to the Assyrian *kuppuru* and the connection of both with ideas of taboo, see R. C. Thompson, *The Devils and Evil Spirits of Babylonia*, London, 1904, ii, pp. 1 *sqq*. It is unnecessary to accept his conclusion that the Hebrew ceremony was directly borrowed from Babylonia. The view advanced in the text as to the antiquity of the Atonement rite may now claim the support of Professor Grimme, who sees in this ceremony one of the oldest elements of the Law and finds the prototype of Azazel in the hairy demons which were believed to haunt the wilderness of northern Arabia. See H. Grimme, "Das Alter des israelitischen Versöhnungstages," *Archiv für Religionswissenschaft*, 1911, xiv, 130–142.

[2] E. Westermarck, "The Popular Ritual of the Great Feast in Morocco," *Folk-lore*, 1911, xxii, 157 *sq*., 180 *sqq*.

The evidence presented in this chapter raises once
more the perplexing and much-debated problem of the
diffusion of culture. The custom of keeping tabooed
days after a death may be properly described as world-
wide, since it exists in all the continents. And the
observance as Sabbaths of periods devoted to the propitiation or expulsion of spirits, though less common,
has been also traced among many half-civilized tribes
of Oceania, Asia, and Africa, as well as in classic Greece
and Rome. Within contiguous areas, for example, in
Borneo and the adjoining islands, or among related
peoples, such as the American and Asiatic Eskimo, it
is reasonable to ascribe the uniformity of custom to
long-continued borrowing. Again, the close resemblance between the Greek and the Roman superstitions
relating to unlucky days — the ἀποφράδες ἡμέραι and the
dies religiosi — is satisfactorily accounted for by the
hypothesis of a common inheritance from prehistoric
antiquity. But where tabooed days are observed for
the same reasons by unrelated peoples, who, as far as
our knowledge reaches, have never been in cultural contact, the student is obliged to conclude that the beliefs
underlying the custom in question have not been
narrowly limited but belong to the general stock of
primitive ideas. In such cases the doctrine of the
fundamental unity of the human mind seems alone to
be capable of explaining the astonishing similarity of
its products at different times and in different parts of
the world.

CHAPTER III

THERE exists, perhaps, no shorter road to the comprehension of a religion as a social product than through the study of its festivals. They are preëminently social in character; they give expression to the feelings of an entire community, whether clan, tribe, or nation; and in their development they are closely associated with the general progress of society. As civilization develops, festivals tend to increase in number, to elaborate their ritual, and to fix more precisely the time and order of their celebration. It becomes the business of a particular class — the priesthood — to establish and maintain a calendar of sacred seasons. We may assume with some confidence that the priestly attitude in such matters has not been entirely disinterested. The holy day, observed with worship, sacrifice, and offerings, must contribute directly to the well-being and prestige of the sacerdotal order.

"The Greeks and the barbarians," declares an ancient geographer, "have this in common, that they accompany their sacred rites by a festal remission of labour."[1] In fact most festivals are celebrated as holidays, when men give up secular occupations and devote themselves to religious exercises and relaxation. Festivals, in consequence, assume with advancing culture a great significance from the economic and sociological standpoint. For the peasant and the artisan they provide welcome relief from physical exertion, and for all ranks of society their pageants and processions, their games, feasts, and merry-makings

[1] Strabo, *Geographica*, x, 3, 9.

give an outlet to the play instincts of mankind. We must not conclude, however, that the remission of labour accompanying a festival has always been dictated by practical and non-superstitious considerations. It has been already pointed out that in some fairly rude communities abstinence from work is a part of the regular procedure for facing a crisis and the spiritual dangers supposed to characterize such an occasion. The rest is a measure of protection and propitiation, quite as much as the fasts, the sacrifices, and the prayers by which it may be attended. Where ideas of this nature prevail, all labour becomes *tabu*.

As we pass from savagery to barbarism and from animism to polytheism, the notion of taboo, at first vague and indeterminate, tends to differentiate into the twin concepts of impurity and holiness. This differentiation, indeed, is never perfectly accomplished even by peoples which have reached some measure of civilization; and the lower races find still greater difficulty in distinguishing between what is dangerous, because polluted, and what is dangerous, because sacred. The "holy" thing and the "unclean" thing possess alike the mystic potency, the magico-spiritual power, the *mana* or *orenda*, to employ a terminology which expresses early man's sense of being ever surrounded by unknown agencies, among which he must walk warily, if he is to walk in safety.[1]

To the primitive mind the sanctity which attaches to the divine chief and king, to such objects of special reverence as bull-roarers, idols, and altars, and also to certain places and shrines, is sufficiently material to be transmissible and to be capable of infecting with its mysterious qualities whatever is done at a particular time. The notion of the transmissibility of holiness

[1] The best study of holiness in its relation to the concept of taboo is still that of W. Robertson Smith (*The Religion of the Semites*,² London, 1894, chaps. iv–v). See further N. Söderblom, "Holiness (General and Primitive)," Hastings's *Encyclopædia of Religion and Ethics*, vi, 731–741.

might seem of itself to furnish a sufficient reason for abstaining from ordinary occupations on a sacred day : the power that blesses can also blast. In practice, however, this idea appears to mingle quite inextricably with the opposite though related conception that what is holy can be contaminated by contact with the secular and the profane. Furthermore, when holy days come to be definitely consecrated to deities, who at such times are believed to be present among their worshippers, it is easy to see how the belief arises that a god is pleased and flattered by the enforced idleness of his devotees. Abstinence from work then takes its place among other rites as a recognized way of expressing a proper reverence for the divinity; while, conversely, to labour on his holy day implies a disrespectful attitude toward him. These are sentiments reasonably certain of continued development, as priestly influence becomes predominant in any community. "The Lord thy God is a jealous God." [1]

The consecration of a particular day to a divinity is a common feature of polytheistic cults. Had we definite information concerning the origin and development of the great deities of the higher religions, it would probably appear that in most instances their connection with particular days is a secondary rather than a primary formation. In other words a period dedicated to a god and observed by his worshippers with absti-

---

[1] "In economic theory," writes Dr. Thorstein Veblen, "sacred holidays are obviously to be construed as a season of vicarious leisure performed for the divinity or saint in whose name the *tabu* is imposed and to whose good repute the abstention from useful effort on those days is conceived to inure. The characteristic feature of all such seasons of devout vicarious leisure is a more or less rigid *tabu* on all activity that is of human use. . . . Sacred holidays, and holidays generally, are of the nature of a tribute levied on the body of the people. The tribute is paid in vicarious leisure, and the honourific effect which emerges is imputed to the person or the fact for whose good repute the holiday has been instituted. Such a tithe of vicarious leisure is a perquisite of all members of the preternatural leisure class and is indispensable to their good fame. *Un saint qu'on ne chôme pas* is indeed a saint fallen on evil days" (*The Theory of the Leisure Class*, New York, 1899, pp. 309 *sq.*).

nence from labour may once have been a season of
taboo for other and quite different reasons. Some per-
tinent instances of tabooed days which grew into holy
days have already engaged our attention.[1] Thus, in the
comparatively well-developed religious system of the
Hawaiians the New Year's festival was consecrated to
the god Lono; but the same festival in Fiji was not
associated with any particular divinity. Again, the
Hawaiians observed in every month four *tabu* periods,
which were severally dedicated to the great gods of the
native pantheon, Ku, Hua, Kaloa, and Kane. That
these Sabbaths had originally no connection with any
divinity and arose in consequence of superstitious beliefs
regarding lunar phenomena is a highly probable conclusion, when we recall the numerous taboos attaching to the
phases of the moon, for instance, among the Dyak tribes
of Borneo. Once more, the attribution of the Bontoc
Igorot *tengao*, or rest day, to Lumawig, the only god
throughout the Bontoc culture area, cannot be earlier
than the emergence of this supreme being from the
crowd of spirits in which the native so firmly believes.
Lastly, we have seen how, in the case of the Athenian
Anthesteria, the attribution of the festival to Dionysus
and the cheerful associations with which the fancy of
the Greeks invested it represent a comparatively late
development.

If many holy days of polytheistic cults were once
tabooed days, it follows that a taboo element may be
looked for in various religious celebrations which in outward semblance have only a festive, happy character.
Particularly does this seem to be true of the numerous
rites observed by the Dravidian peoples of India.
The Kota, an aboriginal tribe of the Nilgiri Hills, hold
an annual feast, called *kambata* or *kamata*, in honour of
Kamataraya. It lasts about a fortnight. On the
second day of the festival no work may be done except
digging clay and making pots.[2] The Uraon keep three

[1] Above, pp. 13, 15, 47, 49, 79. *Primitive Tribes and Monuments of*
[2] J. W. Breeks, *An Account of the* *the Nilagiris*, London, 1873, p. 44.

great feasts during the year. The first, known as
sarhul, occurs in May. Its object is said to be the
celebration of the mystical marriage of the sun-god
with the earth-goddess, in order that they may become
fruitful and consequently bestow good crops. At the
same time the Uraon take care to propitiate all the
village spirits, lest the latter should frustrate the efforts
of Sun and Earth to increase and multiply. On the
eve of the appointed day no one is allowed to plough
his fields.[1] In Bengal, Mother Earth is the object of
much devotion. The goddess generally manifests herself as the benignant source of all things, the giver of the
fruits of the earth. But sometimes she brings disease
and hence requires propitiation. The chief festival
in her honour occurs at the end of the hot season, when
she is supposed to suffer from the impurity common
to women. All ploughing, sowing, and other work
cease at this time, and Bengali widows refrain from
eating cooked rice.[2] A very similar festival, called
ucharal, is celebrated by the natives of the Malabar
coast at the end of January, when Mother Earth has
her annual menstruation. For three days at this time
the people stop all work, except hunting: the house
may not be cleaned; the daily smearing of the floor
with cow-dung is discontinued; and even gardens may
not be watered.[3] The village rites observed by the
Telugu, Kanarese, and Tamil peoples of southern India,
in honour of their local deities, though unattended by
compulsory abstinence from labour, are clearly of a
propitiatory character. In this respect they are analogous to the *genna* customs in Assam. Usually the
people hold no regular festival, but perform their rites
of sacrifice only when some great misfortune — an outbreak of cholera, smallpox, cattle disease, or drought —

[1] P. Dehon, in *Memoirs of the Asiatic Society of Bengal*, 1906, i, no. 1, p. 144.
[2] W. Crooke, *Natives of Northern India*, London, 1907, p. 232.

[3] C. K. Menon, "Some Agricultural Ceremonies in Malabar," Madras Government Museum, *Bulletin*, 1906, v, 104 *sq.*

has convinced them that evil spirits are about and
active. "I have dignified," writes the Bishop of
Madras, "the periodical sacrifices to the village goddesses by the name of festivals. But the term is a
misnomer. There is really nothing of a festal character about them. They are only gloomy and weird
rites for the propitiation of angry deities or the driving
away of evil spirits, and it is very difficult to detect
any traces of a spirit of thankfulness or praise. Even
the term worship is hardly correct. The object of
all the various rites and ceremonies is not to worship
the deity in any true sense of the word, but simply
to propitiate and avert its wrath." [1] The propitiatory
feature is not absent from some of the purely Hindu
festivals, which in this respect may have been affected
by the cults of the aboriginal peoples of India. [2]

One of the Hebrew agricultural festivals described
in the Old Testament furnishes an instance of what
seem to be ancient taboos surviving in a developed religious ritual. In the post-Exilic calendar the Day
of First-fruits, inaugurating the Feast of Weeks, was
declared to be a time of "holy convocation," when no
"servile work" was allowable. [3] Now, primitive peoples
quite commonly observe various ceremonies in connection with first-fruits, particularly a sacramental eating
of them preliminary to general use. [4] With advancing

[1] Henry Whitehead, "The Village Deities of Southern India,"
Madras Government Museum, *Bulletin*, 1907, v, 128 *sq.* The whole
subject of these Dravidian festivals
has now been carefully investigated
by my former pupil Mr. W. T.
Elmore. See his monograph
"Dravidian Gods in Modern Hinduism," *University Studies*, Lincoln, Nebraska, 1915, xv, 1–152.

[2] Several of the Hindu festivals
are accompanied by prayer, fasting,
bathing, and oblation. One of the
minor ceremonies during the month
of February is intended to "avert

smallpox." See E. W. Hopkins,
The Religions of India, Boston,
1895, p. 452 *n.*[2]; H. H. Wilson,
*Essays aud Lectures chiefly on the
Religions of the Hindus*, London,
1862, ii, 209 *sq.*

[3] *Leviticus*, xxiii, 21; *Numbers*,
xxviii, 26.

[4] The ethnographic evidence relating to first-fruits has been very
fully collected by Sir J. G. Frazer
(*Spirits of the Corn and of the Wild*,
London, 1912, ii, 48–137). See
also J. A. MacCulloch, "First-
fruits (Introductory and Primitive)," Hastings's *Encyclopædia of*

culture this rite tends to be replaced by an act of definite sacrifice of a portion of the first-fruits to the spirits or the gods, who have it in their power to give or to withhold the crops. The rite of first-fruits marks a time of peculiar solemnity, when gratitude to the supernatural powers mingles with fear of the hostile influences which may affect injuriously the grain that lies still ungathered. So critical an epoch is frequently inaugurated by a ceremonial cleansing or purgation of the community; and the rite itself may require fasting and continence on the part of those who celebrate it. In at least one case previously noticed, the ceremonial inbringing of first-fruits formed an occasion for abstaining from all secular activities.[1] Since a like restriction was attached to the Hebrew Day of First-fruits, we may surmise with some probability that abstinence from labour at this time was observed by the early Hebrews as a primitive taboo long before the festival was definitely consecrated to Jehovah. It is difficult to avoid the same conclusion with respect to the sabbatarian rules which invested other agricultural festivals of the Hebrews.[2]

The Greeks in late classical times appear to have regarded their religious festivals much as we regard our holidays. "The gods," said Plato, "in pity for the toils which our race is born to undergo have appointed holy festivals, by which men alternate rest and labour."[3] With this remark, indicating that for the philosophic thinker the process of rationalization had begun, it is interesting to compare the statement of a modern scholar that among the Greeks "the time occupied by the feast of the gods was as sacred, *i.e.*, as much subject to taboos, as was the whole of the Jewish Sabbath."[4]

Religion and Ethics, vi, 41–45; E. N. Fallaize, "Harvest," *ibid.*, vi, 520–525.

[1] On the Tongan *inachi* see above, pp. 18 *sq.*

[2] Below, pp. 250 *sq.*

[3] Plato, *Leges*, ii, 653.

[4] E. E. Sikes, "Folk-lore in the 'Works and Days' of Hesiod," *Classical Review*, 1893, vii, 390. The Hesiodic injunction (*Opera et dies*, 742–743):

μηδ᾽ ἀπὸ πεντόζοιο θεῶν ἐν δαιτὶ θαλείῃ

The unlucky days (ἀποφράδες ἡμέραι) observed by the Athenians included the twenty-fifth or twenty-ninth of Thargelion, a day devoted to the celebration of the Plynteria, the washing festival of their patron goddess. On this occasion Athene's image was borne in procession to the sea, divested of its adornments, and laved in the purifying waters. Plutarch's biography of Alcibiades contains a significant reference to the cere-

αὖον ἀπὸ χλωροὖμνειν a rθίωνι σι-
ρῳ δή

stripped of its metaphorical setting, means simply, "Do not cut your nails with iron on a joyous festival of the gods." This taboo may be compared with the rule observed by the Flaminica Dialis at Rome, who, during the celebration of the festival called the Vestalia, might not cut her hair or nails (Ovid, *Fasti*, vi, 225–226). The Roman antiquarian, Pliny the Elder, refers to the belief that it is ominous to pare the nails on market days (*nundinæ*), but to cut the hair on the 17th and 29th days of the month is a preventive of baldness and headache (*Historia naturalis*, xxviii, 5). These pagan superstitions have passed into modern European folklore, being widely current, for example, in England (W. Henderson, *Notes on the Folklore of the Northern Counties of England and the Borders*, London, 1879, pp. 17 *sq.*), as in the familiar lines:

"Better a child had ne'er been
    born
  Then cut his nails on a Sunday
    morn!"

Or, as another old English rhyme runs:

"Sunday shaven, Sunday shorn,
  Better hadst thou ne'er been
    born!"

In certain parts of Ireland people will not shave on Sunday (G. H. Kinahan, in *Folk-lore Record*, 1881, iv, 105). Besides Sunday, Friday is often considered an unlucky day for cutting hair or nails, and sometimes a distinction is made between the two days, as in Northumberland, where it is unlucky to cut hair on a Friday or to pare nails on a Sunday (*Denham Tracts*, ed. J. Hardy, ii, 343). In Macedonia Wednesday and Friday are the two days when the nails should not be cut, while Sunday is unpropitious for bathing (G. F. Abbott, *Macedonian Folk-lore*, Cambridge, 1903, p. 190). Similar taboos are found outside of Europe. The Egyptians hold Saturday to be particularly unfavourable for shaving and cutting the nails (E. W. Lane, *Manners and Customs of the Modern Egyptians*,[1] London, 1871, i, 331), while the Jews in Jerusalem think that the nails should be cut early in the week, so that they may not start growing on the Sabbath (Miss A. Goodrich-Freer, in *Folk-lore*, 1904, xv, 187). These superstitions may rest ultimately on the notion that such acts as hair-cutting, shaving, and nail-paring are ritually unclean, and hence that their performance on a sacred day would defile the festival. See in general on this subject, E. E. Sikes, "Hair and Nails," Hastings's *Encyclopædia of Religion and Ethics*, vi, 474–476.

mony. At the time when that brilliant though shifty Greek returned from exile to his native city, the people were holding the Plynteria, in Athene's honour. On that day "the Praxiergidæ solemnize their secret rites: they remove all the ornaments from her image and cover it up. Hence the Athenians regard this day as most unlucky, and do no work on it. It seemed as though the goddess were receiving him in no friendly fashion, for she hid her face from his as if to banish him from her sight." Xenophon, also, referring to the return of Alcibiades at the time of the Plynteria, declares that "none of the Athenians would venture to transact any serious business on this day." And Pollux informs us that the sanctuaries were roped round at the Plynteria, as at other unlucky times, doubtless to avoid their being tainted with the pollution of the day.[1] The Athenians themselves ascribed the unluckiness of the day of the Plynteria to the fact of Athene's absence from the city during the festival. It is probable, however, that the Plynteria was at one time a rite of purification preliminary to the bringing-in of the first-fruits, and hence a rite which must have existed long before its ascription to the protecting deity of Athens.[2] So considered, the Plynteria as a rest day affords a close parallel to the Tongan *inachi* and the Hebrew Day of First-fruits.

With the Plynteria may be profitably compared the better-known Roman festival of the Vestalia. The Athenian ceremonies came in May, the Roman, in June, but they were alike in content. The nine days devoted to the Vestalia were ill-omened (*religiosi*). During their celebration the innermost sauctnary of Vesta, shut all the rest of the year, was opened to the matrons of Rome, who crowded to it barefooted, while the Vestals themselves offered the sacred cakes made

[1] Plutarch, *Alcibiades*, 34; Xenophon, *Hellenica*, i, 4, 12; Pollux, *Onomasticon*, viii, 141.
[2] Compare Miss Jane E. Harrison, *Prolegomena to the Study of Greek Religion*, Cambridge, 1903, pp. 114 *sqq.*.

of the first ears of corn plucked a month previously. On the ninth day (June 15) the temple was swept and the refuse thrown into the Tiber. Then the *dies religiosi* came to an end, as soon as the last act of cleansing had been duly performed — *Quando stercus delatum fas*, "When the rubbish has been carried away."[1]

The Roman religious festivals, of which a few, as we have seen, were celebrated on *dies religiosi*,[2] went collectively under the name of *feriæ* (*dies feriati*).[3] The public *feriæ*, numbering sixty-one in republican times, were all consecrated to deities of the state cults. As illustrating the Roman prejudice against even numbers as unlucky, it is interesting to note that, with two exceptions, all these older *feriæ* occurred on days which, reckoning from the beginning of the month, would be denoted by odd numbers. The same superstition required that, where a festival occupied more than one day in a month, there should be an interval of one or three days between the beginning and close of its celebration, as in the case of the Lemuria on the ninth, eleventh, and thirteenth of February. The ferial days were of prehistoric origin, though the testimony of tradition assigned them to Romulus and particularly to Numa, the priestly king who was believed

---

[1] Varro, *De lingua Latina*, vi, 32; Ovid, *Fasti*, vi, 219 *sqq.*, 707 *sqq.*; Festus, *De verborum significatione*, ed. C. O. Müller, p. 250; Fowler, *Roman Festivals*, pp. 145 *sqq.*

[2] In addition to the Parentalia, Lemuria, and Vestalia, the occasions on which the Salii performed their dances in March and October (Ovid, *Fasti*, iii, 393 *sqq.*; Livy, xxxvii, 33; Suetonius, *Otho*, 8) and the two days succeeding the *feriæ Latinæ* (Cicero, *Ad Qu. frat.*, ii, 4, 2) were included among the *dies religiosi*.

[3] See G. Wissowa, *Religion und Kultus der Römer*, Munich, 1902, pp. 365–381; *idem*, in Pauly-Wissowa's *Real-Encyclopädie der classischen Altertumswissenschaft*, vi, coll. 2211–2213; A. S. Wilkins, in Smith, Wayte, and Marindin's *Dictionary of Greek and Roman Antiquities*,[3] ii, 836–838; and especially C. Jullian, in Daremberg and Saglio's *Dictionnaire des antiquités grecques et romaines*, iv, 1042–1066. The plural form *feriæ* indicates that the festival day recurs periodically; compare the similar usage as respects *nundinæ* (below, p. 120). *Feria* seems to have been first written *fesia*, whence the word *festus*. On the derivation of *feriæ* see A. Walde, *Lateinisches etymologisches Wörterbuch*,[2] Heidelberg, 1910, pp. 270 *sq.*

to have organized the Roman religion. Considering the great antiquity of the *feriæ*, it becomes a legitimate inquiry how far they resemble the festivals observed in modern times by peoples scarcely inferior in culture to the Romans at the dawn of their history. What likeness, in other words, can be traced between the *feriæ* and days *tabu?*

The ancients made a fundamental distinction between public and private *feriæ*. The former included all festivals which were celebrated by the community at large, the latter, those which appertained to individuals, families, *gentes*, sacred colleges, and other social groups within the body politic. Since the Roman state religion was based on the religion of the family and the *gens*, we are entitled to believe that the *feriæ privatæ* provided the model for the *feriæ publicæ;* and this view is confirmed by numerous analogies elsewhere.[1] The festivals observed by *gentes* are little known and appear to have become obsolete at an early date; the family festivals, on the other hand, flourished throughout antiquity. All important epochs in the life of a Roman housefather and his children — birth, naming, assumption of the *toga virilis*, marriage, and death — were kept as ferial days. The *feriæ denicales* are especially noteworthy, for they show that the Romans shared the superstitious notions of many primitive peoples concerning the noxious influence of death. These ceremonies, which took place a few days after the funeral, were for the purpose of purifying the house and its inmates from the death contagion.[2] Abstinence from labour formed a special feature of all family festivals: they were rest days for both man and beast. As that model economist, Cato the Elder, remarked, "For mules, horses, and asses there are no other holidays

---

[1] Above, pp. 25, 38 *sq.*, 43 *sq.*, 53.

[2] Festus, *De verborum significatione: denicales feriæ colebantur, cum hominis mortui causa familia purgabatur* (ed. Müller, p. 70); compare Cicero, *De legibus*, ii, 22, 55. It was not lawful to bury a corpse on a public holiday, doubtless through fear of polluting the sacredness of the occasion. See Columella, *De re rustica*, ii, 22, 5.

than those of the family." [1] However, we must probably include, as an exception to Cato's statement, the festival of the Paganalia, or *feriæ sementivæ*, which came in January after the seed had been sown. During this time the plough rested by command of the gods, and not the farmer only, but also his slaves and animal servants, enjoyed holiday idleness. The festival had a distinctly prophylactic character, being marked by prayers, offerings, and other rites designed to ward off evil influences from the crops.[2] The Paganalia, as its name indicates, was an old village rite which survived into historic times and became incorporated in the public *feriæ* of the Roman city. But before turning to this division of our subject it may be pointed out that among the private *feriæ* were also included those which were observed by individuals only, as a means of removing the taint of some impurity which rested upon them. A man who had pronounced accidentally the names of certain mysterious divinities was expected to celebrate a private festival as a means of expiation (*ferias observabat*). The Flaminica, or wife of the Flamen Dialis, who with her husband was subject to many restrictions, became tabooed — *feriata* — if she heard thunder, and might not engage in her religious duties until she had performed an act of lustration (*donec placasset deos*).[3]

The public *feriæ* were also occasions for abstinence, purification, and propitiation. On the calendars they

[1] Cato, *De agri cultura*, 138. Compare the Mosaic injunction relating to the Sabbath (*Deuteronomy*, v, 14).

[2] Ovid, *Fasti*, i, 664 *sq.*:

Pagus agat festum: pagum lustrate, coloni;
Et date paganis ennua liba focis.

Some ancient authorities (Varro, *De lingua Latina*, vi, 26; Macrobius, *Saturnalia*, i, 16, 6) appear to distinguish the Paganalia from the *feriæ sementivæ*. On this festival see Fowler, *Roman Festivals*, pp. 294 *sqq.; idem, The Religious Experience of the Roman People*, London, 1911, pp. 61 *sq.*

[3] Macrobius, *op. cit.*, i, 16, 8. On the taboos affecting the Flamen and Flaminica see F. B. Jevons, *Plutarch's Romane Questions*, London, 1892, pp. lxxiii *sqq.;* Sir J. G. Frazer, *Taboo and the Perils of the Soul*, pp. 13 *sq.* The Flamen was in a condition of permanent taboo — *Dialis cotidie feriatus est* (Gellius, *Noctes Atticæ*, x, 15, 16).

are marked *nefasti*, indicating that at such times all
political and judicial business must be suspended.
In the later period of the Roman Republic unscrupulous
consuls sometimes put this regulation to a base use
by ordering special *feriæ* for all comitial days, so as to
stave off legislation by their rivals.[1] The gods, on
ferial days, demanded the service of men by visits to
the temples and by prayers and sacrifices. Hence
the *feriæ* formed public holidays, when even slaves
enjoyed a cessation of toil. "Let contentions of every
kind cease on the sacred festivals, and let servants
enjoy them with a remission of labour; for this purpose
they were appointed at certain seasons."[2] These
words of Cicero reflect, however, not the original purpose of the *feriæ* but only the interpretation put upon
them by a rationalistic thinker in a sophisticated age.
We may assume with confidence that the ferial days
were not established as a boon to the labourer. The
regulations enforced on the *feriæ* indicate how, in Roman
belief, it was essential that their holiness should not be
polluted by unseemly activity. The *rex sacrorum* and
flamines, whose lives were passed in an odour of sanctity,
were not allowed even to see any work being done during the celebration of *feriæ*; hence, when these officials
went out, heralds preceded them to enjoin the people
from working in their presence. An accidental neglect
of such admonitions was punished with a fine and
atonement was made by the sacrifice of a pig. An
intentional disobedience constituted a crime beyond
the power of atonement.[3]

In the later centuries of the republic, with the decay
of supernaturalism, questions began to be raised as
to what kinds of work might legitimately be done on
the public *feriæ*. The pontiff Umbro declared that it

[1] Appian, *Bellum civile*, i, 55;
Plutarch, *Sulla*, 8; Dio Cassius,
xxxviii, 6.
[2] Cicero, *De legibus*, ii, 8, 19;
compare ii, 12, 29; *idem, De
divinatione*, i, 45, 102.

[3] Macrobius, *op. cit.*, i, 16, 9:
*Pollui ferias, si . . . opus aliquod
fieret;* Festus, *s.v. præciamitatores:
ut homines se ab opere abstinerent,
quia his opus facientem videre ir-
religiosum erat* (ed. Müller, p. 248).

H

was no violation of them for a person to do any work
which had reference to the gods, or the offering of
sacrifices — *ad deos pertinens sacrorumve causa.*[1] All
labour was likewise allowable which was necessary to
supply the urgent wants of life. The pontiff Scævola
held that any work might be done, if suffering and
injury were caused by its neglect or delay — *licet quod
prætermissum noceret.* If a house threatened to tumble
down on a ferial day, the inhabitants might take the
requisite measures to repair it at this time. And
should a man's oxe fall into a pit, he might employ work-
men to lift it out without polluting the *feriæ.*[2] Cato
thought that on holidays a farmer might repair ditches,
pave the public roads, and make everything neat and
clean about his premises.[3] Vergil, writing when this
rationalistic movement had culminated, asserts that
"even on holy days some work is permitted by the laws
of God and man. The strictest worshipper has never
scrupled to drain the fields, plant a hedge to protect a
crop, set snares for birds, fire the brambles, or wash his
bleating sheep for health's sake in the stream."[4] Such
interpretations indicate that in late classical antiquity
the burdens of the old tabooed days were being gradually lifted, and their observance adjusted to the social
and economic needs of a progressive community.

Corresponding to the private *feriæ* observed by individuals on special occasions were those public holidays
which had to be kept by the community at large, in
consequence of some unusual and terrifying event.
Certain natural phenomena resulted in the cessation of
all activity by the people and the institution of extraordinary festivals (*feriæ imperativæ*). These were

---

[1] Macrobius, *op. cit.*, i, 16, 10.
[2] *Ibid.*, i, 16, 11; compare
Matthew, xii, 11; *Luke*, xiv, 5.
[3] Cato, *De agri cultura*, ii, 4.
[4] Vergil, *Georgica*, i, 268-272,
with the commentary of Servius.
An entire chapter of Columella's
treatise on husbandry (*De re rustica*,

ii, 22) is devoted to a discussion
of what may and what may not be
done by a farmer on ferial days.
The pontifical law in such matters
was as minute, tyrannical, and ab-
surd as the rabbinical ordinances
relating to the proper observance
of the Sabbath. See below, p. 263.

decreed by the magistrates, acting on the advice of the priests and with the consent of the Senate. Festivals of this sort were anonymous; they were dedicated neither to god nor goddess — *sive deo sive deæ* — for the divine author of the portent was obviously unknown. Numerous instances of the celebration of extraordinary *feriæ* are noticed by classical historians, especially by Livy. During the reign of Tullus Hostilius, the third of Rome's legendary kings, a rain of stones on the Alban Mount led to the institution of a nine days' festival. Shortly after the establishment of the republic an aurora borealis so terrified the people that they kept a three days' festival. About half a century after the sack of Rome by the Gauls a rain of stones, accompanied by an obscuration of the sun, made it necessary for the Senate to appoint a dictator whose special business it was to appease the supernatural powers by appointing holidays and performing ceremonies. When Hannibal was in Italy, threatening the life of the Roman commonwealth, Heaven seemed to multiply portents, and Livy particularly mentions two occasions when a shower of stones provoked compulsory holidays for the usual period (*novemdiales feriæ*). Earthquakes always aroused superstitious fears and made it necessary to celebrate propitiatory *feriæ*. In the year 193 B.C. the frequent earthquakes led to the institution of so many festivals that all public business was blocked; the Senate could not meet and the consuls were constantly employed in rites of propitiation. Under these circumstances, so Livy tells us, the people grew weary, not only of the earthquakes but also of the *feriæ* appointed to expiate them, and an edict was passed that, whenever *feriæ* were ordered to be observed on a certain day, in consequence of an earthquake, no fresh disturbance of the sort was to be reported on that same day. Only a year after the publication of this amusing edict the Romans were terrified by earthquake shocks which lasted for thirty-eight days, a period which was marked by a total cessation of business. And more than two hundred years later the emperor Claudius, when an earthquake happened at Rome, never failed to appoint holidays for sacred rites. Similar ceremonies, *pro valetudine populi*, were sometimes performed to drive away a devastating pestilence.[1]

To the ancient Romans the celebration of ferial days thus provided an appropriate and effectual method of meeting a crisis. Like the tabooed days observed in Polynesia, Indonesia, and southeastern Asia at the present time, the *feriæ* were occasions for the propitiation of supernatural and hostile powers. As such they must have been, originally, periods of gloom and not of joy. That subsequently, when superstition had in some measure relaxed its grip, they became festive occasions, celebrated so luxuriously that both Sulla and Augustus felt themselves obliged to promulgate laws restricting expenditures in connection with them,[2] may be taken as only another instance of man's ineradicable tendency to convert his fast days into feast days.

---

[1] Livy, i, 31, iii, 5, vii, 28, xxi, 62, xxv, 7, xxxiv, 55, xxxv, 40, xli, 21, xlii, 2; Suetonius, *Divus Claudius*, 22. Many more instances are given by Julius Obse-quens in his curious work, *De prodigiis*, 22, 33, 54, 58, 68, 104, 111.
[2] Gellius, *Noctes Atticæ*, ii, 24, 11; compare Horace, *Carmina*, ii, 3, 6–9.

CHAPTER IV

MARKET DAYS

Rest days, more or less regular in occurrence and following at short intervals after periods of continuous labour, are frequently observed by primitive agriculturists. Sabbaths of this sort seem to be unknown among migratory hunting and fishing peoples or among nomadic pastoral tribes.[1] A wandering hunter requires no regular day of rest, since his life passes in alternations of continuous labour, while following the chase,

[1] The Indians of Cape Flattery, state of Washington, are said to keep the month of August as a period of repose when no berries are picked and no fish are taken from the sea, except occasionally by children (J. G. Swan, in *Smithsonian Contributions to Knowledge*, xvi, no. 220, p. 91). Perhaps the practice was consciously designed to establish a "close season," though this is probably attributing too much foresight to the Indian. The fish or berries may have been considered unfit for eating in August. After gathering the yam harvest the Bini of Benin keep the first month of the dry season as a time of idleness (R. E. Dennett, *At the Back of the Black Man's Mind*, London, 1906, p. 216). Here a period of rest is observed by an agricultural people because they have no special labour to perform. Among the Akikuyu of British East Africa there are three months in the year when little or no work is done, since the crops are then ripening (K. R. Dundas, in *Man*, 1909, ix, 38). The Yuchi Indians, now in the state of Oklahoma, keep autumn as "a period of combined rest, hunting, and enjoyment." The winter, also, is passed in idleness and recreation (F. G. Speck, *Ethnology of the Yuchi Indians*, Philadelphia, 1909, p. 67). Dr. C. G. Seligmann has sent to me, in manuscript, some curious information regarding a division of time observed by the Sinaugolo, a hill-tribe to the east of Port Moresby, British New Guinea. It seems that long ago, according to Sinaugolo tradition, the people had to labour incessantly and enjoyed no opportunity to celebrate their dances and other festive ceremonies. So they instituted what was called the *kaba* period as a relaxation from the hard work of ordinary life. During this period, which recurred every other year or oftener, the Sinaugolo danced and held their most important feasts. The division of time into *kaba* and *dauka* (specially devoted to labour) has now lapsed.

and of almost uninterrupted idleness, after a successful
hunt. For the shepherd there can be no relaxation
of the diurnal duties, for every morning the cattle
must be driven abroad to pasture, they must be watched
and watered, and at night they must be milked. And,
as Rudolf von Ihering has suggested, the shepherd,
compared with the farmer, scarcely needs a regular
rest day; his occupation causes him so little continuous exertion that he can pursue it all the year round
without any injury to his health. A farmer, however,
is benefited by a period of rest recurring more or less
regularly, and, though agricultural pursuits are dependent on the seasons and weather, he is usually
able to postpone his work for a brief period without
serious loss. It might be argued, therefore, that the
change from pastoral to agricultural life would itself
be sufficient to call into existence the institution of a
periodic rest day.[1] The evidence to be submitted
suggests, however, that the connection of the rest day
with the farmer's pursuits is secondary, rather than
direct, and is due to the obvious fact that the Sabbath
institution implies a settled life, a more or less developed
form of social organization and government, and something approaching a calendar system.

The greater number of periodic rest days observed
by agricultural peoples in the lower stages of culture
are associated with the institution of the market.[2]
Days on which markets regularly take place are not

[1] *The Evolution of the Aryan*, translated by A. Drucker, London, 1897, p. 117.

[2] On primitive markets see Karl Andree, *Geographie des Welthandels*, Stuttgart, 1867, i, 40–81; C. Köhne, "Markt-, Kaufmanns- und Handelsrecht in primitiven Kulturverhältnissen," *Zeitschrift für vergleichende Rechtswissenschaft*, 1895, xi, 196–220; R. Lasch, "Das Marktwesen auf den primitiven Kulturstufen," *Zeitschrift für Socialwissenschaft*, 1906, ix, 619–627, 700–715, 764–782; H. Schurtz, *Das afrikanische Gewerbe*, Leipzig, 1900, pp. 115–122; P. J. Hamilton Grierson, *The Silent Trade*, Edinburgh, 1903, pp. 54–62; H. L. Roth, "Trading in Early Days," *Bankfield Museum Notes*, Halifax (Eng.), 1908, no. 5, pp. 23 *sqq.*; N. W. Thomas, "The Market in African Law and Custom," *Journal of the Society of Comparative Legislation*," 1908, n.s., no. 19, pp. 90–106.

infrequently characterized by sabbatarian regulations. It is necessary, therefore, to present in some detail the evidence for market weeks and market days in various parts of the world.[1]

Some Australian tribes have established trade centres, where there are periodical meetings for the purpose of exchanging the products and manufactures of neighbouring communities. More or less bartering occurs also in connection with great tribal convocations, especially those for the initiation ceremonies.[2] Necessarily, such gatherings take place at infrequent intervals. The beginnings of regular markets may, however, be traced in certain parts of New Guinea and among some of the Melanesian Islands. The natives of the Mekeo District of British New Guinea are said to hold markets, every fifth day at Mawaia and Mohu (on the banks of the Angabunga River), and at other intervals elsewhere. Women from several villages will assemble at some appointed place, usually on the boundary between two tribes, and there will exchange their products for commodities from other localities. The bartering lies entirely in the hands of the women, who, however, are accompanied by a few armed men acting as a guard.[3] The Kerepunu of Hood Peninsula, to the east of Port Moresby, are described by a missionary who knew them well as most industrious farmers: every morning men, women, and children go to work in the fields and return only at nightfall. "They have a rule, to which they strictly adhere all the year round, of working for two days and resting the third."[4] The

[1] Some observers use ambiguous language, when referring to the length — four, five, six days, etc. — of market weeks. Throughout this chapter I have regularly translated by "every fifth day" such expressions as "tous les cinq jours," "de cinq en cinq jours," "alle fünf Tage," "einmal in fünf Tagen," and "einmaal in de vijf dagen."

[2] A. W. Howitt, The Native Tribes of South-east Australia, London, 1904, pp. 714 sqq. On Australian barter see G. C. Wheeler, The Tribe and Intertribal Relations in Australia, London, 1910, pp. 93–97.

[3] A. C. Haddon, Head-hunters, Black, White, and Brown, London, 1901, pp. 265, 269.

[4] James Chalmers, in Chalmers and Gill, Work and Adventure in

Kerepunu rest day may have originated in a practice, now lapsed, of holding a market every third day, since there is evidence for the former existence of markets in the neighbourhood of Port Moresby.[1] The natives of Patipi and Roembatti, on the MacCluer Gulf in the extreme western part of Dutch New Guinea, have markets, which as a rule recur every fifth day.[2] In the Gazelle Peninsula, Bismarck Archipelago, markets at which the women buy and sell take place every third day.[3] In New Caledonia, where each tribe is divided into sea-folk and bush-folk, the former being cocoa-tree planters and fishers, the latter being yam-growers, there is said to be a lively market conducted each week by the women. "The ladies [sic] of each section of the tribe sit down in rows with their produce before them, and barter is transacted in dances, with a good deal of manœuvring."[4] In some parts of old Polynesia markets were held at stated periods, but, unfortunately, no record seems to have been made of the time intervals in popular use.[5]

Markets take place in Celebes,[6] Sumatra, and Java, usually every fifth day, but sometimes at shorter inter-

---

New Guinea, London, 1885, pp. 40 *sq.* Compare M. Krieger, *Neu-Guinea,* Berlin, 1899, p. 335. Sir William MacGregor observes that the institution of the Sabbath, as a day of rest, "is not quite new to the Papuan, but . . . the Papuan Sabbath of Keapara [Kerepunu] exceeds the Hebrew in dividing time into weeks of three days. The great majority of the tribes, however, do not seem to have a regular week, and work or rest capriciously" (*British New Guinea,* London, 1897, pp. 44 *sq.*). See above, p. 26 *n.*[1]

[1] C. G. Seligmann, *The Melanesians of British New Guinea,* Cambridge, 1910, pp. 48, 94 (Koita).

[2] J. S. A. van Dissel, in *Tijdschrift van het koninklijk neder-*landsch aardrijkskundig genootschap, 1904, second series, xxi, 644.

[3] J. Graf Pfeil, *Studien und Beobachtungen aus der Südsee,* Brunswick, 1899, p. 116.

[4] J. J. Atkinson, in *Folk-lore,* 1903, xiv, 245. Mr. Atkinson in this passage probably has in mind the European week introduced into New Caledonia by the French.

[5] Basil Thomson, *The Fijians,* London, 1908, p. 288; Wilkes, *Narrative of the U.S. Exploring Expedition,* iii, 300 *sq.* (Somu-Somu, in the Fiji group); J. J. Jarves, *History of the Hawaiian or Sandwich Islands,*[2] Boston, 1843, p. 77.

[6] P. Sarasin and F. Sarasin, *Reisen in Celebes,* Wiesbaden, 1905, ii, 324.

vals. Among the Batta of Sumatra a market occurs every third, fourth, or fifth day, according to a regular succession and in a designated place, until the round of participating villages has been made. At Batta markets all hostilities are suspended, and it is sometimes required that every man who carries a musket in the market place shall put a green bough in the muzzle, as a token of his peaceful intentions.[1] The Javanese *pasar*, or market week, consisted of five days — *lege* (or *manis*), *pahing* (or *pa*), *pon*, *wage*, and *kaliwon*. The principal use of the Javanese week was to determine the markets or fairs held in the important towns.[2]

The *pasar* spread from Java to the island of Bali, where it is employed in combination with the week of seven days.[3] In the Malay Peninsula, side by side with the ordinary seven-day week, there is a popular cycle of five days used for the determination of lucky and unlucky days. The names of the days are those of Hindu divinities, but the cycle itself is probably of Javanese origin.[4]

Markets recurring every fifth day are found among the Indo-Chinese, as in Tonkin [5] and the various Lao states of northern Siam.[6] Among the Shan all work

[1] W. Marsden, *The History of Sumatra*,[3] London, 1811, pp. 379 *sq.*; F. Junghuhn, *Die Battaländer auf Sumatra*, Berlin, 1847, pp. 227 *sq.*; J. v. Brenner, *Besuch bei den Kannibalen Sumatras*, Würzburg, 1894, p. 291; B. Hagen, in *Petermanns Mitteilungen*, 1883, xxix, 173 (Batta of Lake Toba); W. Volz, *Nord-Sumatra*, Berlin, 1909, i, 267.

[2] Sir T. S. Raffles, *History of Java*,[3] London, 1830, i, 531; P. J. Veth, *Java*,[3] Haarlem, 1907, iv, 296 *sqq.* The names of the days in the *pasar* were considered to bear a mystical relation to colours and the divisions of the horizon, the first day (white, east), the second (red, south), the third (yellow, west), the fourth (black, north), and the fifth

day a mixed colour, and *focus*, or centre. See John Crawfurd, *History of the Indian Archipelago*, Edinburgh, 1820, i, 289 *sq.* These fancies must be explained by the colour symbolism which so frequently attaches to the cardinal points.

[3] R. Friederich, in *Journal of the Royal Asiatic Society*, 1878, n.s., x, 88 *sqq.*; compare *ibid.*, 1876, n.s., viii, 198.

[4] W. W. Skeat, *Malay Magic*, London, 1900, pp. 545 *sq.*

[5] J. Richard, *Histoire naturelle, civile, et politique du Tonquin*, Paris, 1778, i, 151.

[6] Lillian J. Curtis, *The Laos of North Siam*, Philadelphia, 1903, p. 132.

ceases on market days, except what is necessarily involved in buying and selling. Every native tries to be in his own village when the market takes place there, not only to trade but also to exchange news and gossip. The centre of the village becomes a forum, where every subject is fully discussed.[1] "The Shan is a born trader, and the great feature of life in this country is the bazaar, which is held on every fifth day at all the chief villages of the states."[2] Another traveller tells us that on the first three of the five days constituting the Shan market week small bazaars are held in different parts of the country, but no trading takes place anywhere on the fourth day.[3] The Khasi of Assam have a great market every eighth day, from which circumstance they have developed a week of eight days. "The reason of the eight-day week is because the markets are usually held every eighth day. The names of the days of the week are not those of planets, but of places where the principal markets are held, or used to be held, in the Khasi and Jaintia hills."[4] It may be regarded as certain that this eight-day period arose from a doubling of an earlier four-day cycle, as has been the case among certain African peoples. Even now in the Wár country, lying to the south of the Khasi and Jaintia District, markets are usually held every fourth day.[5]

Throughout the central parts of Africa, from the British and German possessions in the east to those of the Portuguese and French in the west, there are numerous market places where neighbouring communities

[1] Mrs. Leslie Milne, *The Shans at Home*, London, 1910, p. 132.

[2] C. E. D. Black, in *Geographical Journal*, 1895, vi, 30 (Shan of Upper Burma). Compare also *Gazetteer of Upper Burma and the Shan States*, edited by Scott and Hardiman, Rangoon, 1900, pt. i, vol. i, p. 536 (Shan of Lower Burma).

[3] R. G. Woodthorpe, in *Journal of the Anthropological Institute*, 1897, xxvi, 19.

[4] P. R. T. Gurdon, *The Khasis*, London, 1907, p. 189. According to C. Becker (*Anthropos*, 1909, iv, 894) the market is called *jeu duh*.

[5] Gurdon, *op. cit.*, p. 190. Compare Sir J. D. Hooker (*Himalayan Journals*, London, 1891, p. 487), who attributes the fourth-day markets to the Khasi generally.

meet regularly to exchange their productions. Usually every fourth day is a market day, observed with the cessation of ordinary occupations, and by the Wanika of British East Africa, according to missionary testimony, with feasting and carousing.[1] In the same part of British East Africa the Wagiriama possess a week of four days, each with its name.[2] Among the Akikuyu, who employ thirty-day months beginning with new moon, there is a week of four days, the latter being indicated by the names of the different markets held on them. Each market is held on the fourth day of the cycle, and no two markets in the same neighbourhood occur on the same day.[3] The Akikuyu market places in populous districts are often not more than seven miles apart. The site chosen for a market is usually a hill-top, sufficiently open and accessible to accommodate the natives who may assemble there to the number of four or five thousand. All in all the market forms a very important feature of Akikuyu society.[4] The Wachaga of German East Africa, who dwell on the southern slopes of mighty Kilimanjaro, the highest mountain in Africa, hold a daily market, so ordered as to recur every third day in one of three neighbouring settlements. The days of this three-day week are separately named, and hence the Wachaga always know where the market is to be held. The markets, which are said to be very ancient, are visited only by women.[5] The English missionary, David

---

[1] J. L. Krapf, *Travels, Researches, and Missionary Labours*, London, 1867, pp. 82, 365.

[2] W. W. A. Fitzgerald, *Travels in the Coastlands of British East Africa*, London, 1898, p. 111, quoting W. E. Taylor, *Vocabulary of the Giryama Language*, London, 1897. The name applied to the first day of the week — *jumwa* — is directly taken from the Arabic *al jum'a* (Friday, the Mohammedan day of worship), from which circumstance it may be concluded

that the Wagiriama observe *jumwa* both as a market day and a rest day. Similarly, the name of the weekly market held at Antananarivo, the capital of Madagascar, is *zoma*, or Friday (*Antananarivo Annual*, 1889–1892, iv, 372).

[3] K. R. Dundas, in *Man*, 1909, ix, 38.

[4] W. S. Routledge and Katherine Routledge, *With a Prehistoric People*, London, 1910, pp. 105 *sq.*

[5] A Widenmann, in *Petermanns Mitteilungen*, 1899, Ergänzungsheft,

Livingstone, has described the markets held by the
Manyema, who occupy part of the territory between
Lake Tanganyika and the Congo. As many as three
thousand people, chiefly women, may sometimes be
seen in the *chitoka*, or market place. The market is
held to-day in one locality, to-morrow in another, and
so on till the cycle of four days is completed.[1] Among
the natives on the lower Lomami River, near the equa-
tor, markets are described as recurring every third
day,[2] and among the Bakuba (Bushongo), who occupy
the valley of the Sankuru River, every fifth day.[3] The
Baluba, whose territory lies between the Sankuru and
Kasai rivers, hold important markets. A German
explorer who was present at one of them described the
market place as neutral ground, where even members
of hostile tribes might appear without danger. The
chief, in whose honour this primitive fair was held,
kept peace and order, assisted by half a dozen stalwart
guards carrying broad axes on their shoulders. Whenever any dispute arose, these policemen were immediately on the scene of action.[4] The four-day market
week is found among various tribes, such as the Bayaka,[5]
Bambala,[6] and Bahuana,[7] occupying the region between
the Loange and Kwango rivers, tributaries of the
Kasai.

no. 129, p. 69; M. Merker, *ibid.*,
1902, no. 138, p. 25; G. Volkens,
Der Kilimandscharo, Berlin, 1897,
p. 239; B. Gutmann, "Feldbau-
sitten und Wachstumsbräuche der
Wadschagga," *Zeitschrift für Ethnologie*, 1913, xlv, 502.

[1] Horace Waller, editor, *The
Last Journals of David Livingstone
in Central Africa*, New York, 1875,
p. 367. See also V. L. Cameron,
Across Africa, London, 1877, ii, 3.

[2] E. Torday, in *Mitteilungen der
anthropologischen Gesellschaft in
Wien*, 1911, xli, 192.

[3] H. v. Wissmann *et al.*, *Im
Innern Afrikas*,[2] Leipzig, 1891,
p. 252.

[4] H. v. Wissmann, *My Second
Journey through Equatorial Africa*,
London, 1891, p. 125.

[5] Torday and Joyce, in *Journal
of the Anthropological Institute*,
1906, xxxvi, 44. Each day of the
Bayaka week bears a name, the
last being *pungu*, or market day
(*ibid.*, p. 47).

[6] Torday and Joyce, *ibid.*, 1905,
xxxv, 413. The Bambala year
consists of thirteen lunar months,
each divided into seven weeks of
four days, the last day of each week
being *pika*, or market day.

[7] Torday and Joyce, *ibid.*, 1906,
xxxvi, 291.

The market week (*lumingu*[1]), four days in length, appears to be generally diffused among the peoples on both banks of the lower Congo. A missionary, long resident in this part of Africa, tells us that here the week consists of four days, named *nkandu, konzo, nkenge,* and *nsona* in the cataract region. The markets are designated after the days of the week and the towns near which they are held. For instance, the Manyama market is known as *nsona a Manyama,* because it is held on *nsona* day. The great trade markets, however, usually occur every eighth day, for the convenience of traders and to insure a good attendance. At the smaller, local markets, held every fourth day, exchanges are limited to goats, fowls, and foodstuffs. Every one wants to increase the attendance at these local markets; hence it may be declared a penal offence for a woman to go to her farm on the market day. "In some parts another day of the short week is declared to be an unlucky day for farming operations. This is no lingering trace of the idea of a Sabbath, for the day fixed is most arbitrary, two adjacent villages avoiding different days, while in others the women will work any day."[2] An early explorer, referring to the custom of observing *nsona* as a rest day, declares that "on this day they refrain from working in the plantations, under the superstitious notion that the crop would fail; they, however, perform any other kind of work."[3] In Loango, where the natives have a month of twenty-eight days reckoned from new moon, seven weeks are counted to the month. The four weekdays are called, respectively, *nsona, nduka, ntono,* and *nsilu,* the first being regarded as a day of rest.[4] Another writer describes *sona* (*nsona*) as the men's day

[1] Sir H. H. Johnston, *The River Congo,* London, 1884, p. 455.

[2] H. H. Bentley, *Pioneering on the Congo,* London, 1900, i, 399 *sq.*

[3] J. K. Tuckey, *Narrative of an Expedition to explore the River Zaire,* New York, 1818, p. 238.

[4] E. Pechüel-Loesche, in *Die Loango-Expedition,* dritte Abteilung, erste Hälfte, Stuttgart, 1907, p. 139. See also A. Bastian, *Die deutsche Expedition an der Loango-Küste,* Jena, 1874, i, 209.

of rest, but the women's market day, when the latter
buy and sell in the market.   At this time it is regarded
as wrong for husbands to have intercourse with their
wives. On another day, *ntona* (*ntono*), the women
may not plant, and burials take place.[1] With these
accounts it is interesting to compare the statement of
an old writer, according to whom the Loango negroes
"never work above three days in succession; the fourth
is for them a general rest day, during which they are
not allowed to engage in tillage. The men, who repose habitually, work still less on that day. They
walk, sport, and go to market. ·The missionaries have
been unable to procure from the negroes any explanation of this period of four days, which forms their
week."[2]

The market is a well-developed institution among
the semi-civilized negroes about the Gulf of Guinea.
In this part of Africa the sabbatarian character of the
market day is specially pronounced. Markets every
third, fifth, eighth, or tenth day have been noticed
in the interior districts of Kamerun. Market days
are observed with abstinence from work of every sort,
including farm labour; indeed, says an observer,
they may be considered the Sundays of the native

[1] R. E. Dennett, *At the Back of the Black Man's Mind*, London, 1906, pp. 64, 140; idem, *Notes on the Folklore of the Fjort*, London, 1898, pp. 8, 137. Among the lower Congo tribes, generally, the dead are buried only on two of the four weekdays (J. H. Weeks, in *Folklore*, 1909, xx, 61; compare idem, *Among the Primitive Bakongo*, Philadelphia, 1914, p. 249).

[2] L. B. Proyart, *Histoire de Loango, Kakongo, et autres royaumes d'Afrique*, Paris, 1776, p. 116. A still earlier reference to this African Sabbath will be found in G. A. Cavazzi da Montecuccoli, *Istorica descrizione de' tre regni Congo, Matamba, et Angola*, Bologna,

1687, p. 24. For further details relating to markets and market weeks among the lower Congo peoples see Herbert Ward, *Five Years with the Congo Cannibals*, London, 1890, p. 59; J. H. Weeks, *Congo Life and Folklore*, London, 1911, pp. 227 sq.; H. Nipperdey, "Zur Bedeutung der Wochen-Märkte am Congo," *Revue coloniale internationale*, 1887, v, 205-214; A. Thonnar, *Essai sur le système économique des primitifs d'après les populations de l'état indépendant du Congo*, Brussels, 1901, pp. 82-114; A. Cureau, *Les sociétés primitives de l'Afrique équatoriale*, Paris, 1912, pp. 295 sqq.

calendar.[1] . In Old Calabar the week consists of eight
days. The weekdays are named from peculiar rites
of the *egbo* secret society performed thereon, or from
the markets which occur on them. That the week
here originally contained four days only is obvious
from the circumstance that the names applied to the
second group of four days are the same as those which
the four days of the first group receive, except for being
preceded in each case by the adjective "little."[2]
The Ibo and other tribes of the Niger Delta (Southern
Nigeria) observe *eke*, the first day of the four-day week,
as the appropriate time for abstaining from toilsome
labour and for marketing. Natives are forbidden
to climb a cocoanut tree on *eke*.[3] Among the Asaba
people, a branch of the powerful Ibo tribe, there seems
not to be any communal regulation respecting the
observance of *eke*: "the days for rest, for public market,
and for work vary with the individual according to the
particular governing *juju* [fetish] as determined by the
medicine man."[4] Among the Edo, or Bini, of Southern
Nigeria the week is everywhere a recognized period
of time. It is, properly speaking, four days in length,
this being the interval between the two markets in any

[1] F. Hutter, *Wanderungen und
Forschungen im Nord-Hinterland
von Kamerun*, Brunswick, 1902,
pp. 266, 360; compare Preuss, in
Deutsches Kolonialblatt, 1898, ix,
456.

[2] W. F. Daniell, in *Journal of the
Ethnological Society*, 1848, i, 222 *sq.*

[3] A. G. Leonard, *The Lower
Niger and its Tribes*, London, 1906,
pp. 305, 375; William Allen,
*Narrative of the Expedition sent by
Her Majesty's Government to the
River Niger in 1841*, London, 1848,
i, 398; N. W. Thomas, *Anthropological Report on the Ibo-speaking
Peoples of Nigeria*, London, 1913, i,
127. Seven weeks are here counted
to the month of twenty-eight
days (W. F. Baikie, *Narrative of an

Exploring Voyage*, London, 1856,
p. 316). An early missionary to
west Africa observes that among
the Ibo, Igara, and other Nigerian
tribes the week consists of four days,
viz. *eke*, a market day and unlucky
for the *ata*, or chief, to see strangers,
ede, a lucky or good day, *afo*, an
unlucky day, and *uko*, a lucky day.
Besides these days of good and
evil omen the Mohammedans have
made the natives believe that Friday is an unlucky day to undertake any work of importance
(S. A. Crowther, in *The Church
Missionary Intelligencer*, 1865, n.s.,
i, 55).

[4] J. Parkinson, in *Journal of the
Anthropological Institute*, 1906,
xxxvi, 317.

given locality. Occasionally, as in the Ida District, markets are found every eighth day, "but the names applied to the intervening days clearly show that a four-day week was the primary one." One of the four days is commonly known as the rest day, when men often stay at home — though farm work is not absolutely forbidden — and when women go to the market.[1]

The excellent studies of the late Lieutenant-Colonel Ellis, supplemented by later accounts, furnish a considerable amount of information regarding the rest days observed by the Yoruba-speaking and Ewe-speaking peoples of the Slave Coast and by the Tshi-speaking and Ga-speaking peoples of the Gold Coast. Some of these African Sabbaths are kept only by families or by the inhabitants of a single locality. Among the Tshi, for example, on the day sacred to the tutelary deity of a family all its members wear white or light-coloured clothes, mark themselves with white clay, and abstain from work. The day sacred to the tutelary deity of a town is celebrated in the same manner.[2]

[1] N. W. Thomas, *Anthropological Report on the Edo-speaking Peoples of Nigeria*, London, 1910, i, 18 *sq.* That the eight-day week of the Bini has developed from a more ancient four-day week is also the opinion of R. E. Dennett (*At the Back of the Black Man's Mind*, pp. 214, 364). The Bini week has been stated to consist of five days (Cyril Punch, quoted in H. L. Roth, *Great Benin*, Halifax [Eng.], 1903, p. 52 *n.*[1]), but this is certainly an error. An early traveller among the Bini declares that their Sabbath "happens every fifth day, which is very solemnly observed by the great with the slaughter of cows, sheep, and goats, whilst the commonalty kill dogs, cats, and chickens, or whatever their money will reach to. And of whatever is killed, large portions are distributed to the necessitous, in order to enable them, as every person is obliged to celebrate this festival" (David van Nyendael, "A Description of Rio Formosa, or the River of Benin," in W. Bosman, *A New and Accurate Description of the Coast of Guinea*, London, 1705, p. 456).

[2] A. B. Ellis, *The Tshi-speaking Peoples*, London, 1887, pp. 89, 93. On the Gold Coast white seems to be the special colour appropriate for holy or festive days. On a man's birthday, which is sacred to his *kra*, or tenanting spirit, he abstains from work, puts white clay on his face, and dons a white cloth (*ibid.*, p. 156). On the Tshi holy days, observed by families or private persons only, see further Bosman, *op. cit.*, p. 153; W. Hutton, *A Voyage to Africa*, London, 1821, p. 166 *n.*[2] (Ashanti); E. Perregaux, *Chez les Achanti*, Neuchâtel,

In this part of west Africa particular days of the week are assigned to the gods worshipped by different classes of the community. The Yoruba keep the first day of the week as a general Sabbath, but each of the remaining days is a period of rest only for the followers of the god to which it is dedicated.[1] For the adherents of a god to violate the day sacred to him is a serious offence, punishable with a fine, and in former times, with death. The notion prevails that, if the honour of the god is not vindicated by his followers, all will suffer for the neglect. "The Sabbath-breaker is, in fact, killed by the other worshippers of the god from motives of self-protection."[2] While the first day of the Tshi week is a general Sabbath, *bna-da*, the second day, is the fishermen's holiday. Any fisherman who ventures forth on this day is fined and his catch thrown into the sea. In former times he would have been put to death.[3] The fifth day, *iffi-da*, of the Tshi week is the regular rest day for farmers.[4] Similarly, among the Ewe every tribal deity, with one exception, has a sacred day, observed by his followers to the accompaniment of much eating, drinking, and dancing.[5]

All these west African peoples divide the month into weeks and keep one weekday as a general Sabbath. Among the Yoruba, whose week is said to consist of five days,[6] the first day (*ako-ojo*) "is considered un-

---

1906, p. 272; J. Parkinson, in *Man*, 1911, xi, 2 (Appolonians).

[1] Ellis, *The Yoruba-speaking Peoples*, London, 1894, p. 145.

[2] *Ibid.*, p. 149.

[3] Ellis, *Tshi-speaking Peoples*, pp. 220 *sq.* Beecham declares that were the fishermen to go out to sea on this day, "the fetish would be angry and spoil their fishing" (*Ashantee and the Gold Coast*, London, 1841, p. 186). Compare also Bosman, *op. cit.*, p. 160; Miss Mary H. Kingsley, *West African Studies*,[2] London, 1901, p. 145.

[4] Ellis, *Tshi-speaking Peoples* pp. 220, 304.

[5] *Idem, The Ewe-speaking Peoples*, London, 1890, pp. 41, 79.

[6] *Ako-ojo*, "First Day"; *ojo-awo*, "Day of the Secret," sacred to Ifa; *ojo-ogun*, "Day of Ogun," the god of iron; *ojo-shango*, "Day of Shango," the god of thunder; *ojo-obatala*, "Obatala's Day." A holy day is called *ose* (*se*, to disallow), and because each holy day recurs weekly, *ose* has also come to mean the week of five days (Ellis, *Yoruba-speaking Peoples*, pp. 145 *sq.*). According to an

I

lucky, and no business of importance is ever undertaken on it. On this day all the temples are swept
out, and water, for the use of the gods, is brought in
procession." [1] The Ewe of Dahomey are said to observe every fourth day as a holiday, "not kept holy,
but devoted to the will of the working classes; in short,
a sort of remuneration to the slave for the three days'
labour." [2] Weeks of four, five, and six days, usually
ending in a general market day which is also a rest day,
have been observed in various parts of Togo.[3]

earlier writer *osse* (*ose*), or holy day,
comes from a word signifying
silence. This expression was transferred to the Christian Sunday,
with which the Yoruba became
familiar after the year 1822, when
many of them emigrated to Sierra
Leone (Miss Sarah Tucker, *Ab-
beokuta; or Sunrise within the
Tropics*,[2] London, 1853, p. 37
n.). Whether the Yoruba week
really consists of five days seems
open to grave doubt. Bishop
James Johnson, a native African,
substantiates Ellis by giving the
names of the five days (quoted in
Dennett, *At the Back of the Black
Man's Mind*, p. 245), and also
speaks of "every fifth day, which
is the close of a week of *oses*, or
worshipping days" (*ibid.*, p. 251).
But Mr. Dennett himself, in his
latest work, cites three native
informants in favour of a week of
four days. Moreover, Shango's
(Jakuta's) Day is described by Mr.
Dennett as the Yoruba "Sunday."
The first day of the week is Ogun's
Day, the other weekdays following in the order given by Ellis.
It is to be noted that Ogun's Day,
the first, fifth, ninth, and so on, is
the regular market day. The god
Ogun in some parts of Yorubaland
has taken the place of another
deity, Odudua, whom Mr. Dennett
found to be universally regarded
as the originator of the system of

weekdays (*Nigerian Studies*, London, 1910, pp. 72–80). A five-day
week has been noted among the
Jebu of southeastern Yorubaland
(D'Avezac, in *Mémoires de la
société ethnologique*, 1845, ii, pt. ii,
81), and Burton refers to the same
institution among the Egba, by
whom the terminal day is called
ose (R. F. Burton, *Abeokuta and the
Camaroons Mountains*, London,
1863, i, 205).
[1] Ellis, *Yoruba-speaking Peoples*,
p. 145.
[2] F. E. Forbes, *Dahomey and the
Dahomans*, London, 1851, p. 181.
For every fourth day as the market day at Whydah see P. E. Isert,
*Neue Reise nach Guinea und den
Caribäischen Inseln in Amerika*,
Berlin, 1790, p. 132. Bosman (*op.
cit.*, p. 352) makes the Fida
(Whyda) market recur every third
day. A great market every sixth
day is said to be held in the district
about the town of Ardrah (Allada),
Dahomey (John Adams, *Remarks
on the Country extending from Cape
Palmas to the River Congo*, London,
1823, p. 88).
[3] Four-day weeks: R. Plehn,
*Beiträge zur Völkerkunde des Togo-
Gebietes*, Halle, 1898, p. 9; J.
Spieth, *Die Ewe-Stämme*, Berlin,
1906, p. 311 (Ho); five-day weeks:
R. Plehn, in *Mitteilungen von
Forschungsreisenden und Gelehrten
aus den deutschen Schutzgebieten*,

The week of seven days is not unknown to the Guinea negroes. Its presence in the hinterland of Togo is clearly due to the influence of Islam; in fact, the market day here recurs on Friday, the Mohammedan Sabbath.[1] Some of the Ewe peoples nearer the Slave Coast also use a seven-day cycle, which appears to have been borrowed by them from their neighbours, the Tshi tribes of the Gold Coast.[2] The Tshi keep *adjwo-da*, the first day of their seven-day week, as a general Sabbath.[3] The Ga of the Gold Coast, who also have the seven-day week, observe the first day as a communal Sabbath. Its name, *dsu*, means "purification," a term which seems also to have been used as a title of the moon.[4]

1896, ix, 123; six-day weeks: von Zech, *ibid.*, 1898, xi, 128; Christaller, in *Mitteilungen der geographischen Gesellschaft für Thüringen*, 1890, viii, 121; L. Conradt, in *Petermanns Mitteilungen*, 1896, xlii, 15 (Adele). The Akposo, who have a week of five days, keep the fifth day sacred to their creator-god, Uwolowo, whose name it bears. The other gods are worshipped on the second day of the week, a time when no work may be done (F. Müller, in *Anthropos*, 1907, ii, 201).

[1] A. Mischlich, in *Mitteilungen von Forschungsreisenden und Gelehrten aus den deutschen Schutzgebieten*, 1896, ix, 83.

[2] E. Henrici, *Lehrbuch der Ephe-Sprache*, Stuttgart, 1891, pp. 59 *sq.* The names of the seven weekdays in the Ewe and Tshi languages are almost identical. See the lists in Henrici, *op. cit.*, pp. 59 *sq.*, and Ellis, *Tshi-speaking Peoples*, p. 218. The Ewe have borrowed from the Tshi not only the names of the weekdays but also the custom of giving to private persons names derived from those of the weekdays (Henrici, *op. cit.*, p. 60).

[3] Ellis, *Yoruba-speaking Peoples*,

pp. 146 *sq.*; *idem*, *Tshi-speaking Peoples*, p. 218.

[4] Ellis, *Yoruba-speaking Peoples*, p. 147. For the names of the Ga weekdays, see *ibid.*, p. 143. An early writer, whose observations were confined to Akkra on the Gold Coast, speaks of *haughbah* (*ho-gba*) as one of the two sacred days of the seven-day week. It is compulsory for all ranks and sexes, but is especially observed by the women. "Under the supposition that some malign potency pervades the surrounding country on this day, more particularly directed against the pregnant women, their daily avocations are restricted within the walls of their domiciles, no egress being tolerated either for the purposes of travelling or other exterior occupations. Not many people, therefore, presume to violate these injunctions by issuing forth early in the forenoon, and none resort to their familiar haunts in the markets or public thoroughfares, until the prohibition has been withdrawn, by the well-known sign of a declining sun" (W. F. Daniell, in *Journal of the Ethnological Society*, 1856, iv, 23).

Although market weeks of varying length have been reported among some of the other Sudanese negroes south of the Niger,[1] it is clear that the Mohammedan advance in this region has brought with it the week of seven days and the custom of holding a market every seventh day.[2] Similarly, in other parts of Africa, as on the lower Congo, the European week of seven days has taken the place of the shorter native cycles, with the result that, where earlier the market came every fourth day, at present it recurs every seventh day.[3] These facts make it practically certain that the seven-day week, found among the Ewe, Tshi, and Ga, was originally taken over from Islam. Lieutenant-Colonel Ellis, indeed, regarded it as a purely African institution,[4] but he himself pointed out that Mohammedan states were formed to the north of the forest country

[1] R. A. Freeman, *Travels and Life in Ashanti and Jáman*, Westminster, 1898, p. 176 (market every fourth day among the Gaman, a Tshi-speaking people); M. Monnier, *France noire*, Paris, 1894, p. 209 (market every fifth day in Kong); L. G. Binger, *Du Niger au golfe de Guinée*, Paris, 1892, i, 370 (market every fifth day among the Diulasu); L. Desplagnes, *Le plateau central nigérien*, Paris, 1907, p. 377 (market every sixth day among the Habbe). A market every ninth day is described as being held at Bocqua in Northern Nigeria (R. Lander and J. Lander, *Journal of an Expedition to explore the Course and Termination of the Niger*, London, 1832, iii, 73, 82). For a general account of markets among the Nigerian peoples see A. Hovelacque, *Les nègres de l'Afrique sus-équatoriale*, Paris, 1889, pp. 355 *sqq.*

[2] A. Mischlich, *Lehrbuch der hausanischen Sprache*, Berlin, 1902, p. 127 (Hausa); J. S. Gallieni, *Voyage au Soudan français, Haut-Niger, et pays de Segou*, Paris, 1885, p. 436 (Segu); R. Callié, *Travels through Central Africa to Timbuctoo*, London, 1830, i, 323, 346 (Mandingo); A. Hacquard, *Monographie de Tombouctou*, Paris, 1900, p. 55; O. Lenz, *Timbuktu*, Leipzig, 1884, i, 154. The Bali market is said to be held every seventh day, *i.e.*, on Friday. Here, again, Mohammedan influence is to be suspected (F. Hutter, *Wanderungen und Forschungen im Nord-Hinterland von Kamerun*, Brunswick, 1902, p. 361).

[3] C. van Overbergh, *Les Mayombe*, Brussels, 1907, p. 353; A. de Calonne Beaufaict, *Études Bakango*, Liége, 1912, p. 79; J. H. Weeks, *Among the Primitive Bakongo*, Philadelphia, 1914, pp. 248 *sq.* Some of the Galla tribes have been so far affected by Arabic influences as to hold their markets every seventh day (P. Paulitsche, *Ethnographie Nordost-Afrikas. Die materielle Kultur der Danâkil, Galla, und Somâl*, Berlin, 1893, p. 313).

[4] Ellis, *Tshi-speaking Peoples*, p. 217. So also B. Cruickshank (*Eighteen Years on the Gold Coast of Africa*, London, 1853, ii, 189 *sq.*).

of the Gold Coast as early as the eleventh century A.D., and that the period since then has been long enough to allow the new mode of reckoning to become known throughout the entire country. The Tshi, who seem to have moved from the Sudan interior to the coast districts at no very remote period, doubtless took with them their septenary mode of reckoning, which, as we have seen, they communicated to the Ewe and the Ga.

The market, with its accompaniments, the market week and the market day, has thus been shown to prevail throughout equatorial Africa, on the Guinea coast, and in the basin of the Niger and the Nile.[1] The wide diffusion of this institution is doubtless in large measure the outcome of borrowing from tribe to tribe. A market, however, tends naturally to come into existence whenever neighbouring peoples have goods to exchange and the willingness to exchange them. The market place is originally in some neutral district on the tribal borders, where all hostilities must cease. In process of time the increasing friendliness between communities makes it possible for the market to be held in the different settlements according to a definite and well-known sequence. With the regular market is inseparably connected the market week, the length of which varies from three to ten days. The shorter intervals of three, four, and five days reflect the simple economy of primitive life, since the market must recur with sufficient frequency to permit neighbouring communities, who keep on hand no large stocks of food and other necessaries, to obtain them from one another. The longer cycles of six, eight, and ten days, much less common, apparently arise by doubling the

[1] No evidence for markets has been discovered among the Bantu tribes south of the Zambesi. The absence of markets elsewhere is sometimes specifically noted by our authorities; see F. Thonner, *Im afrikanischen Urwald*, Berlin, 1898, p. 33 (Mondunga, on the Dua River, Belgian Congo); J. Maes, in *Anthropos*, 1913, viii, 357 (Mongelima, on the Aruwimi River, Belgian Congo); A. J. N. Tremearne, *The Tailed Head-hunters of Nigeria*, London, 1912, p. 245 (Kagoro and other pagan tribes of Northern Nigeria).

earlier period, whenever it is desired to hold a great market for the produce of a wide area. That the recurrence of the market determines the length of the week is made obvious by the practice of naming the several weekdays from the markets that take place on them.[1] Thus there comes into existence a definite and recognized cycle of time, shorter than the lunar month and in origin unconnected with it, a true periodic week, running continuously from month to month and from year to year.

A market day is necessarily more or less of a rest day. Those who attend a market must abandon for the time being their usual occupations. It is also a holiday, affording opportunities for social intercourse, sports, and amusements of all sorts. Such seems to be the character of most of the market days found in southeastern Asia and the adjacent islands, as well as in some parts of Africa. On the lower Congo, however, the market day sometimes bears an unlucky character, and a distinct tendency exists to attach various restrictions to it. In the Guinea region the market day often, though not always, coincides with the general day of rest observed by an entire community. As such it may be consecrated to a god. The same practice, we have seen, prevails in respect to the holy days of individuals, families, towns, and particular classes of the community. This extensive development of sabbatarian regulations appears to be peculiar to west Africa.

The market week and the market day, though apparently unknown to the ruder tribes of America, formed a feature of those more advanced civilizations which were developed in the valleys of Mexico and Central America, and on the lofty tablelands of Colombia and Peru. Each important pueblo of Mexico held a market (*tianguiztli*) every fifth day, it being provided that neighbouring pueblos should observe different days, in order to secure a regular sequence of markets. All

___
[1] Above, pp. 107, 109, 111.

MARKET DAYS

0MARKET DAYS

0adults were obliged by law to resort to the *tianguiztli*, and severe penalties were imposed on those who exchanged commodities anywhere but at the appointed place and at the appointed time. The market days of old Mexico thus appear as compulsory holidays, when the people relinquished their usual occupations and assembled in great numbers, not only to buy and sell, but also, as we are told, to engage in games and festivities.[1] The five-day market week also existed in various parts of Central America.[2] In the Colombian Andes, among the Muysca (Chibcha) of Bogota, who had attained a degree of civilization far in advance of that reached by the other aborigines of Colombia, regular markets took place, apparently every third day.[3] If the Muysca week consisted only of three days, that of the Peruvians extended to ten days, ending in a holiday which was also a market day. The institution was attributed to the Apu-Ccapac-Ynca, whose beneficent activities gained for him the appellation of Pachacutec, "Reformer of the World." To

[1] D. F. S. Clavigero, *Storia antica del Messico*, Cesena, 1780, ii, 62, 163; B. de Sahagun, *Historia general de las cosas de Nueva España*, transl. Jourdanet and Siméon, Paris, 1880, pp. lxxiii, 290 *sq.*; A. von Humboldt, *Vues des Cordillères*, Paris, 1816, ii, 340; G. Brühl, *Die Culturvölker Alt-Amerikas*, New York, 1887, p. 234; J. Kohler, "Das Recht der Azteken," *Zeitschrift für vergleichende Rechtswissenschaft*, 1895, xi, 75, 87; E. J. Payne, *History of the New World called America*, Oxford, 1892–1899, ii, 359. A greater market or fair was sometimes held once in every cycle of twenty days, that is, on every fourth ordinary market day. Eighteen market months were included in the solar year. How such "months" may arise is illustrated by a Yoruba mode of computing time by periods of

seventeen days, that being the number of days in four market weeks, when the first and fifth days of each cycle are counted in (Ellis, *Yoruba-speaking Peoples*, pp. 149 *sq.*).

[2] Brasseur de Bourbourg, *Histoire des nations civilisées du Mexique et de l'Amérique-Centrale*, Paris, 1858, iii, 464.

[3] A. von Humboldt, *op. cit.*, i, 340, ii, 227; Brühl, *op. cit.*, p. 239; compare p. 326, where a market every fourth day is stated to have been held in Turmequé. In Sorotoca the market took place every eighth day (*ibid.*). But authentic details concerning the Chibcha calendar are not to be had. According to von Humboldt (*op. cit.*, ii, 244) ten of the Muysca "weeks" formed a lunation called *suna*. The *suna* began, not at new moon, but at full moon.

an old chronicler, himself of Ynca blood, this Peruvian
Sabbath appeared to be devised solely for utilitarian
ends. "In order that labour might not be so continuous as to become oppressive, the Ynca ordained that
there should be three holidays every month, in which
the people should divert themselves with various games.
He also commanded that there should be three fairs
every month, when the labourers in the field should
come to market and hear anything that the Ynca or his
council might have ordained. They called these
assemblies *catu*, and they took place on the holidays."[1]
Considering how frequently eight and ten-day weeks
have arisen by doubling periods of four and five days,
respectively, it seems not unlikely that the Peruvian
decade grew out of an earlier market week of five days
similar to the Mexican institution.

Another important instance of the market week and
the market day in archaic civilizations is that of the
Roman *nundinum* and *nundinæ*.[2] The nundinal cycle,

[1] Garcilasso de la Vega, *Comen-
tarios reales de los Incas*, pt. i, bk. vi,
ch. 35; C. R. Markham, *First Part
of the Royal Commentaries of the
Yncas*, London, 1871, ii, 206. It
is an old error, for which Garcilasso
de la Vega (*op. cit.*, pt. i, bk. ii,
ch. 23) appears to be responsible,
that the Peruvians had a week of
seven days, following the successive
phases of the moon. But Acosta,
who visited Peru soon after the
Spanish conquest of that country, is
better informed and says clearly
that neither Peruvians nor Mexicans had a seven-day week (J. de
Acosta, *Historia de las Indias*, bk. vi,
ch. 3; *The Natural and Moral History of the Indies*, edited by C. R.
Markham, London, 1880, ii, 396).

[2] See G. E. Marindin, in Smith,
Wayte, and Marindin's *Dictionary
of Greek and Roman Antiquities*,[3]
ii, 251 sq.; M. Besnier, in Daremberg, Saglio, and Pottier's *Dictionnaire des antiquités grecques et

romaines*, vii, 120–122; E. Huschke,
*Das alte römische Jahr und seine
Tage*, Breslau, 1869, pp. 288–312;
R. Flex, *Die älteste Monatseinteilung der Römer*, Jena, 1880, pp. 16
sqq.; and especially P. Huvelin,
*Essai historique sur le droit des
marchés et des foires*, Paris, 1897,
pp. 84–99. According to the
Roman system of inclusive reckoning — which may be compared
with that sometimes employed in
Yorubaland (p. 119 n.[1]) — the
market fell on the ninth day, as
the derivation of the word *nundinæ*
(from *novem*) indicates. It has
been suggested by H. Diels (*Sibyl-
linische Blätter*, Berlin, 1890, p. 41
n.[1]) that the choice of the ninth
day was influenced by the symbolism attaching to the number nine
among the Romans, as among other
Indo-European peoples; compare
the Nones, or the ninth day before
the Ides, and the nine days' festivals (*novemdiales feriæ*). Prob-

eight days in length, began (or closed) with a day when the peasants came to Rome for purposes of trade. The nundinal day, however, was more than a market day. At this time the ordinary occupations were interrupted; schoolchildren enjoyed a holiday; and sumptuous banquets celebrated the festive occasion.

The origin and early development of the *nundinæ* are veiled in obscurity. The institution enjoyed a high antiquity, tradition ascribing it now to Romulus, now to Servius Tullius, and now to the first consuls.[1] In historic times the *nundinæ* present themselves as the market days and holidays of a laborious peasantry; it may be questioned, indeed, whether they were ever anything else. It seems probable that, at least from the middle of the fifth century B.C., the *nundinæ* could be used for the settlement of judicial business, as is indicated by a passage in the Twelve Tables referring to them.[2] Furthermore, there is reason to believe that, until the passage of the Hortensian law in 287 B.C., the nundinal days were available for meetings of the public assemblies. This unfortunate piece of legislation effectually debarred the rural voters from participation in law-making on the very occasions when the largest number of them would naturally be in the capital city.[3] The classical writers were uncertain whether

ably, however, the Roman market week consisted originally of four days only, and later was doubled to form the cycle employed in historic times. The nundinal days were not named, but were indicated in the calendars by letters of the alphabet from A to H.

[1] Macrobius, *Saturnalia*, i, 16, 32 *sq.*; Dionysius Halicarnassensis, *Antiquitates Romanæ*, ii, 28, vii, 58; compare Varro, *De re rustica*, ii, præf. Cicero attributes the institution of markets to Numa (*De republica*, ii, 14, 27).

[2] *Tertiis nundinis partis secanto* (*Tabula* iii, 6, in Gellius, *Noctes Atticæ*, xx, i, 49).

[3] Macrobius, *op. cit.*, i, 16, 30; Pliny, *Historia naturalis*, xviii, 3. I accept the view that the *lex Hortensia* converted the *nundinæ* into *dies fasti non comitiales*, that is, forbade comitial meetings on these dates, though allowing judicial business to be done thereon. For this explanation see G. W. Botsford, *The Roman Assemblies*, New York, 1909, pp. 139, 315, 471; Marquardt-Wissowa, *Römische Staatsverwaltung*, Leipzig, 1885, iii,[2] 290. It has been maintained that toward the

the *nundinæ* should properly be included among the ferial days, that is, among the days which belonged to gods and not to men.[1] In Varro's time the pontiffs held that the *nundinæ* were not *feriatæ*, but many writers, cited by Macrobius, maintained the contrary opinion.   The *nundinæ* certainly never became public festivals in the technical sense, though they were dedicated to Jupiter, to whom the Flaminica Dialis sacrificed a bull on their recurrence.[2]   In this consecration to a deity the *nundinæ* further resembled some of the west African market days.

The Roman *nundinum* and *nundinæ* have much historic interest. The eight-day cycle, as a periodic week unconnected with the lunar month, presented a close parallel to the Jewish week of seven days. Further parallels existed in the absence of names for the weekdays, Roman and Jewish, and in the special observance of one day of each week by abstention from the customary occupations. It is scarcely surprising to find, therefore, that the Roman *nundinæ*, together with the *feriæ*, contributed to the development of the Christian Sunday. The earliest Sunday law is the brief edict of Constantine (321 A.D.), enacting that magistrates, city people, and artisans were to rest "on the venerable day of the Sun."[3] This legislation by Constantine probably bore no relation to Christianity; it appears, on the contrary, that the emperor, in his capacity of Pontifex Maximus, was only adding the day of the Sun, the worship of which was then firmly

end of the republican period the prohibition referred to was no longer observed (P. Groebe, in Drumann-Groebe, *Geschichte Roms*,[2] Berlin, 1899-1906, iii, 779).

[1] Above, pp. 94 *sqq*.

[2] Macrobius, *op. cit.*, i, 16, 30. According to Plutarch (*Quæstiones Romanæ*, 42), the *nundinæ* were consecrated to Saturn.

[3] *Omnes judices urbanæque plebes et cunctarum artium officia venera-* *bili die Solis quiescant* (*Codex Justinianus*, iii, 12, 3). The prohibition of holding court on Sunday was relaxed by Constantine in the same year so far as to permit such legal proceedings as the emancipation and manumission of slaves to take place at this time (*Codex Theodosianus*, ii, 8, 1). Eusebius (*Vita Constantini*, iv, 18-20) tells us that the emperor forbade all military exercises on Sunday.

established in the Roman Empire, to the other ferial days of the sacred calendar. Much significance must be attached to that part of Constantine's edict permitting agricultural labour on Sunday, "since it frequently happens that the sowing of grain and planting of vines cannot be so advantageously performed on any other day." In this particular the emperor was following the long-accepted rule as to the observance of the *feriæ* in country districts.[1] Another regulation of Constantine's, expressly appointing markets to be held on Sunday, doubtless represents an effort to assimilate the old Roman nundinal day to the new weekly Sunday.[2] With the final triumph of Christianity over paganism the old *feriæ* and the *nundinæ* were abolished, Sunday, with the other Christian festivals, being substituted in their place.[3]

[1] Above, p. 98.

[2] *Provisione etiam pietatis su[a]e nundinas die Solis perpeti anno constituit (Corpus inscriptionum Latinarum*, iii, no. 4121, p. 523). Markets were held on Sunday in many parts of Europe until late in the Middle Ages, in spite of numerous edicts, ecclesiastical and civil, forbidding the practice (Huvelin, *op. cit.*, pp. 46, 156 *sq.*).

[3] The date of the obsolescence of the *nundinæ* is not definitely known. The *fasti Philocali* (354 A.D.) marks the days of the seven-day week by the letters A–G, and gives side by side the old nundinal letters A–H (*Corpus inscriptionum Latinarum*, i, pt. i,[2] 256 *sqq.*). This arrangement had probably become a feature of the state calendar since the Sunday legislation of Constantine.

CHAPTER V

LUNAR SUPERSTITIONS AND FESTIVALS

THERE is good reason for believing that among many primitive peoples the moon, rather than the sun, the planets, or any of the constellations, first excited the imagination and aroused feelings of superstitious awe or of religious veneration. The worship of the moon is widespread; and in various mythologies that luminary, often conceived as masculine, plays the most important part among the heavenly bodies.[1] "That the moon has certain effects on moist substances, that they are apparently subject to her influences, that, for instance, increase and decrease in ebb and flow develop periodically and parallel with the moon's phases, all this is well known to the inhabitants of seashores and seafaring people. Likewise physicians are well aware that she affects the *humores* of sick people, and that the fever-days revolve parallel with the moon's course. Physical scholars know that the life of animals and plants depends upon the moon, and experimentalists know that she influences marrow and brain, eggs and the sediments of wine in casks and jugs, that she excites the minds of people who sleep in full moonlight, and

[1] P. Ehrenreich, *Die allgemeine Mythologie und ihre ethnologischen Grundlagen*, Leipzig, 1910, pp. 114–127; S. Arrhenius, "Über den Ursprung des Gestirnkultus," *Scientia*, 1911, ix, pp. 424 *sqq.*, Sir J. G. Frazer, *Adonis, Attis, Osiris*,³ London, 1914, ii, 140–150; E. J. Payne, *History of the New World called America*, Oxford, 1892–1899, i, 547 *sqq.*; W. H. Roscher, *Über Selene und Verwandtes*, Leipzig, 1890, pp. 1–16, and *Nachträge*, Leipzig, 1895, pp. 1–19. For the ideas of civilized children relating to the moon see J. W. Slaughter, "The Moon in Childhood and Folklore," *American Journal of Psychology*, 1902, xiii, 294–318; G. S. Hall, "Note on Moon Fancies," *ibid.*, 1903, xiv, 88–91.

that she affects (?) linen clothes which are exposed to it. Peasants know how the moon acts upon fields of cucumbers, melons, cotton, etc., and even make the times for the various kinds of sowing, planting, and grafting, and for the covering of the cattle depend upon the course of the moon. Lastly, astronomers know that meteorologic occurrences depend upon the various phases through which the moon passes in her revolutions." [1] This succinct statement, by a learned Mohammedan of the eleventh century, of the reasons which led early philosophers to attach a special signif-icance to the moon, may well serve as a text for elucida-tion and illustration.

It is a widespread and ancient belief, found among peoples in all stages of culture, that the lunar rays are deleterious, especially to little children. Some Brazil-ian Indians, for instance, believe that the moon makes babies ill; hence mothers, immediately after delivery, will hide themselves and their infants in the thickest part of the forest, in order to prevent the moonlight from falling on them. [2] Yao boys, when undergoing initiation into manhood, are told to avoid not only a menstruating woman but also the sight of the new moon, since both are dangerous. [3] Greek nurses took special pains never to show their charges to the moon. [4] In

[1] Albîrûnî, *India*, translated by C. E. Sachau, London, 1888, i, 346 *sq.* Compare the fine passage in Apuleius (*Metamorphoses*, xi, 1).

[2] Spix and Martius, *Reise in Brasilien*, Munich, 1823–1831, i, 381, iii, 1186.

[3] K. Weule, *Native Life in East Africa*, London, 1909, p. 188. On the other hand, children of the Bageshu, a Bantu people of British East Africa, are expected to take part in new-moon dances, since it is thought that they derive benefit from the moon (J. Roscoe, in *Journal of the Anthropological Institute*, 1909, xxxix, 193). A Ba-

ganda mother believes that her child will grow strong and healthy, if it is shown the first new moon after its birth (*idem*, *The Baganda*, London, 1911, p. 58). Similarly, it is said that in the island of Kiri-wina, the largest of the Trobriand group to the east of New Guinea, a mother always presents her child to the first new moon after its birth, in order that it may grow fast and talk soon (George Brown, *Melanesians and Polynesians*, London, 1910, p. 37).

[4] Plutarch, *Quæstiones conviviales*, iii, 10, 3.

modern Germany it is an injunction of peasant folk-lore never to point out the moon to young children.[1]

Moonshine may also be deemed injurious to adults. Certain Queensland aborigines will not stare long at the moon, for by doing so a heavy rain is likely to result.[2] The Bushmen of South Africa avoid looking at the moon.[3] The Chukchi of northeastern Siberia believe that a man who looks too long at the moon may be bereft of his wits, or may be carried away altogether. The moon, think the Chukchi, has a lasso with which he catches the unlucky starer.[4] When an English traveller in Arabia was noticed gazing at the radiant desert moon, the Bedouin said, "Look not so fixedly on him; it is not wholesome."[5] The same idea seems to have found expression in one of the most beautiful of the *Psalms*: "The sun shall not smite thee by day, nor the moon by night."[6] Two New Testament passages illustrate the belief that epilepsy may be caused by the lunar rays.[7] Similarly, the Babylonians believed that Sin, the moon-god, could provoke leprosy, dropsy, and, above all, fever, which, like the lunar phases, has its periods of growth, culmination, and decline.[8] Plutarch refers to the assumed fact that those who sleep abroad under the beams of the moon are not easily wakened, but seem stupid and senseless.[9] This fear of the noxious influences of moonshine may be traced from classical times to the present day. French peasants consider it dangerous to sleep in the moon-

[1] A. Wuttke, *Der deutsche Volks-aberglaube der Gegenwart*, edited by E. H. Meyer, Berlin, 1900, p. 391 (Oldenburg).

[2] W. E. Roth, *North Queensland Ethnography, Bulletin*, 1903, no. 5, p. 7.

[3] W. H. I. Bleek and Lucy C. Lloyd, *Specimens of Bushman Folk-lore*, London, 1911, pp. 67 *sq.*

[4] W. Bogoras, in *Memoirs of the American Museum of Natural History*, xi, 306.

[5] C. M. Doughty, *Travels in Arabia Deserta*, Cambridge, 1888, i, 444.

[6] *Psalms*, cxxi, 6. Another Biblical passage (*Hosea*, v, 7), possibly referring to the moon, is most obscure.

[7] *Matthew*, iv, 24, xvii, 15. The Greek verb used here is σεληνιάζομαι.

[8] E. Combe, *Histoire du culte de Sin en Babylonie et en Assyrie*, Paris, 1908, pp. 36 *sqq.*

[9] *Quæstiones conviviales*, iii, 10, 3.

light.[1] German peasants subject themselves to a long list of restrictions: no work, and especially no spinning, must be done in the moonlight, for the spun yarn would not hold, or the spinner would be spinning for her child a hangman's halter or the linen of a shroud; no waggon or tools should be left exposed to the moonshine, for they would soon be broken; washed clothes should not be hung out to dry in the moonlight, for he who wore them would become moonstruck; one who sews by moonlight sews his own graveclothes; water from a spring or well in which the moon shines should not be drunk, since this would be to absorb the evil influences of the moon; one should never look long at the moon, under penalty of getting a goitre; the lunar rays should never penetrate into the kitchen, or otherwise the maid would break many dishes.[2] So numerous, indeed, are these lunar superstitions that throughout Germany Monday, as partaking of the qualities of the moon from which it is named, is generally an unlucky day.[3] In various parts of the United States the belief prevails that it is dangerous to sleep with the moon shining on the face. If fish are exposed to moonshine, they will spoil.[4]

Various peoples have noticed that monthly periodicity belongs to women and moon alike, and, joining these observations, have supposed that the lunar changes cause menstruation, or that the first appearance of the menses is the result of defloration induced by the moon. As a natural outcome of such beliefs the moon is credited with the power of impregnation and is associated with childbirth.[5] Such superstitions

[1] P. Sébillot, Le folk-lore de France, Paris, 1904–1907, i, 45.

[2] Wuttke-Meyer, op. cit., p. 301.

[3] Ibid., p. 59. In Voigtland, central Germany, the assaults of witches are especially looked for and dreaded on Mondays (R. Eisel, Sagenbuch des Voigtlandes, Gera, 1871, p. 210).

[4] Fanny D. Bergen, Current Superstitions, Boston, 1896, p. 120.

[5] For the belief that impregnation can be accomplished by the sun, see Sir J. G. Frazer, Balder the Beautiful, London, 1913, i, 74 sqq.

are widespread.   In the native legends of the Euahlayi, a tribe of New South Wales, Bahloo, the moon, is a very important personage. He it is who creates the girl babies. Euahlayi mothers are very careful not to look at the full moon or to let their babies do so, for an attack of thrush, an affection common in newly born children, would be the result. Bahloo has also a spiteful way of punishing a woman who stares at him by sending to her the dreaded twins.[1] In Saibai and Yam, two islands in Torres Straits, it is believed that the moon, in the shape of a man, embraces a girl when she is full-grown, and that the halo around the moon represents her blood. This story is also told on the neighbouring coast of British New Guinea.[2] Here, as well as in some parts of Melanesia, natives ascribe menstruation to the moon.[3] The Tuhoe, a Maori tribe, believe that the moon is the permanent (or true) husband of all women, because the latter menstruate when the moon appears. "According to the knowledge of our ancestors and elders," say the Tuhoe, "the marriage of man and wife is a matter of no moment, the moon is the real husband." And the women themselves, on seeing the new moon, say, "The *tane* (husband) of all women in the world has appeared."[4] The Jaluo, a tribe of Nilotic stock living in the district of Kavirondo, British East Africa, ascribe menstruation to the influence of the new moon and believe that women can become pregnant only at this time.[5] The

[1] Mrs. K. L. Parker, *The Euahlayi Tribe*, London, 1905, pp. 50, 64, 98.

[2] C. G. Seligmann, in *Reports of the Cambridge Anthropological Expedition to Torres Straits*, v, 206 *sq.* The word for moon, *ganumi*, is sometimes used as a synonym of *nanamud*, the proper expression for menstrual blood (*ibid.*). Compare A. Hunt, in *Journal of the Anthropological Institute*, 1899, xxviii, 11.

[3] C. G. Seligmann, in *Journal of the Anthropological Institute*, 1902, xxxii, 303 *sq.* (Sinaugolo of the Rigo District); E. Beardmore, *ibid.*, 1890, xix, 460 (Mawatta of the Daudai District); A. Baessler, *Neue Südsee Bilder*, Berlin, 1900, p. 383 (Santa Cruz Islands).

[4] E. Best, "Notes on Procreation among the Maori People of New Zealand," *Journal of the Polynesian Society*, 1905, xiv, 210 *sq.*

[5] C. W. Hobley, in *Journal of the Anthropological Institute*, 1903, xxxiii, 358.

Baganda suppose that menstruation is caused by the moon, either when new or waning.[1] Similar beliefs are entertained by the negroes of the western Sudan, who commonly give to this female function the name of the moon.[2] The Greenlanders believe that the moon, conceived as a masculine divinity, possesses the power of impregnation; as a consequence young girls are afraid to look long at this luminary, "imagining they might get a child by the bargain."[3] The Lengua Indians of the Paraguayan Chaco associate the moon with marriage. Young girls will address the moon with the appeal "Moon, moon, I want to get married."[4] Indian women in Peru are said to have prayed to the moon to give them an easy delivery.[5] In old Egyptian belief the moon was supposed to make women fruitful, and the waxing moon to develop the germ in the mother's body.[6] The association of human fertility with the moon may perhaps explain why Ishtar, the mother-goddess of Babylonian mythology, came to be regarded as a daughter of Sin, the moon-god. In this capacity she presided over childbirth.[7] The Iranian peoples supposed that the moon contained a bull whose semen was another form of *haoma*, the intoxicating decoction of the moon-plant.[8] The position of

[1] J. Roscoe, *ibid.*, 1901, xxxi, 121.

[2] Thomas Winterbottom, *An Account of the Native Africans in the Neighbourhood of Sierra Leone*, London, 1803, ii, 206 (Mandingo, Susu, etc.).

[3] Hans Egede, *A Description of Greenland*, London, 1745, p. 205.

[4] W. B. Grubb, *An Unknown People in an Unknown Land*, London, 1911, p. 139.

[5] P. J. de Arriaga, *Extirpación de la idolatria del Piru*, Lima, 1621, p. 32.

[6] H. Brugsch, *Religion und Mythologie der alten Ägypter*, Leipzig, 1885, p. 335. The sacred bull Apis, which the Egyptians regarded as an image of the soul of

Osiris, a god often identified with the moon, was supposed to be born of a virgin cow impregnated by a divine influence emanating from the moon (Plutarch, *Quæstiones conviviales*, viii, 1, 3; *idem*, *De Iside et Osiride*, 43). On the discovery of an Apis the Egyptians kept a holiday (Herodotus, iii, 28).

[7] W. H. Roscher, "Aphrodite," in Roscher's *Ausführliches Lexikon der griechischen und römischen Mythologie*, i, coll. 390 *sq.*

[8] L. H. Gray, in *Spiegel Memorial Volume*, Bombay, 1908, pp. 160–168. Râkâ and Sinivali, two of the Vedic goddesses identified with the lunar phases, seem to have been associated with child-

Hera as a goddess of marriage and childbirth has been explained by the assumption that she played an ancient rôle as a moon-deity. Artemis, with whom Selene, or the divine personification of the moon, came to be identified, was regularly associated with childbirth. The Roman Juno was connected with the moon as Juno-Lucina, it being held that she aided women during confinement. Ancient mythologers found it easy to identify the Italian Diana, originally a goddess who looked after women in their time of peril, with the Greek Artemis, who had the same functions.[1] Modern French folklore still contains references to the idea that the moon can cause impregnation; in Basse-Bretagne, for example, it is thought that a young woman who exposes her person to the lunar rays may conceive and bear a child.[2]

The influence of the moon on the tides furnishes another element of mystery in the lunar phenomena. So primitive a people as the Andaman Islanders habitually refer tidal movements to the action of the moon; and the same connection between things lunar and things terrestrial has been recognized by other peoples, such as the Hawaiians, the ancient Babylonians, and the modern Chinese.[3] That changes in the moon are associated with weather changes as cause and effect is an ancient superstition not yet obsolete in rural communities.[4]

Comparative studies have shown how very general

birth (*Rig-Veda*, ii, 32; transl. H. Grassmann, i, 41).

[1] Plutarch, *Quæstiones conviviales*, iii, 10, 3; *idem, Quæstiones Romanæ*, 77. See further, W. H. Roscher, *Juno und Hera*, Leipzig, 1875, pp. 40–59; *idem, Über Selene und Verwandtes*, pp. 55–61; *idem,* "Mondgöttin," *Ausführliches Lexicon der griechischen und römischen Mythologie*, ii, coll. 3150 *sqq.*

[2] Sébillot, *op. cit.*, i, 41.

[3] E. H. Man, in *Journal of the Anthropological Institute*, 1883, xii, 337; Sheldon Dibble, *History of the Sandwich Islands*, Lahainaluna, 1843, p. 109; N. B. Dennys, *The Folk-lore of China*, London, 1876, p. 118; M. Jastrow, *The Religion of Babylonia and Assyria*, Boston, 1898, p. 358.

[4] H. A. Hazen, "The Origin and Value of Weather Lore," *Journal of American Folk-lore*, 1900, xiii, 191–198; E. G. Dexter, *Weather Influences*, New York, 1904, pp. 10–26.

is the belief that the moon exerts great influence on growth, particularly on the growth of vegetation, and on all human life and activity.[1] For this opinion there appear to have been two principal causes. Observation showed that moisture in the air and soil are favourable to organic growth and, further, that atmospheric moisture is greater at night than during the day. It was reasonable to suppose the moon itself to be the source of dew and moisture, especially when it was also noticed that the dew is heaviest on cloudless nights. These beliefs were entertained by the ancients, who attributed heat to the sun, but moisture to the moon.[2]

Another fallacy has had an even greater part in generating these lunar fancies. The apparent growth of the moon in the first half of the lunation is associated with the ripening of plants and fruits, the increase of animals, and hence with the prosperous issue of human undertakings. From this doctrine of lunar sympathy have arisen numerous rules for the guidance of shepherds and husbandmen, which had a wide prevalence in antiquity and still survive with almost undiminished vigour among the superstitious classes of to-day.[3]

The doctrine of lunar sympathy, by a natural extension, may also account for the common belief that "the same things which grow with the waxing, dwindle with the waning, moon,"[4] and therefore that all busi-

[1] Payne, op. cit., i, 547 sq.; Sir E. B. Tylor, Primitive Culture,[4] London, 1903, i, 130; W. G. Black, Folk-medicine, London, 1883, pp. 124 sqq.; A. E. Crawley, "Dew," Hastings's Encyclopædia of Religion and Ethics, iv, 698–701.
[2] Roscher, Über Selene und Verwandtes, pp. 49 sqq., 61–67. The New Zealanders believed that it was in the night that everything grew (R. Taylor, Te Ika A Maui, London, 1855, p. 175). The single Old Testament passage which may possibly embody a like conception is Deuteronomy, xxxiii, 14: "and for the precious things put forth by the moon." See W. von Baudissin, Jahve et Moloch, Leipzig, 1874, p. 24.
[3] For many illustrations see Frazer, Adonis, Attis, Osiris,[2] ii, 131 sqq.; J. Grimm, Teutonic Mythology, London, 1883, ii, 708–716.
[4] Gellius, Noctes Atticæ, xx, 8: Eadem autem ipsa, quæ crescente luna gliscunt, deficiente contra defiunt.

ness done in the latter half of a lunation is doomed to
failure. The Toda appear to regard the first half of
the month as the auspicious time for their numerous
ceremonies. "I met with no case," says Dr. Rivers,
"in which any ceremony was appointed for the period
of the full moon or for the second half of the moon's
period."[1] The Andaman Islanders abstain from work
during the first few evenings of the third quarter of
the moon.[2] The Buriat are said never to undertake
anything of importance between the full and the new
moon.[3] The Tatars, according to the account of an
Italian friar who in the thirteenth century made an
adventurous journey to Mongolia, began any new
enterprise "at new moon, or when the moon is full."[4]
The Mandingo paid great attention to the changes of
the moon and thought it "very unlucky to begin a
journey or any other work of consequence in the last
quarter."[5] Of the Sudanese negroes, generally, it
is said that they are much influenced in their undertakings by the appearance of the new moon. For
instance, a journey which has been decided upon during the last quarter of the moon is always postponed
until the new moon. No chief would presume to lead
out his tribesmen on a war party before the appearance
of the crescent.[6] The Nandi celebrate their very
important circumcision festival, as well as all marriage ceremonies, during the waxing moon, but perform their mourning rites during the waning moon.[7]
The Hova and other tribes of Madagascar regard the
waning of the moon as "an unfavourable time for any

[1] The Todas, London, 1906, p. 411.
[2] E. H. Man, in Journal of the Anthropological Institute, 1883, xii, 152 sq. It is also said of the Andamanese that they do no work, except what is noiseless, between dawn and sunrise (ibid.).
[3] Peter Dobell, Travels in Kamtchatka and Siberia, London, 1830, ii, 16.
[4] Joannes de Plano Carpini, in R. Hakluyt, The Principal Navigations, Traffiques, and Discoveries of the English Nation, i, 141 sq. (Glasgow reprint, 1903–1905).
[5] Mungo Park, Travels in the Interior Districts of Africa, London, 1816, i, 266.
[6] L. G. Binger, Du Niger au golfe de Guinée, Paris, 1892, ii, 116.
[7] A. C. Hollis, The Nandi, Oxford, 1908, pp. 52, 60, 71.

important undertaking."[1] Similar beliefs were entertained by the early Germans, who, according to Cæsar, despaired of victory if they engaged in battle before the new moon.[2] Tacitus, with fuller knowledge, declares that the Germans considered the new moon and the full moon as the most auspicious seasons for beginning any enterprise.[3] This superstition seems still to linger in some districts of Germany, where it is commonly held that any work begun when the moon is on the increase is sure to succeed, and that the full moon brings everything to perfection; whereas business undertaken during the waning moon is doomed to failure.[4] A like belief was that of the Scottish Highlanders, to whom the moon in her increase, full growth, and wane was "the emblem of a rising, flourishing, and declining fortune. At the last period of her revolution they carefully avoid to engage in any business of importance; but the first and the middle they seize with avidity, presaging the most auspicious issue to their undertakings."[5] On the other hand the people of

[1] J. Sibree, "Malagasy Folk-lore and Popular Superstitions," *Folk-lore Record*, 1879, ii, 32.

[2] *De bello Gallico*, i, 50.

[3] *Germania*, 11. The rule of the Spartans never to march out to war before the full moon (Herodotus, vi, 106; Pausanias, i, 28, 4) prevented them from sending aid to the Athenians at the time of the battle of Marathon. Though the Spartans always knew how to make use of their religious scruples, during their festivals they really did ostentatiously abstain from expeditions which might have been profitable to them. See A. Holm, *History of Greece*, London, 1895, ii, 26, referring to Thucydides, iv, 5, v, 75.

[4] Kuhn and Schwartz, *Norddeutsche Sagen, Märchen, und Gebräuche*, Leipzig, 1848, p. 457.

[5] The Rev. John Grant, in Sir John Sinclair's *The Statistical Account of Scotland*, Edinburgh, 1794, xii, 457. See also Charles Rogers, *Familiar Illustrations of Scottish Character*,[2] London, 1865, p. 172 (as to Orkney). In the Calendar of Coligny, the most important of the Celtic inscriptions of ancient Gaul, the lunation is divided into two parts by the full moon, and nearly all the important activities of the month are crowded into the first fortnight, apparently because of the ill luck associated with a waning moon. See Sir John Rhŷs, "The Coligny Calendar," *Proceedings of the British Academy*, 1909–1910, pp. 221, 265. It has been pointed out that most of the Greek festivals known to us fell in the first half of the month, and especially on the twelfth day. "Zugrunde liegt die weit verbreitete Vorstellung, dass alles, was gedei-

Thermià (Kythnos), one of the Cyclades, believe that you should never do any work, if you can help it, on the days preceding full moon, while for grafting, planting, cutting trees, and bleaching clothes those days are best which follow the full moon.[1] And an English antiquarian of the seventeenth century declares that, according to the rules of astrology, "it is not good to undertake any business of importance in the new of the moon; and not better just at the full of the moon; but worst of all in an eclipse."[2]

Eclipses of the moon are sometimes considered unfavourable for work, and may also be accompanied by fasting and other forms of abstinence. During such times of uncanny and terrifying darkness it is thought to be wise to avoid every sort of activity, as well as the consumption of food which may be tainted with mysterious evil.[3] Among the Wasania, a tribe of British East Africa, no cohabitation takes place during an eclipse.[4] Lunar and solar eclipses are among the phenomena which require a Naga community to declare a *genna* and give up its ordinary occupations.[5] When the Toda know that an eclipse is about to occur, they abstain from meat and drink; when it is over, they have a feast and eat a special food prepared on all ceremonial occasions.[6] In southern India it is a common custom, when an eclipse occurs, for the people to retire into their houses and remain behind closed doors. "The time is in all respects inauspicious, and no work begun or completed during this period can meet with success; indeed, so great is the dread, that

hen und zunehmen soll, während des zunehmenden Mondes vorgenommen werden soll" (M. P. Nilsson in *Archiv für Religionswissenschaft*, 1911, xiv, 441 *sq.*).

[1] J. T. Bent, *The Cyclades*, London, 1885, p. 438.

[2] John Aubrey, *Remaines of Gentilisme and Judaisme*, edited by J. Britten, London, 1881, p. 85.

[3] On the superstitions attaching to eclipses, generally, see R. Lasch, "Die Finsternisse in der Mythologie und im religiösen Brauch der Völker," *Archiv für Religionswissenschaft*, 1900, iii, 97–152.

[4] W. E. H. Barrett, in *Journal of the Anthropological Institute*, 1911, xli, 35.

[5] Hodson, *Nāga Tribes*, pp. 166 *sq.* See above, pp. 50 *sq.*

[6] Rivers, *op. cit.*, pp. 580, 592.

no one would think of initiating any important work at this time." [1] The natives of northern India are said to consider it a great crime to partake of food, drink water, or answer the calls of nature during an eclipse.[2] Such a period is considered most unlucky for commencing any business of importance. A pregnant woman will do no work during an eclipse, as otherwise her child would be deformed. Among high-caste Hindus no food which has been in the house during an eclipse of the sun or the moon may be eaten. It must be given away, and all earthen vessels in use in the house at the time must be broken.[3] The Chinese formerly observed lunar eclipses by a general suspension of business.[4] The fatal delay which led to the destruction of the Athenian fleet and army before Syracuse was the result of a lunar eclipse, as interpreted by the soothsayers and the incompetent, superstitious Nicias.[5] Among the Jews there were formerly many who abstained from food on the day of an eclipse of the moon, a portent which they regarded as evil.[6] This belief, as has been noted, prevailed in England at least as late as the seventeenth century.[7]

---

[1] *Madras Weekly Mail*, 15th October, 1908, quoted by Edgar Thurston, *Omens and Superstitions of Southern India*, London and Leipzig, 1912, p. 44.

[2] R. G. Chaube, "Some of the Most Popular Beliefs and Superstitions of the Hindus of Northern India," *Journal of the Anthropological Society of Bombay*, v, 326.

[3] W. Crooke, *The Popular Religion and Folk-lore of Northern India*,² Westminster, 1896, i, 21 *sqq.*; compare *idem*, *Natives of Northern India*, London, 1907, p. 203. See also H. G. Rose, "Hindu Pregnancy Observances in the Punjab," *Journal of the Anthropological Institute*, 1905, xxxv, 277 *sq.*

[4] John Barrow, *Travels in China*, London, 1804, p. 287.

[5] Thucydides, vii, 50; Plutarch, *Nicias*, 23.

[6] J. Buxtorf, *Synagoga Judaica*,² Basel, 1680, p. 477: *Defectum lunæ pro pessimo habent signo, quod aliquid mali et inauspicati ab hostibus et inimicis suis portendat. Ideo ejusmodi die animas vulgo jejunio affligunt et ab hostibus suis a Deo defendi postulant.*

[7] Above, p. 134. During a solar eclipse Swabian peasants totally abandon their usual occupations and shut up their cattle in the stalls (A. Birlinger, *Volksthümliches aus Schwaben*, Freiburg-i.-B., 1861–1862, i, 189). In Ober-Pfalz and Bohemia at such a time it is believed to be dangerous to

Various peoples have supposed that the moon, during the period of her invisibility, descends to the underworld. This conception has played a noteworthy part in generating superstitions concerning tabooed and unlucky days. The Akamba, a tribe of British East Africa, believe that on the day which completes the month no child is born and no domestic animal gives birth. One of the Akamba clans is called *mu-mwei* (*mwei* signifying moon), and by the members of this clan no house may be swept on the last day of the month.[1] The Akikuyu, a tribe related to the Akamba, regard the moon as the sun's wife, and suppose that when the moon comes to maturity the sun fights with her and kills her. While she is "dead," as the natives say, no journeys are undertaken, no sacrifices are offered, and no sheep are killed. It is further considered that goats and sheep will not bear on the day after the disappearance of the moon.[2] The Wagiriama keep as Sabbaths the odd days at the end of the month, before the appearance of the new moon.[3] Some tribes of equatorial Africa believe that the new moon is especially ill-humoured and hungry on the day when she emerges from darkness. "She looks down over our country," the natives declare, "and seeks whom she can devour, and we poor black men are very much afraid of her on that account, and we hide ourselves from her sight on that night." People who die between new and full moon are said to be those whom the new moon saw at this fateful time, in spite of all the precautions they took.[4] The missionary, David Liv-

eat anything or even to go outside the house, unless one's mouth is securely covered with a cloth (Wuttke-Meyer, *op. cit.*, p. 302).

[1] C. W. Hobley, *Ethnology of A-Kamba and other East African Tribes*, Cambridge, 1910, p. 53.

[2] W. S. Routledge and Katherine Routledge, *With a Prehistoric People*, London, 1910, p. 284.

[3] W. W. A. Fitzgerald, *Travels in the Coastlands of British East Africa*, London, 1898, p. 111, quoting W. E. Taylor, *Vocabulary of the Giryama Language*, London, 1897. The name of these rest days — *jumwa* — is Arabic; see above, p. 107 n.[2]

[4] P. B. Du Chaillu, *In African Forest and Jungle*, New York, 1903, pp. 96 *sq.*

ingstone, while sojourning at Lake Nyassa, discovered
that the natives in this region regarded the *interlunium*
as distinctly unlucky. On one occasion his men de-
layed an expedition till they had seen the new moon.
We must have the new moon, they said, for a lucky
starting.[1] The "dark day" of the moon was considered by the Zulu as inauspicious for engaging in battle.[2]

A superstitious attitude toward the *interlunium*
appears to be very prevalent among the Dravidian
peoples of India. The Kanarese of Hyderabad and
Mysore do not work in the fields on the last day of
the month. If a child is born at this time, they believe
that some one in the family will die. If a cow or a
buffalo has a calf at such a time, it must be sold. On
the evening before new moon no one may eat cooked
food. The new moon is consecrated to the dead.[3]
The Saoria of the Rajmahal Hills, who regard Sunday
as unlucky and do not work in the fields, pay visits,
or get married on this day, observe much the same
restrictions during the period of the moon's invisibility. Marriages will not be fruitful if consummated
during the dark of the moon, and in general the time
is associated with bad luck and sickness.[4] The same
belief is found elsewhere in northern India, sometimes
with beneficial results, as appears from the following
description, which applies to the district of Rohtak.
"To-day (29th November, 1883), in passing through
the Jât and Ahîr villages in Rohtak, I noticed that no
work was being done at the wells or in the fields, and
that the peasants, usually so hard at work, were idling

[1] Horace Waller, editor, *The Last Journals of David Livingstone in Central Africa*, New York, 1875, p. 273.

[2] J. Y. Gibson, *The Story of the Zulus*, London, 1911, p. 175.

[3] Gengnagel, "Volksglaube und Wahrsagerei an der Westküste Indiens," *Ausland*, 1891, lxiv, 871 *sq.* Another observer declares that if a cow calves on the new-moon day, her milk, it is believed, will kill the owner (P. Kershasp, "Some Superstitions prevailing among the Canarese-speaking People of Southern India," *Journal of the Anthropological Society of Bombay*, vii, 84).

[4] R. B. Bainbridge, in *Memoirs of the Asiatic Society of Bengal*, 1907, ii, 50.

in the village instead. On inquiring the reason, I was told that to-day was the *amâwas*, the last day of the moon, and that on this day of the month the bullocks are always given a rest. The men themselves do any work that is to be done without using the cattle, but no one yokes his bullocks in the plough or at the well, or, if he can help it, in the cart. I noticed that some of the peasants were busy making thorn-fences, or doing other light work, but no bullocks were at work anywhere, and as there is little to be done at this season without their help, the custom practically gave the men a rest also, and the unusual idleness gave the villages a sort of Sunday look. The bullocks are given this rest once a month, on the last day of the moon, and also on the *makar kâ sankrânt*, which comes about January, when the sun enters into the sign of Capricorn (*makar*), and on the *diwâli* and *gôrdhan* (the day after the *diwâli*) in the middle of Kârtik (October). Except on these fifteen days it is lawful for a man to yoke his cattle on all other days of the year, but these particular days are strictly a Sabbath for the cattle, and no one thinks of yoking them on these days. If any one did, it would be a sin (*pâp*), and his fellows would at once stop him. There is no such Sabbath for man, and it is not thought wrong (*pâp*) for a man to work on any day of the year, though, of course, there are many holidays (*têohâr*), on which little work is done." [1]

These superstitions relating to the dark of the moon have not been confined to the natives of Africa and the aborigines of India. They meet us among peoples of archaic civilization and they survive among the peasantry of European lands. To the Babylonians, who paid particular attention to all lunar phenomena, the disappearance of the moon at the end of the month occasioned much anxiety. The day when the moon could no longer be seen in the heavens was called the

---

[1] J. Wilson, in *Indian Antiquary*, 1897, xxvi, 308 (from *Punjab Notes and Queries*, 1883).

"day of sorrow" (*ûm bubbuli*, literally, the "day of the snatching away"). The absence of the moon was reckoned at three days, and during this time prayers were recited and solemn expiatory rites were prescribed, primarily for the king, who, as the representative of his people, had to take special care not to provoke the gods to anger at so critical a season. We still have one of the prayers recited by the ruler in his sanctuary and addressed to the moon-god Sin. The thirtieth day of the month is here described as the god's "holy day" or "festival." The prayer concludes with an allusion to an eclipse, from which it appears that the Babylonians, knowing neither the cause nor nature of such a phenomenon, supposed that, unless the gods were pacified during the moon's temporary obscuration, there would follow the more terrifying portent of an eclipse.[1] Modern Arabs consider the last day or last three days of the month to be unfavourable for any sort of undertaking.[2] By the Athenians these three days were called ἀσέλινοι, because on them the moonlight was extinguished. They were classed with the other unlucky days (ἀποφράδες ἡμέραι) of popular superstition. During the ἀσέλινοι it was necessary to sacrifice to the underworld gods in order to avoid their anger.[3] Selene at this time was supposed

---

[1] M. Jastrow, *Aspects of Religious Belief and Practice in Babylonia and Assyria*, New York, 1911, pp. 214, 333 *sqq.*; idem, *Die Religion Babyloniens und Assyriens*, Giessen, 1905–1912, i, 440, ii, 510 *sqq.* Compare L. W. King, *Babylonian Magic and Sorcery*, London, 1896, pp. 5 *sq.*

[2] I. Goldziher, in *Archiv für Religionswissenschaft*, 1910, xiii, 44 *n.*[4] For the Abyssinian beliefs see E. Littmann, *ibid.*, 1908, xi, 314 *sq.*

[3] E. Rhode, *Psyche*,[6] Tübingen, 1910, i, 234 *n.*[1], 269 *n.*[3]; E. Caillemer, in Daremberg and Saglio's

Dictionnaire des antiquités grecques et romaines, i, 332. G. F. Schoemann denies that the ἀσέλινοι were truly ill-omened, since there are instances of popular assemblies being fixed for these days (*Griechische Alterthümer*,[4] edited by J. H. Lipsius, Berlin, 1897–1902, ii, 457 *n.*[4]). It would seem, however, that the Athenians, like the Romans, sometimes distinguished between days popularly considered unlucky and those officially recognized as such in the state calendars. Friday is for us a most unlucky day, but, excepting Good Friday, it is not a *dies non*.

to descend to the underworld and the abode of shades; hence the moon came to be associated with Persephone.[1] The Romans do not appear to have marked the *interlunium* or *intermenstruum* by any special observances. European folklore, however, still preserves traces of the ancient superstition, as in the Cornish belief that a child, so unfortunate as to be born at this time, will never live to attain the age of puberty. Hence the saying, "No moon, no man."[2] Similar beliefs would seem to survive in the very common idea that the three days before the new moon are especially unlucky and likely to be attended by storms and winds.[3]

We may well believe that the different appearances of the moon were the first celestial phenomena observed with any degree of continuous attention by primitive man. Not only are the phases of the moon marked by striking variations in her form and in the amount of light she radiates, but from night to night she follows a regular path through the sky, changing her elevation above the horizon and appearing to occupy at her successive phases different quarters of the heavens. Such phenomena present elements of mystery not found in the sun's prosaic course. A survey of the anthropological evidence appears to indicate, as might indeed be expected, that of the lunar phases it is particularly the new moon which awakens interest and attention. The first appearance of that luminary in the western sky after sunset is often hailed with various

---

[1] Roscher, *Über Selene und Verwandtes*, pp. 46 *sqq.* The interlunar days were selected by the ancients for the celebration of the sacred marriages of the gods and goddesses and, particularly, of the sun and moon. At least from the time of Thales the conjunction of the two luminaries was indicated by the same term σύνοδος (*coitus*) which was applied to the act of procreation (*ibid.*, pp. 76 *sqq.*).

[2] T. F. T. Dyer, *English Folklore*, London, 1878, p. 41; Thomas Hardy, *The Return of the Native*, London, 1895, p. 29.

[3] H. A. Hazen, in *Journal of American Folk-lore*, 1900, xiii, 192. American folklore contains the injunction never to kill cattle or pigs, or even wild game, by the "dark of the moon"; it is most unlucky, and the meat will come to no good (Bergen, *Current Superstitions*, p. 121).

ceremonial observances. The Indians of the Ucayali River in Peru are said to greet the appearance of the new moon with great joy. They make long speeches to her, accompanied with vehement gesticulations, imploring her protection and begging that she invigorate their bodies.[1] Certain tribes of southern California, afterwards gathered into the Mission of San Juan Capistrano, celebrated the new moon with dances, saying, "As the moon dieth and cometh to life again, so we also, having to die, will again live."[2] The Dakota and other Plains Indians, when the moon does not shine, "say the moon is dead; and some call the three last days of it the naked days. The moon's first appearance they term its coming to life again." At this time they stretch forth their hands toward the moon and repeat joyful expressions.[3] The Creek and Cherokee Indians, according to an early writer, "assemble and feast at the appearance of the new moon, when they seem to be in great mirth and gladness, but, I believe, make no offerings to that planet."[4] Similar observances have been noted in various parts of Africa. An old traveller recites how, at the appearance of every new moon, the Congo negroes, "fall on their knees, or else cry out, standing and clapping their hands, 'So may I renew my life as thou art renewed.'" But if the sky was clouded, they did nothing, believing that the moon had lost its virtue.[5] The Mandingo, on the first appearance of the new moon, "which they look upon to be newly created," say a short prayer.[6] The Bushmen had their special seasons of merry-making, when the dance was never neglected. "Dancing began with the

[1] W. Smythe and F. Lowe, *Narrative of a Journey from Lima to Para*, London, 1836, p. 230.

[2] Father G. Boscana, "Chinigchinich," in *Life in California by an American*, New York, 1846, pp. 298 sq.

[3] Jonathan Carver, *Travels through the Interior Parts of North America*, London, 1781, pp. 250, 252.

[4] W. Bartram, in *Transactions of the American Ethnological Society*, 1853, iii, pt. i, 26.

[5] Merolla, "Voyage to Congo," in Pinkerton's *Voyages and Travels*, xvi, 273.

[6] Mungo Park, *op. cit.*, i, 265.

new moon, as an expression of joy that the dark nights
had ended, and was continued at the full moon, that they
might avail themselves of the delicious coolness after the
heat of the day, and the brilliancy of the moonlight in
this portion of the southern hemisphere." [1]

It has been suggested that in many cases the ceremonies at new moon have a magical aspect. On this
theory the first appearance of the luminary, with its
promise of growth and increase, would be greeted
with rites intended to renew and strengthen, by means
of sympathetic magic, the life of man.[2] Though it is
true that in process of time ideas of a magico-religious
character may attach themselves to lunar phenomena,
and especially to new moon, there seems to be little
reason for assuming them to be original and primary.
Most of the foregoing examples, indeed, may be more
simply interpreted as a naïve expression of man's
delight at the return of the moon to the world, after
an absence at once mysterious and portentous. Still
less necessary is the assumption, so commonly made,
that all lunar ceremonies are acts of worship addressed
to the moon as a divinity. Religious festivals appear
in the first instance to be fixed at new moon or full
moon because these are the two most striking periods
of the lunation and mark, respectively, the beginning
and middle of the lunar month.

[1] G. W. Stow, *The Native Races
of South Africa*, London, 1905,
p. 112. For further examples of
new-moon and full-moon celebrations see P. Kolben, *The Present
State of the Cape of Good Hope*,
London, 1731, i, 96 (Hottentots);
J. Bonwick, *Daily Life and Origin
of the Tasmanians*, London, 1870,
pp. 186 *sqq.*; Seligmann, *Melanesians of British New Guinea*, p. 193
(Koita); Carl Ribbe, *Zwei Jahre
unter den Kannibalen der Salomo-
Inseln*, Dresden, 1903, p. 163
(Shortland Island); Taylor, *Te
Ika A Maui*, p. 93 (Maori);
Turner, *Samoa*, p. 67; A. E. Jenks,
in *Ethnological Survey Publications*,
i, 206 (Bontoc Igorot of Luzon);
V. Solomon, in *Journal of the
Anthropological Institute*, 1902,
xxxii, 213 (Nicobarese); W. Bogo-
ras, in *Memoirs of the American
Museum of Natural History*, xi, 378
(Chukchi); J. v. Klaproth, *Reise
in den Kaukasus und nach Georgien*,
Halle, 1814, ii, 602 (Osetes); A.
von Humboldt, *Vues des Cordillères*,
Paris, 1816, ii, 244 (Muysca of
Colombia).

[2] Frazer, *Adonis, Attis, Osiris*,[2]
ii, 140.

Among many peoples in both the lower and the higher culture the time of new moon and full moon, much less commonly of each half moon, forms a season of restriction and abstinence. The lunar day is sometimes a holy day dedicated to a god, who may be identified with the moon itself. Instances of this sort are to be correlated with the general course of religious development, involving, as it does, the emergence of polytheistic cults and the schematization of the ritual. But under more primitive conditions the lunar day is a tabooed day, quite independent of any association with a deity. It seems idle to seek a particularistic explanation for the taboos observed on such an occasion. We have already noticed the sympathetic influence which the waxing and waning of the moon is supposed to exert on human activities. Furthermore, we have seen that the new moon, rising as it were from the dead, is thought to be pregnant with meaning for the life of man. Her very newness is an element of interest; her contrasts, in shape, size, and position in the heavens, to the old moon further deepen the impression of her significance; and her function of inaugurating the month not only gives to her a special place in primitive calendar systems but also invests her with the emotional importance belonging to the commencement of any new period. These ideas of lunar influence are naturally extended to the full moon, which, as will be shown, is commonly regarded as marking the division of the lunar month into two equal parts, and in some instances to the half moons, as indicating the other prominent stages in a lunation. The phases of the moon thus come to be considered critical times and to be marked not only by religious exercises but also by fasting and cessation of the customary occupations.[1]

[1] The vice of seeking particularistic explanations of widespread social phenomena is illustrated by Nielsen, who, with misdirected ingenuity, has argued that the early Semites founded their Sabbaths on the observation that the moon (conceived as a divinity)

Lunar taboos, involving abstinence and quiescence, are commonly observed in Polynesia and Indonesia.[1] Various African peoples likewise entertain pronounced beliefs regarding the unfavourable influence of the moon's changes on human activities. The Zulu welcome the first appearance of the new moon with demonstrations of joy, but on the day following they abstain from all labour, "thinking if anything is sown on those days they can never reap the benefits thereof."[2] The Bapiri, a tribe of the Bechuana stock, stay at home at new moon and do not go out to the fields. "They believe that if they should set about their labour at such a season, the millet would remain in the ground without sprouting, or that the ear would fail to fill, or that it would be destroyed by rust."[3] Of another Bechuana tribe, the Makololo, in the neighbourhood of the Leeambye River, Livingstone remarks, "There is no stated day of rest in any part of this country except the day after the appearance of the new moon, and the people then refrain only from going to their gardens."[4] An earlier writer, referring to the Bechuana, says that when the new moon appears, "all must cease from work,

rests four times in a lunation. Days on which the deity rested were to be likewise observed by his worshippers as days of rest (D. Nielsen, *Die altarabische Mondreligion und die mosaische Überlieferung*, Strassburg, 1904, pp. 63 *sqq.*). It is true that the moon looks full for a day or two before and for a day or two after she is full; similarly, the changes in her form at the beginning of a lunation are scarcely perceptible. The moon, therefore, might be said to "rest" at these two periods. But neither astronomical science nor untutored observation lends any support to the idea that the moon "rests" at the close of each and every phase. Such a hypothesis, were it true, would not account for the other forms of abstinence, in addition to the cessation of labour, which occur in connection with the moon's changes. And, as we shall see, the observance of lunar taboos may be quite dissociated from true moon-worship and probably long antedates the latter cult.

[1] Above, pp. 14 *sq.*, 20, 32 *and n.[2]*, 34 *and n.[1]*, 37, 52 *n.[1]*
[2] Lieutenant Farewell, in W. F. W. Owen, *Narrative of Voyages to explore the Shores of Africa, Arabia, and Madagascar*, London, 1833, ii, 397; compare Dudley Kidd, *The Essential Kafir*, London, 1904, p. 110.
[3] G. W. Stow, *The Native Races of South Africa*, London, 1905, p. 414.
[4] *Missionary Travels and Researches in South Africa*,[25] New York, 1870, p. 255.

and keep what is called in England a holiday." [1] To the north of the Bechuana, in the upper basin of the Zambesi, live the Barotse, by whom the new moon is made an occasion for great festivities. "It is a general holiday; men of all ranks sing and dance, while the women assemble apart and give vent to strident howls of their own." [2] Similarly, among all the people from Nyassaland to Ujiji on Lake Tanganyika the first night of the new moon is a public festival, sometimes celebrated by a dance in which the men alone participate. [3] The Baziba, who dwell to the west and southwest of Lake Victoria Nyanza, are said to be one of the few tribes in this part of Africa having "a recognized day of rest, independently of the Christians' Sabbath. The two first days of every moon are universal holidays." [4]

A superstitious observance of the new-moon day is found among some of the tribes and peoples occupying British East Africa. The Akamba, whose beliefs regarding the *interlunium* have been already mentioned, [5] also consider it very unlucky to move cattle or livestock of any kind from one place or another, or even to give presents of any stock, during the first four days of the new moon. [6] Well-marked Sabbaths are kept by some sections of the Baganda, the great tribe, or rather nation, occupying Uganda. At the temple estate of the god Mukasa, the most important Baganda deity, there was a weeks' rest, *bwerende*, on the appearance of each new moon; no special gatherings were held during this period, but the people did the minimum of work, even the cutting of firewood being forbidden. All preparations for the festival were made beforehand, in order that the women should not be obliged to perform any labour other than cook-

[1] John Campbell, *Travels in South Africa*, London, 1822, ii, 205.

[2] L. Decle, *Three Years in Savage Africa*, London, 1900, pp. 85 *sq.*

[3] *Ibid.*, p. 295.

[4] J. F. Cunningham, *Uganda and its Peoples*, London, 1905, p. 294.

[5] Above, p. 136.

[6] Hobley, *op. cit.*, p. 104.

L

ing.[1] In Budu, a district of Uganda, there is a curious
worship of the python, conducted by members of the
Heart clan. The sacred snake, which bears the title
of Selwanga, is kept in a temple and receives worship
at the new moon. When this appears, the people
repair to the shrine of the python and make their
offerings. No work may be done on the estate for
seven days.[2] Again, the principal chief of the district
of Singo, who was shield-bearer to the king of the
Baganda, "had to observe a taboo each full moon,
namely, to abstain from food from noon of the day of
the full moon until the following morning, and also to
live apart from his wives during that time. 'It is
full moon, the Mukwenda may not eat,' was a saying
among the people."[3] The Banyoro, a Bantu people
related to the Baganda, who inhabit the country to
the northwest of Uganda, performed every full moon a
ceremony which has been thus described: "In the
afternoon all the drums in the place were beaten, and
everybody shouted, as no one dared keep silent for
fear of offending the moon. The king posted men at
the cross-roads and seized every one who passed along.
These unfortunate folk were brought in to him and
offered as a propitiatory sacrifice for the whole country
to the evil spirits. The hair of the victims was put
into cow horns and their blood was poured on to it,
the horns being then kept by different people as charms
against sickness and trouble. After this the king appeared swathed in barkcloths, taking up his position
in his council hall, his subjects coming to do obeisance
to him. A dead silence prevailed, for no one was allowed to even cough in his presence. . . . As the
full moon rose the feasting began, and the drinking
and dancing continued till dawn. The king's chief
wife had to sit by her intoxicated spouse and pinch

---

[1] John Roscoe, *The Baganda*,
London, 1911, pp. 297, 299, 428;
idem, in *Journal of the Anthropological Institute*, 1902, xxxii, 76.

[2] Roscoe, *Baganda*, pp. 320 *sqq.*;
idem, "Python Worship in Uganda," *Man*, 1909, ix, 88 *sqq.*

[3] *Idem, Baganda*, pp. 249 *sq.*

his arm or bite his finger, to prevent sleep; for a man to slumber during full moon brought disaster to the household." [1] New moon, as well as full moon, seems to have been observed by the Banyoro, for Speke found the palace of the king of Unyoro shut up, because the new moon had been seen for the first time on the preceding evening.[2] The same explorer describes a like custom found among the Bahima, or Wahuma, of Ankole, a region lying to the southwest of Uganda. "On the first appearance of the new moon every month, the king shuts himself up, contemplating and arranging his magic horns — the horns of wild animals stuffed with charm-powder — for two or three days. These may be counted his Sundays or church festivals which he dedicates to devotion." [3]

New-moon and full-moon festivals, accompanied by abstinence from secular activities, are thus seen to form a common feature of native life in southern and eastern Africa. The custom of keeping them as rest days is apparently confined to Bantu peoples, who arose from a mixture of Hamites with the true negroes. No sabbatarian regulations are discoverable among the Bushmen, representing the aborigines of southern Africa, or among the non-Bantu tribes of eastern Africa. It may be argued, therefore, that these African Sabbaths are of foreign parentage, being derived remotely from Hamitic and Himyaritic (Semitic) immigrants into Africa. The argument is strengthened by the fact that lunar festivals may be traced to a remote antiquity, both in Egypt and in western Asia. In any case, however, they must have been much modified with their transmission from tribe to tribe and from century to century.

[1] Mrs. A. B. Fisher, *Twilight Tales of the Black Baganda*, London [1912], pp. 37 *sq.*

[2] J. H. Speke, *Journal of the Discovery of the Source of the Nile*, Edinburgh, 1863, p. 523.

[3] *Ibid.*, p. 259. According to Speke this custom is also observed by the king of Uganda, who, on the first day after the appearance of the new moon, examines and arranges his *mapembe*, or fetishes (*ibid.*, p. 372).

None of the natives of southern and eastern Africa who observe new moon and full moon as seasons of abstinence appear to be familiar with the market week and the market day. On the other hand, in central and western Africa, where markets are so generally found and where the market day is kept as a holiday, lunar festivals accompanied by a cessation of labour are very rare.[1] Lieutenant-Colonel Ellis, who was much impressed with the resemblance of the west-African rest day to the Hebrew Sabbath, supposed that both were once lunar festivals, connected with moon-worship and celebrated on the first day of the new moon. "This holy day, before the invention of weeks, recurred monthly, but after the lunar month was divided, it recurred weekly, and was held on the first day of the week."[2] His theory, however plausible at first sight, breaks down when we remember that the keeping of moon-days as Sabbaths does not necessarily imply worship of the moon as a deity; that full moon, as well as new moon, may be observed festively with abstinence from labour; and, finally, that the market week did not arise as a subdivision of the month, but was in origin quite independent of the lunation. The restrictions attending market days have nothing to do with superstitions relating to the moon.

Lunar taboos are not unknown in modern India. The natives of northern India regard the new moon as an unfavourable time for undertaking important business.[3] The Kanarese, whose customs and beliefs relating to the last day of the lunar month have already been noticed, do not plough their fields at new

[1] The Mendi of the hinterland of Sierra Leone are said to hold a new-moon festival and at it to abstain from all work, "alleging that if they infringed this rule corn and rice would grow red, the new moon being a 'day of blood.'" Ellis, who cites this instance without giving his authority, adds the further fact that the Mendi recognize no weeks (*Yoruba-speaking Peoples*, p. 146).

[2] *Ibid.*, Ellis presented his arguments more fully in an article "On the Origin of Weeks and Sabbaths," *Popular Science Monthly*, 1895, xlvi, 329–343.

[3] W. Crooke, *The Popular Religion and Folk-lore of Northern India*,[2] Westminster, 1896, i, 23.

moon and full moon.[1] The Badaga of the Nilgiri Hills in southeastern India think that children born on the day of the new moon, the full moon, or any one of the three days immediately preceding the full moon, will be unfortunate throughout life.[2] The Korava regard the day after new moon as unlucky for starting out from home.[3] Similar superstitions are doubtless to be found among other Dravidian peoples.

The Aryans of ancient India observed two sacred periods in every month, new moon and full moon, with sacrifices to the gods.[4] The simpler forms of the rite were gradually extended into an elaborate ritual. Every Brahmanical householder was required to perform two half-monthly sacrifices for a period of thirty years, after he had set up a home of his own. According to some authorities these sacrifices were obligatory for the rest of his life. The ceremony usually occupied the greater part of two consecutive days. While the first day was to be chiefly occupied with preparatory rites and the taking of the vow of abstinence (vrata) by the sacrificer and his wife, the second day was reserved for the performance of the main ceremony.[5] Since it was permitted to compress the two days' rites of the full-moon sacrifice into a single day, the conjec-

[1] Gengnagel, "Volksglaube und Wahrsagerei an der Westküste Indiens," *Ausland*, 1891, lxiv, 871 *sq.*

[2] F. Jagor, in *Verhandlungen der Berliner Gesellschaft für Anthropologie, Ethnologie, und Urgeschichte*, 1876, p. (201) (bound with *Zeitschrift für Ethnologie*, vol. viii).

[3] Thurston, *Omens and Superstitions of Southern India*, p. 22.

[4] *Rig-Veda*, i, 9, 1, i, 94, 4 (transl. H. Grassmann, ii, 8, 95); *Atharva-Veda*, vii, 79, 3, vii, 80, 1–4 (transl. W. D. Whitney, pp. 444–446); Martin Haug, *The Aitareya Brahmanam of the Rig-Veda*, Bombay, 1863, ii, 5; A. Weber, "Zur Kenntnis des vedische

Opferrituals," *Indische Studien*, 1868, x, 329 *sqq.;* H. Zimmer, *Altindisches Leben*, Berlin, 1879, pp. 364 *sq.;* A. Hillebrandt, *Das altindische Neu- und Vollmondsopfer*, Jena, 1879; *idem*, in Bühler's *Grundriss der indo-arischen Philologie und Altertumskunde*, Strassburg, 1901, ii, pt. ii, pp. 75 *sq.* The new-moon day was called *darśa*, the day of the full moon, *pūrṇamāsa.*

[5] The first day was called *upavasatha*, a fasting or fast day (compare Sanskrit *upa*, an adverbial adjunct, signifying to refrain from, abstain, hence, to fast). The second day's ceremony was known as the *darśapūrṇamāsa* sacrifice.

ture is plausible that originally only one day was
assigned to the observances of abstinence and sacrifice.[1] The ritualistic requirements for this ceremony
do not expressly include the cessation of labour by the
Brahmanical householder and his family. It might
be argued, therefore, that the new-moon and full-
moon observances were not originally dictated by a
superstitious regard for the lunar phases. The fasting
on the *upavasatha* day would then be merely a rite
preliminary to the sacrifice on the following day; and
the association of the two ceremonies with new and
full moon would mean only that these two divisions
of a lunar month were selected as convenient and conspicuous periods for the performance of religious duties.
But the evidence at our disposal enables us to attach a
deeper significance to the ancient Aryan rite.

In the first place it is well known that the *upavasatha*
was a fast preparatory to the offering of the "moon
plant," the intoxicating *soma*, whose personification
and deification are assigned to a date earlier than that
of the Vedas themselves. A very competent scholar,
after pointing out that in Vedic literature the moon
takes a much higher rank than the sun, being regarded
as the creator and ruler of the world, has argued that
everywhere in the *Rig-Veda soma* and the moon are
identified, and that the terrestrial plant is merely a
symbolic representation of the luminary. According
to this view the moon-god as Soma forms the centre
of Vedic religion.[2] The theory, thus unequivocally
stated, has not won wide acceptance; according to
the commoner view Soma as a god is ordinarily celebrated in the Vedic hymns only as a personification
of the beverage; and his identification with the moon
is to be explained as a secondary mythological formation. Certain instances of such identification are met
in a few of the latest hymns of the *Rig-Veda;* and in the

---

[1] *Satapatha-Brâhmana*, i, 1, 1,
1 *sqq.* (*Sacred Books of the East*,
xii, 1 *sq.;* compare also 374 *sq.*).

[2] A. Hillebrandt, *Vedische Mythologie*, Breslau, 1891–1899, i,
267 *sqq.*, 313, 366 *sqq.;* ii, 209–240.

Atharva-Veda Soma several times means the moon. Post-Vedic writings regularly refer to Soma as the moon, which, when drunk by the gods, begins to wane.[1]

In the second place the two half-monthly sacrifices were characterized by restrictions which can best be described as taboos. The Brahmanical householder was obliged to abstain from certain kinds of food, especially meat, and from sexual intercourse. He might not cut hair, beard, or nails. He should sleep, not on a bed, but on the ground. The directions for the ceremonies, as given in the *Grihya-sûtra of Gobhila*, further require the worshipper not to set out on a journey; if he is away from home even at a distant place, to return to his house; not to sell goods (though he may buy them from others); and to speak as little as possible.[2] It is obvious that the scrupulous observance of all these regulations would convert the *upavasatha* day into a Sabbath, marked, not only by fasting, but also by the cessation of most secular activities.

In post-Vedic times the sabbatarian quality of lunar days becomes increasingly prominent. In the *Institutes of Vishnu* the new moon is mentioned as a penitential fast day.[3] A variety of lunar penances is prescribed in the *Laws of Manu*.[4] The same lawbook sets forth that "on the (night of) new moon and the eighth (lunar day), and also on the (night of) full moon and the fourteenth (lunar day), let a Brahman who has finished his student's course be always (as) a student, even in season," that is, let him remain chaste.[5] According to the *Vishnu Purana*, a relatively late production of Brahmanical thought, there

[1] A. Bergaigne, *La religion védique*, Paris, 1878, i, 157 *sqq.*; A. A. Macdonell, *Vedic Mythology*, Strassburg, 1897, pp. 112 *sqq.*; E. W. Hopkins, *The Religions of India*, Boston, 1895, pp. 112 *sqq.*; J. Muir, *Original Sanskrit Texts,* London, 1884, v, 270 *sq.* Compare *Satapatha-Brâhmana*, i, 6, 4, 5 *sqq.* (S. B. E., xii, 176 *sqq.*).

[2] *Grihya-sûtra of Gobhila*, i, 5, 1–26 (S. B. E., xxx, 25–28).

[3] *Institutes of Vishnu*, xlvii, 3 (S. B. E., vii, 152).

[4] *Laws of Manu*, xi, 217 *sqq.* (S. B. E., xxv, 474 *sq.*).

[5] *Ibid.*, iv, 128 (S.B.E., xxv, 149).

are "certain days on which unguents, flesh, and women
are unlawful, as the eighth and fourteenth lunar days,
new moon and full moon, and the entrance of the sun
into a new sign. On these occasions the wise will
restrain their appetites, and occupy themselves in the
worship of the gods, as enjoined by holy writ, in meditation, and in prayer; and he who behaves differently
will fall into a hell where ordure will be his food." [1]
It is also said that he who attends to secular affairs
on the days of the *parvans* (new moon and full moon)
will be punished hereafter in a hell of blood.[2] For
modern Brahmans the new-moon and full-moon days
are regularly fast days.[3]

With the development of the complex ritual of
Brahmanism holy and unlucky days became almost
identical with days when the sacred books should not
be read.   The code of Manu requires a learned Brahman
not to recite the Veda on the new-moon day, or on the
fourteenth and eighth days of each half-month, or
on the full-moon day.   It is said that "the new-moon
day destroys the teacher, the fourteenth day the pupil,
the eighth and full-moon days destroy all remembrance
of the Veda; let him therefore avoid reading on those
days." [4]   This injunction, moreover, is repeated for a
great variety of other critical occasions: during a
heavy thunderstorm; during an eclipse; and when
an earthquake occurs. A like prohibition is enforced
after events causing pollution; a Brahman, for example, should not read the Veda in a village through
which a corpse has been taken, or near a burning-
ground.[5] Similar prohibitions are set forth at great
length in the lawbook of Gautama. The Veda ought
not to be studied and recited when there is a thunderstorm, an earthquake, an eclipse or a fall of meteors;

[1] *Vishṅu Purāṅa*, iii, 11 (the
translation by H. H. Wilson,
edited by F. Hall, London, 1865,
iii, 132 *sq.*).
[2] *Ibid.*, ii, 6 (Wilson-Hall, ii, 219).
[3] J. A. Dubois, *Hindu Manners,*
Customs, and Ceremonies, Oxford,
1906, p. 270.
[4] *Laws of Manu*, iv, 113 *sq.*
(S. B. E., xxv, 147).
[5] *Ibid.*, iv, 101 *sqq.* (S. B. E.,
xxv, 144 *sqq.*).

on the day of the new moon (on the latter occasion reading may be interrupted for two days); on the full moon of three months of the year, and so forth.[1] In the *Vishnu Purana* we read that "on the days called *parvans*, on periods of impurity, upon unseasonable thunder, at the occurrence of eclipses or atmospheric portents, a wise man must desist from the study of the Vedas."[2] Some of these taboos have endured till the present time, the eighth day of each fortnight, held sacred to the goddess Durga, being a period when no study is allowable for a pious Hindu.[3]

The Vedic ceremonies at new moon and full moon appear to have influenced the Hindu festival of Bhaskara Saptami, which takes place on the twenty-second of the month Magha, the seventh day of the light fortnight (4th of February). "This day is in an especial degree sacred to the sun. Abstinence is to be practised on the day preceding; and in the morning before sunrise, or at the first appearance of dawn, bathing is to be performed until sunrise; a rigid fast is to be observed throughout the day, worship is to be offered the sun, presents are to be made to the Brahmans, and in the evening the worshipper is to hold a family feast; one of the observances of the day is abstinence from study, neither teacher nor scholar being allowed to open a book."[4] For the proper observance of the festival it is also necessary that the sun should be worshipped in his own temple, with prayers and offerings on the sixth day, during which abstinence is to be practised, and at night the worshipper should sleep on the ground. In upper India the festival day is also called Achala Saptami, the

[1] Gautama, xvi, 22, 35–37 (*S. B. E.*, ii, 258 *sqq.*). Compare Apastamba, i, 3, 9, 28: "at the new moon (he shall not study) for two days and nights" (*S. B. E.*, ii, 36).

[2] *Vishnu Puráña*, iii, 12 (Wilson-Hall, iii, 143).

[3] Sir M. Monier-Williams, *Brāhmanism and Hindüism*,[4] New York, 1891, p. 433.

[4] H. H. Wilson, "The Religious Festivals of the Hindus," in *Essays and Lectures chiefly on the Religion of the Hindus*, edited by R. Rost, London, 1862, ii, 194.

fixed or immovable seventh, or Jayanti Saptami, the victorious seventh, and so forth. "Whatever the designation, the worship of the sun is the prominent ceremony of the seventh of the light half of Magha. The same may be said, however, of the seventh lunar day throughout the year, chiefly of one seventh in each fortnight, that of the moon's increase; but also of the seventh day of the moon's wane." [1] The religious books declare that whoever worships the sun on the seventh day of the moon's increase, with fasting and offerings of white oblations, as white flowers and the like, and whoever fasts on the seventh of the moon's wane and offers to the sun red flowers and articles of a red colour, is purified from all iniquity and goes after death to the solar sphere. "The worship of the sun, on the seventh of the dark fortnight, seems to have gone out of use, but that on the seventh of the light fortnight is strongly recommended in various authorities, beginning with this seventh of Magha and continuing throughout the year." [2] The selection of the seventh day of each fortnight as the time of the festival may have been due to the symbolic significance of that number, while the choice of the sun as the object of adoration doubtless reflects the commanding position which that luminary assumed in post-Vedic times. The close resemblance between these Hindu ceremonies of sun-worship and those prescribed in the Vedas for the observance of new moon and full moon suggests, however, that there has been a partial fusion of the two festivals.

The Vedic observance of new moon and full moon survived in the ritual of both Jainism and Buddhism, the two great monastic sects which arose in the sixth century B.C. out of the bosom of Brahmanism. The Jain ceremony, known as *posaha*, is declared to have been specially instituted for those who said that "we

[1] H. H. Wilson, "The Religious Festivals of the Hindus," in *Essays and Lectures chiefly on the Religion*   *of the Hindus*, edited by R. Rost, London, 1862, ii, 197.
[2] *Ibid.*, p. 199.

cannot, submitting to the tonsure, renounce the life of a householder and enter the monastic state, but we shall strictly observe the *posaha* on the fourteenth and eighth days of each fortnight (on the new-moon and) full-moon days." [1] The faithful householder "should never neglect the *posaha* fast in both fortnights, not even for a single night." [2] In the Jain scriptures, the *posaha* is further defined as the observance of a fast or the eating once only on the two holy days of each fortnight, "after having given up bathing, unguents, ornaments, company of women, odours, incense, lights, etc., and assumed renunciation as an ornament." The *posaha* is thus distinguished by the four abstinences from food, bodily attentions, sexual intercourse, and daily work.[3] The keeping of the *posaha* at the present day is especially connected with the holy fast of Pajjusaṇa at the close of the Jain religious year. The observance of the rite at other times by laymen appears to be dying out.[4]

The Buddhist Sabbath, or *uposatha*, like the Jain *posaha*, owed its existence remotely to the Vedic lunar rites. As celebrated anciently in India and in modern times in Nepal and Ceylon, the *uposatha* falls on the day of the new moon, on the day of the full moon, and on the two days which are eighth from new and full moon. The *uposatha* is marked not only by fasting but also by abstinence from secular activities: during its continuance buying and selling, work and business, hunting and fishing are forbidden, and all schools and courts of justice are closed. Whoever observes the *uposatha* rigidly must abstain from food between sunrise and sunset. Since no cooking is allowed to taint the sanctity of the *uposatha*, the pious Buddhist pre-

[1] *Sûtrakṛtâṅga*, ii, 7, 17; compare, ii, 2, 76 (S. B. E., xlv, 428 *sq.*, 383).
[2] *Uttarâdhyayana*, v, 23; compare ix, 42 (S. B. E., xlv, 23, 39).
[3] H. Jacobi, *Gaina Sûtras*, Oxford, 1895, pp. xix, 23 n.[2] (S. B. E., vol. xlv).
[4] Margaret Stevenson, "Festivals and Fasts (Jain)," Hastings's *Encyclopædia of Religion and Ethics*, v, 875 *sq.*

pares his evening meal in the early morning before the sun appears.[1]

The *uposatha*, as contrasted with the *upavasatha*, is a ceremony attached to all four of the lunar phases, instead of to two only; moreover, it is a rest day as well as a fast day. How may it be shown that the Buddhist institution forms a natural outgrowth of the earlier Brahmanical rite?

The origin of the custom of observing four days in the lunar month as *uposatha* is involved in some obscurity. According to Buddhist tradition the monks of non-Buddhistic sects were accustomed to assemble at the middle and close of every half-month for the purpose of proclaiming their teachings. The Buddhists also adopted the custom of these periodical meetings on the fourteenth or fifteenth and eighth day of each half-month, a custom by them attributed to the Buddha himself.[2] There seems to be not the slightest ground for supposing that the number of Buddhist Sabbaths was originally two, but was afterwards increased to four in every month. The words of the canon are: "I prescribe that you assemble on the fourteenth, fifteenth, and eighth day of each [half] month."[3] In the *Dhammika Sutta* the wording is: "Then having with a believing mind kept abstinence (*uposatha*) on the fourteenth, fifteenth, and eighth

---

[1] H. Kern, *Der Buddhismus und seine Geschichte in Indien*, Leipzig, 1884, ii, 256 *sqq.*; *idem, Manual of Indian Buddhism*, Strassburg, 1896, pp. 99 *sq.*; R. C. Childers, *A Dictionary of the Pali Language*, London, 1875, *s.v. uposatho*.

[2] *Mahâvagga*, ii, 1, 1–4 (S. B. E., xiii, 239 *sq.*; compare p. x).

[3] *Ibid.*, ii, 1, 4 (S. B. E., xiii, 240). This rule is to be understood as requiring an assembly to be held on the fourteenth *or* the fifteenth of each half-month, according as the month had twenty-nine or thirty days. In other words an *uposatha* service on the fourteenth day of a short month was to be followed by a celebration on the fifteenth of the following long month. Compare *ibid.*, ii, 34, 1. The important word "half," which has been inserted above, was omitted by an unfortunate oversight in the translation of this passage from the *Mahâvagga*, as given in the *Sacred Books of the East*. It appears, however, in Mr. H. C. Warren's rendering of the same passage (*Buddhism in Translations*, Cambridge [Mass.], 1909, p. 404).

days of the half-month," etc.[1] When Buddhism arose, the custom of keeping the eighth day of each lunar fortnight, in addition to new moon and full moon, appears to have been well-established in both Brahmanism and the non-Buddhistic sects, a circumstance which led to the adoption of all four periods by Buddhists as well.[2] Two of these days (at new moon and full moon) are devoted to the special ceremony of reading, in an assembly of at least four monks, the *patimokkha*, or the disciplinary and penal code of Buddhism, according to the regulation laid down by the Buddha.[3]

In the *Sutta Nipâta*, a collection of seventy didactic poems belonging to the Pitakas, or sacred books of the southern Buddhists, Eight Precepts or Moral Commandments are enumerated. Five of these are binding on every Buddhist, whether mendicant or layman, but the remaining three are not obligatory for the

---

[1] *Sutta Nipâta*, ii, 14, 26 (S. B. E., x, pt. ii, 66).

[2] The eighth day of the waning moon (*áṣṭakā*) is distinctly mentioned in the Vedas, as forming with new moon and full moon the regular festival periods. Compare *Atharva-Veda*, xv, 16, 2 (transl. W. D. Whitney, p. 790); Zimmer, *op. cit.*, p. 365; H. Oldenberg, *Die Religion des Veda*, Berlin, 1894, p. 439. Of these, the full-moon day seems to have enjoyed most importance (Oldenberg, *loc: cit.*), and similarly in Buddhism. Compare *Mahâ-Sudassana Sutta*, i, 11: "On the Sabbath day, on the day of full moon" (S. B. E., xi, 251 *sq.*). Elsewhere the *uposatha* service is referred particularly to the fifteenth day of the month, "it being full moon" (*Sutta Nipâta*, iii, 12), proem. (S. B. E., x, pt. ii, 131 *sq.*). In very early times the Hindus had named and deified as goddesses the four phases of the moon. See *Rig-Veda*, ii, 32 (transl. H. Grassmann, i, 41); *Satapatha-Brâhmana*,

ix, 5, 1, 38 (S. B. E., xliii, 264); C. Lassen, *Indische Alterthumskunde*,[2] Leipzig and London, 1867-1874, i, 986.

[3] *Mahâvagga*, ii, 4, 1-2 (S. B. E., xiii, 246 *sq.*). The *patimokkha* is one of the oldest parts of the Buddhist canonical compositions. The Pali version has been translated in full by Professors Rhys Davids and Hermann Oldenberg (S. B. E., vol. xiii) and the part for monks, by J. F. Dickson (*Journal of the Royal Asiatic Society*, 1876, n.s., viii, 62-130). For a description of these ceremonies as witnessed March 27, 1893, at the Malwatta monastery in Kandy see E. M. Bowden, "The *uposatha* and *upasampadâ* Ceremonies," *ibid.*, 1893, n.s., xxv, 159-161. Mr. Bowden notes that at the Malwatta monastery the *uposatha* service is held more frequently on the day which precedes the new and the full moon than on the new and full-moon days.

laity. The precepts are: (1) not to destroy life; (2) not to commit theft; (3) not to tell lies; (4) not to drink intoxicating liquors; (5) not to indulge in unlawful sexual intercourse; (6) not to eat unseasonable food at night; (7) not to wear garlands or use perfumes; and (8) not to sleep on a raised couch.[1] These precepts are said to constitute the eight-fold fast, or *uposatha*, declared by the Buddha. Their special observance on the *uposatha* day is inculcated, and to break any of them on that day is considered highly irreligious. Instead of observing lunar taboos, the Buddhists were to keep the *uposatha* by a special fulfillment of the moral law, with clean garments and with clean minds; one of the many instances in which the founder of Buddhism gave a spiritual meaning to an earlier superstitious rite. That the *uposatha*, marked as it was by fasting, avoidance of sexual intercourse, and refraining from wearing wreaths and using perfumes, should have come to be regarded as a rest day seems to be only the natural result of its observance as a season of abstinence. The *uposatha* is thus discovered among the earliest institutions of Buddhism; in its origin it could have owed nothing to Jewish or Christian influence; in its diffusion throughout southeastern Asia it appears to have remained unaffected by the influence of Islam. If these conclusions be accepted, the Buddhist Sabbath dates back, remotely, to taboos observed at changes of the moon.

Buddhism was early introduced into Ceylon. The Sabbath still observed there by the Sinhalese falls on the four *poya* days of the month, the days of the changes

---

[1] *Sutta Nipâta,* ii, 14, 19–26 (S. B. E., x, pt. ii, 65 *sqq.*). See also T. W. Rhys Davids, *Buddhism,* London, 1890, pp. 137 *sqq.;* Childers, *op. cit., s.v. silam.* The prohibition of drinking intoxicating liquors was directed against the ancient *soma* sacrifice on the second day of the *upavasatha* ceremony. See *Satapatha-Brâhmana,* 1, 6, 4, 5 *sqq.* (S. B. E., xii, 176 *sqq.*). On the other hand the last precept is identical with one of the regulations for the *upavasatha,* where the celebrant is distinctly enjoined to sleep on the ground (or a shakedown of grass, a blanket). See *Satapatha-Brâhmana,* i, 1, 1, 11 (S. B. E., xii, 6).

of the moon.[1] Missionaries from Ceylon carried the new faith to Burma, at least as early as the fifth century A.D. According to an old traveller the "eighth day of the increasing moon, the fifteenth or full moon, the eighth of the decreasing moon, and the last day of the moon, are religiously observed by Birmans (*sic*) as sacred festivals. On these hebdomadal holidays no public business is transacted in the Rhoom : mercantile dealings are suspended ; handicraft is forbidden ; and the strictly pious take no sustenance between the rising and the setting of the sun ; but the latter instance of self-denial is not very common, and, as I understood, is rarely practised, except in the metropolis, where the appearance of sanctity is sometimes assumed as a ladder by which the crafty attempt to climb to promotion."[2] According to a more recent and sympathetic account there are "four *ubone*, or duty days, in every lunar month, on which all good Burmans are expected to go and worship at the pagodas. These are the eighth of the crescent, the full moon, the eighth of the waning, and the change, of which the second and the fourth are the more sacred. As the monks have nothing to do with looking after the spiritual state of the people, it is entirely a matter to be settled by one's self whether any particular worship day is to be ob-

[1] Mahony, in *Asiatic Researches*, 1803, vii, 40 *sq.*; Edward Upham, *Sacred and Historical Books of Ceylon*, London, 1833, iii, 161 *sqq.*; R. S. Hardy, *Eastern Monachism*, London, 1850, pp. 236 *sqq.*; *idem*, *Manual of Buddhism*, London, 1880, pp. 22, 50, 52; C. F. Köppen, *Die Religion des Buddha und ihre Entstehung*, Berlin, 1857–1859, i, 563 *sq.*; D. J. Gogerly, "The Laws of the Buddhist Priesthood," *Journal of the Ceylon Branch of the Royal Asiatic Society*, 1858–1859, iii, 253–261. By the Kandian, who occupy the interior of Ceylon, not only the *poya* days, but all unlucky days (*vitti*) as well, are observed with abstinence from agricultural labour (P. Kehelpannala, in *Journal of the Anthropological Institute*, 1896, xxv, 108).

[2] Michael Symes, *An Account of an Embassy to the Kingdom of Ava*, London, 1800, p. 335. See further Hiram Cox, *Journal of a Residence in the Burman Empire*, London, 1821, p. 241 ; Sangermano, *A Description of the Burmese Empire*, translated by W. Tandy, Rome, 1833, p. 92; C. J. F. S. Forbes, *British Burma*, London, 1878, pp. 169 *sqq.*

served or not. If you conclude that strict religious
observances are only necessary for your spiritual well-
being on the day of the full moon, or at any rate that
you may leave out the eighth of the crescent and waning moon, then the *ubone* does not concern you at all,
and you may proceed about your ordinary business
without being considered a reprobate. The very
devout may go to the pagoda on all the four sacred
days of the month; but if you choose to omit one or
several, or substitute an ordinary day for that provided by religious custom, there is no one to take you
to task for it. Were a Burman never to go to the pagoda at all, or fail to do so for any considerable time,
he would indeed soon get a very bad character among
his neighbours, and might even be formally excommuni-
cated by the *yahan*. There is, however, practically
no constraint save the force of public opinion. But
the duties of worship are so light, and so dependent in
their details upon yourself, and there is so much amusement to be got out of a visit to the pagoda on an *ubone*,
that few, even of the most worldly-minded, miss any
great number of the appointed days, and a special
festival is always carefully observed. . . . It must
not, however, be supposed that all the people take this
easy-going and frivolous view of duty days. Diligent
seekers after *kutho* behave very differently. They do
not merely limit themselves to the customary forms of
worship and offerings. They sleep little, or not at
all, the night before; telling their beads instead, and
reading good books, some of the discourses of the
Buddha, or portions of the greater *zat*. All necessary
business is transacted the day previous to the *ubone*,
and neighbours are exhorted to observe the festival
properly. After one simple dish in the morning, they
eat nothing for the rest of the day; or perhaps on certain occasions do not break their fast till after midday, a custom very general on the first day of Lent.
Instead of staying in the noisy *zayat*, where the assembled people are talking of light matters, laughing and

diverting themselves, they retire to a *tazaung* on the
pagoda platform or to some place shaded by trees;
there they finger the hundred and eight beads of their
rosary, muttering, 'All is transient, sorrowful, and
vain; the Lord, the Law, the Assembly; the three
precious things'; and meditate on the example of the
Lord Buddha and the excellence of his Law. To vary
the monotony of this performance, they go for an hour
or two to one of the monasteries to talk with the prior
or some learned brother, or perhaps to hear him read
and expound one of the *jataka*, or birth-stories. So the
duty day passes. By sunset most of the worshippers
are making their way back to their homes; but a
few zealous spirits remain all night in the *zayat*, and
only return with daylight on the following morning.
This simple round of celebration is repeated four times
in every lunar month, with here and there a feast day
of some particular shrine thrown in, when the only
difference is that there is greater ceremony and a more
or less large influx of strangers, according to the sanctity of the pagoda." [1]

The Siamese Sabbath (*wan phra*) was also an institution introduced by Buddhist missionaries. An old
writer describes it as follows: "Their Sunday, called
by them *vampra*, is always the fourth day of the moon;
in each month they have two great ones, at the new
and full moon, and two less solemn, on the seventh
and twenty-first. This day does not exempt them
from labour, since only fishing is forbidden to them.
Those who transgress this prohibition pay a fine and
are thrown into prison, as having profaned the sanctity
of the day." [2] A later writer declares that hunting
is also forbidden, and adds that on these days one can-

[1] Shway Yoe [Sir J. G. Scott],
The Burman: his Life and Notions,
London, 1910, pp. 217-220. The
Tungthu of Tenasserim have bor-
rowed these "duty days" from the
Burmese (*Gazetteer of Upper Burma
and the Shan States,* edited by

Scott and Hardiman, Rangoon,
1900, pt. i, vol. i, p. 558).
[2] F. H. Turpin, *Histoire civile et
naturelle du royaume de Siam,* Paris,
1771, i, 45 *sq.* The "fourth day" of
the moon must here be counted from
the astronomical new moon. The

M

not find fresh fish and meat in the shops.[1] In former times the temples were crowded with worshippers, who brought their offerings and listened to the hymns, prayers, and moral discourses addressed to them by the Buddhist priests.[2] But we are told that now a majority of the temples stand empty on the *wan phra*, and what worshippers there are consist invariably of women. Since the adoption of the solar calendar in 1889 the *wan phra* has been superseded to a large extent for civil purposes by Sunday.[3] The Buddhist Sabbath is also found in Cambodia.[4]

In some districts of Tibet the monthly Buddhist festivals (*du-zang*) are four in number, following the successive phases of the moon. In other parts of the country only three festivals are celebrated — at new moon, first quarter, and full moon. On these days no animal food ought to be eaten and no animal killed ; those who break this rule are threatened with severe punishment in a future existence. "To abstain from worldly occupations is, however, not enacted, and as the Buddhist laymen in the Himalaya and western Tibet are not very fond of passing the whole day in prayers and in the temples, these holy days are not particularly marked in the habits of the population." [5] As elsewhere in Buddhist lands the new-moon and full-

uposatha in Siam, as in Ceylon and Burma, falls regularly on the eighth and fifteenth days of the waxing moon and on the eighth and fourteenth or fifteenth days of the waning moon.

[1] J. B. Pallegoix, *Description du royaume Thai ou Siam*, Paris, 1854, i, 249.

[2] John Crawfurd, *Journal of an Embassy*, London, 1830, ii, 75; Sir John Bowring, *The Kingdom and People of Siam*, London, 1857, i, 158.

[3] J. G. D. Campbell, *Siam in the Twentieth Century*, London, 1904, p. 224 n.[1]; G. E. Gerini, "Festivals and Fasts (Siamese)," Hast-ings's *Encyclopædia of Religion and Ethics*, v, 885.

[4] J. Moura, *Le royaume de Cambodge*, Paris, 1883, i, 321. The Malays of the Malacca Peninsula regard the fourteenth and fifteenth days of each lunar month as unlucky. On these two days no work in the rice fields is allowed, a prohibition which only increases the native tendency to laziness (C. O. Blagden, "Notes on the Folk-lore and Popular Religion of the Malays," *Journal of the Straits Branch of the Royal Asiatic Society*, 1896, no. 29, p. 6).

[5] E. Schlaginweit, *Buddhism in Tibet*, Leipzig and London, 1863, p. 237.

moon Sabbaths are of most importance, since on these occasions the *patimokkha* is recited in the monasteries, accompanied by a public confession of sins.[1] However, in Tibet there appears never to have been much uniformity as to the times for the observance of the *uposatha*, the practice varying with different provinces and sects.[2] In Bhutan, where Buddhism was introduced by missionaries from Tibet, the eighth, fourteenth, twenty-fourth, and thirtieth of the month are said to be the holy days, while the Mongolians have the thirteenth, fourteenth, and fifteenth, the three days being brought together perhaps because of the great distance which separates the monasteries from the temple.[3] Among the Kalmucks on the Volga, to the north of the Caspian, the *uposatha* is generally observed thrice a month — the eighth day after new moon, the fifteenth, and the thirtieth.[4]

The *uposatha* is not unknown among the Buddhists of China. The Chinese *Ts'ing-kwei*, or "Regulations of the Priesthood," a Buddhist document, enumerates, among others, four festivals to be kept each month, at new moon and full moon, and on the eighth and twenty-third days. These are called *kin-ming si-chai*, "the four feasts illustriously decreed"; they may be regarded as a variant of the *uposatha*.[5] Among non-Buddhists there is another custom of observing on the new and full moon of each month a ceremony, anciently in honour of the moon, but now particularly

[1] L. A. Waddell, *The Buddhism of Tibet, or Lamaism*, London, 1895, p. 501; W. W. Rockhill, in *Journal of the Royal Asiatic Society*, 1891, n.s., xxiii, 207 n.[2]

[2] Marco Polo refers to five days or four days or three days in each month when the lamas or clergy of Tibetan Buddhism shed no blood and abstain from animal food (Sir Henry Yule, *The Book of Ser Marco Polo*,[3] London, 1903, i, 220, 223). Compare N. Prejevalsky, *Mongolia*, London, 1876, i, 65.

[3] Köppen, *op. cit.*, i, 564.

[4] P. S. Pallas, *Reise durch verschiedene Provinzen des russischen Reichs*, Frankfort, 1776, i, 295.

[5] Joseph Edkins, *Chinese Buddhism*,[2] London, 1893, p. 206. In Buddhist monasteries the *patimokkha* is regularly recited at new moon and full moon. The ceremony is known as *posadha* (J. J. M. de Groot, "Buddhism in China," Hastings's *Encyclopædia of Religion and Ethics*, iii, 554).

addressed to various deities, especially the gods of
wealth. It was formerly the rule to sacrifice a bullock
to the moon at this time. During the festival the
courts of justice and *yaman*, or government residences,
are closed. Offerings are made in the Confucian temples, and even the family gods receive their meed of
worship. The householder on this day enjoys a better
meal than usual, without, however, intermitting his
ordinary occupations.[1] There is no reason to believe
that this Chinese festival owes anything to contact
with Buddhism. Its independent origin, in connection with an early cult of the moon and perhaps at a
remote period with various lunar taboos, becomes,
therefore, something more than a conjecture.

The Buddhist Sabbath penetrated to Japan. An
old writer tells us that in Japan there are three monthly
holidays connected with the moon, though now immovable feasts. "The first is called *isitatz*, and is the
first day of each month. It deserves rather to be called
a day of compliments and mutual civilities, than a
church or Sunday." The second holiday is on the
fifteenth of each month, "being the day of the full
moon. The gods of the country have a greater share
in the visits the Japanese make on this day, than their
friends and relations." The third festival occurs on
the twenty-eighth of each month, "being the day of
the new moon, or the last day of the decreasing moon.
Not near so much regard is had to this, than there is
to either of the two former, and the Sintos [Shinto]
temples are very little crowded on it. There is a
greater concourse of people on this day at the Budsos
[Buddhist] temples, it being one of the monthly holidays sacred to Amida." [2]

Buddhism and Brahmanism, spreading beyond the

[1] J. H. Gray, *China*, London,
1878, i, 263 n.[1]; C. Pitou, *La Chine*,
Lausanne and Paris [1902],
pp. 27 *sqq*. See also W. Grube,
Religion und Kultus der Chinesen,
Leipzig, 1910, p. 66; J. D. Ball,
The Celestial and his Religions,
Hongkong, 1906, p. 25; J. Edkins,
Religion in China,[2] London, 1878,
pp. 48 *sq*.
[2] E. Kaempfer, *History of Japan*,
ii, 21 *sq*. (Glasgow reprint, 1906).

confines of continental Asia, carried the custom of keeping lunar festivals into some parts of Indonesia. In Bali, where the *padanda*, or Brahmans, have preserved many features of the old Vedic religion, fasts and sacrifices are still obligatory on the householder at new moon and full moon.[1] In Kar Nicobar Buddhist influence from Burma is seen in the custom of observing a rest day on the seventh day of the moon, at full moon, and on the twenty-second day of the moon, but only during seven lunar months of the year.[2] The Nicobarese have given to this imported Buddhist Sabbath their native name *anoiila*, which is regularly applied to the rest days or holidays observed by them on various critical occasions.[3]

We pass now from the lunar festivals found in ancient and modern India and in those countries of southeastern Asia which have been long affected by the cultural influence of India to similar observances among peoples of archaic civilization. The ancient Iranians appear to have celebrated four lunar days in each month, for the oldest part of the Avesta contains the following passage: "I dedicate, I perform (the sacrifice) for the month (gods), the time-divisions of Asa, for the between-moon [*i.e.*, the new moon], . . . for the full moon, and for the intervening seventh(s)," in other words, for the first, eighth, fifteenth, and twenty-third days, which were all dedicated to Ahura Mazda.[4]

---

[1] R. Friederich, in *Journal of the Royal Asiatic Society*, 1876, n.s., viii, 197 *sq.* Most priests also observe with prayer and fasting every fifth day (*kaliwon*) of the Javanese five-day market week, which has been introduced into Bali (Friederich, *loc. cit.*).

[2] E. H. Man, in *Indian Antiquary*, 1897, xxvi, 269 *n.*[20] According to this account the Nicobarese do not observe new-moon ceremonies. Other authorities, however, refer to sacrifices and celebrations at this time. See V.

Solomon, in *Journal of the Anthropological Institute*, 1902, xxxii, 204, 213; W. Svoboda, in *Internationales Archiv für Ethnographie*, 1893, vi, 22.

[3] Above, pp. 40 *sqq.*

[4] *Yasna*, i, 8 (so also *ibid.*, ii, 8; compare *Yast* vii, 4). See L. H. Gray, "Festivals and Feasts (Iranian)," Hastings's *Encyclopædia of Religion and Ethics*, v, 872; L. H. Mills, in *Sacred Books of the East*, xxxi, 198, 205; W. Geiger, *Civilization of the Eastern Irānians*, London, 1885, i, 146 *n.*[1] The

The choice of these four lunar days was due to the division of the Avesta thirty-day month into two unequal parts, containing fourteen and sixteen days, respectively, and to the further subdivision of each part so as to form two groups of seven days and two of eight days. This arrangement had the practical advantage of permitting a quadripartite division of the month without a remainder. There is no evidence that the four groups formed civil weeks, or that the first day of each group was observed as a Sabbath.[1]

Although the Egyptians had abandoned the old lunar year and lunar month, perhaps as early as the beginning of the fourth millenium B.C., the people continued for many centuries to observe as festivals the first and fifteenth days of the month. In the earlier calendar these would have coincided with the two significant epochs of the lunation, namely, new moon and full moon. The "monthly feasts" and the "half-monthly feasts" are mentioned in the very ancient texts preserved in the pyramids at Sakkara of kings

term *vishaptatha,* here translated "the intervening seventh" refers to the seventh day between the new moon (on the 1st) and the full moon (on the 15th), that is, to the 8th day of the month (E. Bartholomae, *Altiranisches Wörterbuch,* Strassburg, 1904, col. 1472). The theories as to the meaning of *vishaptatha,* advanced by J. Darmesteter, have not won the acceptance of scholars (*Sacred Books of the East,* xxiii, 90 n.[1]; *Le Zend-Avesta,* Paris, 1892–1893, i, 12 n.[M]).

[1] R. Roth, "Der Kalender des Avesta und die sogenannten gahanbâr," *Zeitschrift der deutschen morgenländischen Gesellschaft,* 1880, xxxiv, 710; L. H. Gray, "Der iranische Kalender," Geiger and Kuhn's *Grundriss der iranischen Philologie,* ii, 675 *sq.* There is extant a Pehlevi tract, said to have been composed in Persia during the fourth century A.D., which mentions among other matters five days in every month, namely, the 1st, 7th, 14th, 22d, and 30th, as times to be observed by abstinence from all worldly business. The manuscript sets forth in detail the peculiar virtues of all the days of one of the Zoroastrian months. "Some are best for beginning a journey or voyage, others for the regulation of matters of domestic economy, some again for social gatherings and festivities, and others again for the pursuit of learning, while not a few are reserved for rest and pious contemplation." These precepts are no longer observed; in fact, their very existence is unknown to most Parsis at the present day. See D. F. Karaka, *History of the Parsis,* London, 1884, i, 132 *sqq.*

of the Sixth Dynasty.[1] They are referred to in the *Book of the Dead*, in the directions requiring special chapters of that work to be recited on the first day of the month, apparently when it coincides with new moon, and on the last day of the sixth month of the Egyptian year, when that day coincides with the full moon.[2] That they were practised under the Twelfth Dynasty appears clearly from the well-known inscription of Khnumhotep II, cut on the walls of the chapel chamber in his tomb at Benihasan. Khnumhotep II, a local ruler of the sixteenth nome in Upper Egypt, sets forth in this inscription a somewhat vainglorious account of his buildings and his piety. Among other things he says, "I endowed him [the mortuary priest] with fields and peasants; I commanded the mortuary offering of bread, beer, oxen, and geese, at every feast of the necropolis: at the feast of the first of the year, of New Year's Day, of the great year, of the little year, of the last of the year, the great feast, at the great Rekeh, at the little Rekeh, at the feast of the five intercalary days, at ———— ——, at the twelve monthly feasts, at the twelve mid-monthly feasts; every feast of the happy living, and of the dead." [3] Again, there is an explicit reference to new-moon festivals under the Thirteenth Dynasty in a celebrated inscription placed by Thothmes III (1501–1447 B.C.) on the walls of the great temple of Amon at Karnak. This inscription describes the numerous campaigns made by the Egyp-

[1] *Pyramid Texts*, § 521 (= Teti, l. 12); compare *ibid.*, § 1453 (= Pepi, l. 657 = Mernere, ll. 763–764). Professor J. H. Breasted of the University of Chicago has very kindly furnished me with a translation of these passages, based on the monumental edition of the texts prepared by K. Sethe (*Die altägyptischen Pyramidentexte*, Leipzig, 1908–1910).
[2] *The Book of the Dead* (Theban Recension), chs. cxxxv, cxl (*The Chapters of Coming Forth by Day*,

translated by E. A. W. Budge, London, 1898, pp. 218, 230). See also H. Brugsch, "Über die Hieroglyphe des Neumondes und ihre verschiedenen Bedeutungen," *Zeitschrift der deutschen morgenländischen Gesellschaft*, 1856, x, 676.
[3] J. H. Breasted, *Ancient Records of Egypt*, Chicago, 1906, i, 285. See further E. Mahler, *Études sur le calendrier égyptien*, Paris, 1907, p. 128; *idem*, in *Zeitschrift der deutschen morgenländischen Gesellschaft*, 1908, lxii, 35.

tian king in Syria. The account of the battle of
Megiddo opens as follows: "Year 23, first (month) of
the third season (ninth month), on the twenty-first
day, the day of the feast of the new moon, corresponding to the royal coronation, early in the morning, behold,
command was given to the entire army to move." [1]
The significance of this lunar festival is further set
forth in the inscriptions on the ceiling of the pronaos of
the temple of Dendera, where the phases of the moon are
portrayed together with other astronomical matters.
The thirty days of the month are here given their
eponymic names and are arranged in two divisions,
according as they belong to the decreasing or to the
increasing moon. Four lunar days are brought into
special prominence as associated with the chief phases
of the moon, viz., 1st lunar day = "festival of new
moon"; 7th lunar day = "festival of the first quarter"; 15th lunar day = "festival of the fifteenth,"
and 23d lunar day = "festival of the third quarter."
In this inscription full moon on the fifteenth of the lunar
month, repeatedly mentioned in poetical terms as "the
eye of the moon," seems to have been regarded as the
most significant of the lunar phases.[2] The oldest
traces of this important list of lunar days belong to the
Eighteenth and Nineteenth dynasties; the latest
date from Ptolemaic and Roman times.[3] The evidence,
then, fully warrants the conclusion that from the earliest period the Egyptians included the celebrations at
new moon and full moon among the most important
of their religious ceremonies.[4] In late classical times
the lunar festivals appear to have been consecrated to
Osiris, whose identification with the moon is reason-

[1] Breasted, op. cit., ii, 184; for an earlier translation see S. Birch, in Records of the Past, ii, 43.
[2] H. Brugsch, Thesaurus inscriptionum Ægyptiacarum, Leipzig, 1883–1891, pt. i, 30 sqq., 49 sqq.; idem, Die Ägyptologie, Leipzig, 1891, pp. 332 sq.

[3] Brugsch, Thesaurus, pt. i, 52; idem, Ägyptologie, p. 332.
[4] Compare idem, Ägyptologie, p. 334; E. Meyer, "Ägyptische Chronologie," Abhandlungen der königlich-preussischen Akademie der Wissenschaften, 1904, p. 7.

ably certain.[1] But to what extent, if any, they were accompanied by the imposition of taboos remains problematical.

The evidence for lunar rites among the Greeks must be pieced together from scattered references in the classical writers. The day of the visible new moon (νουμηνία), marking the beginning of the lunar month, appears to have been ceremonially observed throughout the Greek world.[2] The Noumenia was particularly associated with Apollo and also with Hera, a goddess who seems to have had an ancient rôle as a moon deity. The antiquity of the Noumenia may be judged from the references to it in the *Odyssey*, where no other general festival than that of Apollo is mentioned. In the island of Ithaca a feast of Apollo on the new-moon day was in progress at the time of the trial of Odysseus's bow. Is it not the holy day of Apollo, ask the suitors? Who on such a day could stretch the bow?[3] The first of the month is holy, declares Hesiod.[4] In Athens, and doubtless in other Greek cities, the Noumenia continued to be in historic times a day of repose, when all public activities, except of a religious character, were intermitted.[5] Private business, however, was not suspended on the Noumenia; the markets, especially those for the purchase of slaves, were then particularly

[1] Herodotus, ii, 47; Plutarch, *De Iside et Osiride*, 8, 43, 52; Frazer, *Adonis, Attis, Osiris*,[2] ii, 129–131; Budge, *Osiris and the Egyptian Resurrection*, i, 384–396.

[2] J. Meursius, *Græcia feriata, sive de festis Græcorum*, Lugduni Batavorum, 1619, pp. 210–214; F. G. Welcker, *Griechische Götterlehre*, Göttingen, 1857, i, 554 *sq.*; W. H. Roscher, *Über Selene und Verwandtes*, pp. 110 *sq.*; idem, in *Philologus*, 1898, lvii, 216, 218; E. Saglio, "Noumenia," Daremberg and Saglio's *Dictionnaire des antiquités grecques et romaines*, iv, 108. The word νουμηνία occasionally was used in the sense of the true or

astronomical new moon (Thucydides, ii, 28).

[3] *Odyssey*, xxi, 258 *sq.*: νῦν μὲν γὰρ κατὰ δῆμον ἑορτὴ τοῖο θεοῖο ἁγνή · τίς δέ κε τόξα τιταίνοιτ';
Compare *ibid.*, xiv, 158–162, xx, 156, 276–278.

[4] *Opera et dies*, 770.

[5] Aristophanes, *Nubes*, 615–619; idem, *Acharnenses*, 999; idem, *Vespæ*, 96; Demosthenes, *Adv. Aristogiton*, i, 99; Athenæus, *Deipnosophistæ*, xii, 76; Plutarch, *Quæstiones Romanæ*, 25; idem, *De vitando ære alieno*, 2; Porphyry, *De abstinentia*, ii, 16; Theophrastus, *Characteres*, 14; Lucian, *Icaromenippus*, 13; idem, *Lexiphanes*, 6.

frequented; the time was regarded as the most favourable for marriage; and in the homes there was much feasting and good cheer.[1] The Dichomenia (διχομηνία), or full-moon day, appears also to have been a regular monthly festival in Greece, though of lesser importance than the Noumenia.[2]

The Roman month was originally lunar, and at all periods was divided by the real or imaginary phases of the moon. The Kalends, or day of the visible new moon, were sacred to Juno, a goddess, who, like the Greek Hera, was particularly associated with the moon.[3] On the Kalends one of the pontiffs performed a sacrifice, with the assistance of the *rex sacrorum*.[4] Pious Romans also celebrated the new-moon day with offerings and prayers to the family gods.[5] The Ides, or day of the full moon, were consecrated to Jupiter, but the Nones, which may originally have marked the moon's first quarter, were not sacred to any deity.[6] The Kalends of March, June, and October, the Nones of July, and the Ides of all the months were numbered among the *feriæ publicæ*, or sacred festivals attended by a compulsory remission of labour, of the Roman state religion.[7]

The taboos which at Rome invested the lunar phases appear to have lingered into the historic age under yet another guise. Among the unlucky days (*dies religiosi* [8]) of the Roman calendar were those following the Kalends, Nones, and Ides. The thirty-six *dies*

---

[1] Aristophanes, *Vespa*, 171; idem, *Equites*, 43 *sq.*; Alciphron, *Epistolæ*, iii, 38; Porphyry, *De abstinentia*, ii, 129; Proclus, on Hesiod, *Opera et dies*, 780; Suidas, *s.v.* νουμηνία (ed. G. Bernhardy, Halle, 1853, ii, 1010).

[2] *Hymni Homerici*, xxxii, 11; Plutarch, *De gloria Atheniensis*, 7; idem, *Dion*, 23. Hesiod (*op. cit.*, 819, compare 794 *sqq.*) describes the 14th of the month as "above all a holy day" (περὶ πάντων ἱερὸν ἦμαρ).

[3] Above, p. 130.

[4] Macrobius, *Saturnalia*, i, 15, 9.

[5] Ovid, *Fasti*, i, 47; Plutarch, *Quæstiones Romanæ*, 24; Vergil, *Bucolica*, i, 43 *sq.*; Horace, *Carmina*, iii, 23, 1 *sq.*

[6] Macrobius, *op. cit.*, i, 15, 15; Ovid, *op. cit.*, i, 48 *sq.*; Lydus, *De mensibus*, iii, 7.

[7] Wissowa, *Religion und Kultus der Römer*, p. 369; compare T. Mommsen, in *Corpus inscriptionum Latinarum*, i, pt. i,[2] 297.

[8] Above, pp. 80 *sq.*, 94.

postriduani were regarded as unsuitable for many purposes, both public and private: for battles, levies,
sacred rites, journeys, and marriages.[1] We are told
that they owed their unlucky quality to a pronounce-
ment of the Senate and pontiffs, in consequence of the
grave defeat of the Allia on the 18th of Quinctilis
(July). According to the story preserved by Gellius
one of the senators publicly declared that on the day
following the Ides the Roman commander had performed sacred rites with a view to engaging the Gauls,
only to experience an overwhelming defeat two days
later. Many other senators called to mind that on
sundry occasions, when sacrifices on the day following
the Kalends, Nones, or Ides had been performed to
secure the favour of the gods in battle, not victory but
disaster followed. In consequence these days were
declared unfit for public sacrifices.[2] It is obvious
that this traditional explanation of the *dies postriduani* must be far from the real truth. Unlucky days
are not generated in such an artificial fashion or on so
wholesale a scale. We may with some confidence
regard the prohibitions accompanying these days as
real survivals of primitive taboos at new moon, first
quarter, and full moon, their assumed historic significance being only the conscious fiction of a later and
more sophisticated age.[3]

[1] Varro, *De lingua Latina*, 29; Ovid, *Fasti*, i, 59 *sq.;* Livy, vi, 1; Plutarch, *Quæstiones Romanæ*, 25; Gellius, *Noctes Atticæ*, iv, 9, 5; Macrobius, *Saturnalia*, i, 16, 18. These days were also described as *atri vel vitiosi*. The greater num-ber of them were available for judicial business, but not for meetings of the assemblies (*dies fasti non comitiales*). Many Ro-mans also regarded as ominous the fourth day before the Kalends, Nones, and Ides; according to one account because the battle of Cannæ took place on the fourth day before the Nones of the month Sextilis (Gellius, *op. cit.*, v, 17, 3).

[2] Verrius Flaccus, *ap.* Gellius, *op. cit.*, v, 17; Macrobius, *op. cit.*, i, 16, 21.

[3] On this point I am happy to find myself in agreement with Dr. W. Warde Fowler, who also regards the traditional explanation of the *dies postriduani* as an ætiological myth. "The fact that the authori-ties of the state had made one or two days *religiosi* as anniversaries of disasters, supplied a handy ex-planation for a number of other *dies religiosi* of which the true ex-

The scanty records on which we must rely for our knowledge of the heathen inhabitants of central and northern Europe, before they came into contact with Rome and Christianity, furnish no certain evidence that they celebrated lunar festivals. According to Strabo the Celtiberians and their neighbours to the north sacrificed every full moon to a nameless god, the ceremony taking place at night and being accompanied by dancing.[1] Again, Tacitus, who mentions the custom of the Germans of holding their assemblies on "fixed days" (*certi dies*), either at the new moon or the full moon, also refers to the *certi dies* on which they think it lawful to propitiate Mercury, their chief god, with human sacrifices.[2] Such statements may mean much or little. Having traced lunar festivals among the Aryans of India, the Iranians, the Greeks, and the Romans, it might reasonably be supposed that the Celts and Germans were also familiar with them.

But the festive observance of the two great epochs of the lunation was by no means confined in antiquity to Indo-Germanic peoples. The Chinese and Egyptian festivals at new moon and full moon reach back into the past as far as the historical eye can follow them; while in Semitic lands, as we shall learn, the same rites occupied a most conspicuous place in the religious calendar. Not unjust was the remark of Isidore of Seville, a famous scholar of the Middle Ages, that the ancients, just as the Hebrews, were accustomed to celebrate the beginnings of all the months — *apud veteres enim omnium mensium principia colebantur, sicut et apud Hebræos.*[3]

---

planation had been entirely lost; but that there was such a true explanation, resting on very primitive beliefs, I have very little doubt" (*The Religious Experience of the Roman People*, London, 1911, p. 40). Dr. Fowler in a letter (under date Dec. 9, 1911) tells me that he regards as "quite probable"

the suggestion in the text that these days were originally tabooed in consequence of lunar superstitions attaching to them.

[1] *Geographica*, iii, 4, 16.
[2] *Germania*, 9, 11.
[3] Isidorus Hispalensis, *Etymologiæ sive origines*, v, 33.

CHAPTER VI

LUNAR CALENDARS AND THE WEEK

THE calendar forms one of the most important of social institutions and registers in its gradual improvement from age to age the onward march of culture. The first attempts at calendar-making were naturally of the rudest sort, for they were based on the untutored experience and observation of common men. With the progress of society the regulation of calendrical matters tended to fall into the hands of the sacerdotal class, partly because priests alone enjoyed the leisure necessary for prolonged researches, but chiefly because the calendar, on which depends the orderly sequence of holy days and festivals, was itself an affair of religion.[1]

It is clear that the alternations of night and day must have furnished man with his most elementary conceptions of the passage of time. A longer cycle was naturally suggested by the lunar phenomena, so striking, so obvious, and marked by stages so readily determined. A survey of the anthropological data indicates that among savage and barbarous peoples the moon is the measure of time, and that the period of a lunation furnishes the customary unit for longer reckon-

[1] J. K. Fotheringham, "Calendar (Introductory)," Hastings's *Encyclopædia of Religion and Ethics*, iii, 61–64; F. K. Ginzel, *Handbuch der mathematischen und technischen Chronologie*, Leipzig, 1906–1911, ii, 121–159; E. Meyer, *Geschichte des Altertums*, Erster Band, Erste Hälfte, Berlin, 1907, pp. 231–243; R. Schram, "Jahrform und Zeitrechnung verschiedener Völker," *Mitteilungen der kaiserlich-königlichen geographischen Gesellschaft in Wien*, 1884, xxvii, 481–498; M. Hubert, "Étude sommaire de la représentation du temps dans la religion et la magie," in Hubert and Mauss, *Mélanges d'histoire des religions*, Paris, 1909, pp. 189–229.

ings.[1] Lunar months are general throughout Australia, Melanesia, Polynesia, Africa, and America, wherever primitive calendars have not been supplanted by more refined calculations borrowed from advanced peoples. The computation of time by moons naturally formed the basis of those early calendars which were framed by peoples just rising into civilization. In Mexico and Yucatan the year of twelve moon-months preceded the introduction of the solar year; and the ancient Peruvians, in some respects so advanced, always continued to reckon by the succession of lunations.[2] There can be no doubt that the solar calendar in use among the Egyptians at the very dawn of their history had been preceded by a more primitive reckoning of the year in lunations. It is enough to point out in this connection that the Egyptians regularly employed the figure of a crescent moon as the hieroglyph for "month."[3] The calendars of Semitic peo-

---

[1] The lunar or synodic month, determined by the synodic revolution of the moon, is the time between two successive conjunctions of that luminary with the sun, and may be measured from new moon to new moon or from full to full. It varies about thirteen hours by reason of eccentricities of the moon's orbit and of that of the earth about the sun, but its mean value is 29 days, 12 hours, 44 minutes, and 3 seconds. The length of the "light month," or period of the moon's visibility, though commonly taken at three days, is a variable quantity. It is the usual practice to assume that the moon becomes visible on the first evening when she is more than thirty hours old at sunset. Her mean age when first seen is, therefore, 30 hours $+ \frac{24}{2}$ hours = 1 day, 18 hours. See J. K. Fotheringham, "On the Smallest Visible Phase of the Moon," *Monthly Notices of the Royal Astronomical Society*, 1910, lxx, 527–531.

[2] E. J. Payne, *History of the New World called America*, Oxford, 1892–1899, ii, 329, 331; E. Förstemann, in *Bulletin of the Bureau of American Ethnology*, 1904, no. 28, p. 523 (Maya pre-solar calendar).

[3] Horapollo, *Hieroglyphica*, i, 4; compare H. Brugsch, in *Zeitschrift der deutschen morgenländischen Gesellschaft*, 1856, x, 676; C. R. Lepsius, *Die Chronologie der Ägypter*, Berlin, 1849, i, 156 *sq.*, 219; E. Meyer, "Ägyptische Chronologie," *Abhandlungen der königlich-preussischen Akademie der Wissenschaften*, Berlin, 1904, pp. 5 *sqq.* Papyri discovered by Professor W. M. Flinders Petrie at Kahun, belonging to the age of Sesostris III, show that a lunar year of three hundred and fifty-five days was still recognized as late as the Twelfth Dynasty. These papyri relate to the temple revenues, which the priests, with characteristic religious conserva-

ples, notably those of the Babylonians and Hebrews, were based on the moon;[1] and the prophet Mohammed, when enjoining on his followers the observance of the pure lunar year, in place of the lunisolar year used by the Arabians before the Hegira, was in reality reverting to a still more primitive mode of counting time. Lunisolar calendars, in which the primary unit is the lunation, were known, long before the Christian era, to every civilization in the Old World from the Roman in the west to the Chinese in the east. Linguistic researches indicate that in most, if not all, Indo-European languages, the names for moon and month originally coincided.[2] In Max Müller's poetical language the moon was "the golden hand on the dark dial of heaven."

The need of observing the moons, apart from religious or superstitious reasons, was no doubt mainly connected with economic considerations. To the savage it is of supreme importance to be able to anticipate the different periods of the year which bring with them different supplies of natural food; and for this purpose the moons afford a convenient basis of reckoning. Hence we find that very generally among primitive peoples the moons are named after the moulting, migrating, and pairing of animals, or after the budding, blossoming, and ripening of the fruits of the earth. Again, most shepherd tribes reckon time by moons. In the pastoral stage it is probable that the necessity of calculating the various periods of gestation and the proper time for breeding, so that young animals might be brought into the world at seasons most favourable to their health and maintenance, contributed to the observation of the moon and to the formation of lunar

tism, were accustomed to reckon according to lunar months (seven of thirty days and five of twenty-nine days). See L. Borchardt, in *Zeitschrift für ägyptische Sprache*, 1899, xxxvii, 92–95.
[1] Below, pp. 226, 247.

[2] O. Schrader, *Prehistoric Antiquities of the Aryan Peoples*, translated by F. B. Jevons, London, 1890, p. 306; *idem, Reallexikon der indogermanischen Altertumskunde*, Strassburg, 1901, p. 547.

calendars. If the desirability of observing the successive moons was felt by frugivorous and pastoral peoples, it will be readily seen how the introduction of agricultural operations, often accompanied by religious ceremonies and festivals, rendered definite and clearly marked divisions of time a matter of the greatest moment. It is therefore probable that rude popular calendars based on the moon were in use long before more accurate observations were made by primitive astronomers. There is much evidence for the practice of naming the moon-months after the different agricultural operations, such as planting and harvesting, which occur in them. Among the Chinese, Japanese, Babylonians, Hebrews, Celts, Germans, and Slavs, the early epithets of some or all of the months are connected with agriculture and the farmer's life. And the Roman Aprilis, Maius, and Junius, from which our own month-names have been taken, are believed to have been originally seasonal designations, referring to the sprouting, growth, and maturity of vegetation.

A lunar month does not necessarily imply a lunar year. Of not a few savage and half-civilized peoples it is expressly said that they have but vague notions of a year as a fixed period of time, and that they can refer to events more than a few months past only as happening after some noteworthy event, such as a flood, a drought, an earthquake, a comet, or the death of a chief. The foundation of yearly reckonings must be sought in the observation of rhythmical natural phenomena — the alternation of the seasons, the recurrence of periodical winds, the varying length of day as determined by the sun's elevation, and especially the rising and setting of the Pleiades.[1] In order to adapt the same moons to the same seasons as they succes-

---

[1] R. Andree, "Die Plejaden im Mythus und in ihrer Beziehung zum Jahresbeginn und Landbau," Globus, 1893, lxiv, 362–366; Sir J. G. Frazer, Spirits of the Corn and of the Wild, London, 1912, i, 307–319; E. Förstemann, "The Pleiades among the Mayas," Bulletin of the Bureau of American Ethnology, 1904, no. 28, pp. 523 sq.

sively occurred, or to the course of the sun, or to the rising and setting of the Pleiades, the number of moons was usually taken at twelve, giving the lunar year of three hundred and fifty-four days.[1]

It is unnecessary in this connection to discuss fully the various methods which have been employed to adjust the pure lunar year of twelve synodic months to the seasonal or solar year. Some primitive peoples adopt the expedient of counting thirteen lunations to the year. A more common and accurate procedure is to intercalate the thirteenth month, usually in every second or third year. Familiar illustrations are furnished by the Hindus, Babylonians, Jews, and Greeks in antiquity; among modern peoples, by the natives of Burma, Siam, China, and Japan.[2] The methods of intercalation employed are historically numerous, the details are often obscure, and in no instance were the results wholly successful. The difficulties arising from such attempts to coördinate incoördinable quantities must have been the prime cause of the adoption of calendars in which the month, instead of denoting the moon's synodic revolution, received an arbitrary num-

---

[1] The lunar year of twelve synodic months consists, exactly, of 354 days, 8 hours, 48 minutes, and 36 seconds. The Maori have a legend to the effect that their ancient year contained ten months only, until a certain teacher, full of divine wisdom, instructed them to make their year twelve months long (E. Tregear, *The Maori Race*, Wanganui [N.Z.], 1904, p. 143). The Chinese have a similar tradition of a ten-month year (H. A. Giles, *A Glossary of References on Subjects connected with the Far East,*[3] Shanghai, 1900, p. 183). The Roman "year of Romulus" consisted of ten months and (commonly) three hundred and four days (Censorinus, *De die natali,* xx, 2–3; Lydus, *De mensibus,* i, 16).

Sceptical modern historians are inclined to dismiss the Roman tradition as a mere figment of the imagination.

[2] The thirteenth month is referred to in the *Rig-Veda* (i, 25, 8; transl. H. Grassmann, ii, 25) as the "later-born month"; compare *Atharva-Veda,* v, 6, 4, xiii, 3, 8 (transl. W. D. Whitney, pp. 230, 729). This intercalary month bears a distinctly unfavourable character, being regarded as unfit for any religious undertaking (Haug, *Aitareya Brahmanam,* ii, 26). Among the Loango negroes the thirteenth month, inserted every three years, is likewise regarded as an evil time (E. Pechuël-Loesche, *op. cit.,* pp. 138 *sq.*).

N

ber of days approaching the twelfth part of a solar year.

The period of a lunation seems to have been generally estimated, in the first instance, at thirty days, a calculation found in the lunar calendars of many half-civilized peoples, and still employed at the present day on all occasions when absolute accuracy is not considered necessary. Indeed, if lunations be used, it is more exact to count by thirty days than by twenty-nine. When the moon's synodic revolution came to be more accurately measured by calculating an average from the number of days comprised in several successive lunations, the true length (about twenty-nine and one-half days) could be conveniently calendarized only by periods of twenty-nine and thirty days in alternation. Such vacillating months were used by the Hawaiians and the New Zealanders; they were familiar to the Jews, the later Babylonians, and the Greeks; and they are still found throughout the Mohammedan world, and among various peoples of southeastern Asia.[1]

People who reckon by moons naturally begin their lunar month with the first appearance of the luminous

---

[1] The old Roman arrangement of the months, though based on the lunar year, is *sui generis*. Four of the twelve months, viz., March, May, July, and October, had thirty-one days, and the rest twenty-nine days, except February, which had twenty-eight days. All the months thus had an odd number of days, save February, which was specially devoted to purificatory ceremonies and the cult of the dead. This peculiar arrangement appears to have been based on an old belief that odd numbers are of good omen, even numbers, of ill omen (T. Mommsen, *Die römische Chronologie bis auf Cæsar*, Berlin, 1858, p. 13; Marquardt-Wissowa, *Römische Staatsverwaltung*, iii,² 284). The superstition, alluded to by Vergil in a famous line — *Numero deus impare gaudet* (*Bucolica*, viii, 75) — is supposed to have been derived from Pythagorean speculations regarding the cosmic properties of numbers. It may better be considered a genuinely Italian notion, since like beliefs are found in the folklore of other peoples, notably the old Arabs and the modern Hindus. See I. Goldziher, in *Globus*, 1901, lxxx, 31; Crooke, *Popular Religion and Folk-lore of Northern India*,² ii, 51. The choice of 355 days, rather than 354 days, as the length of the Roman lunar year, was undoubtedly determined by the prevalence of the same superstition (Censorinus, *De die natali*, xx, 4).

crescent in the western sky.[1] The real moon being invisible for two or three days, various expedients are adopted in order to secure regularity in lunar reckonings. Thus, the Toda keep a record of the number of days from new moon to full moon and from that to the next new moon. The full moon is counted as being on the fifteenth day after the new moon, and the new moon as being on the sixteenth day after the full moon.[2] The Basuto begin their month on the day when the new moon is visible, though they count two more days when the moon cannot be seen at all in the heavens.[3] Still other devices were employed in antiquity by the Babylonians, Hebrews, and Romans.[4]

[1] This custom explains the widespread practice of beginning the civil day at sunset or, more accurately, in the interval between the going-down of the sun and complete darkness. The necessities of a calendar system requiring that the first day of the month should be counted from the same moment that the month itself is supposed to begin, it follows that the other days of the month must also be calculated from evening to evening. The noctidiurnal cycle is widespread throughout the lower culture, being found, generally, among the North American Indians, the Melanesians and Polynesians, and in Africa. The same cycle obtained among many peoples of archaic civilization. The Babylonian day began with the evening, and this is still the custom among the Arabs and throughout the Mohammedan world. Modern Jewish communities, in beginning their ritual day in the evening, retain a practice illustrated by several Old Testament passages (*Genesis*, i, 5; *Psalms*, lv, 17). Various festivals and fasts, such as the Sabbath, the Day of Atonement, and the Feast of Unleavened Bread, were so arranged as to begin and end with the evening. Among most of the Indo-Germanic peoples the civil day, or nycthemeron, commenced at sunset; and the practice, which still survives in Iceland, was not abandoned in Italy and some other parts of Europe until about a century ago. Our English words "fortnight" and "sennight" are reminiscent of this ancient custom. See G. A. Wilken, "Het tellen bij nachten bij de volken van het maleisch-polynesische ras," *Bijdragen tot de taal-land-en volkenkunde van Nederlandsch-Indië*, 1886, fifth series, pt. i, 378-392; A. Fischer, "'Tag und Nacht' im arabischen und die semitische Tagesberechnung," *Abhandlungen der philologisch-historischen Klasse der königlich-sächsischen Gesellschaft der Wissenschaften*, 1909, xxvii, 741-758; O. Schrader, *Reallexikon*, p. 845; S. Reinach, "Die," in Daremberg and Saglio, *op. cit.*, iii, 168 *sq.*, G. Bilfinger, *Der bürgerliche Tag*, Stuttgart, 1888.

[2] Rivers, *Todas*, pp. 590 *sqq.*

[3] J. Sechefo, "The Twelve Lunar Months among the Basuto," *Anthropos*, 1909, iv, 931 *sqq.*

[4] Below, pp. 184, 226 *sq.*, 248 *sq.*

The lunar month, which in rude communities provides a satisfactory chronological unit, does not meet the needs of an advancing society. Shorter periods become desirable, and these may be found in the division of the lunation. There is much evidence that primitive peoples watch the lunar phases with keen interest, often name them, and sometimes use them for the purpose of reckoning time. The natives of Victoria are said to employ ordinal numbers only in numbering the days of the month for making appointments. As their months are marked by the reappearance of the moon, their ordinal numbers do not go beyond twenty-eight.[1] The Dieri and related tribes of South Australia reckon by lunar phases; "when anticipating a grand ceremony they refer to the first or last quarter of the moon."[2] The central Australians, who regard the moon as a male deity, have distinct names applied to new moon, first quarter, full moon, and last quarter.[3] In German New Guinea the phases of the moon are employed for all time-units greater than a day.[4] The natives of New Britain are close observers of the phases of the moon (kalang) and have separate terms for them.[5] The New Caledonians count by lunar months, "each divided into four weeks, following the four phases of the moon."[6] The Kayan on the Mendalam River in Dutch Borneo name eight phases of the waxing and waning moon.[7] The Dyak tribes on the Mahakam and Barito rivers in Dutch Borneo "reckon their time by the full moon, half moon, and new moon."[8] In those parts of Sumatra where the seven-day week has not been introduced,

[1] James Dawson, Australian Aborigines, Melbourne, 1881, p. xcix.
[2] S. Gason, in Journal of the Anthropological Institute, 1895, xxiv, 174.
[3] Spencer and Gillen, The Native Tribes of Central Australia, London, 1897, pp. 25, 564 sq.
[4] B. Hagen, Unter den Papua's, Wiesbaden, 1899, p. 244.
[5] George Brown, Melanesians and Polynesians, London, 1910, p. 332.
[6] V. de Rochas, La Nouvelle-Calédonie, Paris, 1862, p. 191.
[7] Nieuwenhuis, op. cit., i, 317.
[8] C. Bock, Head-hunters of Borneo,[2] London, 1882, p. 212.

it is a common practice to calculate by the days of the moon's age.[1]   The very primitive peoples occupying Nias and the Mentawi Islands off the western coast of Sumatra distinguish four phases of the moon and give to them appropriate names.[2]   Not only do the Nicobarese possess terms to denote the chief phases of the lunation, but they are also able to indicate any particular day in the lunar month with perfect clearness, since each day has its particular name.[3]   The Andaman Islanders, possessing no extended enumeration, do not count the moons in the year, but nevertheless employ appropriate words to designate the lunar phases.[4]   The Bontoc and Ibaloi Igorot have noted and named eight phases of the moon; these, however, are said to be seldom used for counting time.[5] Throughout the Caroline Islands (Yap, Lamotrek, Ponape, Uleai) the successive days of the month receive names indicating the moon's age.[6]   In Polynesia every night in the month had its distinct name derived from the changing aspects of the moon.[7]   The Nandi of

[1] William Marsden, *The History of Sumatra*,⁸ London, 1811, p. 194; compare B. Hagen, *Die Orang Kubu auf Sumatra*, Frankfurt-a.-M., 1908, p 154.

[2] E. Modigliani, *Un viaggio a Nias*, Milan, 1890, pp. 4, 484; A. Maass, *Bei liebenswürdigen Wilden*, Berlin, 1902, p. 93.

[3] E. H. Man, in *Indian Antiquary*, 1897, xxvi, 270 *sq.*

[4] *Idem*, in *Journal of the Anthropological Institute*, 1883, xii, 337.

[5] A. E. Jenks, in *Ethnological Survey Publications*, Manila, 1905, i, 219; O. Scheerer, *ibid.*, ii, 158.

[6] F. W. Christian, *The Caroline Islands*, London, 1899, pp. 387 *sq.*, 392 *sqq.*; M. Girschner, in *Baessler-Archiv*, 1911, ii, 175 *sq.*

[7] The Maori counted twenty-eight "nights" of the moon, including: 1. *noni hope*, the moon is in the *reinga*, or underworld; 4. *he oho ata*, the moon is visible; 5. *ouenuku*, it begins to rise a little way; 6. *maweti*, it rises still higher; 14. *he atua*, full; 19. *he ohika*, the moon begins to wane; 24. *tanagaroa a roto*, it sinks into the sea; 28. *he o mutu*, it disappears (Taylor, *Te Ika A Maui*, p. 177). To the Society Islanders the fifteenth day was *omarae*, or the moon with a round and full face; the thirtieth day, *oterieo*, was the time when the moon dies or is changed (Ellis, *Polynesian Researches*, i, 87 *sq.*). In the Hervey group several of the moon nights were sacred to the gods. The twenty-eighth day was called *mauri* — ghost; the twenty-ninth, *omutu* — ended; the thirtieth, *otire o avaiki* — lost in the depths of *avaiki*, or Hades (W. W. Gill, *Myths and Songs from the South Pacific*, London, 1876, p. 318).

British East Africa similarly designate the successive
nights of a lunar month.[1] The Bini of Southern
Nigeria even appoint special persons to observe the
changes of the moon.[2] The Ho tribes of Togo and the
Hottentots of South Africa employ separate terms for
all the lunar phases.[3] In South America the Karaja
of Brazil, in addition to noting and naming the four
most conspicuous phases of the moon, also distinguish
a fifth phase, which occurs between first quarter and
full moon.[4] Of the North American Indians it has
been said, generally, that the "alternations of day and
night and the changes of the moon and the seasons
formed the basis of their [calendar] systems." [5] In
the words of the *Koran* the phases of the moon are
"indications of time for men." [6]

Since new moon and full moon are the most conspicuous lunar phases, it has been a common practice to
recognize two periods in the lunation, as marked by the
waxing and the waning moon.[7] This two-fold division

For a table of the days of the
moon's age in the Maori, Moriori,
Hawaiian, Tahitian, Marquesan,
and Rarotongan languages see
Tregear, *Maori-Polynesian Comparative Dictionary*, p. 666.

[1] Hollis, *Nandi*, pp. 95 *sq.*

[2] Dennett, *At the Back of the
Black Man's Mind*, p. 186.

[3] J. Spieth, *Die Ewe-Stämme*,
Berlin, 1906, p. 556; L. Schultze,
Aus Namaland und Kalahari, Jena,
1907, p. 370. The Hottentots now
use the European week (Schultze,
op. cit., p. 372).

[4] F. Krause, *In den Wildnissen
Brasiliens*, Leipzig, 1911, p. 339.

[5] C. Thomas, "Calendar," *Handbook of American Indians*, pt. i,
189 (*Bulletin of the Bureau of
American Ethnology*, no. 30).

[6] *Koran*, ii, 185. Even at the
present time the south Arabians
determine the day of the month by
observation of the moon's phases,
the first quarter being called, for

example, the seventh day, and the
last quarter, the twenty-first day
(Nielsen, *Altarabische Mondreligion*,
p. 85, referring to Dr. Glaser's observations).

[7] The mean age of the moon
when first seen being 30 hours
$+ \frac{24}{2}$ hours = 1 day, 18 hours
(above, p. 174 *n.*[1]), and the mean
age of the moon when full being
$\frac{29\,days,\,12 + hours}{2}$ = 14 days, 18
hours, it follows that the mean
interval between the first appearance of the moon and the full of
the moon is about 13 days. "In
other words the moon becomes full
on an average at the end of the
thirteenth day and the beginning
of the fourteenth night. Hence,
where the days are reckoned from
sunset, we should expect the fourteenth day of the month to be
regarded as the day of the full
moon. And it is in fact one of the

of the month does not seem to be employed for calendrical purposes by the Australian aborigines, but in some parts of Melanesia the two halves of the lunation receive appropriate names and the full moon itself bears a particular designation.[1] The Maori of New Zealand, who sometimes "divide the month into halves or fortnights by 'moon-growing' and 'moon-lessening,'"[2] are the only Polynesian people to adopt this mode of reckoning. It is met, also, in Malaysia (Java, Sumatra, Bali, Nias, etc.), but only where Indian culture has penetrated.[3]

The division of the month into two parts is found among most Indo-European peoples. In India the recognition of the "light" and "dark" halves of the month goes back to Vedic antiquity.[4] Modern Hindus divide the month into two fortnights, the days of which are reckoned continuously as those of the increasing

days most commonly so regarded. The fifteenth is a date obtained more simply. Fifteen is half thirty and, as the middle of the month, should be the date of full moon. In calendars based on calculations the month is frequently reckoned from the actual new moon, and in these the fifteenth is more correct than the fourteenth for the mean date of full moon." It should be noted, also, that, as a general rule, the nearer the autumnal equinox, the later the first appearance of the moon and the shorter the interval between the visible new moon and full moon. If the first appearance is late, as it often is in September, the moon might be full on the night following the eleventh day. See J. K. Fotheringham, in *Proceedings of the British Academy*, 1909-1910, pp. 283, 286.

[1] R. Thurnwald, *Forschungen auf den Salomo-Inseln und dem Bismarck Archipel*, Berlin, 1912-1913, i, 330 *sq.*

[2] E. Tregear, in *Journal of the Anthropological Institute*, 1890, xix, 114.

[3] L. H. Gray, "Calendar (Polynesian)," Hastings's *Encyclopædia of Religion and Ethics*, iii, 130; J. v. Brenner, *Besuch bei den Kannibalen Sumatras*, Würzburg, 1894, p. 233; R. Friederich, in *Journal of the Royal Asiatic Society*, 1878, n.s., x, 93 *sq.*; Modigliani, *op. cit.*, p. 464.

[4] A. Weber, in *Indische Studien*, 1853, ii, 166 *n.*; H. Zimmer, *Altindisches Leben*, Berlin, 1879, p. 364; G. Thibaut, "Astronomie, Astrologie, und Mathematik," Bühler's *Grundriss der indo-arischen Philologie und Altertumskunde*, iii, pt. ix, 12. This lunar fortnight of the Hindus attracted the attention of the Romans, and Quintus Curtius speaks of it as a noteworthy fact (*Historia Alexandri Magni*, viii, 9). References to it are also found in mediæval literature; compare Albîrûnî, *op. cit.*, i, 359.

or decreasing moon. The full-moon day (*amavus*) is
held in great sanctity.[1] Like customs prevail in Ceylon, Burma, Siam, Indo-China, and other parts of
Asia.[2] The bipartite division of the month was familiar to the ancient Persians [3] and to the early Greeks.[4]
The fifteenth of the month was regularly called by
the Greeks the full-moon day (Dichomenia, διχομηνία)
even after the introduction of the sequence of twenty-
nine day and thirty-day months.[5] In "hollow" months
of twenty-nine days the full moon, of course, would
fall on the fourteenth day, except when an extra day
was intercalated every thirty-two or thirty-three
months.[6] The Roman *kalendæ* and *idus* corresponded
to the Greek νουμηνία and διχομηνία.[7] The Kalends
were so named because in early times the pontiffs had
been accustomed to make a public announcement
(*calare*) whether five or seven days should be reckoned
from new moon to the first quarter.[8] The Ides thus

[1] G. E. Balfour, *The Cyclopædia
of India,*[2] ii, 981; Sewell and
Dikshit, *The Indian Calendar*, London, 1896, p. 4.
[2] Childers, *Dictionary of the Pali
Language, s.v. parācadasi;* A. Cabaton, in Hastings's *Encyclopædia of
Religion and Ethics*, iii, 136 (as to
the Siamese); Shway Yoe, *The
Burman,*[2] p. 550; A. Cabaton,
in Hastings's *Encyclopædia of Religion and Ethics*, iii, 113 *sq.* (as to
the Cambodians, Chams, and
Laotians); H. Vámbéry, *Die primitive Cultur des turko-tatarischen
Volkes*, Leipzig, 1879, p. 160;
Carl Hiekisch, *Die Tungusen*, St.
Petersburg, 1879, p. 94. In Tibet
the fifteenth day of the lunar month
receives a special name (A. Csoma
de Körös, *A Grammar of the Tibetan
Language*, Calcutta, 1834, p. 157).
[3] *Yašt*, vii, 2 (S. B. E., xxiii, 89).
[4] *Odyssey*, xiv, 162; xix, 307:
τοῦ μὲν φθίνοντος μηνός, τοῦ δ᾽ ἱσταμέ-
νοιο; Hesiod, *Opera et dies*, 780:
μηνὸς δ᾽ ἱσταμένου τρισκαιδεκάτην.

[5] G. F. Unger, "Zeitrechnung
der Griechen und Römer," Iwan
von Müller's *Handbuch der klassischen Altertumswissenschaft*, i, 563.
However, evidence is not wanting
for the observance of the fourteenth
day, and even of the sixteenth day,
as that of the full moon. See A.
Mommsen, *Chronologie*, Leipzig,
1883, pp. 99 *sqq.*
[6] The Greeks never knew the
exact mean measurement of a
lunation and, owing to their neglect
of the odd minutes and seconds in
the lunar month, they were obliged
occasionally to intercalate an additional day. From a passage in
Aristophanes it would appear that
this pious duty to the gods was not
always performed (*Nubes*, 610
sqq.).
[7] T. Mommsen, *Römische Chronologie*, pp. 13 *sq.*, 215 *sq.*; Marquardt-Wissowa, *Römische Staatsverwaltung*, iii,[2] 282 *sq.*
[8] Macrobius, *Saturnalia*, i, 15,
10; Varro, *De lingua Latina*, vi, 27.

fell on the thirteenth or fifteenth day of the month, according as the Nones occurred on the fifth or seventh day. The Roman belief in the virtue of odd numbers doubtless explains this choice of dates for both Nones and Ides.[1] Among the ancient Germans new moon and full moon appear as the most prominent lunar phases.[2] The division of the lunation into two parts, the first of fifteen days, the second of fourteen or fifteen days, according as the month had twenty-nine or thirty days, is clearly indicated for the Celtic peoples.[3] In the Calendar of Coligny the days of each half-month are numbered consecutively, following what must have been the old Indo-European practice. The second half of the month is always preceded by the title *atenoux*, doubtless indicating full moon, and variously translated "great night" or "renewal."[4] That this Gallic calendar presents no exceptional custom is obvious from the constant occurrence in the literature of the insular Celts of such expressions as the Welsh *pythewnos*, a fortnight (literally "a fifteen night"), and the Irish *cóicthiges*, which has the same meaning.[5] With these

[1] The *nonæ*, or Nones, were so called because, by the Roman inclusive reckoning, they fell on the ninth day (*nonus*) before the Ides (Varro, *loc. cit.*). Plutarch's derivation from *novus*, new or young, referring to the waxing moon, is without justification (*Quæstiones Romanæ*, 24). On the etymology of *idus* see Walde, *Lateinisches etymologisches Wörterbuch*,[2] p. 375. The Romans had no name, corresponding to *nonæ*, for the last quarter of the moon. It has been argued, therefore, that the Nones never marked the first quarter and that they were introduced, quite artificially, during the regal period (R. Flex, *Die älteste Monatseinteilung der Römer*, Jena, 1880, pp. 5 *sq.*, 24 *sqq.*, 36, 42).

[2] Tacitus, *Germania*, 11: *cum aut inchoatur luna aut impletur.*

[3] J. Loth, "L'année celtique d'après les textes irlandais, gallois, bretons, et le calendrier de Coligny," *Revue celtique*, 1904, xxv, 131; R. Thurneysen, "Die Namen der Wochentage in den keltischen Dialecten," *Zeitschrift für deutsche Wortforschung*, 1901, i, 191.

[4] The long inscription, engraved on a bronze tablet, which forms the Calendar of Coligny, was discovered in 1897 near the city of Lyons. See S. de Ricci, "Le calendrier gaulois de Coligny," *Revue celtique*, 1898, xix, 213–223; R. Thurneysen, "Der Kalender von Coligny," *Zeitschrift für celtische Philologie*, 1899, ii, 523–544; Sir John Rhŷs, "The Coligny Calendar," *Proceedings of the British Academy*, 1909–1910, pp. 207 *sqq.*

[5] Loth, *loc. cit.*; Rhŷs, *Celtic Heathendom*,[2] London, 1898, pp. 360 *sq.*

terms may be compared our English "fortnight" (O. E. *feówertȳne niht*).

The bipartite division of the month may be traced even more widely. It was recognized by the Egyptians, who appear to have counted the days by the decreasing and increasing moon and to have regarded the full moon (*mḥ*) as the most important of the lunar phases.[1] For Semitic peoples, notably the Babylonians and Hebrews, new moon and full moon enjoyed significance not only as religious festivals but also as the most conspicuous periods of the lunation. A primitive cycle of thirteen days used for ritual purposes by the ancient Mexicans may have been originally suggested by the number of months in the lunar year, but the choice of this number seems also to have been affected by the recognition of thirteen visible stages of the moon's increase (*mextozoliztli*, the moon's waking) and thirteen visible stages of her decrease (*mecochiliztli*, the moon's sleep).[2] In both Colombia and Peru the half-months were reckoned by the waxing and the waning of the moon.[3]

[1] Horapollo, *Hieroglyphica*, i, 4; Brugsch, *Ägyptologie*, p. 331; E. Mahler, in *Journal of the Royal Asiatic Society*, 1901, n.s., xxxiii, 55 *sqq.* Mahler's hypothesis that the Egyptians looked upon the full moon as the completion of the lunation is not improbable; there are several passages in the Vedas where the full moon is indicated as the end of the month and at the same time as the beginning of the next month (Thibaut, *op. cit.*, p. 12). The evidence yielded by the Calendar of Coligny has been thought to imply that originally the Sequani of Gaul counted the months from full moon to full moon (R. Thurneysen, in *Zeitschrift für celtische Philologie*, 1899, ii, 526). The Melanesians of New Georgia do not seem to calculate long periods of time at all: "one full moon to another is as far as they usually go" (B. T. Somerville, in *Journal of the Anthropological Institute*, 1897, xxvi, 404).

[2] Payne, *op. cit.*, ii, 310, 323 *sqq.*, 355 *sqq.*; J. de Acosta, *op. cit.*, bk. vi, ch. 2 (ed. C. R. Markham, ii, 393); H. H. Bancroft, *The Native Races of the Pacific States of North America*, ii, 515 *sq.* For other and less plausible reasons leading to the choice of the number thirteen, see C. P. Bowditch, *The Numeration, Calendar Systems, and Astronomical Knowledge of the Mayas*, Cambridge (Mass.), 1910, pp. 266 *sq.*

[3] V. Restrepo, *Los Chibchas antes de la conquista española*, Bogota, 1895, p. 162; Garcilasso de la Vega, *op. cit.*, pt. i, bk. ii, ch. 23 (transl. C. R. Markham, i, 181).

From the division of the month into two fortnights, at once the simplest, earliest, and most widespread form of the week, we pass to the consideration of those shorter cycles of time which are found in various parts of the world. It might appear at first sight that all civil weeks of five, six, seven, eight, nine, and ten days would likewise have a natural origin in divisions, either of the true lunation or of the conventional month. But the evidence which has been presented for the existence of market weeks shows that these arose quite independently of the lunar month, and that only at a subsequent period, when they came into general use for calendrical purposes, were they adjusted to the length of the moon's monthly course. Some interesting examples of this process of adjustment may be studied among the negroes of west Africa. Thus, the Yoruba week consists of five days, and six of them are supposed to make a lunar month. As a matter of fact, since the first day of the first week always commences with the appearance of the new moon, the month really contains five weeks of five days' duration, and one of four days and a half, approximately.[1] Again, the Tshi tribes of the Gold Coast, having chosen seven-day weeks, find it necessary to begin them at different hours of the day. Some of their weeks, termed *n'ehsŭn*, "It is seven," may have eight days and six nights, others the reverse, and others seven days and nights, with a fractional part of a day or night.[2] Such are the expedients adopted by some semi-civilized peoples, whose months are strictly lunar, to avoid the difficulty presented by the fact that the length of the lunation

[1] Ellis, *Yoruba-speaking Peoples*, pp. 143 *sq*. The Benin tribes are said to employ the same method of reckoning.

[2] *Idem, Tshi-speaking Peoples*, pp. 215 *sq*. The Ga tribes have an exactly similar mode of measuring time, though their names for the days of the week are not the same as those used by the Tshi. With both the Tshi and Ga the full moon marks the commencement of the third week of 7½ days and, with the Yoruba, the commencement of the fourth week of 5 days, in each case marking the lapse of half a month.

(twenty-nine and a half days) does not permit of sub-division into exactly equal parts.

One of the most common forms of the week is the decade. When not based on the institution of the market, it seems reasonable to suppose that this cycle was originally suggested by the increase, culmination, and decrease of the moon, as shown by the waxing crescent, the more or less full disk, and the waning crescent. If it be held that the arrangement by dec-ades was based rather on denary arithmetic, we may at least feel confident that it would not have been chosen except for its close approximation to the length of the lunar month. As a matter of fact, such a sequence represents the true course of the lunation in days more correctly than a nine-day, or an eight-day, or even a seven-day week. A division of the month into decades is definitely attributed to the Maori of New Zealand, who doubtless were obliged to count only nine days in the third and last decade of every other month.[1] The arrangement of the four Hawaiian *tabu* periods, of which the first three came at intervals of ten days, ar-gues strongly in favour of a division of time into decades, or *anahulu*. This term, though now obsolete, occurs frequently in ancient legends and songs as a measure of time comprising ten days. The fourth monthly *tabu* period, sacred to the god Kane, was celebrated on the twenty-seventh of the month, only three days after the festival of Kaloa, from which circumstance it has been plausibly regarded as of later introduction than the others.[2] A curious division of the month into

---

[1] R. Taylor, *Te Ika A Maui*, London, 1855, p. 177. When the Maori adopted the European week, they gave native names to three of the weekdays. Sunday they called "the week," *te wiki*, because on that day the week began, Saturday was *te ra horoi*, or washing and cleaning-up day, a name derived from their obser-vation of European customs at that time, and Friday was *te ra oka*, or bleeding day, so named because the missionaries killed their pigs on Friday in order to be able to cut them up on Saturday and dispose of them before Sun-day. The remaining weekdays had naturalized names, viz., *manei*, *turei*, *wenerei*, and *tairei* (*ibid.*, pp. 176 *sq.*).

[2] Malo, *Hawaiian Antiquities*,

three parts prevails in some of the Caroline Islands. In Yap, for instance, the thirty-day month is divided into *pul*, or new moon, lasting thirteen days, *botrau*, or full moon, lasting nine days, and *lumor*, or darkness, continuing to the end of the month.[1]   Lunar decades are found in southeastern Asia.   The Chingpaw or Kachin of Upper Burma, whose primitive year consists of twelve lunar months uncorrected by intercalation and arbitrarily adjusted to the successive seasons, recognize three divisions of the month, each of ten days' duration.   The first, called *shitta pyaw*, includes ten days of the waxing moon; the last, called *shitta si*, includes ten days of the waning moon.   The intervening period bears no special name, though the full moon itself is called *shitta lai*.[2]   The peoples of French Indo-China (Cochin-China, Anam, and Tonkin) regularly divide the month into three decades, but this arrangement is now being gradually superseded by the European week of seven days.[3]   Probably the Indo-Chinese custom was borrowed from the Chinese, among whom it has long been a common practice to speak of anything as happening in the first, middle, or last decade of any particular month.[4]   A similar system has not yet become obsolete in Japan, where the ten-day periods are known as the upper, middle, and lower decades.[5] Various African peoples use the ten-day cycle.   Among the Wagiriama of British East Africa the three decades

p. 54; N. B. Emerson, in *ibid.*, p. 200; Fornander, *Account of the Polynesian Race*, i, 120 *sq*.   On the Hawaiian Sabbaths see above, pp. 14 *sq*., 88.

[1] Christian, *Caroline Islands*, p. 394.

[2] *Gazetteer of Upper Burma and the Shan States*, edited by Scott and Hardiman, pt. i, vol. i, p. 434; H. J. Wehrli, *Beitrag zur Ethnologie der Chingpaw (Kachin) von Ober-Burma*, Leiden, 1904, p. 68 (*Internationales Archiv für Ethnographie*, vol. xvi, Supplement).

[3] A. Cabaton, "Calendar (Indo-Chinese)," Hastings's *Encyclopædia of Religion and Ethics*, iii, 110.

[4] T. L. Bullock and L. H. Gray, "Calendar (Chinese)," *ibid.*, iii, 83. The names of the three decades are said to be *shang*, *chung*, and *hea* (Robert Morrison, *A View of China for Philological Purposes*, Macao, 1817, p. 104).

[5] E. W. Clement, "Calendar (Japanese)," Hastings's *Encyclopædia of Religion and Ethics*, iii, 115.

(*makumi*) exist side by side with the market week four days in length.[1] The Sofalese of Portuguese East Africa are said to have divided the month into three periods each of ten days, the first day of the first week being the festival of the new moon.[2] Among the Tofoke, a Congo tribe, the lunar month consists of three parts, reckoned, respectively, from new moon to the increasing half moon, from this to the decreasing half moon, and thence to the end of the month. Each of these phases bears a distinct name.[3] The Ahanta of the Gold Coast divide the lunar month into three periods, two of ten days' duration, and the third lasting till the next new moon appears, that is, for about nine days and a half.[4] These decades seem to be quite independent of the market weeks, sometimes ten days' long, which are also found in Africa. On the other hand the Peruvian decades, previously noticed, were clearly connected with the institution of the market.[5] The sole instance of a week discoverable among the Indians of North America is found among the Zuñi of northeastern New Mexico, a Pueblo tribe leading a sedentary existence and in many respects advanced in culture. By the Zuñi "the month is divided into three parts, each part being called *topinta as temla*, 'one ten.'"[6]

[1] Fitzgerald, *op. cit.*, p. 111.

[2] De Faria, in Astley's *A New General Collection of Voyages and Travels*, London, 1746, iii, 397. The eighth day of the new moon was considered most unlucky by the Sofalese. No one on that day was allowed to attend court or even speak to the king (*ibid.*).

[3] E. Torday, in *Mitteilungen der anthropologischen Gesellschaft in Wien*, 1911, xli, 200.

[4] Ellis, *Yoruba-speaking Peoples*, p. 144. The first period, called *adai*, is considered lucky; the second, called *ajamfo*, is unlucky; while *adim*, the third period, has a neutral character (John Beecham, *Ashantee and the Gold Coast*, London, 1841, p. 187). An old writer asserts that the negroes living inland from the Gold Coast count in every month the "great fortunate time," nineteen days in length, and the "lesser fortunate time," of seven days' duration. Between these periods come seven ill or unfortunate days which serve as "a sort of vacation to them, for then they do not travel, till their land, or undertake anything of consequence, but remain altogether idle" (W. Bosman, *A New and Accurate Description of the Coast of Guinea*, London, 1705, p. 160).

[5] Above, pp. 119 *sq.*.

[6] Mrs. M. C. Stevenson, in *Twenty-third Annual Report of the*

A ten-day week was employed in antiquity by the Egyptians. The hieroglyphic expression meaning "the ten days" is found in inscriptions belonging to the age of the Pyramid-builders. The names applied to each of the three decades — *hati*, that of the beginning, *abi*, that of the middle, and *pahu*, that of the end — are perhaps somewhat less ancient, the earliest definite use of these appellations being found in the time of the Tenth Dynasty. The decades ran continuously from month to month. Since the Egyptian year consisted of three hundred and sixty-five days, it was necessary, however, in alternate years to begin the reckoning of the decades on the sixth, instead of on the first, of the month. According to an inscription dating from the time of the Third Dynasty, the first day of each decade was marked by sacrifices, and later records contain frequent instances of a religious observance of this day.[1]

The Greek decades betray in their names, μὴν ἱστάμενος (waxing), μεσῶν (central), and φθίνων (waning), an association with the moon. The days of the last decade were usually counted backward; in "hollow" months, the day corresponding to the twenty-ninth of "full" months was omitted, so that the decade really contained only nine days. By the Athenians

Bureau of American Ethnology, p. 108. It is only right to add that Dr. J. W. Fewkes, an eminent authority on the Pueblo Indians, expressed to me in conversation (July, 1912) his doubts as to the correctness of Mrs. Stevenson's statement.

[1] Lepsius, *Chronologie der Aegypter*, i, 131 *sqq.*; Brugsch, *Thesaurus*, pt. i, 488 *sqq.*; *idem, Aegyptologie*, p. 364. On the astrological connection between the thirty-six decades of the twelve months and certain constellations see G. Daressy, "Une ancienne liste des décans égyptiens," *Annales du service des antiquités de l'Égypte*, 1900, i,

79-90. The old and once popular theory, based upon a misunderstanding of certain passages in classical writers (Herodotus, ii, 82; Dio Cassius, xxxvii, 19), that the Egyptians originally possessed a week of seven days has now been entirely abandoned. For some monumental evidence, dating from the Twenty-second Dynasty, which may possibly refer to an hebdomadal cycle then used in astronomical speculations, see G. Daressy, "La semaine des Égyptiens," *Annales du service des antiquités de l'Égypte*, 1909, x, 21-23, 180-182.

the last day of the third decade was styled ἔνη καὶ νέα ("old and new moon"), as being the day which belonged in part to the preceding (theoretical) month of twenty-nine and a half days and in part to the following month. No clearer illustration could be afforded of lunar weeks adjusted to the lunar month.[1] The Greek arrangement by decades must have been very old. Unknown to Homer, it appears in Hesiod's *Works and Days* side by side with the still earlier division of the month into two parts determined by full moon. Hesiod, who tells his Bœotian farmer to avoid the thirteenth of the waxing month for the commencement of sowing, and who declares that the fourth, whether of the waning or of the waxing month, is "a very fateful day," also uses such expressions as the "first sixth," "first ninth," "middle third," "middle fourth," and "the fourth which follows the twentieth of the month."[2] This unequivocal evidence for the use of the decades as early as the middle of the eighth century B.C. seems to dispose of the theory[3] that they were an importation from Egypt.

The evidence for the existence of weeks of nine days is very obscure. They are found in west Africa, but only as market weeks unconnected with the lunation. Efforts have been made to discover traces of such periods among various Indo-Germanic peoples, particularly the Greeks of the Homeric and pre-Homeric age.[4] There are, indeed, numerous illustrations in the

[1] Pollux, *Onomasticon*, i, 63; G. F. Unger, in Iwan von Müller's *Handbuch der klassischen Altertumswissenschaft*, i, 563 *sqq.*; M. P. Nilsson, "Die älteste griechische Zeitrechnung, Apollo und der Orient," *Archiv für Religionswissenschaft*, 1911, xiv, 432 *sq.*

[2] Hesiod, *Opera et dies*, 765 *sqq.*; compare A. W. Mair, *Hesiod*, Oxford, 1908, pp. 165 *sq.*; A. Mommsen, *Chronologie*, Liepzig, 1883, p. 43.

[3] E. Curtius, *History of Greece*, New York, 1871, ii, 58; C. E. Ruelle, "Calendarium," Daremberg and Saglio's *Dictionnaire des antiquités grecques et romaines*, ii, 832.

[4] W. H. Roscher, "Die enneadischen und hebdomadischen Fristen und Wochen der ältesten Griechen," *Abhandlungen der philologisch-historischen Klasse der königlich-sächsischen Gesellschaft der Wissenschaften*, Leipzig, 1903, xxi, no. 4, pp. 14 *sqq.*; idem, "Die Sieben- und Neunzahl im Kultus und

older literature of cycles of nine days (as also of nine years), but no evidence at all that these were ever employed for civil purposes as regular divisions of the month. The same remark applies to the so-called weeks of nine days among the ancient Germans,[1] and to the frequent mention in old Irish and Welsh texts of periods of three days and nights and of nine days and nights.[2]

Market weeks, eight days in length, which seem to have developed from earlier periods of four days, are found in Assam, in certain parts of Africa, perhaps at one time among the Indians of Colombia, and in antiquity among the Romans.[3] Such market weeks are independent of the moon and run unfettered through the months and years. On the other hand a week of eight days, called 'sāmēn, which exists among the northern Abyssinians, is clearly adjusted to the length of the lunation. Every month consists, theoretically, of four weeks, of which the first two are those of the

---

Mythus der Griechen," *ibid.*, 1904, xxiv, no. 1, pp. 54, 69, 83.

[1] K. Simrock, *Handbuch der deutschen Mythologie*,[2] Bonn, 1887, p. 156; E. Siecke, *Die Liebesgeschichte des Himmels*, Strassburg, 1892, pp. 47 *sqq.*; K. Weinhold, "Die mystische Neunzahl bei den Deutschen," *Abhandlungen der königlich-preussischen Akademie der Wissenschaften*, Berlin, 1897, pp. 40 *sqq.*

[2] R. Thurneysen, "Die Namen der Wochentage in den keltischen Dialecten," *Zeitschrift für deutsche Wortforschung*, 1901, i, 191. J. Loth, however, regards the Celtic periods as having been employed as ordinary weeks ("L'année celtique d'après les textes irlandais, gallois, bretons, et le calendrier de Coligny," *Revue celtique*, 1904, xxv, 136). He accepts Roscher's theory of the sidereal month having furnished the basis for such nine-day periods as are found among the Celts, and argues that subsequently, when the sidereal month had been abandoned for the synodic month, the nine-day periods became artificial units, independent of any connection with the moon. But so strange a transition as that from the sidereal to the synodic month cannot be supported by any Celtic evidence and has no analogy among other peoples. For another theory see Sir John Rhŷs, *Celtic Heathendom*,[2] London, 1898, pp. 361-366.

[3] Above, pp. 106, 109 *sqq.*, 119 n.[2], 120 *sq.* The theory advanced by Theodor Mommsen that the Roman *nundinum* originally represented a quadripartite division of the lunation (*Römische Chronologie*, pp. 240 *sq.*) was afterwards abandoned by its author (*Römisches Staatsrecht*, iii, 373). Compare also R. Flex, *Die älteste Monatseinteilung der Römer*, Jena, 1880, pp. 18 *sqq.*

o

increasing moon and the last two those of the decreasing moon. In practice, however, the people are compelled to count only six days in their fourth and last week.[1] This Abyssinian cycle possibly may have originated as a market week, since elsewhere in Africa market weeks of four or more days have been adjusted, somewhat artificially, to the length of the lunation.

Six-day weeks, connected with the market and probably derived from an earlier week of three days' duration, are found in Africa.[2] There are also a few instances of the same cycle where a connection with the market does not certainly appear. The Lolo, Pula, and other aboriginal tribes of southwestern China keep a "Sabbath," as a rule every sixth day. No ploughing may take place at this time, and in some places the women are not allowed even to sew or wash clothes.[3] The Bawenda, who occupy the northeast corner of the Transvaal, are said also to use a week of six days, though only three of these are separately named.[4]

The numerous five-day weeks found in the Malay Archipelago, southeastern Asia, and Africa all exist in connection with the market.[5] On the other hand this cycle seems to be sometimes independent of the market. An Egyptian calendar, belonging to the second century B.C. but probably based on much older material, divides the year for astrological purposes into weeks of five days, each week corresponding to the sixth part

[1] E. Littmann, "Sternensagen und Astrologisches aus Nordabessinien," *Archiv für Religionswissenschaft*, 1908, xi, 302 *sq.*, 319. In order to adapt the ʿsâmên to the imported hebdomadal cycle, Sunday is counted twice.

[2] Above, pp. 114 *and n.*[3], 116 *n.*[1]

[3] A. Henry, in *Journal of the Anthropological Institute*, 1903, xxxiii, 105. The Muhso, a Lao hill tribe, "have a twelfth-day Sabbath or sacred day, not very definitely marked" (Daniel McGilvary, *A Half Century among the Siamese and the Lão*, New York [1912], p. 323). Did this "Sabbath" originate as a market day, which at first recurred every sixth day?

[4] E. Gottschling, in *Journal of the Anthropological Institute*, 1905, xxxv, 382.

[5] Above, pp. 103 *sqq.*, 108, 110, 113 *and n.*[3], 114 *and n.*[1], 116 *n.*[1]

of one of the signs or constellations of the zodiac. The calendar also gives the name of the presiding deity of each sign, together with the omens, portents, and favourable or unfavourable characteristics that belong to it.[1] A five-day period, *khamushtu*, employed as a sixth of the month, appears to have been familiar to the Assyro-Babylonians in the third millenium B.C. We do not know how far the *khamushtu* entered into the civil life of the Mesopotamian peoples, but from the circumstance that this system of computing short time-intervals was used in mercantile and monetary transactions it may be surmised that we here have to do with a very ancient form of the market week.[2] Babylonian and Assyrian cuneiform texts also contain traces of five-day periods associated with the successive changes of the moon and dedicated to various divinities; but it is not certain that these later cycles were derived from the *khamushtu*.[3] The whole subject is obscure and may well await future discoveries for its complete elucidation. Finally, there is evidence that the old Scandinavian peoples employed time-intervals of five days, of which six were counted to the month. Here, again, we are at a loss to determine how far this pentad, called *fimt*, was regularly used as a civil week in heathen times. After the introduction of the

[1] *The Oxyrhynchus Papyri*, edited by Grenfell and Hunt, London, 1903, pt. iii, 126-137.

[2] The data relating to the *khamushtu* are found in some Cappadocian tablets discovered by Golénischeff and others in mounds not far from Kaisariyeh. This city was a colony of Assyria and the last outpost of Assyrian power in the northwest. The tablets are in Babylonian cuneiform script belonging to the age of Hammurabi. Professor A. H. Sayce in 1897 was the first to show that the term *khamushtu* in these documents represented a continuous succession of five-day periods; and Professor

Hugo Winckler later made, independently, the same discovery. See Sayce, in *Proceedings of the Society of Biblical Archæology*, 1897, xix, 288; *idem*, in *Babyloniaca*, 1907, ii, 1-45; Winckler, *Altorientalische Forschungen*, Leipzig, 1898-1900, ii, 91 *sqq.*, 354 *sqq.*

[3] For references to the cuneiform evidence see P. Jensen, "Die siebentägige Woche in Babylon und Nineveh," *Zeitschrift für deutsche Wortforschung*, 1901, i, 150 *sq.*; W. Muss-Arnolt, in *Journal of Biblical Literature*, xi, 94; A. Jeremias, *The Old Testament in the Light of the Ancient East*, London, 1911, i, 65.

hebdomadal cycle into northern lands, the term survived as a standing phrase in Norse laws and popular
sayings.[1]

The preceding pages have presented much evidence
to show how carefully primitive peoples watch the
changes of the moon and describe them by appropriate
names. The four lunar phases provide, indeed, an
obvious means of calculating the passage of time; and
they are often used for this purpose in the absence of
any recognized calendrical unit shorter than the lunar
month. The length of the lunation being approximately twenty-nine and a half days, a single phase
occupies about seven and three-eighths days, which
must be calendarized as seven days, since it is necessary
to employ a round number. It is not a valid argument against the natural origin of the hebdomadal
cycle to urge that seven does not form an exact division
of the lunar month. No other number will divide
the lunation without a remainder. However, the
hebdomad furnishes a less satisfactory time-unit than
the decade, the former falling short of a quarter of
the month by more than nine hours, the latter exceed-
ing a third of the lunation by rather less than four
hours. This circumstance may account for the otherwise remarkable fact that, while the ten-day lunar
week is found in many parts of the world, the week of
seven days occurs in the lower culture and among peoples of archaic civilization only as a borrowed institution, which can be traced ultimately to Semitic
lands and Semitic antiquity.

The prevalence of the seven-day week throughout
the world furnishes a most impressive instance of the
diffusion of a cultural element. Its introduction into
the Pacific area during the nineteenth century and

[1] G. Vigfússon, *An Icelandic-English Dictionary*, Oxford, 1874, s.v. *fimt*; Vigfússon and Powell, *Corpus Poeticum Boreale*, Oxford, 1883, i, pp. cxx, 428; F. B. Gum-mere, *Germanic Origins*, New York, 1892, p. 418; T. F. Troels-Lund, *Livsbelysning*, Copenhagen, 1904, pp. 13, 198. For the translation of this last reference I am indebted to Mr. N. H. Debel.

among the aborigines of America as the result of their contact with European civilization is well known.[1] In Africa it has been spread by Judaism, Christianity, and Islam; in southeastern Asia and the Malay Archipelago the original disseminators were Hindus, followed later by Arabs and Europeans. This imported week has sometimes provided a cycle of time shorter than the lunar month, where none existed before; in other cases it has supplanted a native cycle usually associated with the market. Together with the week has often gone the Jewish, Christian or Mohammedan rest day.

In Madagascar and along the east coast of Africa Arab influence, continuing for many centuries, naturally left its impress on the calendar. The names of the Malagasy weekdays are of Arabic origin.[2] Previous to the introduction of Christianity under Radama I (1810–1828) no rest day was communally observed, though each god had a sacred day when those who were its special votaries abstained from work.[3] The Swaheli, who occupy the coast lands north and south of Zanzibar, use a seven-day week, beginning with Friday, the Mohammedan Sabbath.[4] Some peculiar arrangements are found among the Masai of eastern equatorial Africa, a warlike race clearly distinguished by

[1] The Stseelis, an Indian tribe of British Columbia, have a singular tradition that their ancestors used to observe a kind of Sabbath ceremony long before the coming of the whites. The people assembled every seventh day for dancing and praying. It is impossible to explain this tradition apart from European influence at some remote time (C. Hill-Tout, in *Journal of the Anthropological Institute*, 1904, xxxiv, 329).

[2] L. Dahle, "The Influence of the Arabs on the Malagasy Language," *Antananarivo Annual*, 1875–1878, i, 205. In addition to the Arabic seven-day week with its numbered weekdays, the Malagasy also use, for astrological purposes, the planetary designations of the weekdays. Of these, three are good or lucky days, three are unlucky, and one has a neutral character. See J. Sibree, "Divination among the Malagasy," *Folklore*, 1892, iii, 220 *sq*.

[3] Soury-Lavergne and de la Devèze, in *Anthropos*, 1913, viii, 310 n.[4]; James Sibree, *The Great African Island*, London, 1880, p. 281.

[4] O. Kersten, editor, *Baron Carl Claus von der Decken's Reisen in Ost-Afrika*, Leipzig, 1869, i, 101.

language, customs, and appearance from the Bantu
peoples. The Masai seem to be connected with the
so-called Nilotic group, and their ancient home has
been placed in the region between Lake Rudolf and
the Nile. At the present time they dwell much farther
south both in British and German territory. The
Masai count time by moon months, generally taken at
thirty days in length. The month does not begin
with the visible new moon, but on the fourth day
thereafter. In addition they have a week of seven
days, each one separately named. The seventh day,
which ends, and does not begin, the week, is called
essubat 'n oloñ, "the good day." According to Masai
tradition this week in remote times began on the new-
moon day, but now it is reckoned continuously without regard to the lunation. Furthermore, the Masai
appear to have once divided the months into decades,
as is still indicated by their expression, *negera*, applied
to the tenth, twentieth, and thirtieth days. This
term comes from a verbal form meaning "to be silent." [1]
There can be little question that the Masai seven-day
week was borrowed from Jewish or Christian sources,
while the decade arrangement may have been affected
remotely by cultural contact with peoples influenced
by ancient Egypt. Most of the interior tribes of
British East Africa recognize no subdivision of the
lunar month. But among the Rendile and Burkeneji,
who inhabit the steppes east of Lake Rudolf, we find
a week of seven days. Three of these days are marked
by restrictions. The first day, *hahat*, is a fast day,
at which time animals cannot be slaughtered for food.
On the second day, *hura hakhan* (*hura* in the Rendile
language means sun), no work may be done, except
the slaughtering of food animals. On the fifth day,
ser hakhan, people will not travel, move their grazing
grounds, or make cattle-medicine. The natives are
unable to identify the particular days of their week

[1] M. Merker, *Die Masai*,² Berlin,   Sir Charles Eliot, in A. C. Hollis,
1910, pp. 157 *sq.*, 327 *sq.*; compare   *The Masai*, Oxford, 1905, p. xiv.

with those of the European cycle.[1] Many of the Galla tribes between Shoa, a kingdom of southern Abyssinia, and the Tana River of British East Africa, are said to show great respect for Saturday and Sunday, and on these days do not work in the fields. Here we may legitimately assume Jewish and Christian influences from Abyssinia, especially since the nomadic Galla of equatorial Africa do not seem to keep any special rest days.[2] Other eastern Hamitic peoples, the Somali, Afar, and Danakil, use the seven-day week with Arabic names and observe Friday, the Mohammedan Sabbath.[3] The seven-day week found among the natives of Kaffa, a region of eastern Africa on the borderland between the British and Italian spheres of influence, appears to have been introduced a few centuries ago by Christian immigrants from Amhara, the central province of Abyssinia.[4] The spread of Islam among the Sudanese and Guinea negroes has resulted in the introduction of the hebdomadal cycle and of the custom of holding markets on the seventh day.[5]

The seven-day week in India has a long history. The original division of the Hindu lunar month was, as we have seen, into two equal parts, determined by the waxing and the waning moon. This arrangement, which still prevails in India, appears to have been the only one in calendrical use until long after the beginning of the Christian era. It is true that even in Vedic

[1] C. W. Hobley, *Ethnology of the A-Kamba and Other East African Tribes*, Cambridge, 1910, p. 163.

[2] J. L. Krapf, *Travels, Researches, and Missionary Labours*, London, 1867, p. 82.

[3] J. W. C. Kirk, *A Grammar of the Somali Language*, Cambridge, 1905, p. 134; P. Paulitschke, *Ethnographie Nordost-Afrikas. Die geistige Kultur der Danâkil, Galla, und Somâl*, Berlin, 1896, p. 224.

[4] F. J. Bieber, in *Revue des études ethnographiques et sociologiques*, 1909, ii, 38, 63.

[5] Above, pp. 115 *sqq.* For further instances see Anne Raffenel, *Nouveau voyage dans le pays des nègres*, Paris, 1856, i, 350 (Bambara); H. Gaden, in *Revue d'ethnographie et de sociologie*, 1912, iii, 52 (Toucouleur and Mohammedan Peul of Senegal). Among the Vey of Liberia the week of seven days must be due to Christian influence (J. Büttikofer, *Reisebilder aus Liberia*, Leiden, 1890, ii, 317).

times the eighth day after the full moon was regarded
as one of the festival days of the month, and that, at
least as early as the rise of Jainism and Buddhism in
the sixth century B.C., the eighth day after new moon
was added to the list of holy days.[1] The celebration
of four lunar festivals does not, however, imply the use
of a civil week by the Hindus, any more than in the
case of the Persian festivals, which likewise were adjusted to the phases of the moon.[2] The hebdomadal
cycle in India was entirely a borrowed institution,
derived from the planetary or astrological week, the
days of which are named after five planets and the sun
and moon. By the middle of the third century A.D.,
the planetary week was well known in the Roman
world, and somewhat later it was introduced as an
astrological device into India. Who the intermediaries
were — whether Hindus who visited Mediterranean
lands or learned Greeks who made the voyage to
India — it is impossible to say. The earliest-known
genuine instance of a planetary name of a day in India
occurs in an inscription belonging to the year 484 A.D.
By the end of the eighth century there are perhaps ten
other inscriptional records, coming from various parts
of India and from Indian settlements in Java, Cochin-
China, and Cambodia, of the assignment of the weekdays to the planets. After 900 A.D., instances of this
practice are more numerous, indicating that the seven-
day week had now become something more than an
astrological device and was generally recognized for
civil purposes as a part of the Hindu calendar.[3] In

[1] Above, p. 157 and n.[2]
[2] Above, p. 166.
[3] J. F. Fleet, "The Use of the
Planetary Names of the Days of
the Week in India," Journal of the
Royal Asiatic Society, 1912, n.s.,
xliv, 1039-1046. For lists of the
more common planetary names of
the weekdays, as now found in
India, see Sewell and Dikshit,
The Indian Calendar, London,

1896, p. 2. The celebrated astronomical work in Sanskrit, known
as the Sūrya-Siddhānta, contains
two references to the planetary
week (i, 51-52, xii, 78-79; transl.
Burgess-Whitney, in Journal of the
American Oriental Society, 1860, v,
175-178, 396), and in the Hitō-
padēsa (ed. Johnson, p. 16, l. 411)
there is an interesting passage
which, as A. W. von Schlegel was

modern India every day of the week has its sacred character for the devotees of various gods, Sunday being especially consecrated to the sun, Monday, to Siva, and Saturday, to the monkey-god Hanuman.[1] For Hindus, generally, Sunday, Tuesday, and Saturday are unlucky days, and at such times no important business will be undertaken or any long journey begun.[2]

India was the center from which the planetary week of seven days was first introduced into southeastern Asia — into Ceylon, the Maldive Islands, Nepal, Tibet, Burma, Cambodia, and Siam.[3] The Brahmanist Chams in Cambodia and Anam use the planetary weekdays borrowed from Hinduism, but the Mohammedan Chams sometimes employ the days of the Arabic week and observe Friday as a Sabbath.[4] The Laotians, who have taken over the planetary week from the Siamese, are careful, as pious Buddhists, so to adjust their calendar that Sunday (*van athit*) always falls on the eighth and fifteenth days of the lunar fortnight.[5]

the first to point out (*Indisches Bibliothek*, 1827, ii, 178), refers to Sunday as a sacred day.

[1] Sir M. Monier-Williams, *Brāhmanism and Hindūism*,[4] New York, 1891, p. 433; W. Crooke, *Natives of Northern India*, London, 1907, p. 226; idem, *The Tribes and Castes of the North-western Provinces and Oudh*, Calcutta, 1896, iii, 112.

[2] J. A. Dubois, *Hindu Manners, Customs, and Ceremonies*,[3] Oxford, 1906, p. 382.

[3] R. Percival, *An Account of the Island of Ceylon*, London, 1803, p. 187; H. C. P. Bell, *The Máldive Islands*, Colombo, 1883, p. 119; B. H. Hodgson, *Essays on the Languages, Literature, and Religion of Nepál and Tibet*, London, 1874, p. 8; E. Schlaginweit, *Buddhism in Tibet*, Leipzig and London, 1863, p. 289; Shway Yoe, *The Burman*,[3] London, 1910, pp. 550 *sq.*; E.

Aymonier, *Le Cambodge*, Paris, 1900–1904, i, 42, ii, 19; De la Loubère, *A New Historical Relation of the Kingdom of Siam*, London, 1693, ii, 168.

[4] A. Cabaton, in Hastings's *Encyclopædia of Religion and Ethics*, iii, 113, 345, 450. On the other hand a week of seven days, found in central Asia, has been borrowed from Persia, as its name *hafta* from the Persian *heft*, "seven," indicates (H. Vámbéry, *Die primitive Cultur des turko-tatarischen Volkes*, Leipzig, 1879, p. 160). In northern Asia, again, the Russian advance has begun to lead to the use of the seven-day week by native tribes, such as the Yukaghir of northeastern Siberia (W. Jochelson, in *Memoirs of the American Museum of Natural History*, xiii, 42).

[5] Tournier, *Notice sur le Laos français*, Hanoi, 1900, p. 188.

The Chinese possess no regular division of the month into weeks, though a popular cycle, ten days in length, has long been found among them. The week of seven days is coming into use in commercial centres frequented by Europeans, where, for Monday, Tuesday, etc., native names meaning "first day," "second day," etc., have been coined. The assertion that the Chinese from of old have been familiar with the seven-day week appears to be based on their custom, which is not of extreme antiquity, of applying the names of the twenty-eight lunar mansions to each day of the year in rotation, from which circumstance the same four out of the twenty-eight always fall on Sunday and constitute what has been well described as a perpetual "Sunday letter." [1] On the other hand there is definite evidence that the planetary week was introduced from India to China, where, however, it seems never to have been employed except for astrological purposes. A Chinese translation, made in the eighth century A.D. of an Indian treatise on astrology, apportions the days of the week among the planets, according to the astrological order. Sunday in some Chinese almanacs is still called the "day of Mit," that is, the day of Mithra, the Persian deity associated with the sun. This "Sunday" seems formerly to have had a place in the state calendars issued under imperial auspices at Peking.[2] In this connection it is interesting to note that the famous Nestorian Monument bears witness to the introduction of the Christian Sunday into China by Nestorian missionaries from Persia.[3] But the

---

[1] Robert Morrison, *A View of China for Philological Purposes*, Macao, 1817, pp. 52, 102; *idem, A Grammar of the Chinese Language*, Serampore, 1815, p. 54.

[2] A. Wylie, "On the Knowledge of the Weekly Sabbath in China," *Chinese Researches*, Shanghai, 1897, pt. ii, 86–101; J. Edkins, *Chinese Buddhism*,[2] London, 1893, p. 211.

[3] The Nestorian Monument was set up in 781 A.D. in the department or prefecture of Hsi-an, province of Shen-hsi, northwestern China. At the end of the inscription on it we read: "Erected in the second year of the period Chien-chung of the great T'ang dynasty, the year-star being in Tso-yo, on the seventh day of the first month, being Sunday." See James Legge, *The Nestorian Monument of Hsi-an Fu in Shen-*

week of seven days as a calendrical entity never took root among the Chinese, nor have they ever observed a weekly day of rest.[1]

In old Japan, as in China, the week of seven days was unknown. Shortly after the restoration of the Mikado's power in 1867–1868 there was introduced what were called the *ichi-roku*, or holidays on the "ones" and "sixes" of each month, *i.e.*, on the first, sixth, eleventh, sixteenth, twenty-first, twenty-sixth, and thirty-first days. But this arrangement, borrowed from the Christian Sunday, did not last long, and the copy soon gave way to the original. The Japanese now have the seven-day week with names derived from the Occidental names. Sunday, in vulgar parlance is called *dontaku* (a corruption of the Dutch Zontag) and Saturday, in equally vulgar parlance, is called *han-don*, that is, "half-Sunday" (because the modern English Saturday half-holiday has made its way into Japan).[2] On Sunday government offices and schools are closed. In the cities some of the larger banks and mercantile houses also suspend their business on Sunday, but as a rule country people, artisans, and labour-

hsi, China, London, 1888, p. 29. A replica of this monument, which is a limestone block ten feet in height and of two tons' weight, was taken to the United States in 1908 and now rests in the Metropolitan Museum of Art, New York City. See F. V. Holm, "The Holm Nestorian Expedition to Sian, MCMVII," *Open Court*, 1909, xxiii, 18–28.

[1] "Some persons," writes an experienced observer of the Chinese, "have expressed their surprise that the unceasing round of toil which the Chinese labourer pursues has not rendered him more degraded. It is usually said that a weekly rest is necessary for the continuance of the powers of body and mind in man in their full activity, and that decrepitude and

insanity would oftener result were it not for this relaxation. . . . Yet, in China, people who apparently tax themselves uninterruptedly to the utmost stretch of body and mind, live in health to old age. . . . Nothing like a seventh day of rest, or religious respect to that interval of time, is known among the Chinese, but they do not, as a people, exercise their minds to the intensity, or upon the high subjects, common among western nations, and this perhaps is one reason why their yearly toil produces no disastrous effects" (S. W. Williams, *The Middle Kingdom*,[2] New York, 1883, i, 809 *sq.*).

[2] B. H. Chamberlain, *Things Japanese*,[2] London, 1891, pp. 418 *sq.*

ers observe no weekly day of rest. By people of the middle and highest classes Sunday is preëminently a day devoted to social intercourse, and even Japanese Christians, after attending an early morning church service, feel themselves free to devote the afternoon and evening to any form of legitimate recreation or amusement.[1]

The planetary cycle is not unknown in the Malay Peninsula, though here employed, as it seems, solely for astrological purposes. For civil purposes weeks of seven days, marked by the return of Friday, the Mohammedan Sabbath, are in general use.[2] Curious animistic superstitions sometimes attach themselves to this day. Thus, the Malays of the Patani States believe that the spirits have extra power over mankind on Friday, hence many people will not take shelter under a tree at any time on this day, lest the spirits sitting in the tree dive down into them. This precaution especially applies to travellers, whose bodies are weary and whose souls are therefore weak. Some Malays who have wooden chests in which they store their finery and treasures dare not, on Friday, lift the lid of one of these receptacles, because then the chest's soul (*semangat*) might escape. Henceforth the chest would become a dead thing and all luck would desert its owner. Patani fishermen on Friday always make offerings to the *semangat* of their boats.[3]

The seven-day week in the Malay Archipelago exists both as a Hindu institution of remote origin and also as an outcome of the expansion of Islam over this region. The Achehnese in northern Sumatra have not only borrowed the hebdomad from the Mohammedans, but go so far as to make Friday a day *pantang* for all agricultural work, *pantang* being the native term for taboo.[4] Among the natives of the

[1] Arthur Lloyd, *Every-day Japan*, London, 1909, pp. 371 *sq.*

[2] W. W. Skeat, *Malay Magic*, London, 1900, pp. 548 *sq.*, 554.

[3] Annandale and Robinson, *Fasciculi Malayensis*, London, 1903–1904, i, 80 *sq.*, 100; ii, 30, 55.

[4] C. S. Hurgronje, *The Achehnese*, Leiden, 1906, i, 236, 261.

Kuantan District the seven weekdays bear names derived from the Arabic.[1] On the other hand the Batta of Lake Toba possess a calendar derived from Hindu sources and also a week of seven days, with planetary names clearly taken from the Sanskrit. But the Batta magicians, who use this cycle for astrological purposes, do not now recognize its planetary origin; they know only the sun, the moon, and, possibly, Venus. To the Batta *ari na pitu*, the seventh day, is an evil day, and he who ventures to begin any work upon it will surely be visited by some grave misfortune.[2] In districts of Sumatra where neither Hindu nor Arabic influence has penetrated, a division into weeks is unknown, the natives counting, instead, by the days of the moon's age.[3] In Java the Hindu planetary week was combined with the still earlier market week of five days in the eighth and ninth centuries, A.D., and since that time the Arabic designations of the seven weekdays have also been introduced.[4] A similar combination of the two cycles, yielding a period of thirty-five days, occurs in Bali.[5] In Macassar, a former native kingdom of Celebes, the Mohammedan Sabbath is observed.[6]

The foregoing pages make it clear that the spread of Mohammedan rule both in Asia and Africa has

[1] A. Maass, *Durch Zentral-Sumatra*, Berlin, 1910, p. 513.

[2] J. Winkler, "Der Kalender der Toba-Bataks auf Sumatra," *Zeitschrift für Ethnologie*, 1913, xlv, 441 *sqq.*

[3] W. Marsden, *The History of Sumatra*,[3] London, 1811, p. 194.

[4] E. Metzger, "Über die Zeitrechnung der Javanen," *Deutsche Rundschau für Geographie und Statistik*, 1887, ix, 311; P. J. Veth, *Java*,[2] Haarlem, 1907, iv, 297 *sq.* A recent observer points out that, although the life of a Javanese village is never intensely laborious, it is, in a sense, a life of continuous labour, "for the Javanese does not

feel compelled to abstain from labour entirely upon any day of the week — not even on a Friday — to satisfy his religious beliefs. He works as long as he needs to work; but only too often only just so long. His village holidays are numerous" (A. Cabaton, *Java, Sumatra, and the Other Islands of the Dutch East Indies*, London and Leipzig, 1911, pp. 125 *sq.*).

[5] R. Friederich, in *Journal of the Royal Asiatic Society*, 1878, n.s., x, 89, 93.

[6] *An Historical Description of the Kingdom of Macasar*, London, 1701, p. 149.

introduced the week of seven days into regions where
it had not previously found entrance. The Arabs
themselves adopted the week from the Jews and Christians, presumably at the time of their conversion to
Islam.[1] In the Arabic week the days from Sunday
to Thursday are numbered in their order, Friday is
called *al jum' a* "the meeting" (for worship), and Saturday, *as sabt*, "the Sabbath." On Friday, according
to the rule laid down by Mohammed, the faithful are
to take part in the midday prayer at the mosque and
to listen to the sermon which follows the prayer.
Labour is suspended during the service, but at its
close secular vocations, including marketing, are resumed. The Mohammedean *jum' a*, unlike the Jewish
Sabbath, but like the early Christian Sunday, is not a
day of rest.[2]

The seven-day week has now been traced over a
large part of the globe. It sometimes exists as a
planetary-astrological cycle of pagan derivation; in
other cases its presence is obviously due to Jewish,
Christian, or Mohammedan influence. In no region
does the hebdomadal cycle appear as an independent
product of the native culture. The inquiry into its
remote origin and connection with the cult of the number
ber seven takes us back to the ancient Oriental world.

It is a familiar fact that many people attach to certain numbers a sacred or symbolic meaning.[3] Such

[1] T. Nöldeke, "Die Namen der
Wochentage bei den Semiten,"
*Zeitschrift für deutsche Wortfor-
schung*, 1901, i, 162; J. Wellhausen,
Reste arabischen Heidentums,[2] Ber-
lin, 1897, p. 142.

[2] *Koran*, lxii, 9 *sq.* (S. B. E., ix,
283); T. P. Hughes, *Dictionary of
Islam*, London, 1885, pp. 131, 666;
idem, "The Mosque Life of the
Muslim," *Open Court*, 1906, xx,
335; T. W. Juynboll, "Djum'a," *The
Encyclopædia of Islam*, i, 1061 *sq.*

[3] See in general L. Lévy-Bruhl,
Les fonctions mentales dans les
sociétés inférieures, Paris, 1910,
pp. 235-257; D. G. Brinton, "The
Origin of Sacred Numbers," *American Anthropologist*, 1894, vii, 168-
173; idem, *The Myths of the New
World*,[2] Philadelphia, 1896, pp. 83-
119; W. J. McGee, "Primitive
Numbers," *Nineteenth Annual Report of the Bureau of American
Ethnology*, pt. ii, 821-852; W.
Schultz, "Gesetze der Zahlenver-
schiebung im Mythus und in
mythenhaltiger Überlieferung,"
*Mitteilungen der anthropologischen
Gesellschaft in Wien*, 1910, xl, 101-

mystic numbers, unlike those of ordinary arithmetic, are real categories in which thought naturally rests; they are not fortuitous counts of objects but are rather subjective syntheses — *cadres donnés d'avance* — according to which the mind divides up and parcels out all things visible and invisible. Like names they may become virtual entities endowed with their own functional power. The symbolism and superstitions attaching to certain numbers, which we discover in the records of all archaic civilizations, must be based

150; R. Hirzel, "Über Rundzahlen," *Berichte über die Verhandlungen der philologisch-historischen Klasse der königlich-sächsischen Gesellschaft*, Leipzig, 1885, xxxvii, 1–74; E. Kautzsch, "Zahlen," in Herzog, Plitt, and Hauck's *Realencyklopädie für protestantische Theologie und Kirche*,[3] xx, 598–607; A. Bergaigne, *La religion védique*, Paris, 1883, ii, 114–156; E. W. Hopkins, "The Holy Numbers of the Rig-Veda," in *Oriental Studies*, Boston, 1894, pp. 141–159; E. Wölfflin, "Zur Zahlensymbolik," *Archiv für lateinische Lexikographie und Grammatik*, 1895, ix, 33–353; I. Goldziher, "Über Zahlenaberglauben im Islam," *Globus*, 1901, lxxx, 31–32. For collections of the evidence relating to the sacredness of certain numbers see B. Stade, "Die Dreizahl im Alten Testament," *Zeitschrift für die alttestamentliche Wissenschaft*, 1906, xxvi, 124 sqq.; H. Usener, "Dreiheit," *Rheinisches Museum für Philologie*, 1903, n.s., lviii, 1–47, 161–208, 321–362; Anne W. Buckland, "Four as a Sacred Number," *Journal of the Anthropological Institute*, 1896, xxv, 96–102; F. X. Kugler, "Die Symbolik der Neunzahl bei den Babyloniern," in *Assyriologische und archäologische Studien Hermann v. Hilprecht gewidmet*, Leipzig, 1909, pp. 304–309; A. Kaegi, "Die Neunzahl bei den Ostariern," in *Philologische Abhandlungen für Heinrich Schweizer-Sidler*, Zürich, 1891, pp. 50–70; K. Weinhold, "Die mystische Neunzahl bei den Deutschen," *Abhandlungen der königlich-preussischen Akademie der Wissenschaften*, Berlin, 1897, pp. 1 61; Edgar Thurston, "The Number Seven in Southern India," in *Essays and Studies presented to William Ridgeway*, Cambridge, 1913, pp. 353–364; W. H. Roscher, "Die enneadischen und hebdomadischen Fristen und Wochen der ältesten Griechen," *Abhandlungen der philologisch-historischen Klasse der königlich-sächsischen Gesellschaft der Wissenschaften*, Leipzig, 1903, xxi, no. 4; *idem*, "Die Sieben- und Neunzahl im Kultus und Mythus der Griechen," *ibid.*, 1904, xxiv, no. 1; *idem*, "Die Hebdomadenlehren der griechischen Philosophen und Ärzte," *ibid.*, 1904, xxiv, no 6; *idem*, "Enneadische Studien," *ibid.*, 1907, xxvi, no. 1; *idem*, "Die Zahl 40 im Glauben, Brauch, und Schrifttum der Semiten," *ibid.*, 1909, xxvii, no. 4; *idem*, "Über Alter, Ursprung, und Bedeutung der hippokratischen Schrift von der Siebenzahl," *ibid.*, 1911, xxviii, no. 5; *idem*, "Die Tessarakontaden und Tessarakontadenlehren der Griechen und anderer Völker," *Berichte über die Verhandlungen*, etc., Leipzig, 1909, lxi, 17–206.

on very primitive modes of thinking, since a similar tendency toward mysticism in the use of numbers appears among half-civilized peoples. It is a tendency to whose development no bounds can be set, once the refining ingenuity of the priestly class has begun to elaborate the concept of the "sacred" as opposed to that of the "profane." It seems obvious, therefore, that the systems of sacred numbers, found in ancient India, Babylonia, Greece, and other cultural areas, incorporate many items of folk superstition together with the results of much speculative activity on the part of early organizers of religion.

It would be hard to find any number in the first decade which has not been invested, by this or that society, with a mystical significance. Seven, in particular, has enjoyed a marked importance among many peoples widely separated in space and time.[1] As a symbolic number it occurs among the Babylonians, Greeks, and Hindus at the very dawn of their history; and it still figures prominently in the popular lore of India, China, and southeastern Asia. Cultural influences emanating from the Asiatic mainland appear to have introduced the symbolism of seven into certain parts of Oceania and, notably, into Borneo. Of the Sea Dyak of Sarawak it is said that, after three, their favourite number is seven; while among the Malanau, another Sarawak tribe, seven is very prominent in rites of exorcism.[2] The same number occurs repeatedly in the legends of the Dusun of British North Borneo, and its mystic significance may account in part for the curious system of unlucky days observed by them. The Dusun consider twelve days of the month, beginning with the seventh and including also the fourteenth and twenty-first, as distinctly bad for

[1] For a large collection of evidence see F. von Andrian, "Die Siebenzahl im Geistesleben der Völker," *Mitteilungen der anthropologischen Gesellschaft in Wien*, 1901, xxxi, 225–274.

[2] Brooke Low, in H. L. Roth, *The Natives of Sarawak and British North Borneo*, London, 1906, i, 231; Hose and McDougall, *The Pagan Tribes of Borneo*, London, 1912, ii, 134 *sq.*

agricultural labour. At such times they refrain from going to their rice-fields, under penalty of failure of the crop, but other work than that on the farms may sometimes be performed. The natives cannot furnish any explanation of the evil quality of these days.[1] A peculiar observance of the seventh day is found in some parts of Melanesia. When the first missionaries visited the New Hebrides and introduced the European week with Sunday as a day of rest, the natives were much astonished to learn that the whites were also familiar with their *bugi kai bituki*, or evil day. These Melanesians had never recognized any time-divisions shorter than the lunar month, but it had long been a custom among them to mark the seventh day by certain taboos. The natives would not engage in warfare on the seventh day after the declaration of hostilities; nor would they attempt to execute vengeance on the seventh day after the receipt of an insult.[2] The two prohibitions perhaps represent the broken-down form of a system of taboos at one time much more extensive. Elsewhere in the Pacific area (New Guinea, Australia, and Polynesia) seven does not seem to possess any special significance.

The mystic qualities of seven are recognized in Africa, but only where foreign influences have penetrated. Among the Wachaga of German East Africa the seventh month of the year is most unlucky: houses are not built, or marriages celebrated, or fields planted, or wars begun, during this fateful time.[3] The Wagiriama and Wasania, Bantu tribes living in the southeastern corner of British East Africa, observe the symbolism of seven in birth, circumcision, and mourning ceremonies.[4] The Akikuyu attach a very special

[1] I. H. N. Evans, "Notes on the Religious Beliefs, Superstitions, Ceremonies, and Tabus of the Dusuns," *Journal of the Royal Anthropological Institute*, 1912, xlii, 394 *sq.*
[2] Suas, "Le septième jour aux Nouvelles Hébrides, Océanie," *Anthropos*, 1912, vii, 1057; compare *ibid.*, 50 n.[1]
[3] M. Merker, in *Petermanns Mitteilungen*, 1902, Ergänzungsheft, no. 138, p. 25.
[4] W. E. H. Barrett, in *Journal of the Royal Anthropological Institute*, 1911, xli, 22, 31 *sq.*, 34.

P

ill-luck to the seventh day. A herdsman will not herd his flocks for more than six days, and on the seventh he must be relieved by another man. One who has been away on a journey for six days will not return to his village on the seventh; sooner than do so he will go and sleep at the house of a neighbour a short distance away. Were this rule broken, he would certainly be struck down by some serious illness, and a medicine-man would have to be called in to remove the curse. "This belief," we are told, "makes it easy for the missionaries to explain to the Akikuyu the force of the Christian observance of the Sabbath." [1] Seven is also one of the unlucky numbers of the Nandi.[2] The seven-day periods kept as Sabbaths by some of the Baganda and the seven-day week with three days marked by taboos, found among the Rendile and Burkeneji, have been previously noticed.[3] In some parts of Abyssinia and Somaliland we find not only a week of seven days but also cycles of seven months and seven years, with seven as a distinctively holy number.[4] In west Africa, besides the adoption of a seven-day week as the result of Mohammedan influence, there is also a symbolic use of seven in native folk-tales,[5] thus providing an instructive parallel to the same feature in European stories. The frequent occurrence of the symbolic seven in the magic and astrology of north African peoples must also be attributed to the spread of Islam from the Mediterranean to the Sudan.[6]

If the cult of seven in the Pacific area and Africa appears clearly as a borrowed institution, no other explanation than that of independent origination can account for the fact that some American Indian tribes

[1] C. W. Hobley, ibid., 1910, xl, 439 sq. Seven among the Akikuyu is of all numbers the most unlucky in divination (Routledge and Routledge, With a Prehistoric People, pp. 264, 274).

[2] Hollis, Nandi, p. 89.

[3] Above, pp. 145 sq., 198 sq.

[4] Above, p. 199.

[5] E. Dayrell, Folk Stories from Southern Nigeria, West Africa, London, 1910, nos. xxx–xxxii, xxxiv, xxxviii, etc.

[6] E. Doutté, Magie et religion dans l'Afrique du nord, Algiers, 1909, pp. 184 sqq.

also ascribe a peculiar sanctity to this number. In the opinion of most Americanists the symbolism of seven is here an outgrowth of cosmical conceptions of the four cardinal points, reinforced by conceptions of a central, an upper, and a lower world. Seven is thus the most sacred number because it represents all the regions of the cosmos.[1] This explanation cannot be safely applied outside the American area.

The antiquity of the symbolism of seven in the Old World is attested by its appearance as a sacred number in the earliest literary records of India, Greece, and Babylonia. Numerous references to seven occur in the *Rig-Veda*, where, however, it enjoys less importance than three.[2] Periods of seven days and seven years are frequently mentioned in the *Odyssey*.[3] Hesiod includes the seventh day of the month in his list of holy days (ἑβδόμη ἱερὸν ἦμαρ), "for on the seventh day Leto bare Apollo of the golden sword"; and this particular connection with the seventh day was maintained by the god in the later age of Greek history. Most of his great festivals began on the seventh day, at which time all public business appears to have ceased.[4] Many other illustrations exist of the large

[1] The Zuñi priests preserve a ceremonial diagram of the seven "Ancient Spaces," or primeval cosmogonic areas, representing north, east, south, west, the zenith, the nadir, and the middle. The observer is always supposed to stand in the central space. For illustrations of the seven-cult among the American Indians see J. W. Powell, in F. H. Cushing, *Zuñi Folk Tales*, New York, 1901, pp. xii *sq.;* S. Hagar, "Cherokee Star-lore," in *Boas Anniversary Volume*, New York, 1906, p. 361; J. O. Dorsey, in *Sixth Annual Report of the Bureau of Ethnology*, p. 397 (Osage, Kansa, Omaha, Dakota, and Ponka tribes); Jean L'Heureux, in *Journal of the An-*

thropological Institute, 1886, xv, 303 (Blackfoot); D. G. Brinton, *The Lenâpé and their Legends*, Philadelphia, 1885, pp. 139 *sq.*
[2] E. W. Hopkins, "The Holy Numbers of the *Rig-Veda*," in *Oriental Studies*, Boston, 1894, pp. 141, 144 *sq.;* compare A. Bergaigne, *La religion védique*, Paris, 1883, ii, 123, 127.
[3] *Odyssey*, x, 81, xii, 399, xiv, 252, 288, xv, 477.
[4] *Opera et dies*, 770 *sq.;* Herodotus, vi, 57; Æschylus, *Septem contra Thebas*, 800; Plutarch, *Quæstiones conviviales*, viii, 1, 2; Lydus, *De mensibus*, ii, 12. The seventh day of each month was a holiday for Greek children, in remembrance of Apollo's birth on the seventh of

symbolic rôle played by the number seven in Greece at a remote period.[1] Among the Babylonians, as early as the third millenium B.C., seven appears as a symbolic number in magico-religious rituals, incantations, exorcisms, and mythological narratives.[2] Thus, in the Babylonian version of the Deluge myth, periods of seven days' duration assume a marked importance : the rain continues for six days and ceases on the seventh, when the waters begin to subside ; and seven days again intervene before the Babylonian Noah is able to abandon the Ark and offer sacrifice to the gods for his preservation. The exceptional importance which this number enjoyed in Babylonia lends credibility to the theory that here was the centre from which the lore of seven passed to adjoining regions of western Asia and thence to more distant parts of the ancient world.[3]

Thargelion (Lucian, *Pseudologistes,* 16). The first and twentieth of the month were also consecrated to Apollo, who received in consequence the cult titles Ἑβδομαγένης, Νεομήνιος and Εἰκάδιος. According to Plutarch (*Dion,* 23), a festival of Apollo was also celebrated on the fifteenth of the month. On the seventh day in Greece see, further, L. R. Farnell, *The Cults of the Greek States,* Oxford, 1906–1910, iv, 258 *sq.; idem, Greece and Babylon,* London, 1911, p. 295; O. Gruppe, *Griechische Mythologie und Religionsgeschichte,* Munich, 1906, ii, 939 *sqq.;* M. P. Nilsson, "Die älteste griechische Zeitrechnung, Apollo und der Orient," *Archiv für Religionswissenschaft,* 1911, xiv, 442 *sqq.*

[1] See the exhaustive collection of the evidence, both literary and inscriptional, in Roscher, "Fristen und Wochen," pp. 41–68; *idem,* "Sieben- und Neunzahl," pp. 4–53; *idem,* "Hebdomadenlehren," pp. 7–23. Some students have seen in this sanctity of seven the results of

early intercourse with the Orient through Phœnician channels (V. Bérard, in *Revue de l'histoire des religions,* 1899, xxxix, 426 *sq.;* compare A. Thumb, "Die Namen der Wochentage im Griechischen," *Zeitschrift für deutsche Wortforschung,* 1901, i, 163 *sq.*). The theory of the diffusion of the cult of seven from the East might now be strengthened by substituting Cretan for Phœnician intermediaries. Nilsson argues that the seven-cult, together with the worship of Apollo, reached Greece by way of Asia Minor, "eine Etappe auf dem Wege nach Babylonien" (*Archiv für Religionswissenschaft,* 1911, xiv, 447 *sq.*).

[2] J. Hehn, *Siebenzahl und Sabbat bei den Babyloniern und im Alten Testament,* Leipzig, 1907, pp. 4–44; P. Jensen, *Die Kosmologie der Babylonier,* Strassburg, 1890, pp. 170–184.

[3] The predominance of seven among the Hebrews, if not wholly explained by borrowing from Babylonia, may reasonably be assumed to have been much influenced by

Some Assyriologists have connected the symbolism of seven with the seven stars visible to the naked eye which traverse the celestial zodiac.   For the Babylonian astrologers and astronomers these were the sun, the moon, and the five larger planets, Mercury, Venus, Mars, Jupiter, and Saturn.   There can be no question that the separation of the planets from the fixed stars, one of the enduring contributions which Babylonia has made to civilization, was the outcome of superstitious notions concerning the influence of the heavenly bodies on the life of man.   The Babylonian astrologers who watched night by night the stately procession of the stars across the cloudless skies were animated by no high zeal for scientific knowledge, but rather by the necessity of drawing from the celestial phenomena omens of good or ill for king and country.   Jupiter ·and Venus were probably the first planets to be differentiated, the one because of his brilliant light, the other because of her two appearances when she precedes the rising, and follows the setting, sun.   Saturn, Mercury, and Mars seem originally to have been combined under the one designation Lu-Bat, a term which came to bear the general meaning of "planet" — doubtless on account of the difficulty involved in observing their separate courses.[1]   We do not know when all five planets were set off from the fixed stars, or when they were first connected with the sun and moon to form a group of seven planetary luminaries.   As an eminent Italian astronomer has remarked, both achievements must have required centuries of close and accurate observations; they do not belong to a primitive astronomy.[2]   Hence we may safely conclude that the

Babylonian conceptions.   On the Hebrew cult of this number see Hehn, Siebenzahl und Sabbat, pp. 77–90; O. Zöckler, "Siebenzahl, heilige," in Herzog, Plitt, and Hauck's Realencyklopädie für protestantische Theologie und Kirche,³ xviii, 310–317.

[1] M. Jastrow, Aspects of Religious Belief and Practice in Babylonia and Assyria, New York, 1911, pp. 217 sqq.; idem, Die Religion Babyloniens und Assyriens, Giessen, 1905–1912, ii, 446 sq., 663 sqq.
[2] G. Schiaparelli, Astronomy in the Old Testament, Oxford, 1905,

symbolism of seven, reaching into remote Babylonian antiquity, long preceded the recognition of the seven planets; nay, more, that the symbolic significance of this number imposed itself on Babylonian astronomers and astrologers and compelled them to include in it all the principal stars.

The differentiation of the planets led naturally to their identification with the greater deities of the Babylonian pantheon, whose several names — Nabu, Ishtar, Nergal, Marduk, and Ninib — have come down to us through the Greeks and Romans in their classical equivalents, Mercury, Venus, Mars, Jupiter, and Saturn. It is by no means certain, however, that at all periods of Babylonian history these were the only deities which enjoyed planetary affiliations, or that the same gods were invariably connected with the same planets. The association of planet and god seems to have been quite artificial and arbitrary; at any rate, the omen texts do not show any close correspondence between the character of the deity and the prognostications drawn from the behaviour of his planet. Furthermore, the cuneiform records contain no indication that the Babylonians were familiar with what is known as the astrological order of the planets, the order,

pp. 134 *sq.* The fact that by the Babylonians Venus, as a morning star, was considered masculine and as an evening star, feminine (F. X. Kugler, *Sternkunde und Sterndienst in Babel,* Münster-i.-W., 1907–1910, ii, 19 *sq.*) must point back to a time when the different appearances of that heavenly body at morning and evening were regarded as those of different planets. Such was also the opinion of the early Greeks, who held the morning star, Ἑωσφόρος, and Ἕσπερος, the evening star, to be different bodies. Their identity was not recognized until the time of Pythagoras in the sixth century B.C. (W. H. Roscher, "Planeten," *Ausführliches Lexikon* der griechischen und römischen *Mythologie,* iii, col. 2521). Similar misconceptions are found among primitive peoples. Of the Maori it has been said: "Tawera is their Lucifer and Merimeri their Hesperus, and under these two names the beauty of the planet Venus is frequently celebrated in their poetry" (E. Shortland, *Traditions and Superstitions of the New Zealanders,* p. 219). Additional evidence is found among the aborigines of Sumatra (Marsden, *op. cit.,* p. 194), the Hottentots (Schultze, *op. cit.,* p. 367), and the Cherokee Indians (Hagar, in *Boas Anniversary Volume,* p. 357).

that is, in which they appear as regents of the week-days in the so-called planetary week of seven days. The oldest known list of the Babylonian planets dates from about 700 B.C., and presents the following arrangement: Moon, Sun, Jupiter, Venus, Saturn, Mercury, Mars. The same order is found one hundred and fifty years later, in astronomical texts belonging to the time of the New Babylonian Empire.[1] This seems to be nothing more than the sequence according to which the planets were severally differentiated from the fixed stars. At all events it is not the astrological sequence, which lies at the basis of the planetary week. Nor can the origin of the names of the weekdays be sought in Babylonia. It is true that the Babylonians, like the Egyptians,[2] ascribed to every day in the month its appropriate divinity, but absolutely no evidence exists that they ever applied the names of the seven planetary deities to the days of a septenary cycle. That step was taken at another time and by another people.

The planetary week,[3] an institution which has spread

[1] Kugler, op. cit., i, 13; compare F. Boll, "Zur babylonischen Plane-tenordnung," Zeitschrift für Assyriologie, 1911, xxv, 373. Between 400 B.C. and the opening of the Christian era the order is the same, except that Mercury and Saturn exchange places.

[2] Herodotus, ii, 82.

[3] The history of the planetary week has been treated with exhaustive learning by E. Schürer, "Die siebentägige Woche im Gebrauche der christlichen Kirche der ersten Jahrhunderte," Zeitschrift für die neutestamentliche Wissenschaft, 1905, vi, 1–66. A very valuable survey is that by F. Boll, "Hebdomas," in Pauly-Wissowa's Real-Encyclopädie der classischen Altertumswissenschaft, vii, coll. 2547–2578. Among the earlier discussions those by J. C. H(are), "On the Names of the Days of the Week," Philological Museum, 1832, i, 1–73, and E. Schrader, "Der babylonische Ursprung der siebentägigen Woche," Theologische Studien und Kritiken, 1874, xlvii, 343–353, hold an honourable place. See further W. H. Roscher, "Planeten," Ausführliches Lexikon der griechischen und römischen Mythologie, iii, coll. 2518–2539; A. Bouché-Leclercq, L'astrologie grecque, Paris, 1899, pp. 476–484; Jensen, Nöldeke, et al., "Geschichte der Namen der Wochentage," Zeitschrift für deutsche Wortforschung, 1901, i, 150–193; O. Schrader, "Woche," Reallexikon der indogermanischen Altertumskunde, Strassburg, 1901, pp. 959–965; W. Lotz, "Woche," in Herzog, Plitt, and Hauck's Realencyklopädie für protestantische Theologie und Kirche,³ xxi, 409–414; F. Rühl, Chronologie des Mittelalters

eastward over the Oriental world and westward into Europe, is a product of the speculations of astrologers and philosophers during the Hellenistic, or Græco-Oriental, era. The sequence of its days depends ultimately upon the order of the seven planetary spheres, adopted by Ptolemy in antiquity and after him by astronomers until the discoveries of Copernicus. If the planets are grouped according to their distance from the earth, beginning with the highest and descending to the lowest, we obtain the following order: Saturn, Jupiter, Mars, Sun, Venus, Mercury, Moon. No certain evidence exists that this arrangement was known at an earlier date than the second century before our era.[1] The astrological order, which also begins with Saturn, proceeds next to the fourth planet, or Sun, from which again the fourth planet (by inclusive reckoning) is the Moon. By continuing to select every fourth planet thereafter we obtain at length the regents of the seven weekdays: Saturn, Sun, Moon, Mars, Mercury, Jupiter, Venus.

How, it may be asked, did such an arrangement arise? This question has been answered for us by the Roman historian, Dio Cassius, who interrupts his narrative of the victorious campaign of Pompey the Great in Palestine to furnish a brief account of the planetary week.[2] The institution, says Dio Cassius,

---

und der Neuzeit, Berlin, 1897, pp. 49-63; F. K. Ginzel, Handbuch der mathematischen und technischen Chronologie, Leipzig, 1906-1911, index, s.v. "Woche." The word "week" in various Germanic languages has the general meaning of "change" (Anglo-Saxon wice, Old Frisian wike, Old Norse vika, Danish uge, Old High German wecha, Gothic wiko, etc.). See F. L. K. Weigand, Deutsches Wörterbuch,[5] Giessen, 1910, ii, 1279. The Latin vicis, "change," "turn" (a genitive form) is a related expression. See Walde, op. cit., p. 833.

[1] The reverse order, beginning with the Moon and ending with Saturn, is attributed to Pythagoras by Pliny the Elder (Historia naturalis, ii, 22) and by Censorinus (De die natali, xiii, 3); and according to Macrobius it was adopted by Archimedes in the third century B.C. (Commentarium in somnium Scipionis, i, 19, 2, ii, 3, 13). But the statements of these late writers on the subject may be safely disregarded.

[2] Historia Romana, xxxvii, 18 sq. There is also extant a still earlier explanation of the planetary se-

can be explained in two ways. According to the first explanation the gods are supposed to preside over separate days of the week, following the "'principle of the tetrachord' (which is believed to constitute the basis of music)."[1] The planetary week would thus be one expression of the occult relations supposed to exist between harmonic intervals of music and the seven planetary spheres. Though the idea that the motions of the planets were regulated by the laws of musical harmony had great popularity among some of the Greek schools of philosophy, neo-Pythagorean and neo-Platonist, it is not, however, to this comparatively refined doctrine of the "music of the spheres" that we must look for the origin of the planetary sequence.[2] The second explanation given by Dio Cassius, and also by Vettius Valens, is connected with the astrological theory of "chronocratories," which assigned to the several planets dominion over hours and days as periods of time. If the day is divided into twenty-four hours and each hour is ascribed in turn

quence by Vettius Valens, an astrologer of the age of the Antonines. The one provided by Plutarch, in the seventh chapter of the fourth book of his *Symposiacs*, has been lost. Dio Cassius attributes the origin of the planetary week to the Egyptians; Lydus, a Byzantine antiquarian of the fifth century A.D., hesitates between the Egyptians and the Babylonians (*De mensibus*, ii, 31).

[1] This arrangement — διὰ τεσσάρων — may be illustrated by means of the heptagram. Let the circumference of a circle be divided into seven equal arcs and the signs of the planets — Saturn, Jupiter, Mars, Sun, Venus, Mercury, Moon — be placed at the points of division. If these points are connected by a series of continuous chords, then, beginning with Saturn, the lines of the chords will lead

successively to the signs of the planets in the astrological order. The figure of a seven-branched star, inscribed in a circle, is an ancient device; indeed, the heptagram appears on a clay tablet recently unearthed at Nippur in Babylonia (H. V. Hilprecht, *Explorations in Bible Lands*, Philadelphia, 1903, p. 530), but in this case quite without any indication of its use.

[2] As a matter of fact the gamut, or scale of seven notes comprised within the interval of an octave, rests on no fundamental laws of acoustic phenomena but is itself a product of the all-pervading symbolism of seven. This system of musical numeration has spread from Greece as far east as India and China. See J. Combarieu, *La musique et la magie*, Paris, 1909, pp. 176–200.

to the several planets — Saturn, Jupiter, Mars, Sun, Venus, Mercury, Moon — then Saturn will preside over the first, eighth, fifteenth, and twenty-second hours of the first day, the twenty-third hour will fall to Jupiter, and the twenty-fourth to Mars. The twenty-fifth hour, or the first hour of the second day, will belong to the Sun, the first hour of the third day to the Moon, and so on for the remaining weekdays. The planetary deity found to preside over the first hour of a day is then supposed to give his name to the entire day. This scheme, as far as it depends on the recognition of twenty-four hours, is evidently not of Greek origin, for the mathematical division of the day into fixed parts did not arise in the Occident, but was due to Oriental influences.[1]

The planetary week thus presents itself as a curious amalgam of ideas derived from different sources. Babylonia, the motherland of divination, provided the doctrine of the influence of the stars on human destinies; Greece furnished the mathematical astronomy which grouped the planets according to their distance from the earth; and upon these foundations astrologers of the Hellenistic era, familiar with the cult of seven and with a division of the day into twenty-four hours, built up what was, at the outset, an entirely pagan institution.

The seven-day week (ἑβδομάς, septimana), in its astrological form, has had a varied history. It probably first appeared in the star cults of Mesopotamia

[1] Herodotus (ii, 109) says explicitly that the Greeks learned from the Babylonians to divide the day into twelve parts. This statement agrees with the evidence from the cuneiform records, which show that it was the Babylonian custom to divide the nycthemeron, or cycle of night and day, into twelve kaspu, corresponding to two of our equinoctial hours. On the other hand the Egyptians from very early times were familiar with a division into twenty-four hours, twelve for the night and twelve for the natural day. It is not improbable, therefore, that the astrological use of the twenty-four hours was remotely derived from Egypt. On the entire subject of hour deities see W. Gundel, "Stundengötter," Hessische Blätter für Volkskunde, 1913, xii, 100-131.

and Syria, certainly not before the second century
B.C., passed thence to the cosmopolitan city of Alexandria, the meeting-ground of East and West, and
about the age of Augustus gained an entrance into
Occidental lands. The first reasonably certain evidence of its existence in Italy is found in the so-called
fasti Sabini, the fragments of a calendar drawn up
between the years 19 B.C.–4 A.D. Here the days of
the seven-day week (indicated by the letters *A* to *F*)
and those of the old Roman nundinal cycle (indicated
by the letters *A* to *G*) are set forth in parallel columns
for the months of September and October. All similar
calendars of the same period employ only the lettering
of the eight-day Roman week.[1] The earliest evidence
for the planetary naming of the weekdays is found
in two inscriptions from Pompeii. Of these, the first
gives all the names of the planetary deities in their
Greek form; the second, the names in their more
familiar Latin form, except for the accidental omission
of Wednesday: Saturni, Solis, Lunæ, Martis, Jovis,
Veneris.[2] Indications that the planetary week was
known and used during the second century A.D. occur
in both classical literature and the inscriptions. Dio
Cassius,[3] writing early in the third century (about
210–220 A.D.), declares that the custom of referring
the days to the stars, called planets, had then become
quite familiar to the Romans as well as to the rest of
mankind. The accuracy of this statement is confirmed
by his Christian contemporaries, Tertullian and Clement of Alexandria, who in their writings addressed to
the pagans employ the planetary names of the weekdays.[4]

[1] *Corpus inscriptionum Latinarum*, i, pt. i,[2] 220; G. Gunder-
mann, "Die Namen der Wochentage bei den Römern," *Zeitschrift für
deutsche Wortforschung*, 1901, i, 177.

[2] A. Mau, in *Bullettino dell'
instituto di corrispondenza archeo-
logica*, 1881, p. 30; *Atti della reale
accademia dei lincei, anno 1901,
Serie v, classe di scienze morali*, etc.,
ix, *Notizie degli scavi*, p. 330.

[3] *Historia Romana*, xxxvii, 18.

[4] Tertullian, *Apologeticus*, 16;
idem, *Ad nationes*, i, 13; Clement,
Stromata, vii, 12, 75; compare
Justin Martyr, *Apologia prima*, 67.

The early Christians had at first adopted the Jewish seven-day week with its numbered weekdays,[1] but by the close of the third century A.D. this began to give way to the planetary week; and in the fourth and fifth centuries the pagan designations became generally accepted in the western half of Christendom.[2] The use of the planetary names by Christians attests the growing influence of astrological speculations introduced by converts from paganism. The old beliefs in the power of the stars over human destinies lived on in Christian communities; the heavenly bodies, though no longer deities, were still demons capable of affecting the fate of man. During these same centuries the spread of Oriental solar worships, especially that of Mithra,[3] in the Roman world, had already led to the substitution by pagans of *dies Solis* for *dies Saturni*, as the first day of the planetary week; and Constantine's famous edict, as we have seen, definitely enrolled Sunday among the holidays of the Roman state religion.[4] The change from Saturn's Day to Sunday must have further commended the planetary week in Christian circles, where the Lord's Day (*dies dominica*), beginning the week, had long been observed as that on which Christ, the "Sun of Righteousness,"

[1] The Jews indicated each weekday by its numerical name, as the first day, the second day, and so on; compare *Exodus*, xvi, 5, 22; *Matthew*, xxviii, 1; *Mark*, xvi, 2; *Luke*, xxiv, 1; *John*, xx, 1; *Acts*, xx, 7; 1 *Corinthians*, xvi, 2. The sixth day, preceding the Sabbath, came eventually to be called by Hellenistic Jews ἡ παρασκευή, or "preparation" for the Sabbath; compare *Matthew*, xxvii, 62; *Mark*, xv, 42; *Luke*, xxiii, 54; *John*, xix, 31.

[2] The oldest dated Christian inscription to employ a planetary designation belongs to the year 269 A.D. (*Inscriptiones Christianæ urbis Romæ*, ed. De Rossi, 1861, i, no. 11).

[3] According to the testimony of Celsus, as quoted by Origen (*Contra Celsum*, vi, 21), the seven planets played an important rôle in the Mithraic mysteries. The chief position was naturally assigned to the sun, from which circumstance Cumont concludes, not only that the planetary week was known to Mithraism, but also that the *dies Solis* "était évidemment le plus sacré de l'hebdomade pour les fidèles de Mithra, et, comme les Chrétiens, ils devaient sanctifier le dimanche et non pas le sabbat." See F. Cumont, *Textes et monuments figurés relatifs aux mystères de Mithra*, Brussels, 1896-1899, i, 118 *sq.*, ii, 31.

[4] Above, pp. 122 *sq.*

rose from the dead.[1]   Thus gradually a pagan institution was engrafted on Christianity.

The planetary week became familiar to the barbarians of the West before its adoption by Christianity.
Much monumental evidence exists to show that in Gaul
and Roman Germany the planetary order, beginning
with Saturn, was known from the first half of the third
century.   The same cycle appears to have been introduced into Roman Britain.   In nearly all Romance
countries the planetary names are applied to the weekdays except the first and seventh, for which the ecclesiastical designations, *dies dominica* and *sabbatum*, are
retained.[2]   In most Germanic languages Sunday and
Monday appear as translations of the Latin forms;
Tuesday, Wednesday, Thursday, and Friday represent equations of classical and Germanic deities, based
on the most obvious points of resemblance between
them;[3] while Saturday, for which no corresponding
Germanic god suggested itself, is a corrupt form of

[1] Below, p. 268.

[2] Italian *domenica,   sabbato;*
Spanish *domingo, sabado;* French
dimanche, samedi, etc. But the
heathen names of even these two
days continued for a long time in
popular use, as is evident from the
words of Gregory of Tours: *Ecce
enim dies Solis adest, sic enim bar-
baries vocitare diem dominicam con-
sueta est* (*Historia Francorum,* iii,
15). The other weekdays (Monday to Friday) in the calendar of
the Roman Church follow the
Jewish usage in being numbered,
not named: *feria secunda, feria
tertia, feria quarta, feria quinta,*
and *feria sexta* (Isidore of Seville,
Etymologia sive origines, v, 30).
In Portugal the influence of the
Church was strong enough to secure
the general adoption of this mode
of reckoning, instead of the planetary sequence; and here Monday
is still called *feira segunda,* Tuesday, *feira terça,* etc. It is curious

to find the old Roman term for a
holy day thus employed to refer
to the weekdays that are particularly devoted to secular occupations.
The origin of the practice has not
been satisfactorily explained.

[3] Tiu (Mars), Woden (Mercu-
rius), Thor (Jupiter), Frija (Venus).
The special observance of Thursday as a holy day reflects the commanding place occupied by Thor
in Germanic paganism. His worship on that day is referred to in
documents of the early Middle
Ages as a superstition to be eradi-
cated (*nullus diem Jovis in otio
observet,* etc.), but the modern
Esthonians still consider Thursday as holier than Sunday and in
Sweden, as late as the nineteenth
century, the day was generally
considered sacred. See J. Grimm,
Teutonic Mythology, London, 1882,
i, 191; O. Montelius, "The Sun-
god's Axe and Thor's Hammer,"
Folk-lore, 1910, xxi, 77.

Saturnus.[1] Among the Slavic peoples, whose week begins with Monday, as the first day after rest, the planetary names are unknown, the days being numbered in conformity with the usage of the Greek Church.[2] A similar custom prevails among the Lithuanians and Esthonians, who appear to have borrowed their week from the Slavs. Modern Greeks employ the ecclesiastical designations of the weekdays,[3] but the Finns and Lapps, at the other extremity of Europe, in adopting the week from the Scandinavians, took over also the planetary names of the days.[4]

[1] The Scandinavian name for Saturday, "bath-day" or "wash-day" (Old Norse *laugardagr*), arose from the custom of taking a bath at the end of the week (De la Saussaye, *The Religion of the Teutons*, Boston, 1902, p. 379; P. B. Du Chaillu, *The Land of the Midnight Sun*, New York, 1881, ii, 205 *sqq.*).

[2] In Slavic antiquity Friday, or some day corresponding to it, appears to have been consecrated to a female divinity, whose personality, after the introduction of Christianity, became merged into that of St. Prascovia. "As she is supposed to wander about the houses of the peasants on her holy day, and to be offended if she finds certain kinds of work going on, they are (or at least they used to be) frequently suspended on Fridays. It is a sin, says a time-honoured tradition, for a woman to sew or spin, or weave, or buck linen on a Friday, and similarly for a man to plait bast shoes, twine cords, and the like. Spinning and weaving are especially obnoxious to 'Mother Friday,' for the dust and refuse thus produced injure her eyes." The peasants believe that any work begun on Friday is sure to go wrong (W. R. S. Ralston, *Russian Folktales*, London, 1873, pp. 198 *sq.*).

[3] In Thessaly and Macedonia Saturday (σάββατον) is considered inauspicious for beginning any undertaking. This taboo on the day has been considered as perhaps a reminiscence of the Jewish Sabbath (Sir Rennell Rodd, *The Customs and Lore of Modern Greece*, London, 1892, p. 159). According to Mr. G. F. Abbott, the Macedonians believe it unlucky to finish any work on a Saturday; the end of the week being associated in some way with the end of the owner's life. "People born on a Saturday (hence called Σαββατιανοί or Sabbatarians) are believed to enjoy the doubtful privilege of seeing ghosts and phantasms, and of possessing great influence over vampires" (*Macedonian Folklore*, Cambridge, 1903, pp. 191, 221).

[4] On the week among European peoples see further E. Maass, *Die Tagesgötter im Rom und den Provinzen*, Berlin, 1902; A. Thumb, "Die albanesischen Wochentage," *Zeitschrift für deutsche Wortforschung*, 1901, i, 173–175; R. Thurneysen, "Die Namen der Wochentagen in den keltischen Dialecten," *ibid.*, pp. 186–191; W. Meyer-Lübke, "Die Namen der Wochentage im Romanischen," *ibid.*, pp. 192 *sq.*; C. L. Rochholz, *Deutscher Glaube und Brauch*, Berlin, 1867, ii, 9–63; K. A. Oberle, *Überreste germanischen Heidentums im Christentum*, Baden-Baden, 1883, pp. 13–40; Grimm, *op. cit.*, i, 122–130.

CHAPTER VII

THE BABYLONIAN "EVIL DAYS" AND THE SHABATTUM

IT is time to return to Babylonia. We have seen that here the cult of seven as a symbolic number was long anterior to the recognition of the seven planets; and, furthermore, that the planetary week, instead of being an early creation of Babylonian astrology, arose during the Hellenistic Age from the union of Greek and Oriental speculations. But for many centuries previously a seven-day week, in which the days were numbered, not named, had existed as a Jewish institution in western Asia; and we have still to determine whether this Jewish form of the week was derived remotely from Babylonia, and according to what conceptions the assumed Babylonian original was itself developed.

In the year 1869 the late George Smith, well known as a pioneer student of Assyriology, discovered among the cuneiform tablets in the British Museum "a curious religious calendar of the Assyrians, in which every month is divided into four weeks, and the seventh days, or 'Sabbaths,' are marked out as days on which no work should be undertaken." [1] Six years afterward Sir Henry Rawlinson published this calendar in the fourth volume of his standard collection of cuneiform inscriptions. It appears to be a transcript of a much more ancient Babylonian original, possibly belonging to the age of Hammurabi, which had been made by order of Asshurbanipal and placed in his royal library at Nineveh. The calendar, which is

[1] G. Smith, *Assyrian Discoveries*, London, 1883, p. 12; compare *idem, The Assyrian Eponym Canon*, London, 1875, pp. 19 *sq.*

complete for the thirteenth or intercalary month, called Elul II, and for Markheshwan, the eighth month of the Babylonian year, takes up the thirty days in succession and indicates the deity to which each day is sacred and what sacrifices or precautionary measures are necessary for each day. All the days are styled "favourable," an expression which must indicate a pious hope, not a fact, since the words *ud-khul-gal* or *ûmu limnu* ("the evil day") are particularly applied to the seventh, fourteenth, nineteenth, twenty-first, and twenty-eighth days. The second Elul, being an intercalated month, might be thought to have enjoyed a special significance, as intercalary months have had elsewhere;[1] but such a hypothesis will not explain the inclusion of the month of Markheshwan in the calendar.[2] Hence it is highly probable that at one time the other months were similarly marked, though as yet there is no inscriptional evidence for the observance of the five "evil days" in all the months of the Babylonian year.[3]

With regard to the reasons which dictated the choice of the seventh, fourteenth, twenty-first, and twenty-eighth days, two views have been entertained. It has been held, in the first place, that the "evil days" were selected as corresponding to the moon's successive changes; hence that the seventh day marks the close of the earliest form of the seven-day week, a week bound up with the lunar phases. According to another opinion the setting apart of every seventh day

---

[1] Above, p. 177 *n.*[2]

[2] The first edition (1875) of the fourth volume of Rawlinson's *Cuneiform Inscriptions of Western Asia* contained only a calendar for the month of Elul II, but in the second edition (1891) of this volume there was added, from a number of fragments, a calendar for the month of Markheshwan.

[3] The difficulty which arises in respect to the nineteenth day has been solved to the satisfaction of most Assyriologists by the suggestion that the nineteenth day was regarded as seven times the seventh day (*i.e.*, the forty-ninth from the first of the preceding month). This, of course, would not be strictly true, when the preceding month had only twenty-nine days, but it seems that the early Babylonian month was conventionally taken at thirty days' duration.

was due to the importance ascribed to seven; hence that the seven-day cycles were not regarded as quarters of the lunation but rather as periods containing the symbolic number of seven days, which happened to coincide, roughly, with a fourth part of the lunar month. The second view would be merely an amplification of the first, if we assume, with perhaps the majority of Assyriologists, that the rôle of seven as a symbolic number is ultimately connected with the moon changing her phases at intervals of approximately seven days.

It must be admitted, however, that in the present state of our knowledge we cannot obtain any satisfactory explanation of the origin of a symbolic number. As far as seven is concerned, the American evidence, previously referred to,[1] indicates that cosmical speculations may sometimes account for its significance; while in the Semitic area, again, one root of the cult of seven may lie in the observation of the Pleiades and the early use of Pleiades calendars by the agriculturist.[2] That the Pleiades number seven stars has been noted even by savage peoples, who have also observed that each one of three other prominent constellations, Ursa Major, Ursa Minor, and Orion, contains seven principal stars. Such unexplained coincidences may have served to confirm the impression of the significance of seven in the minds of Babylonian astrologers, even though the mystic quality of that number was based originally on a different set of ideas. But it is unnecessary to discuss further what popular superstitions and priestly speculations gave rise to the symbolism of seven in ancient Babylonia.

[1] Above, pp. 210 sq.

[2] Compare H. Zimmern, in E. Schrader, Die Keilinschriften und das Alte Testament,³ Berlin, 1903, pp. 620 sq. The possible influence of Pleiades cults has been worked out with much ingenuity by H. Grimme (Das israelitische Pfingst-fest und der Plejadenkult, Paderborn, 1907), who discerns in the duration of the Hebrew Pentecost, or Feast of Weeks, as well as in the rites which marked that agricultural festival, the predominance of a septenary division based on the observation of these seven stars.

Q

The month in Babylonia was a lunar month, and the year was a lunisolar year. Unlike the Egyptians, who passed from moon- to sun-reckonings before the dawn of history, the Babylonians always retained the primitive lunar calendar, harmonized with the solar year by the crude method of intercalating an extra month at the necessary intervals. As in all lunar calendars the month began with the visible new moon. So important was this for the determination of the month that *arxu*, the Babylonian expression for "month," meant, properly, the beginning of the month; while Nannar (*nannaru*), one of the names of the moon-god, was originally applied to the new moon.[1] The length of the month was reckoned at thirty days as an approximate average of the duration of the moon's course, a calculation familiar enough to many half-civilized peoples.[2] The ideogram for *arxu* is the number "thirty" enclosed in the ideogram for "day"; and the ideogram for Sin, the moon-deity, is made up of that for "god" and of that for "thirty," which number was sacred to him. When in late mythological syncretism the goddess Ishtar was represented as the daughter of Sin, her sacred number became fifteen, and this, with the determinative of goddess prefixed to it, was often used to express her name.[3]

Though the calendar assigned to each month thirty full days, the actual month must have often included only twenty-nine days, since the reckoning employed was purely lunar. We may assume, in the absence of definite statements as to the way of fixing the length of the month, that the Babylonians at first followed the rough-and-ready method of modern Arabs: on the twenty-ninth of the month, after the sun has gone

[1] W. Muss-Arnolt, "The Names of the Assyro-Babylonian Months and their Regents," *Journal of Biblical Literature*, 1892, xi, 73; E. Combe, *Histoire du culte de Sin en Babylonie et en Assyrie*, Paris, 1908, pp. 8, 13.

[2] Above, p. 178.
[3] W. Muss-Arnolt, in *Journal of Biblical Literature*, 1892, xi, 72 *sqq.*, 82 *sqq.*, 90; E. Meyer, "Astarte," in Roscher's *Ausführliches Lexikon der griechischen und römischen Mythologie*, i, col. 649.

down, they look in the western sky for the faint sickle of the moon; if this is seen, the new month begins forthwith; if it cannot be seen, the following day is also included in the old month, which then contains thirty days. By the middle of the seventh century B.C., and perhaps at an even earlier date, a more exact means of calculating the length of the month had come into use. The royal astrologers, who sent regular reports to the king as to the appearance or non-appearance of the moon at the expected time, appear to have carefully observed the day of the opposition of the sun and moon in the middle of the month; when the full-moon day was known, it became an easy matter to determine how many more days should be counted to the end of the month.[1] It was not until the third or second century B.C., when exact astronomical methods had supplanted purely empirical study of the heavens, that the Babylonians were able to calculate the appearance of the true new moon. By this time, too, the progress of astronomical knowledge allowed them to adopt the more accurate calendarizing of the lunation into months of twenty-nine and thirty days, five of the former, and seven of the latter, length.[2]

These details concerning the Babylonian calendar, in all but its latest form, are enough to indicate that it presents no striking divergence from the general type of lunar reckonings. The Babylonians, like all other peoples of the ancient East, based their calculations of time on the moon. It follows, therefore, that the seven-day periods described in the Rawlinson calendar were also reckoned from the visible new moon; indeed,

[1] R. C. Thompson, *The Reports of the Magicians and Astrologers of Nineveh and Babylon*, London, 1900, ii, pp. xviii *sqq.*, xxvi.

[2] Epping and Strassmeier, *Astronomisches aus Babylon*, Freiburg-i.-B., 1889, p. 179; F. X. Kugler, *Die babylonische Mondrechnung*, Freiburg-i.-B., 1900, pp. 49, 201; F. H. Weissbach, "Zum babylonischen Kalender," in *Assyriologische und archäologische Studien Hermann v. Hilprecht gewidmet*, Leipzig, 1909, p. 281.

this fact is clearly indicated by the description applied
in that calendar to the first day of the month.[1] We
may reasonably assume that the last day of the month
(when the latter actually included only twenty-nine
days) or the last two days of a thirty-day month were
regarded as forming an epagomenal period, interrupt-
ing the regular succession of seven-day cycles. Possibly
the Babylonians may have employed some such device
as that found among the negroes of west Africa, in
order that four of their lunar periods should correspond
exactly to the length of the lunation.[2]

We may next inquire whether additional evidence
exists to indicate that the seven-day periods of the
Rawlinson calendar were definitely associated with
successive phases of the moon. It has already been
noticed that very early in the Assyro-Babylonian cultural area there was in at least occasional use a five-
day cycle, called *khamushtu*.[3] Whether it preceded
the hebdomadal cycle or afterwards supplanted it
(perhaps as forming a closer divisor of the lunation),
or whether the two periods may not have existed
more or less contemporaneously, are matters concerning which the cuneiform records tell us nothing. They
do tell us, however, that a five-day period, possibly
to be identified with the *khamushtu*, was closely associated with the successive appearances of the moon,
as in a text where the first five days of the month
are spoken of as those of the crescent moon, the next
five, as those of the half-moon ("kidney"), and the
five following days as those of the full or nearly full
moon.[4] A similar association with the moon's course
is set forth in the case of a seven-day period in a text
which specifically indicates the seventh, fourteenth,
twenty-first, and twenty-eighth days as those of Sin,

[1] Rawlinson, *op. cit.*, iv,[2] pl. 32,
col. 1, ll. 1–2; W. Lotz, *Quæstiones
de historia Sabbati*, Leipzig, 1883,
p. 39.
[2] Above, pp. 187 *sq.*
[3] Above, p. 195.

[4] Rawlinson, *op. cit.*, iii, 55,
no. 3, ll. 17–26; P. Jensen, "Die
siebentägige Woche in Babylon
und Nineveh," *Zeitschrift für
deutsche Wortforschung*, 1901, i,
150.

the moon-god.[1] Another text connects several days of the month with the moon's course in the following order: first day, new moon; seventh day, moon as "kidney" (half-moon); fifteenth day, full moon.[2] Finally, in the fifth tablet of the Babylonian *Epic of Creation*, a work which in its original form is traced to the close of the third millennium B.C., it is told how the god Marduk, having created and set in order the heavenly bodies, then placed the moon in the sky to make known the days and divide the month with her phases. Although this interesting production, in its present mutilated state, mentions only the seventh and fourteenth days, we are entitled to believe that the original text also referred to the twenty-first and twenty-eighth days of the month.[3]

The cuneiform evidence thus makes it reasonably certain that the cycles of seven days' duration found in the Rawlinson calendar were regarded as divisions of the lunar month. This conclusion does not require us to hold that these cycles originated in the quartering of the lunation. Their choice may conceivably have been dictated in the first instance by the desire to apply the prevailing symbolism of seven to periods

[1] Rawlinson, *op. cit.*, iii, 64, 18 b; Jensen, in *Zeitschrift für deutsche Wortforschung*, 1901, i, 152; Zimmern, in Schrader, *Keilinschriften*,[3] p. 621 *n.*[5]

[2] *Cuneiform Texts from Babylonian Tablets in the British Museum*, pt. xxv, pl. 50 (K. 170); F. Hommel, "Calendar (Babylonian)," Hastings's *Encyclopædia of Religion and Ethics*, iii, 76.

[3] *Enuma elish*, v, ll. 12–18 (transl. L. W. King, *The Seven Tablets of Creation*, London, 1902, i, 78, 81):

"The Moon-god he caused to shine forth, the night he entrusted to him,
He appointed him, a being of the night, to determine the days;

Every month without ceasing with the crown he covered (?) him, (saying):
'At the beginning of the month, when thou shinest upon the land,
Thou commandest the horns to determine six days
And on the seventh day to [divide] the crown
On the fourteenth day thou shalt stand opposite, the half [. . .].'"

For other translations see P. Jensen, *Die Kosmologie der Babylonier*, Strassburg, 1890, pp. 288 *sqq.;* W. Muss-Arnolt, in R. F. Harper, *Assyrian and Babylonian Literature*, New York, 1901, p. 296.

of time; while only later, and as a secondary development, were they brought into connection with the phases
of the moon.   In either case the seven-day periods can
be only loosely and inaccurately described as "weeks."
Nothing in the cuneiform records indicates that the
Babylonians ever employed them for civil purposes.
These periods seem to have had solely a religious significance, as was true also of the four divisions of the
month, similarly connected with the lunar phases,
in the sacred calendars of both Buddhism and Zoroas-
trianism.[1] What we have disclosed in Babylonia is,
not the week itself, but the material out of which such
an institution might be formed.

Each septenary period in the calendar for Elul II
and Markheshwan closed with an unnamed "evil
day."   The symbolism of seven cannot in itself account
for the unlucky quality attaching to this seventh
day. Seven to the Babylonians bore no unlucky
character. It stood, rather, for the notion of completeness or totality, appearing in prayers, incantations,
and exorcisms to indicate the sum total of the gods or
spirits recognized by the worshipper; sometimes marking the length of the period during which such important actions as the dedication of a temple or the mourning for a death must be performed; and often, again,
assuming a mythological rôle, as in the seven gates of
the underworld, the seven names of the goddess Ishtar,
and the periods of seven days' duration found in the
Babylonian Deluge narrative.[2] In these and many
other instances seven appears as a symbolic, but not
as a portentous, number. Assuming, however, that
the seven-day periods of the Rawlinson calendar were
associated with successive phases of the moon —
whether originally or secondarily does not matter —
it is clear that the seventh day, marking the critical
or transition point in each phase, would possess a
special importance. In fact, the negative or prohibitive regulations enforced among the Babylonians on

---

[1] Above, pp. 157, 165 *sq.*   [2] Above, p. 212.

the "evil days" bear a close resemblance to the taboos which many other peoples have observed at the changes of the moon.

Recent students of Semitic magic have shown that the Sumerians and their successors, the Babylonians and Assyrians, were familiar with the idea of taboo; the term *mamit*, which appears frequently in magical texts, is exactly equivalent to *tabu*, since it refers to that state of ritual impurity or ceremonial uncleanness attending certain circumstances or actions.[1] A great part of the so-called *Shurpu* series [2] deals with the methods of removing the condition of *mamit* into which a man may have wittingly or unwittingly fallen. The murderer, the adulterer, or the thief became *mamit* in consequence of his breach of ordinary social morality, but equally cursed was the unlucky person who ran up against another who was under a taboo, slept on his bed, ate out of his plate, or drank from his cup. A man might be contaminated by putting his foot in some unclean water, by treading in some libation that had been poured forth, by touching a bewitched woman, and even by seeing one of unwashen hands. The third tablet of the *Shurpu* series enumerates no less than one hundred and sixty-three taboos, including "those which come from the family, old or young, friend or neighbour, rich or poor; oven, bellows, pots and cups, bed or couch, chariot or weapons. To drink out of an unclean vessel, to sit in the sun, to root up plants in the desert, to cut reeds in a thicket, to slay the young of beasts, to pray with unclean hands, and a host of other common actions, might under certain conditions bring a *tapu* on the man." Such tabooed acts placed the man under an interdiction; if he fell sick, he knew that his sufferings were due to the hostility of some supernatural power; and a professional exorcist would be called in to drive away by magical words, prayers, and rites the divine curse

---

[1] C. Fossey, *La magie assyrienne,* Paris, 1902, pp. 52, 58.

[2] See H. Zimmern, *Die Beschwörungstafeln šurpu,* Leipzig, 1896.

clinging to his person.[1] It seems to be clear, then, that the taboos observed on the "evil days" represented to the Babylonians only a particular application of an ancient and generally accepted superstition.

The calendar for Elul II contains specific directions for the observance of the five "evil days," in each case the same except for differences in the names of the deities.[2] The regulations for the seventh day read as follows:

"An evil day. The shepherd of great peoples shall not eat flesh cooked upon the coals, or bread of the oven.[3] The garment of his body he shall not change, he shall not put on clean [garments]. He shall not bring an offering. The king shall not ride in his chariot. He shall not speak as a ruler (?). The priest shall not give a decision in the secret place. The physician shall not lay his hand on a patient. To issue a malediction it [the day] is not suitable.[4] At night the king shall bring his gift before Marduk and Ishtar, he shall offer a sacrifice. The lifting up of his hands will then be pleasing to god."

It is clear that the rules for the seventh day pre-

[1] R. C. Thompson, *The Devils and Evil Spirits of Babylonia*, London, 1904, ii, pp. xxxix *sqq.*

[2] H. C. Rawlinson, *The Cuneiform Inscriptions of Western Asia*, London, 1891, iv,[2] pl. 32-33. The complete text was first translated by A. H. Sayce ("A Babylonian Saints' Calendar," *Records of the Past*, London, 1876, vii, 157-170) and shortly thereafter by W. Lotz (*Quaestiones de historia Sabbati*, Leipzig, 1883, pp. 39-49). The passage relating to the seventh day has been many times rendered by Assyriologists, not without variations in the result. I have used the version in the scholarly work of R. W. Rogers, *Cuneiform Parallels to the Old Testament*, New York, 1912, p. 189.

[3] The nineteenth day would seem to be particularly tabooed, for then the "shepherd of great peoples" is forbidden to eat "anything which the fire has touched."

[4] Most Assyriologists (Jeremias, Delitzsch, Lagrange, Pinches, Clay) make this sentence read: "The day is unsuitable for any business," a translation which, if correct, converts the seventh day into a veritable Sabbath. To this translation Professor Morris Jastrow now adds the great weight of his authority, pointing out that we must read *ana epasch la na-ṭu*, "'für Arbeit (oder Ausführung) nicht geignet' . . . und nicht, wie man früher annahm, *epesch arrati*, 'zum Fluchen,' was ja ein eigentümliches Verbot wäre" (*Die Religion Babyloniens und Assyriens*, Giessen, 1905-1912, ii, 533 *n.*[1]).

scribe a season of abstinence affecting many royal activities. The "shepherd of great peoples" must not eat any food which has been cooked with fire; he must not change his clothes; and he must not offer a sacrifice until the end of the day. The king is not to speak in public; and he is even forbidden to travel. The Babylonian monarch who observed all these taboos five times a month would have been as strictly secluded as was the Hawaiian ruler, who, likewise, during the four monthly *tabu* periods retired to the inner precincts of his temple.[1]

The Babylonian regulations have been interpreted as survivals from ancient times, when priest-kings were accredited with a divine or supernatural nature, and hence were subjected to numberless restrictions designed to prevent any impairment of their sanctity and magical power.[2] A consideration of the evidence yielded by primitive societies suggests, however, that the Babylonian regulations may have been connected originally with taboos imposed on the entire community. In Hawaii, where the lunar phases were observed as *tabu* periods, the prohibitions affecting the king represented only an intensification of the communal taboos, to be explained by the extreme sanctity attached to the Hawaiian ruler. In Assam, where the *genna* institution enjoys a vigorous life, we find that, besides the prohibitions communally observed at critical times, the *khullakpa*, or priest-chief, is surrounded by many elaborate taboos. Their purpose is "to protect the man who acts on behalf of the whole subdivision or village on the occasions of general *genna*, from any accident which might impair his power." He is subject to various food restrictions, must content himself with only one wife, and must even separate himself from her on the eve of a general *genna*. In one group

[1] Above, p. 15.
[2] For much evidence as to the sacredness of chiefs and kings and as to the accompanying taboos, see Sir J. G. Frazer, *Taboo and the Perils of the Soul*, London, 1911, pp. 1-17; *idem, Psyche's Task,*[2] London, 1913, pp. 6-19.

the headman may not eat in a strange village, nor, whatever the provocation, may he utter a word of abuse. The violation of any one of these taboos is thought to bring misfortune on the entire village.[1] It is not wholly speculative to suggest that, were the natives of Assam to discard their communal taboos as burdensome, the special regulations affecting the *khullakpa* might survive, in deference to old tradition, and might even be increased in severity, if that individual should grow in authority and holiness. The situation would then furnish a very close analogy to what existed in ancient Babylonia. The regulations concerning the "evil days," it may be noted, did not pertain to the king alone. We may reasonably assume that "the shepherd of great peoples" and the king mentioned further on in the calendar are one and the same; but the record also describes certain rules imposed on the priest and on the physician, both important functionaries among the Babylonians. It seems also evident that the day was regarded as unsuitable for any one to lay a curse or ban; according to another, and possibly more accurate, rendering, unsuitable for all business. These considerations increase the probability that at one time some taboos on the seventh day were observed by the entire community.[2]

It is questionable, however, whether in late historic times there was any general abstention from work and other activities on the "evil days." The Babylonians were a highly organized commercial and manufacturing people who would have found such regulations burdensome to the highest degree. Taboos once generally

[1] T. C. Hodson, in *Journal of the Anthropological Institute*, 1906, xxxvi, 98; *idem*, in *Folk-lore*, 1910, xxi, 298; *idem*, *Naga Tribes of Manipur*, pp. 102, 141 *sq.*

[2] For further discussions of the "evil days" see M. J. Lagrange, *Études sur les religions sémitiques*,[2] Paris, 1905, pp. 291 *sqq.*; J. Hehn, *Siebenzahl und Sabbat bei den Babyloniern und im Alten Testament*, Leipzig, 1907, pp. 106-109; J. Meinhold, *Sabbat und Woche im Alten Testament*, Göttingen, 1905, pp. 15 *sqq.*; F. Bohn, *Der Sabbat im Alten Testament*, Gütersloh, 1903, pp. 39-43.

observed may have been gradually relaxed and at last abandoned, just as modern Jews are now neglecting the observance of the Sabbath. The practice might have been kept up, however, by the king and the priests as the special guardians of conservative institutions.[1]

The cuneiform records contain a term *shabattum*, which has been generally accepted as the phonetic equivalent of the Hebrew *shabbāthôn*, perhaps an intensive form of *shabbāth* or Sabbath, referring to a Sabbath of particular solemnity.[2] *Shabattum*, a word

[1] Some painstaking efforts have been made to discover whether during historic times there was any general observance in Babylonia of the "evil days." W. Lotz (*op. cit.*, p. 66), from an examination of 540 dated contract tablets belonging to different months, found that the average of the number of transactions on the 7th, 14th, 21st, and 28th days was 18, which would be also the average for each day of the month. The 19th day, however, had only one contract to its credit. Schiaparelli (*op. cit.*, p. 132 n.[1]) examined about 400 dated documents from the archives of the Babylonian business firm, Egibi and Sons, and showed that there was a real abstention from business only on the 19th day, when no contracts were concluded. The same investigator (*op. cit.*, pp. 175 *sqq.*) also classified according to the day of the month 2764 dates on contract tablets belonging to the period 604-449 B.C. and found again that, while the transactions for the 7th, 14th, and 21st days were considerably above the average (94) and those for the 28th day only slightly below it, the 19th day registered but 12 transactions. It is true that these statistics deal with a late period of Babylonian history and include the reigns of several Persian kings. By this time the general observ-

ance of the custom may have been in decay. The figures, moreover, do not distinguish the sort of business done on the "evil days." Many of the documents are temple records, having to do with offerings, receipts of salaries by priests, etc., and such business may not have been regarded as a violation of the prohibitions in question (C. H. W. Johns, "The Babylonian Sabbath," *Expository Times*, 1906, xvii, 566 *sq.*). For Assyria, during the period 720-606 B.C., 365 dated documents indicate no marked cessation of business on the 7th, 14th, 21st, and 28th days. "They were not kept with puritan respect for the Sabbath, if Sabbaths they really were." Only 2 contracts, however, were made on the 19th, and for one of these the date is doubtful (*idem, Assyrian Deeds and Documents*, London, 1901, ii, 40 *sq.*). Finally, out of 356 dated documents of the Hammurabi era, only 2 were dated on the 19th and only 26 on the four other "evil days" (*idem*, in *Expository Times*, 1906, xvii, 566 *sq.*). It would seem, accordingly, that at this earlier period (about 2000 B.C.) there was a sabbatic observance of all five days, and especially of the 19th day.

[2] *Shabbāthôn* occurs all together ten times in the Old Testament, where it is applied to New Year's Day, the Day of Atonement (above,

which has been found as yet only five or six times in Assyro-Babylonian documents, occurs in a lexicographical tablet containing the equation $shabbattu(m) = \hat{u}m\ n\hat{u}kh\ libbi$.[1] The accepted translation of the latter expression is "day of rest of (or for) the heart" (s.c., "of the angered gods"). Various scholars in England and Germany, intent on discovering Babylonian parallels for all Hebrew institutions, have therefore explained shabattum and its equivalent phrase by the five "evil days" found in the calendar already noticed. This identification was based on the observation that these seemed also to be penitential days, when by special observances the gods must be appeased and their anger averted. The Hebrew Sabbath would therefore represent an institution directly derived from the Babylonian regulations for the "evil days."[2]

Until recently, however, Assyriology has sounded no certain note concerning the etymology and significance of the term shabattum. Thus, Delitzsch holds

pp. 82 sq.), the first and eighth days of the Feast of Tabernacles, and also to the Sabbatical Year (Leviticus, xxv, 4) and to the Sabbath Day proper (Exodus, xvi, 23, xxxi, 15, xxxv, 2; Leviticus, xxiii, 3). Professor Morris Jastrow thinks that shabbāthôn is mistranslated as "solemn rest" and that in fact it is merely an adjectival formation meaning "sabbatical" or "Sabbath-like." The word "belongs to a period prior to the development of a Sabbath institution, celebrated every seventh day without any reference to the phases of the moon" (American Journal of Semitic Languages and Literatures, 1914, xxx, 97 n.[7]).

[1] Rawlinson, op. cit., ii, pl. 32, no. i, 16 a–b (Cuneiform Texts, pt. xviii, pl. 23, 17 [K. 4397]). The discovery of this important equation was made by W. H.

Boscawen; see A. H. Sayce, in Academy, 1875, viii, 555. Shabattu(m) here and elsewhere can be read shapattu(m), without, however, affecting the sense (P. Jensen, in Zeitschrift für Assyriologie, 1900, xiv, 182; H. Zimmern, in Schrader, Keilinschriften,[3] p. 592 n.[5]).

[2] A. H. Sayce, The Higher Criticism and the Verdict of the Monuments, London, 1895, p. 74; idem, The Religions of Ancient Egypt and Babylonia, Edinburgh, 1902, p. 476; F. Delitzsch, Babel and Bible, London, 1903, p. 41. The purely conjectural character of this procedure was long ago pointed out by Francis Brown in his article, "The Sabbath in the Cuneiform Records," Presbyterian Review, 1882, iii, 693. Compare also A. T. Clay, Amurru, Philadelphia, 1909, pp. 55 sqq.

that "the only meaning that may be justifiably assumed is "'ending (of work), cessation, keeping holiday from work.'"[1] As the result of linguistic analysis Hirschfeld concludes, on the contrary, that "the idea of resting for religious reasons after a certain spell of working days is far too complicated to be the original meaning of a primitive root."[2] Jastrow, again, points out that *ûm nûkh libbi*, with which *shabattum* has been equated, was a standing expression for the pacification of a deity's anger. It occurs frequently in Babylonian religious literature, where it is more particularly used in hymns addressed by penitentials to some god who has shown his ill-will toward them. *Shabattum* implies, therefore, a day of propitiation, and the idea of rest involved refers to gods and not to men — a refraining from or cessation of divine anger.[3] Zimmern suggests that *shabattum* may be derived from the verb *shabâtu*, with the sense of "discontinue" or "desist," applied to the anger of the gods.[4] Pinches, on the contrary, believes that the word comes from the Sumerian *shabat*, which probably had no connection with the Semitic verb *shabâtu*.[5] Nielsen goes still further afield for a satisfactory explanation, and considers *shabat* a term taken over from the Arabic *thabat*, from a root meaning "rest," applied to the lunar phases.[6] As the outcome of extensive philological study Hehn argues that *shabattum* meant originally "fulness," "completeness," the notion of rest being

---

[1] *Babel and Bible*, p. 99.

[2] H. Hirschfeld, "Remarks on the Etymology of Sabbāth," *Journal of the Royal Asiatic Society*, 1896, n.s., xxviii, 357.

[3] M. Jastrow, "The Original Character of the Hebrew Sabbath," *American Journal of Theology*, 1898, ii, 316 *sq.*, 351; compare idem, *Hebrew and Babylonian Traditions*, New York, 1914, pp. 134, 149.

[4] H. Zimmern, in Schrader, *Keilinschriften*,[3] p. 593. In one cuneiform list (Rawlinson, *op. cit.*, v, pl. 28, l. e–f) the verb *shabâtu* is equated with *gamâru*, which is thought to mean "be complete," "be full," "cease," though in some other syllabaries it apparently has the sense of "pacify." In the light of the meaning now assigned to *shabattum* both translations appear to be intelligible and harmonious.

[5] T. G. Pinches, *The Old Testament*, London, 1902, p. 327.

[6] D. Nielsen, *Die altarabische Mondreligion*, pp. 87 *sq.*

later and entirely secondary.[1] Still another interpretation makes *shabattum* equivalent to "day of lament."[2] Finally, in a brief, though highly suggestive study, Professor Toy holds that the root idea in the Babylonian expression was that of abstinence, though *shabattum* might also have been regarded as a day of propitiation because of the restrictions attached to it.[3]

These conflicting interpretations scarcely made for confidence in the results of a purely philological analysis. Recent discoveries, however, have thrown new light on the problem. A lexicographical tablet from the library of the Assyrian king Asshurbanipal gives the names attached to several days of the Babylonian month; and among these is the designation *shabattum*, applied to the fifteenth day.[4] Still more recently a similar use of *shabattum* has been found in a text which contains an account of the moon's course during the month. Reference is here made to the first appearance of the new moon, its ash-grey light until about the seventh day thereafter, its opposition with the sun on the fourteenth day, its aspects on the twenty-first, twenty-eighth, and twenty-ninth days, and finally its disappearance on the thirtieth day, being the time of

---

[1] J. Hehn, *Siebenzahl und Sabbat*, p. 98.

[2] S. Langdon, "The Derivation of *Sabattu* and Other Notes," *Zeitschrift der deutschen morgenländischen Gesellschaft*, 1908, lxii, 30.

[3] C. H. Toy, "The Earliest Form of the Hebrew Sabbath," *Journal of Biblical Literature*, 1899, xviii, 190 *sqq.*; compare *idem*, *Introduction to the History of Religions*, Boston, 1913, p. 251.

[4] The text (K. 6012 + K. 10,684) forms a part of the British Museum collection of cuneiform tablets. A portion of the text was published by Rawlinson (*op. cit.*, iii, pl. 56, no. 4) and additions to it, as well as duplicate Babylonian fragments, were subsequently identified by Dr. Pinches, to whom, accordingly, full credit for this important discovery should be ascribed. See T. G. Pinches, "*Sapattu*, the Babylonian Sabbath," *Proceedings of the Society of Biblical Archæology*, 1904, xxvi, 51–56. H. Zimmern, however, had previously pointed out that, according to the Rawlinson text, the fifteenth day of a thirty-day month might have borne the designation *shabattum* (Zimmern, in Schrader, *Keilinschriften*,[3] p. 593 *n.*[1]); compare his comments on Pinches's discoveries (*Zeitschrift der deutschen morgenländischen Gesellschaft*, 1904, lviii, 199–202, 458–460).

conjunction with the sun. In this description, which for minuteness recalls the Polynesian naming of the nights from successive aspects of the moon,[1] the fifteenth day again appears as *shabattum*.[2]

It is clear that the Babylonians recognized, with many other peoples, the two most prominent stages of the lunation, new moon and full moon, and described them by particular names, *nannaru* and *shabattum*. Evidence exists, moreover, showing that these two days from very early times were observed as festivals, particularly in the cities of Ur and Harran. Here were the chief seats of the cult of Sin, the moon-god, always one of the most important members of the Babylonian pantheon and anciently enjoying precedence over Shamash, the sun-god.[3] Certain cuneiform tablets, all written down during the time of the Fourth Dynasty of Ur and dating, therefore, from the third millennium B.C., distinctly refer to sacrifices which were made to the divine kings of Ur on the new-moon day and on the fifteenth of the month.[4] At Harran, where

[1] Above, p. 181 n.[7]

[2] The text (K. 2164 + 2195 + 3510) has been edited with a translation and commentary by E. Weidner, "Zur babylonischen Astronomie," *Babyloniaca*, 1911, vi, 8 *sqq.* It should be observed that it belongs to the same series as the text (K. 170) in which the fifteenth day is expressly described as the day of full moon (above, p. 229). Professor A. H. Sayce has published a table of lunar longitudes (K. 490) which shows how many degrees the moon advances during the first fifteen days of the month and how many degrees it retrogrades during the second half of the month (*Zeitschrift für Assyriologie*, 1887, ii, 337–340).

[3] Combe, *Histoire du culte de Sin*, pp. 46 *sqq.*, 86 *sq.*; Jastrow, *Religion Babyloniens und Assyriens*, i, 66 *sq.*, 72 *sqq.*

[4] H. Radau, *Early Babylonian History*, New York, 1900, pp. 314 *sq.* The text on the statue of Gudea, a chief, or *patesi*, of Lagash (c. 2350 B.C.), bears record of a rest day which has been interpreted as a full-moon day, therefore as a *shabattum:* "No one was struck with the whip, the mother corrected not her child, the householder, the overseer, the labourer . . . the work of their hands ceased. In the graves of the city . . . no corpse was buried. The Kalû played no psalm, uttered no dirge, the wailing women let no dirge be heard. In the realm of Lagash no man who had a lawsuit went to the hall of justice." See A. Jeremias, *The Old Testament in the Light of the Ancient East*, London, 1911, i, 203; compare H. Winckler, *Religionsgeschichtlicher und geschichtlicher Orient*, Leipzig,

the cult of Sin continued to flourish under the Roman
Empire and into the early Middle Ages, four sacri-
ficial days were observed every month, and of these
at least two were determined by the conjunction and
opposition of the moon.[1] Outside the Babylonian
cultural area, but within the general field of Semitic
religion, there is also the interesting evidence yielded
by the inscription of Narnaka, which indicates that as
late as the time of the Ptolemies new moon and full
moon were the chief periods of sacrifice observed by
the Phœnicians.[2]

The choice of the fifteenth day as the *shabbatum* was
obviously determined by the length of the Babylonian
month, which in the earlier period was regularly taken
at thirty days' duration. We have seen, however,
that, where lunar reckonings are employed and the
month begins at sunset with the visible new moon,
the fourteenth day more commonly coincides with
the full of the moon.[3] *Shabattum* being the technical
expression for the fifteenth day as the time of full
moon, it is only reasonable to conclude that, if not the
name, at any rate the observances belonging to this

1906, p. 61. Professor Morris
Jastrow holds, however, that this
passage from the inscription of
Gudea has no reference to the full
moon (*American Journal of Semitic
Languages and Literatures*, 1914,
xxx, 98 n.⁹).

[1] D. Chwolsohn, *Die Ssabier
und der Ssabismus*, St. Petersburg,
1856, ii, 8, 94 *sqq.*, translating the
Fihrist (ix, 1, 5) of Ibn al-Nadīm.
On the Harranians see in general
D. S. Margoliouth, in Hastings's
Encyclopædia of Religion and Ethics,
vi, 519 *sq.* It is curious to find a
Moslem tradition, current about
830 A.D., that "Abraham lived with
his people four-score years and
ten in the land of Harran, worshipping none other than Al Ozza, an
idol famous in that land and adored
by the men of Harran, under the

name of the Moon, which same
custom prevails among them to the
present day" (Sir William Muir,
The Apology of Al Kindy, London,
1887, p. 17).

[2] W. F. von Landau, *Beiträge
zur Altertumskunde des Orients*,
Leipzig, 1899, ii, 46 *sq.*; compare
idem, Die phönizischen Inschriften,
Leipzig, 1907, p. 22 (*Der alte
Orient*, viii, 3).

[3] Above, p. 182 n.⁷ There are
numerous reports by Babylonian
astrologers according to which
any one of five days, from the
twelfth to the sixteenth of the
month, might be taken as the
exact time when the moon became
full, depending, of course, upon how
early or how late was the visible
new moon (Kugler, *Sternkunde und
Sterndienst in Babel*, ii, 14 *sq.*).

day would be often transferred to the fourteenth of the month, or to any other day on which the moon became full. No other hypothesis will explain the outstanding fact that *shabattum* was equated with *ûm nûkh libbi* as a day for appeasing the anger of the deity. And if for practical purposes the fourteenth day might be a *shabattum*, it is not difficult to assume that this was also the case with the days (seventh, twenty-first, and twenty-eighth, perhaps, also, the nineteenth), which marked other characteristic stages of the lunation. In the developed Babylonian cult all these were "evil days," when the gods must be propitiated and conciliated. In the primitive faith of Semitic peoples they were occasions observed with superstitious concern as times of fasting, cessation of activity, and other forms of abstinence.[1]

[1] The Rev. C. H. C. Johns has pointed out that in Babylonian calendars many days are indicated as *sabattu*, a term signifying rest, pause, and especially a god's connubial rest with his consort goddess. "The observance of such days was a bar to attending even to important diplomatic business or setting out on a journey. . . ." It is quite possible that *shabattum* and *sabattum* are from the same root and originally denoted much the same thing — a pause, abstention, from whatever cause or for ceremonial purposes" (*Encyclopædia Britannica*,[11] xxiii, 961 *sq.*). A calendar of the intercalary month of Elul cites the 3d, 7th, and 16th days as the *sabattu* of Marduk and his consort Sarpanit (Lagrange, *op. cit.*, p. 284 n.[6]; Schrader, *Keilinschriften*,[3] p. 371).

CHAPTER VIII

THE HEBREW SABBATH

THE earliest Biblical references to the Sabbath all
indicate that the institution had long been found
among the Hebrews. It appears in the most ancient
documents of the Law, such as the two Decalogues,[1]
the old "Ritual Code," and the nearly related "Book
of the Covenant."[2] It is mentioned in the "Books
of Kings" during the time of the prophet Elisha.[3]
It is noticed in the prophecies of Amos and Hosea.[4]
The antiquity of the Sabbath is further indicated
by the fact that Hebrew tradition preserved no certain
information of its origin. From the Old Testament
we cannot tell whether the Sabbath was hallowed in
remembrance of Jehovah's rest after the Creation,[5]
or whether it was instituted as a memorial of the escape
of the Hebrews from Egypt.[6] Assuming, with most
reputable critics, that the narrative in the first chapter
of Genesis, which divides the work of creation into six
days, is comparatively late, it follows that the Sabbath

[1] The form of the Fourth Commandment in the First Decalogue
(*Exodus*, xx, 8), "Remember the
Sabbath Day, to keep it holy,"
indicates not the institution of a
new day but the sanctioning of an
old one. In the Second Decalogue (*Deuteronomy*, v, 12), the
commandment reads: "Observe
the Sabbath Day, to keep it holy."
The word "holy" in these injunctions has the force of "set
apart ritually," "separated from
common use," *i.e.*, taboo.

[2] *Exodus*, xxxiv, 21, xxiii, 12.

[3] *2 Kings*, iv, 23. This is perhaps the earliest historical reference
to the Sabbath.

[4] *Amos*, viii, 5; *Hosea*, ii, 11.

[5] *Genesis*, ii, 2-3; *Exodus*, xx,
11.

[6] *Deuteronomy*, v, 15; compare
Nehemiah, ix, 14; *Ezekiel*, xx, 12.
The principal Old Testament references to the Sabbath have been
grouped in their assumed historical order by E. G. King, "The
Sabbath in the Light of the Higher
Criticism," *Expository Times*, 1906,
xvii, 438-443.

242

could not have been founded as a reminiscence of the completion of the Creation. The author must have been familiar with the institution of a seven-day week ending in a Sabbath. Its chief characteristic was then that of a day of rest, as appears from the fact that, without mentioning the Sabbath by name, he seeks to glorify it by placing the hallowed character of the seventh day at the beginning of the world. The sanctity of the seventh day is in reality antedated, and the priestly writer wished to adjust artificially the work of creation to it.[1]

An old and still common theory derives the Sabbath institution from the worship of Saturn, after which planet the first day of the astrological week received its designation.[2] The theory is untenable for more than one reason. In the first place the Hebrews did not name their weekdays after the planets, but indicated them by ordinal numbers. In the second place Saturn's Day began the planetary week, while the Jewish Sabbath was regarded as the last day of the seven, a suitable position for a rest day. And in the third place neither the Hebrews nor any other Oriental people ever worshipped the planet Saturn as god and observed his day as a festival. It is true that, besides Venus, another planet familiar to the Hebrews may be recognized in the Old Testament under the

---

[1] M. Jastrow, "The Original Character of the Hebrew Sabbath," *American Journal of Theology*, 1898, ii, 313 *sq.*; S. R. Driver, *The Book of Genesis*,⁵ London, 1906, p. 35. Canon Cheyne suggests that the priestly writer in *Genesis*, ii, 2 *sqq.* appears to accept the anthropomorphic view which finds such frequent expression in Oriental antiquity. Things on earth correspond to things in heaven; if God "rested" on the seventh day, man ought to do likewise (*Traditions and Beliefs of Ancient Israel*, London, 1907, p. 70). Later Hebrew writers carry this idea of correspondence so far as to require the angels to observe all the Jewish festivals (H. P. Smith, *The Religion of Israel*, New York, 1914, p. 229).

[2] F. Baur, "Der hebräische Sabbat und die Nationalfeste des mosaischen Cultus," *Tübinger Zeitschrift für Theologie*, 1832, iii, 145 *sqq.*; A Kuenen, *The Religion of Israel*, London, 1873, i, 262 *sqq.*; Paul de Lagarde, editor, *Psalterium iuxta Hebræos Hieronymi*, Leipzig, 1874, 158 *sqq.*

name Kewan, the Assyrian designation of Saturn.[1]
This name appears in a passage of Amos, where the
prophet has been supposed to be referring to an early
worship of Saturn by the Israelites during the period
of their sojourn in the Wilderness.[2] But a single Old
Testament text, both corrupt and obscure, can scarcely
be cited as proving that Saturn was ever recognized
by the Israelites as a distinct god. If it be held
that Amos had in mind the Hebrews of his own time,
the passage in question can only refer to the adoption
by them of astrological notions derived from Babylonia. These imported superstitions eventually led
Jewish rabbis to call Saturn *Shabbti*, "the star of the
Sabbath," which, however, is not a naming of the day
after the planet, but a naming of the planet after the
day. It was not until the first century of our era, when
the planetary week had become an established institution, that the Jewish Sabbath seems always to have
corresponded to Saturn's Day.[3]

The association of the Sabbath Day with Saturday
was probably one reason why Saturn, a planet in Babylonian astrological schemes regarded as beneficent
rather than malefic, should have come to assume in
late classical times the rôle of an unlucky star (*sidus
tristissimum, stella iniquissima*). The oldest reference to Saturday is found in a verse by the poet Tibul-

[1] Schiaparelli, *Astronomy in the Old Testament*, pp. 48 sq.; P. Jensen, "Astronomy," *Jewish Encyclopedia*, ii, 246.

[2] *Amos*, v, 26; W. R. Harper, *A Critical and Exegetical Commentary on Amos and Hosea*, New York, 1905, pp. 137 sqq.; K. Budde, *The Religion of Israel to the Exile*, New York, 1899, pp. 67 sqq.

[3] J. Fürst, *Kultur- und Literaturgeschichte der Juden in Asien*, Leipzig, 1849, pt. i, 40; W. Nowack, *Lehrbuch der hebräischen Archäologie*, Strassburg, 1894, ii, 142 sq.; E. Schürer, in *Zeitschrift*

für neutestamentliche Wissenschaft, 1905, vi, 6 sq., 19. There is a Talmudic story which tells how Moses, having arranged with Pharaoh for a day of rest to be observed by the Hebrews in Egypt, was asked what day he thought most suitable for the purpose. Moses answered, "The seventh day, sacred to Saturn; work done upon this day never prospers" (Jeremias, *The Old Testament in the Light of the Ancient East*, i, 202; Delitzsch, *Babel and Bible*, p. 102).

lus (d. 19 B.C.), who apparently identifies Saturn's Day with the supposed inauspicious Jewish Sabbath, when he gives as one of his excuses for not quitting Rome the bad omens which detained him "on the sacred day of Saturn."[1] Ovid mentions "foreign Sabbaths" along with the anniversary of the day of the battle of the Allia — *dies Alliensis* — as unlucky occasions.[2] Frontinus, a Roman military officer and tactician (d. about 103 A.D.), says that Vespasian defeated the Jews by attacking them on Saturn's Day, when it was unlawful for them to do anything. Dio Cassius also speaks of the Jews having dedicated to their god the day called the day of Saturn, "on which, among many other most peculiar actions, they undertake no serious occupation."[3]

The Hebrews manifested so little originality in cultural matters and borrowed so heavily from their neighbours that it becomes a natural inquiry whether the Sabbath, with the seven-day week, may not have arisen outside of Israel. Writing in the seventeenth century the learned 'John Spencer argued that Egypt was the original home of the institution, since in various Old Testament passages the Sabbath is declared to have been established to commemorate the exodus from Egypt.[4] But the Egyptians, as we have seen, divided their months into decades, and no evidence exists

---

[1] *Saturni aut sacram me tenuisse diem* (*Elegiæ*, i, 3, 18).

[2] Ovid, *Remedium amoris*, 220; compare *idem*, *Ars amatoria*, i, 415-416; Horace, *Satiræ*, i, 9, 69-70; Persius, *Satiræ*, v, 184.

[3] Frontinus, *Strategematica*, ii, 1, 17; Dio Cassius, *Historia Romana*, xxxvii, 17. Tacitus (*Historiæ*, v, 4) thinks that the Jewish Sabbath may be an observance in honour of Saturn, though he gives an alternative explanation, connecting the day with the escape from Egyptian bondage. For other evidence from classical writers see P. Lejay, "Le sabbat juif et les poètes latins," *Revue d'histoire et de littérature religieuses*, 1903, viii, 305-335; T. Reinach, *Textes d'auteurs grecs et romains relatifs au judaïsme*, Paris, 1895, pp. 104, 243, 266, 287; M. Wolff, "Het oordeel der hellenensch-romeinsche schrijvers over oorsprong, naam, en viering van der Sabbat," *Theologisch Tijdschrift*, 1910, xliv, 162-172.

[4] J. Spencer, *De legibus Hebraeorum ritualibus et earum rationibus*, Cambridge, 1727, i, 67 sqq. (bk. i, ch. v, sect. viii).

that they ever employed for civil purposes any shorter division of the month.[1] A second hypothesis, which makes the week and the Sabbath a direct importation from Babylonia, is likewise without warrant in the light of existing information.[2] The same may be said of the theory that the Sabbath was first taken over from Babylonia by the agricultural inhabitants of Canaan, from whom, in turn, the Israelites borrowed an institution which would have no meaning to a nomadic people.[3] But the opinion, so frequently expressed, that the Sabbath cannot be very primitive, since it "presupposes agriculture and a tolerably hard-pressed working-day life," [4] betrays an imperfect acquaintance with popular superstition. The brief prohibitions of work found in the Pentateuch cannot be separated, by any subtleties of exegesis, from the numerous other taboos with which the institution was invested. The rest on the Sabbath is only one of the forms of abstinence in connection with lunar changes; and, if the Sabbath began as a festival at new moon and full moon, it may well have been observed by the Israelites before their contact with Canaanitish culture. The ancient dwellers in the Arabian wilderness, who celebrated new moon and full moon as seasons of abstinence and rest, little dreamed that in their senseless custom lay the roots of a social institution, which, on the whole, has contributed to human welfare in past ages and promises an even greater measure of benefit to humanity in all future times.

To a shepherd people in tropical or semi-tropical lands the moon appears as a gentle guardian, bringing

[1] Above, p. 191.

[2] Below, pp. 253 sq.

[3] Nowack, op. cit., ii, 144; R. Smend, Lehrbuch der alttestamentlichen Religionsgeschichte, Freiburg-i.-B., 1899, pp. 160 sq.; A. F. von Gall, "Die alttestamentliche Wissenschaft und die keilinschriftliche Forschung," Archiv für Religionswissenschaft, 1902, v, 321.

[4] J. Wellhausen, Prolegomena zur Geschichte Israels,⁶ Berlin, 1905, p. 109; W. E. Addis, Documents of the Hexateuch, London, 1892, i, 139; idem, Hebrew Religion to the Establishment of Judaism under Ezra, London, 1906, p. 85.

restful coolness after the day with its withering heat, and dispelling with her kindly beams the thick darkness which may cloak a lurking foe. "This," writes an intrepid traveller, "is the planet of way for the wayfaring Semitic race. The moon is indeed a watchlight of the night in the nomad wilderness; they are glad in her shining upon the great upland, they may sleep then in some assurance from their enemies." [1] To the Israelites, as to the ancient Egyptians, the moon was preëminently the "wanderer," by whose movements the earliest calendars were framed. [2] One of the Hebrew names for "month" is *yérah*, from *yāréah*, "moon"; it is called, also *hodesh*, which means new moon. One of the most magnificent of the *Psalms* declares that Jehovah "appointed the moon for the seasons"; [3] all the Jewish festivals were determined by the moon. At the same time there is no Biblical testimony to indicate that the Israelites ever conceived of the moon as a divinity and addressed to that luminary specific acts of worship. It was only toward the end of the Hebrew monarchy, when the Chosen People were giving themselves over to astrology, divination, and the worship of the heavenly bodies,

[1] C. M. Doughty, *Travels in Arabia Deserta*, Cambridge, 1888, i, 366.

[2] The Hebrew lunisolar year consisted of twelve months, adjusted to the solar year by the intercalation of a thirteenth month. The name of the latter is first met in the *Mishna*, where it is styled the "second Adar." The months consisted of 29 days (hence called "defective" months), or of 30 days ("full" months), but there seems to have been no uniform sequence of long and short months. The regulation of the month was probably at first in the hands of the priests and later was committed to the Sanhedrin. A solar year of 364 days, i.e., 52 complete weeks, is found in two pseudographia which date probably from Maccabæan times (*Book of Enoch* and *Book of Jubilees*), but it is hardly likely that solar reckonings were then in general use. On this subject consult S. Poznański, "Calendar (Jewish)," in Hastings's *Encyclopædia of Religion and Ethics*, iii, 117 *sqq.*

[3] *Psalms*, civ, 19. Compare *Ecclesiasticus*, xliii, 6–8: "He made the moon also to serve in her season for a declaration of times, and a sign of the world. From the moon is the sign of feasts, a light that decreaseth in her perfection. The month is called after her name, increasing wonderfully in her changing."

that clear evidence of a moon-cult appears in the Old
Testament, where it encounters the denunciation of the
prophets, the prohibitions of the Law, and the repres-
sive measures of a reforming king.[1]

The evidence is quite conclusive that of the lunar
phases it was especially the new moon and the full
moon which first aroused the attention of the Semitic
nomads and evoked feelings of delight and veneration.
Even to-day "the first appearing of the virgin moon is
always greeted with a religious emotion in the deserts
of Arabia."[2] When the Bedouin and Fellahin of
modern Palestine first see the lunar crescent they
exclaim, "God's new moon has appeared in his exalted-
ness. May it be for us a blessed new moon."[3] Modern Jewish ritual prescribes a special service for the
new-moon day, including the recital of psalms of joy.
So familiar an expression as Hallelujah, "praise Jehovah" (Jahweh), is a verbal form of the onomatopoetic
stem hilâl, meaning "new moon," "crescent," with the
addition of the divine name.[4] The Hebrew month,
as among other peoples who count by lunations, began
when the silvery crescent was first discerned in the
evening twilight. In later Judaism, as soon as the
moon's appearance was proved by credible witnesses
before the Sanhedrin at Jerusalem, the feast of the new

[1] Jeremiah, viii, 2; Zephaniah,
i, 5; Deuteronomy, xvii, 3; 2 Kings,
xxiii, 5; G. W. Gilmore, "Moon,"
New Schaff-Herzog Encyclopædia of
Religious Knowledge, vii, 493.
That no trace of the cult of Sin,
the Babylonian moon-god, is discoverable in the Old Testament,
even in the name Sinai, is the
opinion of the latest investigator
of this subject. See E. Combe,
Histoire du culte de Sin, Paris, 1908,
pp. 157 sqq. The custom of kiss-
ing the hand to the moon (Job,
xxxi, 26 sq.) may have meant to the
Hebrews little more than it does
to us. Orthodox Jewish mothers
are said still to teach their sons
to take off their caps to the new
moon.
[2] Doughty, op. cit., ii, 305 sq.;
compare D. Nielsen, Die altarabische Mondreligion und die
mosaische Überlieferung, Strassburg,
1904, p. 50. For the Abyssinian customs see E. Littmann, in Archiv für
Religionswissenschaft, 1908, xi, 313 sq.
[3] Mrs. H. H. Spoer, in Folk-
lore, 1910, xxi, 289.
[4] M. Jastrow, Aspects of Religious Belief and Practice in Babylonia and Assyria, New York, 1911,
pp. 214 n.³, 336 n.³; F. Hommel,
Der Gestirndienst der alten Araber
und die altisraelitische Überlieferung,
Munich, 1901, p. 28.

moon was held, and messengers were sent abroad to announce the opening of the new month. The celebration of the festival would seem, at least occasionally, to have lasted two days, an arrangement obviously dictated by the inability to determine beforehand on which of two successive days the moon might be expected to appear.[1]

The new-moon festival was considered an exceptional solemnity as early as the time of Saul. The twentieth chapter of the *First Book of Samuel* records a conversation between David and Jonathan in which the former says, "Behold, to-morrow is the new moon, and I should not fail to sit at meat with the king." It appears from this chapter that the first two days of the month were marked by feasts at which all members of the household were expected to be present, unless prevented by some ceremonial uncleanness.[2] The occasion was also observed by compulsory abstinence from all servile work.[3] In the time of Elisha the new

[1] I *Samuel*, xx, 27-28; compare *Judith*, viii, 6. On the new-moon festival see Nowack, *op. cit.*, ii, 138 *sqq.*; Wellhausen, *op. cit.*, pp. 107 *sqq.*; I. Benzinger, *Hebräische Archäologie*,[2] Tübingen, 1907, pp. 388 *sq.*; G. Förster, "Die Neumondfeier im Alten Testament," *Zeitschrift für wissenschaftliche Theologie*, 1906, xlix, 1-17; B. Stade, *Biblische Theologie des Alten Testaments*, Tübingen, 1905, i, 176 *sqq.*; A. Dillmann, *Die Bücher Exodus und Leviticus*,[3] edited by V. Ryssel, Leipzig, 1897, pp. 634 *seq.* See also "New Moon" in Hastings's *Dictionary of the Bible*, *Jewish Encyclopedia*, and *Encyclopædia Biblica*.

[2] I *Samuel*, xx, 5-6, 24-29.

[3] *Ibid.*, xx, 18-19. In verse 19 the Hebrew expression *beyom hama 'aseh*, rendered in the Authorized Version (margin) "in the day of the business," appears in the Greek Septuagint, the Latin Vulgate, and the Jewish Aramaic Targum as the designation of a working day, in distinction from the festival day of the new moon. The Douai version of the Scriptures translates accordingly, "in the day when it is lawful to work." Professor H. P. Smith holds that, owing to the corruption of the text, the particular day here intended is no longer intelligible (*A Critical and Exegetical Commentary on the Books of Samuel*, New York, 1899, pp. 190 *sq.*). He has, however, overlooked the fact, that, as my friend and pupil Rabbi Jacob Singer points out to me, the same expression *sheset yeme hama 'aseh* is found in *Ezekiel* (xlvi, 1) as the designation of "the six working days" of the week; see Brown, Driver, and Briggs, *A Hebrew and English Lexicon of the Old Testament*, Boston, 1906, p. 795.

moon seems to have been one of the favourite occasions for consulting the prophets, a circumstance which could be explained if the day were marked by a cessation of the usual occupations.[1]   There are other reasons, presently to be given, for believing that until the Exile, or later, the new moon was a general rest day; and such it still remains for Jewish women, whose conservative instincts have thus preserved a memorial of its ancient observance.[2]

Full moon, as well as new moon, enjoyed a religious significance to the early Hebrews. Two great agricultural festivals, one marking the commencement of the barley harvest, the other, the close of the fruit harvest, must have been celebrated at about the time of full moon, for, when the sacred calendar was framed in post-Exilic times, they were definitely fixed at the middle of the month.[3]   The Passover, observed on the fourteenth day of the first month (Nisan), was followed on the fifteenth day by the Feast of Unleavened Bread, occupying seven days.[4]   The Feast of Tabernacles began on the fifteenth of the seventh month (Tishri) and likewise continued for seven days.[5]

[1] 2 *Kings*, iv, 23. Some Biblical references indicate that on the first day of the month the prophets were supposed to be most under the influence of their divine afflatus; compare *Ezekiel*, xxvi, 1, xxix, 17, xxxi, 1, xxxii, 1; *Haggai*, i, 1.

[2] John Allen, *Modern Judaism*, London, 1830, pp. 390 *sq.*; H. G. F. Löwe, *Schulchan Aruch, oder die vier jüdischen Gesetzbücher*, Vienna, 1896, i, 91; M. Friedmann, in *Jewish Quarterly Review*, 1891, iii, 712; Israel Abrahams, *Jewish Life in the Middle Ages*, London, 1896, p. 374.

[3] That the Old Testament thus contains indirect evidence of the celebration of full-moon day by the early Hebrews was long ago recognized by the learned commentator, August Dillmann. "Von einer Feier des Vollmondes zeigt sich bei den Israeliten keine Spur. . . . Jedoch war er dadurch bevorzugt, dass an ihm das grosse Frühlings- und Herbstfest begann" (*Die Bücher Exodus und Leviticus*,[2] p. 635). A passage in one of the *Psalms* (lxxxi, 3): "Blow the trumpet at the new moon, at the full moon, on our feast-day," probably refers to new moon in the seventh month, or New Year's Day (*Leviticus*, xxiii, 24), and to the first day of the Feast of Tabernacles, which began on the fifteenth of the same month (*ibid.*, xxiii, 39).

[4] *Leviticus*, xxiii, 5–6; *Exodus*, xii, 6 *sqq.*; *Numbers*, xxviii, 16–17.

[5] *Leviticus*, xxiii, 33–36, 39; *Numbers*, xxix, 12.

The religious importance of these two festivals is indicated by the injunction to keep the first and last days of the Feast of Unleavened Bread as times of "holy convocation," when no "servile work" might be done,[1] and by the significant expression *shabbāthôn* ("solemn rest"), which is used in reference to the beginning and end of the Feast of Tabernacles, that is, to the fifteenth and twenty-second of the month Tishri.[2] Furthermore, the Pentateuchal codes contain a passage, the meaning of which was in dispute several centuries before the Christian era, where the word "Sabbath" appears to be used in a sense precisely the same as that of the Babylonian *shabattum*, referring to the fifteenth day of the month. In the twenty-third chapter of *Leviticus* it is prescribed that on "the morrow after the Sabbath" the sheaf of the first-fruits of the harvest is to be brought to the priest, who shall wave it before Jehovah, and that, counting from "the morrow after the Sabbath," fifty days are to elapse before the commencement of the Feast of Weeks.[3] As Professor Jastrow has clearly shown, the word "Sabbath" is here used, not in its later sense of a seventh day of rest, but as a survival of the old designation of the Sabbath as the full-moon day. "The two references in *Leviticus* stand out as solitary signposts of an abandoned road."[4]

In some of the older parts of the Bible, and especially in the earlier prophetical compositions, the new moon and the Sabbath are repeatedly mentioned together. In the pathetic narrative which describes how the Shunammite woman went to seek Elisha that the prophet might restore her son to life, her husband asks, "'Wherefore wilt thou go to him to-day? It is neither new moon nor Sabbath.'"[5] The prophet

---

[1] *Leviticus*, xxiii, 6–8; *Exodus*, xii, 16; *Numbers*, xxviii, 18, 25.
[2] *Leviticus*, xxiii, 39; *Numbers*, xxix, 12, 35.
[3] *Leviticus*, xxiii, 11, 15.
[4] M. Jastrow, "'The Day after the Sabbath,'" *American Journal of Semitic Languages and Literatures*, 1914, xxx, 104.
[5] *2 Kings*, iv, 23. This passage, incidentally, affords proof that at the time it was written the legal

Hosea, promising that the people's unfaithfulness shall be punished, cries out wrathfully, "I will also cause all her mirth to cease, her feasts, her new moons, and her Sabbaths, and all her solemn assemblies."[1] Amos rebukes the oppressors of his people "that would swallow up the needy, and cause the poor of the land to fail, saying 'When will the new moon be gone, that we may sell grain? and the Sabbath, that we may set forth wheat, making the ephah small and the shekel great?'"[2] Isaiah condemns the formalism of the ancient faith in striking words: "Bring no more vain oblations; incense is an abomination unto me; new moon and Sabbath, the calling of assemblies — I cannot bear iniquity with the solemn meeting."[3] Elsewhere, in the same work appears the prophecy: "And it shall come to pass, that from one new moon to another, and from one Sabbath to another, shall all flesh come to worship before me, saith Jehovah."[4]

This remarkable association of the Sabbath with the day of new moon had been previously noticed by such acute critics as Wellhausen and Robertson Smith, who were unable to offer a satisfactory solution of the problem thus presented.[5] When, however, the cuneiform records disclosed the fact that the Babylonian *shabattum* fell on the fifteenth (or fourteenth) day of the month and referred to the day of the full moon, it became clear that in these Biblical passages we have another survival of what must have been the primary meaning of the Hebrew term *shabbāth*.[6] As late, then, as the eighth

---

length of a "Sabbath Day's journey" had not been determined, for from Shunem to Elisha's abode on Carmel was a distance of some thirty to forty kilometres (R. Kittel, *Die Bücher der Könige*, Göttingen, 1900, p. 200).

[1] *Hosea*, ii, 13 (A. V. v. 11).
[2] *Amos*, viii, 4–5.
[3] *Isaiah*, i, 13.
[4] *Ibid.*, lxvi, 23; compare *Colossians*, ii, 16.

[5] Wellhausen, *Prolegomena*,[5] pp. 108 *sq.*; Smith, "Sabbath," *Encyclopædia Britannica*,[9] xxi, 126.
[6] This pregnant suggestion was first made by H. Zimmern in his comments on the discovery by T. G. Pinches (*Zeitschrift der deutschen morgenländischen Gesellschaft*, 1904, lvii, 202 and n.[1]). The hypothesis of the original identity of Sabbath and full-moon day was subsequently elaborated

century B.C., popular phraseology retained a lingering trace of the original collocation of the new-moon and full-moon days as festival occasions characterized by abstinence from secular activities. How long-lived were the old ideas is further illustrated by the provision in Ezekiel's reforming legislation that the inner eastern gate of the new Temple at Jerusalem should be shut during the six working days, but should be opened on the Sabbath and on the new-moon day for the religious assemblage of the people.[1] That the term *shabbāth*, the designation of the full-moon day, should have come to be applied to every seventh day of the month seems to be quite in accord with both Babylonian and Hebrew usage, which, as we have seen, led the month itself to be called after the new-moon day.[2]

The Hebrew seven-day week, ending with the Sabbath, presented so obvious a resemblance to the Babylonian septenary period, which closed with an "evil day," that scholars have felt themselves compelled to seek its origin in Babylonia. The two institutions, nevertheless, show important differences. The Babylonian cycle, as far as we know, was never employed as a chronological unit; the Hebrew week was a true civil week, a definite and well-understood period of time. The Babylonian cycle seems not to have been dissociated from the lunation;[3] the Hebrew week was a periodic week, running unfettered from month to

by J. Meinhold (*Sabbat und Woche im Alten Testament*, Göttingen, 1905), whose main conclusions have been accepted by K. Marti (*Religion of the Old Testament*, London, 1907, pp. 150 *sq.*) and T. K. Cheyne (*Traditions and Beliefs of Ancient Israel*, London, 1907, p. 69). See also E. Mahler, "Der Sabbat," *Zeitschrift der deutschen morgenländischen Gesellschaft*, 1908, lxii, 40, 46 *sq.*; M. Jastrow, *Hebrew and Babylonian*

Traditions, New York, 1914, pp. 154 *sqq.*, 185.
[1] *Ezekiel*, xlvi, 1–3.
[2] Above, pp. 226, 247. *Shabbāth* also appears several times in the Old Testament in the general sense of "week," the name of the principal weekday being used as the designation of the entire cycle of seven days. Compare *Leviticus*, xxiii, 15, xxv, 8.
[3] H. Zimmern, in E. Schrader, *Keilinschriften,*[3] p. 594; compare

month and from year to year. The Babylonian "evil day" was an unnamed unlucky day, observed by the king, by priests, and by physicians, but not certainly by the people at large; the Hebrew Sabbath was a named holy day, dedicated to the worship of the national god and kept by the entire community as a festival. These real divergencies make it certain that the Hebrew week and Sabbath, in the form in which we know them, could not have been taken over without change from Babylonia. The celebration of new-moon and full-moon festivals, which both Babylonians and Hebrews appear to have derived from a common Semitic antiquity, underwent, in fact, a radically unlike evolution among the two kindred peoples. To dissever the week from the lunar month, to employ it as a recognized calendrical unit, and to fix upon one day of that week for the exercises of religion were momentous innovations, which, until evidence to the contrary is found, must be attributed to the Hebrew people alone.

In his able treatise Meinhold has argued that until the age of Ezekiel the Hebrews employed no weeks at all. He then supposes that continuous seven-day weeks were introduced, largely through Ezekiel's reforming influence, and hence that the Sabbath as the last day of the periodic week was a post-Exilic institution.[1] Critics have pointed out that it is highly improbable that so far-reaching a change should have occurred without being recorded; moreover, that the acceptance of such a hypothesis makes it necessary to assume that all places in the Old Testament where the Sabbath is mentioned as the seventh day are either of Ezekiel's time or later. But the problem is simplified if we hold that the Hebrews employed lunar seven-day weeks, perhaps for several centuries preced-

A. H. McNeile, *The Book of Exodus,* London, 1908, p. 122.

[1] Johannes Meinhold, *Sabbat und Woche im Alten Testament,* Göttingen, 1905, pp. 10 *sqq.;* compare *idem,* "Die Entstehung des Sabbats," *Zeitschrift für die alttestamentliche Wissenschaft,* 1909, xxix, 81–112.

ing the Exile; weeks, that is, which ended with special observances on the seventh day but none the less were tied to the moon's course. The change from such cycles to those unconnected with the lunation would not have involved so abrupt and sudden a departure from the previous system of time reckoning as that from a bipartite division of the lunar month to a week which ran continuously through the months and the years.[1]

The establishment of a periodic week ending in a Sabbath observed every seventh day was doubtless responsible for the gradual obsolescence of the new-moon festival as a period of general abstinence, since with continuous weeks the new-moon day and the Sabbath Day would from time to time coincide. This seems to be a more natural explanation than that which regards the complete ignoring of the new-moon festival in the "Book of the Covenant" and in the Deuteronomic legislation as a deliberate act, designed to wean the people away from an observance to which heathenish superstitions were attached. The day of new moon never lost, indeed, its significance in Jewish ritual, for, when all the great festivals were definitely fixed to certain days, the new moon, as marking the beginning of the month, continued to hold a leading place in the sacred calendar. The Priestly Code prescribed special offerings for the new-moon day, and in Ezekiel's legislation the sacrifices marking it exceeded in importance those for the Sabbath.[2] The ancient character of this festival as a season of compulsory abstinence from labour survived in its observance as a

[1] The march of the Israelitish host around Jericho on seven successive days, one of which must have been the Sabbath, if that institution as a weekly rest day was then known to them, would have been a profanation of the Sabbath according to later ideas. See *Joshua*, vi, 4, 14-15; compare Tertullian, *Adversus Judæos*, 4.

But this account may contain a reminiscence of a period of Hebrew history when the week, either lunar or periodic, had not become established in Israel.

[2] *Numbers*, xxviii, 11-15; *Ezekiel*, xlvi, 4-6; compare 1 *Chronicles*, xxiii, 31; 2 *Chronicles*, ii, 4, viii, 13, xxxi, 3; *Ezra*, iii, · 5; *Nehemiah*, x, 33.

rest day by Jewish women, perhaps also in the provision
of the law of *Leviticus* that the first day of the seventh
month, beginning the new year, should be a "solemn
rest," "a memorial of blowing of trumpets, a holy
convocation." [1]

The Sabbath is described in the Pentateuchal codes
as an agricultural institution. It appears there as
a day of rest from farm labour, to be observed not
only by the householder and his family, but also by the
slaves, the cattle, and the stranger within the gates.
In what is generally considered the earlier form of the
Decalogue the keeping of the Sabbath is prescribed,
"that thy man-servant and thy maid-servant may rest
as well as thou"; or, as expressed in another passage,
"that thine ox and thine ass may have rest, and the son
of thine handmaid, and the sojourner may be re-
freshed." [2] From this commandment one might draw
the conclusion that in pre-Exilic times the Sabbath
enjoyed a purely humanitarian character as a season
of repose for man and beast. The omission of any
similar statement in the later form of the Decalogue,
where the prohibition of Sabbath labour is based
solely upon Jehovah's rest on the seventh day,[3] would
then be explained as the outcome of the priestly desire
to exalt the Sabbath as a religious festival at the ex-
pense of its more humane and social aspects. The
further requirement that even in the busiest seasons
of the year no plea of necessity might be accepted in
mitigation of the strict rule of Sabbath observance —
"in ploughing time and in harvest thou shalt rest" [4] —
also would be taken as evidence of the growing rigour
of ecclesiastical ordinances.

Properly considered, however, this priestly attitude
toward the Sabbath was not a radical departure but
rather an intensification of the austere significance
attached from the earliest times to the new-moon and

[1] *Leviticus*, xxiii, 24; compare
Numbers, xxix, 1; *Nehemiah*, viii,
2, 9-12. But see above, p. 82.
[2] *Deuteronomy*, v, 14; *Exodus*,
xxiii, 12. [3] *Exodus*, xx, 8-11.
[4] *Ibid.*, xxxiv, 21.

full-moon days. The Pentateuchal codes contain, in fact, a number of sabbatarian regulations which are meaningless, except when elucidated from the comparative standpoint as taboos. The rule requiring every one to remain indoors on the Sabbath: "Abide ye every man in his place, let no man go out of his place on the seventh day,"[1] is identical with the numerous rules which impose seclusion on tabooed or unlucky occasions, as a means of avoiding physical contact with supernatural and invisible powers of evil.

The prohibition: "Ye shall kindle no fire throughout your habitations upon the Sabbath Day,"[2] which in another passage[3] is amplified into the rule requiring all cooking to be done on the preceding day, may be first compared with the taboos observed by "the shepherd of great peoples" in Babylonia. On four "evil days" he was not to eat roasted meat or baked bread, and on the nineteenth day he might eat nothing which

---

[1] *Exodus*, xvi, 29. On this text Dositheus, the founder of an ascetic Samaritan sect, is said to have based the requirement that, in whatever habit, place, or posture the Sabbath found a man, in this he was to continue till the close of the sacred festival; if he was found sitting, he must sit still all the day, or, if reclining, he must lie down all the day (Origen, *De principiis*, iv, 1, 17). S. Reinach wittily compares the Dosithean injunction to the practice of various animals, which, when in danger and unable to flee, *fait le mort* ("Le sabbat hébraïque," *Cultes, mythes, et religions*, Paris, 1906-1912, ii, 444). For some mediæval stories illustrating the rule of absolute repose on the Sabbath, see R. Basset, "L'observation du sabbat," *Revue des traditions populaires*, 1893, viii, 250-254. [2] *Exodus*, xxxv, 3. [3] *Ibid.*, xvi, 23. The rules forbidding the lighting of fires and cooking on the Sabbath were very strictly observed by the Essenes (Josephus, *Bellum Judaicum*, ii, 8). In the *Mishna* (*Shabbāth*, iv, 1) the prohibition to bake and boil on the Sabbath is interpreted to mean that food may be kept hot on the Sabbath, provided its existing heat is not increased, which would be "boiling." Hence the food must be put only into such substances as would maintain but not increase the heat. The prohibition to kindle a fire on the Sabbath was naturally extended to one of extinguishing a fire, as well as lights and lamps (*ibid.*, xvi, 6). In mediæval times Rabbi Solomon ben Adret had a lock affixed to his stove, and kept the key over the Sabbath to prevent his too-considerate housemaid from lighting a fire on Saturdays (I. Abrahams, *Jewish Life in the Middle Ages*, London, 1896, p. 83). On the modern Jewish custom of kindling lights at the arrival and departure of the Sabbath see M. Friedmann,

s

had been touched by fire.[1] In a remarkable calendar of the unlucky days observed by the Egyptians we find an extensive series of regulations regarding the use of fire. On the fifth of the month of Athyr, fire might not be looked at and, if it went out, it might not be rekindled. On the eleventh of Tybi no one might approach a fire-place, for, said the scribe, on that day the god Ra had once burst into flame to devour his enemies, and the effects of his metamorphosis were felt on every anniversary of the day. These taboos, which reach back into a remote period of Egyptian history, are still found among the peasants of Thebes and the Saîd, who, on certain days of the year, refuse to kindle a fire, and on others avoid approaching the flame, even of a candle or a lamp, and the most timid do not smoke.[2] In Hawaii, as we have seen, during the four *tabu* seasons in each lunar month, "every fire and light was extinguished." The same regulation is attached to periods of abstinence elsewhere in the aboriginal world.[3]

Some of these taboos relating to fire may reflect primitive man's fear of a mysterious element which had not yet been completely tamed and harnessed to human use; but the fact that among various peoples all fires are put out after a death indicates a more probable origin of the prohibition in the fear of attracting evil spirits or influences. In Morocco, when a person has died in the morning, "no fire is made in the whole village until he is buried, and in some parts of the country the inmates of a house or tent where a death has occurred, abstain from making fire for two or three days."[4] Similar customs are found in Polynesia, Borneo, the East Indies, Burma, and various parts of

"The Sabbath Light," *Jewish Quarterly Review*, 1891, iii, 707–721.
[1] Above, p. 232 and n.[2]
[2] F. J. Chabas, *Le calendrier des jours fastes et néfastes de l'année égyptienne*, Chalon-s.-S., 1870, pp. 46, 68; Sir G. Maspero, *New Light on Ancient Egypt*,[3] London, 1909, pp. 130 sq.
[3] Above, pp. 9, 12, 15, 16, 20, 41, etc.
[4] E. Westermarck, *Origin and Development of the Moral Ideas*, ii, 305.

Africa; they were practised by Persians and Greeks in antiquity; and they still survive among the peasants of Calabria and the Scottish Highlanders.[1] It is hardly possible to urge that the putting-out of fires on such occasions is always a necessary result of the widespread custom of fasting after a death and until the corpse is buried; as a matter of fact we find that fires may be extinguished when there is no fasting, and also that the fast is often restricted to the daytime, when evil spirits, and in particular the ghost of the dead man, are presumed to be unable to see.

But, as Professor Westermarck has so ably shown, the widespread custom of fasting is itself often to be explained as due to the desire to prevent pollution.[2] Under certain circumstances to partake of food may cause defilement; hence fasting is only one of the numerous precautions necessary to avoid contamination. These ideas find expression in the rules which, like those prescribing the cessation of labour after a death, require mourners to abstain from eating food infected with the death pollution. Fasting may also be enjoined on other critical occasions, such as an eclipse of the sun or the moon, or during a thunderstorm; and we have seen that it characterizes some of the tabooed days previously considered.[3] Such well-established facts suggest that in the earliest period fasting may have also marked the Hebrew Sabbath.[4] This hypothesis seems first to have been advanced by the "judicious" Hooker, who observes that "it may be a question, whether in some sort they [the Jews] did not al-

---

[1] For a collection of the ethnographic evidence, see Sir J. G. Frazer, "On Certain Burial Customs as Illustrative of the Primitive Theory of the Soul," *Journal of the Anthropological Institute*, 1885, xv, 90; *idem, The Magic Art and the Evolution of Kings*, London, 1911, ii, 267 n.[4]; E. S. Hartland, "Death and Disposal of the Dead (Introductory and Primitive)," Hast-

ings's *Encyclopædia of Religion and Ethics*, iv, 439.

[2] E. Westermarck, "The Principles of Fasting," *Folk-lore*, 1908, xviii, 397 *sqq.; idem, Moral Ideas*, ii, 293 *sqq.*

[3] Above, pp. 15, 17, 39, 44, etc.

[4] Compare M. Jastrow, in *American Journal of Theology*, 1898, ii, 324 *sqq.;* Westermarck, *op. cit.*, ii, 310 *sq.*

ways fast on the Sabbath." [1] He instances a statement
of Josephus that the sixth hour or noon was the time
when "our laws require us to go to dinner on Sabbath-
days." [2] Various pagan writers also refer to the Sabbath as a day of fasting. [3] Such a notion may have
arisen from a misunderstanding of the Biblical rule
forbidding cooking on the Sabbath, or, perhaps, from
a confusion of this festival with the great fast on the
Day of Atonement, which was a *shabbāth shabbāthôn*,
a "Sabbath of solemn rest." [4] Yet it seems difficult
to understand the rule forbidding fasting at new moon
and on the seventh day, [5] except as a reference to a
custom formerly observed but in later times regarded
as an illegitimate rite. Since the Sabbath fell, originally, at the middle of the month, it may be that the
new-moon and full-moon days were once marked by
both cessation of labour and abstinence from food.
The foregoing pages have supplied too many instances
of the transformation of fasts into feasts for such an
explanation to be dismissed as an idle conjecture. [6]

When the notion of a weekly Sabbath was extended,
after the Captivity, to the Sabbatical Year, the seventh
year was to be a "Sabbath of solemn rest" (*shabbāth
shabbāthôn*) for the land, not because of the advantage of allowing soil to lie fallow at regular intervals,
but because the land itself was consecrated as "a
Sabbath unto Jehovah." [7] The regulation does not

[1] *Ecclesiastical Polity*, v, 72.

[2] *De vita sua*, 54.

[3] Suetonius, *Divus Augustus*, 76;
Strabo, *Geographica*, xvi, 2, 40;
Martial, *Epigrammata*, iv, 4;
Justin, xxxvi, 2. Justin speaks of
the Sabbath as having been conse-
crated as a fast day to commemo-
rate a seven days' fast of the
Israelites in the deserts of Arabia.

[4] Above, pp. 81 *sqq*.

[5] *Judith*, viii, 6; *Schulchan
Aruch*, i, 91 *sq*.

[6] The Talmud (*Tractate Pesa-
chim*, 105 a) indicates that some

superstitions attached to the after-
noon of the Sabbath as a dangerous
time for the consumption of food.
During the early Middle Ages
Jews in northern France, Lorraine,
and Germany, but not in Provence,
Narbonne, or Spain, refrained from
eating and drinking on Sabbath
afternoons. See D. Kaufmann,
"Was the Custom of Fasting on
Sabbath Afternoon Part of the
Early Anglo-Jewish Ritual?"
Jewish Quarterly Review, 1894, vi,
754-756.

[7] *Leviticus*, xxv, 4. This law

imply that, as a consequence of a fallow year, the land will produce better harvests on the succeeding year. It is expressly said that the year before the Sabbatical Year is the one to be conspicuous for its fruitfulness: "Then I will command my blessing upon you in the sixth year, and it shall bring forth fruit for the three years." [1] The rule requiring that the produce of the soil should be devoted to the poor and to the cattle [2] perhaps indicates a partial triumph of the utilitarian spirit. During the Jubilee, at the end of seven times seven years, "Ye shall not sow, neither reap that which groweth of itself in it, nor gather the grapes in it of the undressed vines," [3] a regulation which can be explained only as the outcome of the sabbatarian observances attached to the seventh day and the seventh year.

In the Hawaiian Islands and west Africa any one who broke a sabbatarian taboo suffered death. Among the early Israelites the Sabbath-breaker was threatened with a similar penalty: "Every one that profaneth it shall surely be put to death; for whosoever doeth any work therein, that soul shall be cut off from among his people." [4] We are not informed how frequently this stern ordinance was enforced; the case of the woodgatherer on the Sabbath, who, by direction of Moses, acting on a direct revelation from Jehovah, was stoned to death outside the camp, is the only instance of capital punishment for Sabbath desecration which has found its way into the Scriptures as we now have them. [5]

was occasionally productive of great distress (1 *Maccabees*, vi, 48, 53; compare Josephus, *Antiquitates Judaicæ*, xiv, 16, 2).

[1] *Leviticus*, xxv, 21.

[2] *Exodus*, xxiii, 11.

[3] *Leviticus*, xxv, 11. Whether the Jubilee was celebrated after forty-eight years or after forty-nine years is a problem incapable of solution from the Old Testament evidence. As Schiaparelli has well shown (*Astronomy in the Old Testament*, pp. 146 sqq.), the

twenty-fifth chapter of *Leviticus* combines two systems of rules which are not only different but actually irreconcilable with each other, the septennial system of the Sabbatical Year and the Jubilee system of fifty years.

[4] *Exodus*, xxxi, 14; for a similar regulation see *ibid.*, xxxv, 2.

[5] *Numbers*, xv, 32–36. The comments of Philo Judæus on this passage are interesting, if not illuminating (*Vita Mosis*, iii, 27–28).

The instance is an instructive one, as revealing the strong sense of group-welfare and hatred of the non-conformist, characteristic of a religion which had not yet outrun clan and tribal limitations.

The Old Testament affords evidence that the Hebrews kept the Sabbath with varying degrees of rigour in different places and at different times. Under the later prophets a movement appears to have begun toward a stricter observance of the day, as is seen in the effort of Jeremiah to prevent burden-bearing on the Sabbath, and in Ezekiel's constant insistence on the profanation of the Sabbath in his catalogue of the sins of the Israelites.[1] But more than a century after these prophets, in the age of Nehemiah, the people of Judea made wine and gathered the harvest on the Sabbath. All manner of burdens were brought into Jerusalem on that day, and the inhabitants bought and sold with the men of Tyre.[2] These practices indicate that the Sabbath bade fair to become a social institution, divorced from supernatural sanctions.

It is doubtless true that the Exile tended to augment the religious importance of the Sabbath, since even in heathen lands it could be observed by a people who now had neither state nor temple. In the Exilic literature great significance is ascribed to the Sabbath,[3] and in post-Exilic law it is regarded as a sign between Jehovah and the children of Israel that Jehovah is their God. It is impossible, however, to follow those critics who assume that the rigour of the sabbatarian observances after the Exile forms an entirely new development, and that the priestly Sabbath represents something very different from the Sabbath of the "Book of the Covenant" or of *Deuteronomy*.[4] The increased

---

[1] *Jeremiah*, xvii. 19-27: *Ezekiel*, xx. 12, 16, 21, 24, xxii. 8, 26, xxiii. 38.
[2] *Nehemiah*, x. 31, xiii. 15-16. The use of the Sabbath Day for marketing is paralleled by the Mohammedan observance of jum'a (above, p. 206).

[3] *Isaiah*, lvi. 2 sq., lviii. 13.
[4] T. K. Cheyne, *Jewish Religious Life after the Exile*, New York, 1898, p. 60: C. G. Montefiore, *Lectures on the Origin and Growth of Religion as Illustrated by the Religion of the Ancient Hebrews*,[2] London, 1893.

significance of the institution led naturally to a revival of the old taboos with which the day had been always invested, taboos which otherwise might have been expected to disappear with advancing culture and the decay of supernaturalism. Closer contact with Assyria and Babylonia, from the eighth to the sixth century B.C., also may have helped to revitalize the older superstitions and to give to the Sabbath once more an austere character. The day, in fact, seems never wholly to have lost all traces of its severe and sombre origin in a period of taboo; it is significant in this connection that, while the Hebrews had their favourable and unfavourable days, as the expression yōm ṭōb "good day" in holy days shows, the Sabbath is never so described.

The later history of the Sabbath as a holy day commences in the exaggerations of pharisaic Judaism and the extraordinary multiplying of the rabbinical enactments. The Mishna enumerates no less than thirty-nine principal classes of prohibited actions. Some of these are regarded as belonging to as ancient a period as any of the taboos found in the Old Testa-

ment; the majority, however, represent only an elaboration of the scriptural precepts. Two entire works
are devoted to the provisions for Sabbath observance.
The first treatise, called *Shabbāth*, is chiefly remarkable as an illustration of the subtle refinements and
distinctions of which the rabbis were capable. Thus,
the prohibitions to tie or untie a knot being regarded
as too general, it was necessary to define the species
of knot referred to. A camel-driver's knot and a boat-
man's knot rendered the man who tied or untied them
a Sabbath-breaker; but Rabbi Meir said, "A knot
which a man can untie with one hand only, he does
not become guilty by untying." Rabbi Jehudah,
still more liberal of mind, laid down the rule that any
knot which was not intended to be permanent might
be lawfully tied. The second treatise, *Ērūbim*, was
intended to alleviate the extreme rigour of some of the
enactments in the former work. Thus, the limits of
a "Sabbath Day's journey" having been fixed at two
thousand cubits, the rabbis conceded that one who
before the Sabbath had desposited food for two meals
at the boundary thereby removed his habitation from
the town and made that place his new domicile. When
the Sabbath came, he was at liberty to proceed two
thousand cubits beyond it, though he lost the right
to walk the same distance in the opposite direction.
As is well known, literal obedience of the Sabbath
regulations was sometimes carried to such an extreme
as to prove a source of great hardship, danger, and
even death to its devotees.[1]

These legal fictions, these casuistical elaborations
of the simple ordinances of the Pentateuch concerning
the Sabbath, may be paralleled by the growth of pontifical regulations at Rome relating to what might and

---

[1] 1 *Maccabees*, ii, 31 *sqq.;* 2 *Maccabees*, v, 25–26, vi, 11, viii, 26; Josephus, *Antiquitates Judaicæ*, xii, 62. Plutarch refers to the Jews who allowed their enemies to rear scaling ladders and make them- selves masters of their walls, and "so lay still until they were caught like so many trout in the dragnet of their own superstition" (*De super- stitione*, 8).

what might not be done on public ferial days.[1] Like
the Roman *feriæ*, also, the Hebrew Sabbath affords
an instance of what seems to be a very general, perhaps
universal, tendency of the human mind to dwell with
special emphasis on the festive aspects of a holy season, and by some subtle alchemy of the spirit to convert what was once a day of gloom and anxiety into
a day of gladness and good cheer. The post-Exilic
prophet, the so-called second Isaiah, when he urges
his people to "call the Sabbath a delight"[2] presents
it, indeed, as a festival "holy to Jehovah," but capable,
nevertheless, of contributing to man's physical and
mental refreshment. And in later Judaism the strict
observance of the Sabbath rest did not by any means
preclude abstinence from bodily pleasures. Fasting,
as we have seen, was forbidden on that day; three
substantial meals were to be "enjoyed," so Jewish
theologians declared; and the New Testament itself
contains evidence that Pharisees of the strictest type
gave sumptuous entertainments on the Sabbath.[3]
In fact, various Christian Fathers were persuaded that
the Jews observed the Sabbath as a day of violent
excess, and converts to Christianity were cautioned
against applying to the Lord's Day the *luxus sab-
batarius*. "The Jews in our time," says St. Augustine, "observe their Sabbath by a kind of bodily rest,
languid and luxurious. They abstain from labour
and give themselves up to trifles, and, though God
ordained the Sabbath, they spend it in actions which
God forbids. Our rest is from evil works, their rest
is from good works; for it is better to plough than
to dance."[4] We may believe that such criticisms
had slight justification in the real nature of the Jewish

[1] Above, pp. 97 *sq.*
[2] *Isaiah*, lviii, 13.
[3] *Luke*, xiv, 1–24.
[4] Augustine, *In comm. ad Psalm. xcii (Nicene and Post-Nicene Fathers of the Christian Church*, viii, 453). This passage, with others in a similar strain, from St. Chrysostom, Prudentius, and Theodoret, is adduced by the learned ecclesiastical historian Joseph Bingham (*Antiquities of the Christian Church*, London, 1838–1840, vii, 32 *sqq.*).

observance, little more, perhaps, than Plutarch's quaint
notion that the Sabbath must bear some relation to
Dionysus, for, said Plutarch, when the Jews keep the
Sabbath, they invite one another to potations till all
are drunk.[1] It is more satisfying to turn to hundreds
of Jewish hymns where the Sabbath is hailed "as a
day of rest and joy, of pleasure and delight, a day in
which man enjoys some presentiment of the pure bliss
and happiness which are stored up for the righteous
in the world to come, and to which such tender names
were applied as the 'Queen Sabbath,' the 'Bride Sabbath,' and the 'Holy, dear, beloved Sabbath.'"[2]

The Jewish Sabbath appears to have been first
brought to the attention of the Romans as early as
the last century of the republic, when Pompey's sweeping campaigns in the East led to the establishment of
Roman dominion over Syria and Judea. References
to the institution in Tibullus, Horace, and Ovid indicate that its peculiar character as a day of rest was then
generally understood.[3] Their contemporary, Philo,
the Hellenistic Jew of Alexandria, declared that the
seventh day was the festival, not of one city or one
country, but of all the earth, "the birthday of the
world,"[4] and Josephus could write that there was no
city among the Greeks or the barbarians where the
festival of the Sabbath was not celebrated.[5] These
statements, though exaggerated, bear witness to the
success of that Jewish propaganda which, at the very
time when the preaching of Christianity began, carried
this other Oriental faith throughout the ancient world.
The great commercial cities of the Mediterranean

[1] Plutarch, Quaestiones convivialiae, iv. 6. 2.

[2] S. Schechter, in Jewish Quarterly Review, 1902, iii, 762; compare also Studies in Judaism, New
York, 1896, pp. 244 ff.; and
Israel Abrahams, Jewish Life in
the Middle Ages, London, 1896,
pp. 131, 134, 172 ff. See further
J. Mann, "The Observance of the

Sabbath and the Festivals in the
First Two Centuries of the Current
Era according to Philo, Josephus,
the New Testament, and the Rab-
binic Sources," Jewish Review, 1914,
iv. 433-456.

[3] Above, pp. 244 ff.

[4] De vita Mosis, iii; compare
above, The Week, ii, 4.

[5] Contra Apionem, ii, 40.

became seats of thriving Jewish communities where
pagan proselytes adopted Jewish customs, including
the observance of the Sabbath.[1]

The Jewish seven-day week with its numerical indications of the days was adopted by the early Christians, to whom the planetary week, bearing the names
of pagan deities, could scarcely prove attractive.[2]
Friday and Saturday continued to have the designations *παρασκευή* and *σάββατον*, respectively, but Sunday, which by Jewish custom was called "the first
day" after the Sabbath, eventually received the designation *ἡ κυριακὴ ἡμέρα dies dominica*, the Lord's
Day.[3] The New Testament contains unambiguous
evidence that from a very early period "the first day
of the week" was observed by Christians as a day of
assembly for the "breaking of bread" and perhaps for
the collection of free-will offerings.[4] The author of
the *Epistle of Barnabas*, toward the end of the first
century, speaks of keeping the "eighth day" for rejoicing, and justifies its observance as a celebration of the
resurrection of Christ.[5] The *Didache*, or *Teaching of
the Twelve Apostles*, a work which belongs to the early
part of the second century, enjoins meetings "on the
Lord's own day" *κατὰ κυριακὴν δὲ Κυρίου*, for the

---

[1] Compare Juvenal, *Satire*, xiv.
100-106 with J. B. Mayor's
commentary. Tertullian, *Apologeticus*, 16, note, *Ad nationes*, i. 13.

[2] Above, p. xx.

[3] In the New Testament such
phrases as *ἡ μία τῶν σαββάτων*
(Acts, xx. 7, and even *μία σαββάτων*,
1 Corinthians, xvi. 2; compare
Matthew, xxviii. 1; Mark, xvi. 2;
Luke, xxiv. 1; John, xx. 1, 19)
refer to Sunday as "the first day
of the week." An equivalent expression, *πρώτῃ σαββάτου*, is also
found (Mark, xvi. 9). The designation of Sunday as the Lord's
Day — *ἡ κυριακὴ ἡμέρα* — occurs
in a single New Testament passage
(Revelation, i. 10). Some critics

hold that the author of the *Apoca-
lypse* was referring here, not to
Sunday but to the day of Judgment,
called elsewhere *ἡ ἡμέρα ἡ μεγάλη*,
"the great day" (ibid., vi. 17; xvi.
14).

[4] Acts, xx. 7; 1 Corinthians, xvi.
2; compare *supra*, xx. 26.

[5] *Epistle of Barnabas*, 15; compare Justin Martyr, *Dialogue cum
Tryphone*, 138; Tertullian, *De
idololatria*, 14. The "eighth day"
might seem to be a natural designation for the day following the
Sabbath, the seventh day, more
probably, however, it is to be
explained by the ancient practice
of inclusive reckoning.

breaking of bread and giving thanks.[1] Eusebius of Cæsarea, in his *Ecclesiastical History*, preserves a fragment of a letter of Dionysius, Bishop of Corinth (175 A.D.), to Soter, Bishop of Rome, in which the former says, "To-day we passed the Lord's holy day, when we read your epistle"; and the same historian also mentions the fact that Melito, Bishop of Sardis (170 A.D.), had written among other works a treatise on the Lord's Day.[2] Justin Martyr, writing about the middle of the second century, describes how, "on the day called Sunday" (τῇ τοῦ Ἡλίου λεγομένη ἡμέρα), all town and country Christians were wont to assemble for instruction in the holy writings, and for prayer, the distribution of bread and wine, and the collection of alms. The name Sunday commemorates, according to Justin, the first day of creation and the resurrection of Christ from the darkness of the grave.[3] Justin's use of this nomenclature, in a work addressed to the pagans, witnesses to the spread of Oriental solar worship throughout the Roman Empire, leading to the substitution of the day of Sun for Saturn's Day, as the beginning of the planetary week. As we have learned, the Christians themselves adopted eventually the pagan designation of the first day of the week.[4]

[1] *Didache*, xiv, 1. The testimony of Pliny the Younger (*Epistolæ*, x, 98) makes it evident that as early as the year 111 A.D. the Christians of Asia Minor were accustomed to hold religious assemblies on a fixed day (*stato die*), which can hardly have been other than the first day of the week.

[2] Eusebius, *Historia ecclesiastica*, iv, 23, 11, iv, 26, 2.

[3] *Apologia prima*, 67. Tertullian, who found it necessary to answer the objection that Christians worshipped the sun, declares, "Indeed, they made Sunday a day of joy, but for other reasons than to adore the sun, which was no part of their religion" (*Apologeticus*, 16; compare *Ad nationes*, i, 13).

[4] Above, pp. 220 *sq*. On the early history of the Christian Sunday see A. Barry, "Lord's Day," Smith and Cheetham's *Dictionary of Christian Antiquities*, ii, 1042–1053; G. A. Deissmann, "Lord's Day," *Encyclopædia Biblica*, iii, coll. 2813–2816; O. Zöckler, "Sonntagsfeier," Herzog, Plitt, and Hauck's *Realencyklopädie für protestantische Theologie und Kirche*,³ xviii, 521–529; T. Zahn, "Geschichte des Sonntags vornehmlich in der alten Kirche," in *Skizzen aus dem Leben der alten Kirche*,² Erlangen, 1898, pp. 160–208, 351–

Though Jesus regarded the Sabbath as still binding on his followers, his teaching that it was a social institution designed for practical benefit to mankind, and not as a fetish, brought him repeatedly into conflict with the Pharisees, and called forth those utterances which have been so strangely neglected by sabbatarians in after ages: "For the Son of man is lord of the Sabbath"; "The Sabbath was made for man, and not man for the Sabbath"; "My Father worketh [on it] even until now, and I work." [1] Jewish Christians appear at first to have continued the observance of the Sabbath, but this practice met the unqualified condemnation of St. Paul; [2] and one of the *Epistles* of St. Ignatius, who suffered martyrdom about 107 A.D., refers to Christians as "no longer observing the Sabbath, but living in the observance of the Lord's Day (μηκέτι σαββατίζοντες, ἀλλὰ κατὰ κυριακὴν ζῶντες), on which also our life has sprung up again by Him and by His death." [3] However, the Jewish element in the churches of the East was strong enough to secure the ecclesiastical recognition of Saturday as a holy day. It long continued to be observed like Sunday, by religious assemblies and feasting, though not by any compulsory cessation of the ordinary occupations. [4] Tertullian was the first Church Father to declare that Christians ought to abstain on Sunday

376; J. A. Hessey, *Sunday*, [5] London, 1889, pp. 40-49.

[1] *Matthew*, xii, 8; *Mark*, ii, 27; *John*, v, 17.

[2] *Colossians*, ii, 16; compare *Romans*, xiv, 5; *Galatians*, iv, 10-11.

[3] *Epistola ad Magnesios*, 9. The longer recension of this passage, though an interpolation of much later date, expresses the same antagonism toward sabbatizing: "But let every one of you keep the Sabbath after a spiritual manner, rejoicing in meditation on the law, not in relaxation of the body,

admiring the workmanship of God, and not eating things prepared the day before, nor using lukewarm drinks, and walking within a prescribed space, nor finding delight in dancing, and plaudits which have no sense in them" (*Ante-Nicene Fathers*, i, 62 sq.).

[4] *Constitutiones Apostolicæ*, ii, 59, 1, vii, 23, 2, viii, 33, 1; *Concilium Laodicenum*, can. 16 (Labbe-Mansi, *Sacrorum conciliorum collectio*, ii, 567); Socrates, *Historia ecclesiastica*, vi, 8. The church council held at Laodicea in 363 A.D. anathematized as Judaizers those

from secular duties and occupations, lest they should
"give place to the Devil." [1] Tertullian's statement
has sometimes been understood to indicate a sabbatarian spirit on the part of its author; properly considered, however, it means only that Christians should
so carefully observe the duties peculiar to the Lord's
Day as to neglect, if necessary, their worldly business
on that day. Other Church Fathers of the third
century, including Origen and Cyprian, made no reference to Sunday as a day of abstinence from labour.
The earliest Sunday law, the edict issued by Constantine in 321 A.D., bore no relation to Christianity. [2]
What began, however, as a pagan ordinance, ended
as a Christian regulation; and a long series of imperial
decrees, during the fourth, fifth, and sixth centuries,
enjoined with increasing stringency abstinence from
labour on Sunday. The view that the Christian Lord's
Day is but the Jewish Sabbath transferred from the
seventh to the first day of the week found occasional
expression in both the law and the theology of the

who refrained from work on Saturday (*Concilium Laodicenum*, can. 29;
Labbe-Mansi, *op. cit.*, ii, 580).
The anathema did not penetrate
to the ancient Christian kingdom of
Abyssinia, where Saturday is still
strictly observed. "The ox and
the ass are at rest. Agricultural
pursuits are suspended. Household avocations must be laid aside,
and the spirit of idleness reigns
throughout the day. . . . When,
a few years ago, one daring spirit
presumed, in advance of the age,
to burst the fetters of superstition,
his majesty the king of Shoa, stim-
ulated by the advice of besotted
monks, delegated his wardens
throughout the land, and issued a
proclamation, that whoso disturbed
the original dreamy stillness of the
Jewish Sabbath should forfeit his
property to the royal treasury, and
be consigned to the state dungeon"
(W. C. Harris, *The Highlands of
Ethiopia*, New York [1843], p. 272).
The Celts kept Saturday as a day
of rest, with special religious services on Sunday (A. Bellesheim,
*History of the Catholic Church in
Scotland*, Edinburgh, 1887-1890, i,
86).

[1] *De oratione*, 23: *Omni anxie-
tatis habitu et officio cavere debemus,
differentes etiam negotia, ne quem
diabolo locum demus.* Tertullian,
however, elsewhere rejects the im-
plication that Christians should be
sabbatizers, "we, to whom these
Sabbaths belong not, nor the new
moons, nor the feast days once
beloved of God" (*De idolatria*, 14);
compare *idem, Apologeticus*, 16;
idem, Ad nationes, i, 13; *idem, Adversus Judæos*, 4; Augustine, *De
spiritu et littera*, 24.

[2] Above, pp. 122 *sq.*

Middle Ages, and culminated in the sabbatarian excesses of English and Scottish Puritanism.[1]

[1] For the history of Sunday legislation see E. V. Neale, *Feasts and Fasts*, London, 1845; R. E. Prime, "Sunday Legislation," *New Schaff-Herzog Encyclopedia of Religious Knowledge*, xi, 146–151; J. Gairdiner, "Sundays, Ancient and Modern," in Gairdiner and Spedding, *Studies in English History*, Edinburgh, 1881, pp. 286–315; Hans [Johannes] Meinhold, *Sabbat und Sonntag*, Leipzig, 1909, pp. 65–103; Alice M. Earle, *The Sabbath in Puritan New England*, New York, 1891, pp. 245–258.

CHAPTER IX

UNLUCKY DAYS

THE observance of lucky and unlucky days is a familiar phenomenon in primitive society and among peoples of archaic civilization. Under the attenuated form of a survival, the superstition still lingers in civilized and Christian lands. The reasons for the assignment of a good or an evil character to certain days are usually quite obscure; and even where explanations are provided, these are, as a rule, explanations after the event. The attempt to provide a satisfactory origin for them insensibly widens out into an effort to account for the genesis of the great body of popular and anonymous superstitions.

Probably the commonest source of the belief in unlucky days is to be sought in that erroneous association of ideas which underlies so much of savage magic and savage religion. If an event, fortunate or unfortunate, has taken place on a certain day, the notion easily arises that all actions performed on the recurrence of the day will have a similarly favourable or unfavourable issue. Among the Tshi of west Africa, the most unlucky day is the anniversary of the Saturday on which Osai Tutu was slain in an ambush near Acromanti in 1731.[1] In modern Macedonia the superlative ill-luck attending Tuesday is explained by some as due to the fact — historically true — that Constantinople was taken by the Turks on this day of the week.[2]

[1] Ellis, *Tshi-speaking Peoples*, pp. 219 *sq*.
[2] G. F. Abbott, *Macedonian Folklore*, Cambridge, 1903, p. 189. In Greece and Albania, also, Tuesday is an unlucky day for every sort of enterprise (Miss Mary Hamilton, *Greek Saints and their Festivals*, Edinburgh, 1910, p. 190).

The *dies religiosi*, or unlucky days, of the Roman calendar included the anniversary of the battle of the Allia, *dies Alliensis* (July 18), when the republic had suffered grave misfortune. The same date was also observed as the anniversary of the destruction of the Fabii at the Cremera, 477 B.C.[1] After the assassination of Julius Cæsar a decree was made that the Ides of March (March 15) should be called *parricidium*, and henceforth should be observed as an unlucky day.[2] The superstitions which in Christian times have gathered about Friday — at once a holy and an unlucky day — are connected with it as the anniversary of Christ's Passion. In the Middle Ages people were accustomed to date on Friday all the unfortunate events of religious tradition and history. On that day Adam sinned and was driven from Paradise, Cain killed his brother Abel, John the Baptist was beheaded, and Herod slew the Holy Innocents. It was also the day of the Deluge, the Confusion of Tongues, and the infliction of the Plagues upon Egypt. Synchronisms of this sort had a great attraction to the mediæval mind, and numerous lists of them are preserved in old manuscripts.[3] There is a Jewish superstition, reaching back to the

[1] Livy, vi, 1; Tacitus, *Historiæ*, ii, 91; Suetonius, *Vitellius*, 11. Compare Ovid (*Fasti*, i, 49–50):

Omen ab eventu est; illis nam Roma diebus,
Damna sub adverso Marte tristia tulit.

[2] Suetonius, *Divus Julius*, 88.
[3] See "La recommandation du vendredi," *Mélusine*, 1888–1889, iv, 104, 133 *sqq.*, 205 *sq.* However, the Friday superstition may antedate Christianity. In Macedonia it is believed that ablutions on Friday are dangerous, especially for women in childbed (Abbott, *op. cit.*, p. 190). The Brahmans of India share the Friday superstition, saying that "on this day no business must be commenced" (Buchanan, in *Asiatick Researches*, vi, 172). Among the Parsis Tuesday and Friday are inauspicious days, generally avoided for betrothals, marriages, and other happy occasions. Many persons will not begin an important work or start on a distant journey on these days (J. J. Modi, "Omens among the Parsees," *Journal of the Anthropological Society of Bombay*, i, 294). All over Burma Friday is unlucky. "Don't go on Friday" is a current saying (L. Vossion, "*Nat*-worship among the Burmese," *Journal of American Folk-lore*, 1892, iv, 112). For Russian superstitions relating to Friday see above, p. 222 *n.*[2]

T

Talmud, that it is lucky to begin an undertaking on Tuesday, because, in describing the third day of creation, it is said, "God saw that it was good." Contrariwise, it is unlucky to commence anything of importance on Monday, as to which day nothing at all is said.[1] Where such conceptions are rife, they readily lend themselves to divination and astrology, and under the fostering care of practitioners of magical arts may develop into elaborate augural codes.

The observation of natural phenomena sometimes accounts for the unlucky character ascribed to particular occasions. We have already noted many superstitious observances connected with the phases of the moon, her monthly disappearance from the heavens, and her occasional eclipse by the earth. A further illustration of the same subject is found in the astrological doctrine of the moon stations. The old Babylonian astronomers, one of whose duties it was to make very careful observations of the moon, noticed that at each lunation she appears to pass by the same star-groups. It was natural, therefore, to associate the moon with the conspicuous stars and constellations in the vicinity of the moon's path. The names which they received were in time extended to the lunar days themselves; and this apparent connection between the two became the principal basis of astrological forecasts for each day of the sidereal month.[2] The fact is well known that Babylonian astrology and astronomy — for the two were scarcely distinguishable in the earlier period — exerted great influence on the neighbouring peoples of Asia; and hence it has been generally assumed that the lunar mansions, reckoned at twenty-seven or twenty-eight in number, which we find among the Hindus and Chinese, and the

[1] J. Jacobs, "Superstition," *Jewish Encyclopedia*, xi, 599.
[2] The sidereal month, determined by the moon's revolution from any star back to the same star, has a mean length of 27 days, 7 hours, 43 minutes, and 11 seconds. The least duration is 27 days, 4 hours, and the greatest, about 7 hours longer.

augural calendars connected therewith, were derived
ultimately from Babylonia.[1] In modern India the
nakshatra, as they are called, "are consulted at births,
marriages, and on all occasions of family rejoicing,
distress, or calamity. No one undertakes a journey or
any important matter except on days which the aspect
of the *nakshatra* renders lucky and auspicious."[2]
Among the Persians and Arabs the lunar stations have
long been employed for astrological purposes.[3] The
Arabs carried them to Madagascar, where they gave
rise to an elaborate distinction of days lucky and unlucky. Some days were considered absolutely bad;
others were absolutely good; others were indifferent.
Again, some days were not regarded as good in general, though still good enough for special purposes;
one being excellent for a house-warming, another
for marking out the ground for a new town, and
still another was lucky to be born on, but bad for
business. Some days had a special peculiarity of
their own, for instance, children born on a certain
day usually became dumb. The character of a day,
according to the Malagasy astrologers, depended, in
short, on what one of the twenty-eight lunar stations
it represented.[4]

[1] F. K. Ginzel (*Handbuch der mathematischen und technischen Chronologie*, Leipzig, 1906-1911, i, 70 *sqq.*) provides a useful survey, with bibliographies, of the lengthy discussions relating to the origin and diffusion of the moon-stations. See also W. D. Whitney, "On the Lunar Zodiac of India, Arabia, and China," in his *Oriental and Linguistic Studies*, second series, New York, 1874, pp. 341-421.

[2] Sir M. Monier-Williams, *Brāhmanism and Hindūism*,[4] New York, 1891, pp. 345 *sq.*; compare J. A. Dubois, *Hindu Manners, Customs, and Ceremonies*,[3] Oxford, 1906, p. 382.

[3] L. H. Gray, "The Pari-

sian *Burj-Nāmah*, or Book of Omens from the Moon," *Journal of the American Oriental Society*, 1910, xx, 337 *sqq.*; A. de C. Motylinski, *Les mansions lunaires des Arabes*, Algiers, 1899.

[4] J. Sibree, "Divination among the Malagasy," *Folk-lore*, 1892, iii, 230 *sq.* In Madagascar the names of the separate days in the month have been taken directly from the Arabic names for the twenty-eight lunar mansions. It thus appears that these names have both astrological and chronological value (G. Ferrand, "Note sur le calendrier malgache et le *fandruana*," *Revue des études ethno-graphiques et sociologiques*, 1908, i,

The conception of unluckiness may be deduced *a priori* from the assumed critical nature of certain periods, such as epagomenal months and days. The thirteenth month, which many peoples employing lunar calculations find it necessary to intercalate at more or less regular intervals, is sometimes regarded as unlucky.[1] Again, the eleven or twelve days by which the solar year exceeds the lunar year assumed among various Indo-European peoples a portentous and often unfavourable significance.[2] The celebration of the Twelve Nights, in the sense of the Twelve Nights and Days, as a festival before or after the winter solstice, has been assigned to the Aryans of the Vedic age in India on the strength of certain passages in the *Rig-Veda*, where the three Ribhus, generally regarded as the personified seasonal deities who divided up the year, are described as sleeping during these days " in

95. Among the northern Abyssinians lucky and unlucky days are likewise determined by the lunar stations, though only six or seven are reckoned, each containing from two to seven days (E. Littmann, "Sternensagen und Astrologisches aus Nordabessinien," *Archiv für Religionswissenschaft*, 1908, xi, 301 *sq.*).

[1] Above, p. 177 n.[2]

[2] According to A. Jeremias no evidence exists for the recognition of twelve intercalary days in the ancient Oriental world (*Das Alter der babylonischen Astronomie*, Leipzig, 1909, p. 42 n.[1]). However, the Babylonian New Year's festival of Zagmuk, which occupied the first eleven days of the spring month of Nisan, has been compared with the Twelve Days of Indo-European antiquity (H. Winckler, *Altorientalische Forschungen*, Leipzig, 1898, ii, i, 182). What relation, if any, the Babylonian Zagmuk bore to the Babylo-Persian Sacæa and the Hebrew Purim is still a subject of controversy. See the full presentation of the evidence in Sir J. G. Frazer, *The Scapegoat*, London, 1913, pp. 354-407. The Babylonian *Epic of Gilgamesh*, recorded on twelve cuneiform tablets, has been plausibly interpreted as a solar myth, recounting the sun's annual course during the twelve months. Now, a relationship undoubtedly exists between at least three tablets of the poem and the corresponding months of the year, notably in the case of the eleventh tablet, in which the story of the Deluge is told, and the eleventh month, which by the Babylonians was termed the "month of rain" (M. Jastrow, *Religion of Babylonia and Assyria*, pp. 484, 510). It is curious, therefore, to find that in the Hebrew narrative of the Flood the waters cover the earth for the period of a year and eleven days, apparently, here, a lunar year of 354 days plus eleven days (*Genesis*, vii, 11, viii, 14).

the house of the sun." [1] The prophetic character of
the Twelve Days appears to be indicated by their
characterization in various Brahmanical writings as
an "image of the coming year." [2] Some eminent
scholars have thought that the Twelve Days represent
an ancient method of adjusting the lunar year to the
solar year, as practised by the early Aryans before the
custom arose of inserting a thirteenth month, to which
reference is also made in the *Rig-Veda*.[3] This opinion,
though not free from difficulties, is strongly supported
by numerous parallels to the Indian evidence found in
European folklore of the Twelve Days.[4]

Throughout Europe from east to west the Twelve
Days, usually reckoned from Christmas to Epiphany,
are prolific in popular superstitions and customs.
At this time the souls of the dead, sometimes under
animal form, return to the earth and revisit the living;
witches and demons swarm in the mischief-laden air;
werewolves roam about, and the Wild Huntsman rides
in the heavens. Most of the ceremonies performed
during the Twelve Days have a distinctly pagan cast,
such as the constant fire on the domestic hearth, the
village bonfires, and the lighted candles; while others,
such as the sprinkling of the houses with holy water
and the marking of the cross on the doors, have only

[1] *Rig-Veda*, i, 161, 11, 13, iv, 33, 7; compare *Atharva-Veda*, iv, 11, 11 (transl. W. D. Whitney, p. 166).

[2] *Kāthaka*, 7, 5; *Taittirīya-brāhmaṇa*, I, 1, 9, 10; H. Zimmer, *Altindisches Leben*, Berlin, 1879, p. 367.

[3] A. Weber, "Zwei vedische Texte über Omina und Portenta," *Philologische und historische Abhandlungen der königlichen Akademie der Wissenschaften zu Berlin*, 1858, pp. 388 sq.; *idem, Indische Studien*, 1868, x, 242 sq., 1885, xvii, 223 sqq., 1898, xviii, 45; *idem*, "Vedische Beiträge," *Sitzungsberichte der königlich-preussischen Akademie der Wissenschaften zu*

Berlin, 1898, pp. 559 sqq. Compare A. Ludwig, *Der Rigveda*, Prague, 1883, vi, 232; A. Kaegi, *The Rigveda*, Boston, 1886, p. 37; Zimmer, *op. cit.*, pp. 366 sq. For contrary opinions see O. Schrader, *Reallexikon der indogermanischen Altertumskunde*, pp. 391 sq.; G. Thibaut, in Bühler's *Grundriss der indo-arischen Philologie und Altertumskunde*, iii, pt. ix, 9 sq.

[4] J. Lippert, *Christentum, Volksglaube, und Volksbrauch*, Berlin, 1882, pp. 680–685; C. A. Miles, *Christmas in Ritual and Tradition, Christian and Pagan*, London, 1912, pp. 238–246; Frazer, *The Scapegoat*, pp. 313–345.

a thin veneer of Christianity. To a certain extent
the Twelve Days thus form the modern European
representative of those seasons devoted to the expulsion of ghosts and evil spirits which are observed by
peoples of the lower culture.[1] A further resemblance
exists in the distinctly unlucky character often assigned
to the Twelve Days. In Macedonia no marriages are
solemnized during their continuance.[2] In various parts
of Germany they are kept as rest days, when the most
important household occupations and even those on
the farm are omitted. The housewife must not spin,
weave lace, or engage in her usual tasks of washing
and baking; and the farmer must not thresh grain.
Certain foods, especially peas and other legumes, are
carefully avoided; and no meat is eaten. It is not
wise to lend anything out of the house or to remove
refuse and sweepings. One ought not to be short of
anything at this time, else one will be short of everything during the ensuing year. Certain animals,
particularly associated with witches, should not be
called by their right names; hence, you must refer to
the fox as "Mr. Long-tail," and to the mouse as "Floor-
runner." During these fateful days perfect quiet is
essential: no table must be pushed about and no doors
slammed, otherwise the house will be struck by lightning. In this period dreams and other prognostics
are most to be relied on and are most carefully investigated. Everywhere in Germany it is believed that
the weather of the Twelve Days determines what
will be experienced during the following twelve months,
so that they form, in effect, a meteorological calendar
for the new year.[3] This last superstition, however, is

---

[1] Above, pp. 74 sqq.

[2] G. F. Abbott, *Macedonian
Folklore*, Cambridge, 1903, p. 75.

[3] A. Wuttke, *Der deutsche Volks-
aberglaube der Gegenwart*,[3] edited
by E. H. Meyer, Berlin, 1900,
pp. 63 sqq. See also K. Weinhold,
Weihnacht-Spiele und Lieder aus
Süddeutschland und Schlesien, Grāz,
1853, pp. 11 sq.; K. A. Öberle,
*Überreste germanischen Heidentums
im Christentum*, Baden-Baden,
1883, pp. 63 sq.; E. H. Meyer,
Indogermanische Mythen, Berlin,
1887, ii, 526 sqq.

not confined to Germany, being met, for instance, in modern Brittany. In most parts of that country the Twelve Days, here reckoned from the first of January, are popularly termed *gour-deziou*, "male days," an expression which must be understood as meaning supplementary or additional days.[1] A superstitious avoidance of certain kinds of work during the Twelve Days may still be found in remote districts of the British Isles. In Shropshire horses are not set to the plough at this time and no spinning is done.[2] In Aberdeenshire people believe that all work ought, if possible, to be finished before Christmas Day. Between this time and New Year's Eve no bread is baked and no clothes are washed, and the spinning-wheel must be carried from one side of the house to the other.[3] The Twelve Days over and above the year were called in Wales "days of days" *dyddiau dyddiau*. "They are free days, and let any one come from any place he may, he will be free, and exposed to no weapon or strike, since there can be no court and law of country on those days."[4]

The solar year, superseding the lunar year of three hundred and fifty-four days, seems to have been generally assumed in the first instance at the round number of three hundred and sixty days, the earth's periodical course around the sun being taken as a multiple of the moon's course around the earth. In ancient Mexico, where a solar calendar came into use, the three hundred and sixty days were divided into eighteen periods, each of twenty days. As their total did not round out the solar year it became necessary to add five days at the end of the year; and these possessed

[1] J. Loth, "Les douze jours supplémentaires *gour-deziou* des Bretons, et les douze nuits des Germains et des Indous," *Revue celtique*, 1905, xxix, 310-312.

[2] Miss C. S. Burne, editor, *Shropshire Folk-lore*, London, 1883, p. 405.

[3] W. Gregor, *Notes on the Folk-lore of the North-east of Scotland*, London, 1881, p. 156; idem, in *Folk-lore Journal*, 1884, ii, 332.

[4] John Williams ab Ithel, *Barddas*, Llandovery, 1862-1874, i, 424, 425.

an unfavourable character. They were called *nemontemi*, "the superfluous, supplementary days," with
the secondary significance of "the useless days," as
being consecrated to no deity and employed for no
civic business. That they were considered sinister
and unlucky is evident from the abstinence that characterized them. Nothing of any importance was
done on the *nemontemi*. The house was not swept,
no legal case was tried, and any person so unfortunate
as to be born on one of these days was destined to a
poor and miserable life. At the same time, the *nemontemi* possessed a prophetic power for the whole year.
"They were careful," says Father Sahagun, "during
these fatal days not to fall asleep during the day, not
to quarrel together, not to trip or to fall, because they
said that if any of these things befell them, they would
continue to befall them thence forevermore." [1] Among
the Mayas of Yucatan the same abstinence prevailed
on the five *xma kaba kin*, the "days without names."
On these days "men left the house as seldom as possible, did not wash or comb themselves, and took special
care not to undertake any menial or difficult task,
doubtless because they lived in the conviction that
they would be forced to keep on doing it through
the whole ensuing year. The Mexicans were more
passive in regard to these days, inasmuch as they merely
took care to avoid conjuring up mischief for the coming
year, while the Mayas did things more thoroughly.
During these days, so portentous for the entire year,
they banished the evil which might threaten them.
They prepared a clay image of the demon of evil,

[1] E. Seler, "The Mexican Chro-
nology," *Bulletin of the Bureau of
American Ethnology*, no. 28, p. 16.
The passage quoted above is
from Seler's translation of the
Aztec text of Sahagun, which is
more complete than the latter's
Spanish version (*Historia general
de las cosas de Nueva España*, ii,
37; transl. Jourdanet and Siméon,
Paris, 1880, pp. 50, 77, 164, 283,
291). Other Spanish authorities
refer to the *nemontemi* as days
when the people did nothing but
receive and return visits (Clavigero,
Storia antica del Messico, vi. 24;
Acosta, *Historia de las Indias*,
vi, 2).

Uuayayab, that is, *u-uayab-haab* ('by whom the year is poisoned'), confronted it with the deity who had supreme power during the year in question, and then carried it out of the village in the direction of that cardinal point to which the new year belonged." [1]

It is an impressive testimony to the essential unity of primitive culture that in a far distant quarter of the globe an almost identical superstition existed. The Egyptian solar calendar, like the Mexican, was based on a year of three hundred and sixty days, but in Egypt these were grouped into twelve equal months of thirty days each, leaving five supplementary days to be added at the end of the twelfth month — "the five days over and above the year" (*haru duaït hiru ronpit*), as they were styled.[2] Their great antiquity is indicated by another designation, "little month," applied to them; and, in fact, a notice of the epagomenal days occurs in the *Pyramid Texts* belonging to the Sixth Dynasty, where they are referred to as the "five additional days" on which the gods were born.[3] Later monumental records show that the deities associated respectively with these days were the five members of the Osirian cycle, Osiris, Horus, Set, Isis, and Nephthys.[4] The evidence of the *Leiden Papyrus*, setting forth the ceremonies requisite for epagomenal days, indicates that

[1] E. Seler, in *Bulletin of the Bureau of American Ethnology*, no. 28, pp. 16 *sq.*; compare *idem*, in Hastings's *Encyclopædia of Religion and Ethics*, iii, 308. The principal authority for the Maya custom is Diego de Landa, *Relación de las cosas de Yucatan*, ch. xxxv (transl. Brasseur de Bourbourg, pp. 211 *sqq.*).

[2] These five days thus inserted between the "small year" and the "large year" did not interrupt the regular sequence of the three decades into which the Egyptian month was divided; see above, p. 191.

[3] Pepi, 2, l. 754. A still earlier reference is found in an inscription belonging to the time of the Fifth Dynasty (K. Sethe, *Urkunden des alten Reichs*, Leipzig, 1903, i, 24).

[4] H. Brugsch, "Die fünf Epagomenen in einem hieratischen Papyrus zu Leiden," *Zeitschrift der deutschen morgenländischen Gesellschaft*, 1852, v, 254–258; compare *idem*, *Die Ägyptologie*, Leipzig, 1891, p. 362; C. R. Lepsius, *Die Chronologie der Ägypter*, Berlin, 1849, i, 145 *sqq.* The chief classical references to the epagomenal days are Herodotus, ii, 4; Plutarch, *De Iside et Osiride*, 12; and Diodorus Siculus, i, 13, 4.

they enjoyed exceptional importance because of their position at the end of the year. As religious festivals they were consecrated to the dead. Furthermore, they bore a distinctly ominous or unlucky character, and many were the prayers and magical formulas to be recited by the pious worshipper in order to secure divine protection against the malefic influences supposed to characterize them. To positive rites of prayer and sacrifice the worshipper must add cessation of all activity: "during the five days at the end of the year do no work; abstain from everything" — so runs the priestly text.[1] These precautions taken, he might look forward to a happy New Year.

The conquest of Egypt in the sixth century B.C. by the Achæmenian kings seems to have introduced a knowledge of the excellencies of the Egyptian solar reckoning to the Persians. Their five epagomenal days were called the Gāthā-days, each being sacred to one of the five great divisions of the *Gāthās*, or Zoroastrian hymns. A Persian calendar of late date (1687 A.D.) gives the first day as lucky, and the third as unlucky.[2] It is significant that among the Persians, as in ancient Egypt, the epagomenal days particularly belonged to the dead, to whom sacrifices were regularly offered at this time, as well as during the first five days of the new year.[3] The Armenians also had their five supplementary days — *aweleach* — intercalated after the twelfth month, an arrangement doubtless borrowed from the Persians, but these days do

[1] F. J. Chabas, *Le calendrier des jours fastes et néfastes de l'année égyptienne*, Chalon-s.-S., 1870, pp. 102–107. In the *Leiden Papyrus* (i. 346) only the first, third, and fifth days are marked with the same sign as unlucky, but the observances prescribed relate to all five days. Plutarch (*op. cit.*, 12) refers to the third day, that of Set or Tryphon, as inauspicious for Egyptian kings, who did no business on it and took no care of their persons till nightfall. The parallel to the royal observance of the Babylonian "evil days" is instructive (above, pp. 232 *sq.*).

[2] L. H. Gray, "Calendar (Persian)," Hastings's *Encyclopædia of Religion and Ethics*, iii, 129; *idem*, "Divination (Persian)," *ibid.*, iv, 819.

[3] F. Justi, *Geschichte des alten Persiens*, Berlin, 1879, p. 79.

not appear to have been marked by any special observances.[1] The latest attempt to introduce the use of epagomenal days dates from the time of the French Revolution. In their desire to abolish a chronological system bound up with the Christian religion the bold innovators of the National Convention set aside in 1793 the Gregorian calendar, establishing a Republican calendar in which the seven-day week was replaced by the decade and the year was divided into twelve months of thirty days each, according to the old Egyptian arrangement. Five intercalary days, popularly called *sansculottides*, came at the end of the year (six days at the end of every fourth year); they were dedicated to Virtue, Genius, Labour, Opinion, and Reward; and were observed as holidays. But this calendar, which John Quincy Adams described as an "incongruous composition of profound learning and superficial frivolity, of irreligion and morality, of delicate imagination and coarse vulgarity," had a short life. In 1802 the week of seven days returned into general use, and three years later an edict of Napoleon ordered the restoration of the Gregorian calendar.[2] In our own time, however, serious proposals have been made looking toward the reformation of the present awkward calendar, and among them is the suggestion that we adopt the ancient Egyptian system of months and epagomenal days.

It has been repeatedly noticed in the preceding pages that oftentimes no clear line of demarcation can be drawn between days *tabu* and days considered "unlucky." Both may involve ideas of contagion, the sanctity or pollution attaching to the one being conceived as scarcely less transmissible than the vaguer "unluckiness" which belongs to certain periods and affects everything done during their continuance.

[1] F. Macler, "Calendar (Armenian)," Hastings's *Encyclopedia of Religion and Ethics*, iii, 70.

[2] J. Levering, in *Proceedings of the American Academy of Arts and Sciences*, 1873, viii, 348–364; "Calendrier républicain," *La grande encyclopédie*, viii, 908–910.

How some of the so-called unlucky days, still lingering in contemporary civilization, have descended from the holy days of antiquity is aptly illustrated by the superstitions relating to the certain days of March and of August, as observed at the present time in south-eastern Europe. In Macedonia the peasants during the first three days and the last three days of these two months do not plant: they cut no tree or vine, for fear lest it should wither: they do not bathe in the sea, or their bodies would swell; and they even refrain from washing clothes.[1] In various parts of Greece and the Ægean it is considered necessary to abstain from particular kinds of work on certain days of August, and occasionally of March. During the first five days of August the people of Epirus do not wash clothes or go into the fields to work. In Crete the period is longer, for here on the first six and last six days of August clothes are not washed and grapes are not gathered.[2] In Cos on the first three days of August the women do no work, for it would not prosper, and wash no clothes, for these would soon wear out. The eleven days which follow are supposed to foreshadow the weather during the succeeding eleven months: as the fourth day is, so will September be; the fifth day prognosticates the weather for October, and so on. The fifteenth of August is celebrated as the Feast of the Assumption, closing a fortnight's strict fast.[3] The Cypriotes observe the first three or six days of August as times when no trees are cut or peeled to obtain resin, when the use of water for washing clothes or the body is forbidden, and when no one travels by water. The severity of the regulations has led to the days being called the "evil days of August."[4]

[1] Abbott, op. cit., pp. 21, 23. The Macedonians observe the same restrictions on the Wednesdays and Fridays of these two months.
[2] Miss Mary Hamilton, Greek Saints and their Festivals, Edinburgh, 1910, pp. 187 sq.
[3] W. H. D. Rouse, "Folklore from the Southern Sporades," Folk-lore, 1899, x. 170.
[4] J. C. Lawson, Modern Greek Folklore and Ancient Greek Religion, Cambridge, 1910, pp. 152 sq.

All these taboos thus show much similarity, relating in particular to abstention from work which has to do with water or with vines and trees. From this fact it becomes a plausible inference that the unlucky days were originally sacred to the tree-nymphs and water-nymphs, whose festivals were celebrated in pagan antiquity. At the present time the days are associated with the crystal mysterious spirit supposed to be abroad on them, and probably to be identified with the arvant of classic mythology.

The likeness between tabooed days as periods of abstinence and some unlucky days may be further illustrated by much ethnographic evidence drawn from different culture areas. The Maori, we are told, endeavour to determine by divination whether the day set for a journey is favourable or unfavourable. The fisherman is hopeless of making a catch on an unfavourable day. At such a time no cress will be commenced no seine cast no fish-pool bailed no ground turned up no seed sown distant visit made hair cut or dressed timber cut canoe formed or even food partaken of. The Batta of Sumatra possess elaborate calendars of days favourable, unfavourable, and of a doubtful character; and these are regularly consulted by the Batta magician in order that his clients may know when to commence any important undertaking such as sowing and harvesting house-building erection of a new village removal to another village preparation of sacrifice at birth name-giving burial betrothal and marriage and all other great occasions. A day may be wholly unlucky for one thing but not for another; for instance a day which could not safely be used for the celebration of a sacrifice might still be used for the inauguration of agricultural labour. On the other hand there are certain days indicated in the calendar when all activity ceases except the entertainment of relatives and mon-

J. E. Polack, Manners and Customs of the New Zealanders, London, page ...

pensable harvest work. If a man should meet with misfortune on one of these fatal days, a sacrifice must be offered to the supernatural power supposed to be responsible for the visitation. The Batta calendar in its existing form is derived from India, but the people seem formerly to have possessed their own rude calendar, which was used to determine the lucky and unlucky days in a lunar month. Even at the present time the calendar is not employed for the fixation of dates in the European sense, but only in the service of popular superstition.[1]

The Mohammedan Malays of the Malay Peninsula possess a number of divinatory calendars, one specifying seven unlucky days in every month, a second, twelve other most inauspicious days in every year, while a third gives all the days of the year classified under the heads lucky, somewhat unlucky, most unlucky, and neutral.[2] Chinese popular calendars set forth a similar classification of the days of the month as very lucky, neither lucky nor unlucky, unlucky, and very unlucky.[3] Furthermore, the first, fifth, and ninth months are considered unfavourable by the Chinese, who will not marry or change houses during

---

[1] J. Winkler, "Der Kalender der Toba-Bataks auf Sumatra," Zeitschrift für Ethnologie, 1913, xlv, 436-447. Among the Batta dwelling inland from the Bay of Tapanuli the priest or magician, whose duty it is to announce propitious days, is a most important functionary in every village. The people "will not engage in any undertaking, however trifling, or make the smallest alteration in their domestic economy, without first consulting him" (Burton and Ward, in Memoirs of the Royal Asiatic Society, 1827, i, 500).

[2] W. W. Skeat, Malay Magic, London, 1900, p. 549.

[3] N. B. Dennys, The Folk-lore of China, London, 1876, pp. 30 sq.

In China there is also the state almanac, which is annually prepared at Pekin under the direction of a bureau attached to the Board of Rites. By making it a penal offence to issue a counterfeit or pirated edition of this almanac, the government astrologers have monopolized the management of the superstitions of the people in regard to the fortunate or unfortunate conjunction of each day and hour. "No one ventures to be without an almanac, lest he be liable to the greatest misfortunes, and run the imminent hazard of undertaking important events on black-balled days" (S. W. Williams, The Middle Kingdom,[2] New York, 1883, ii, 79 sq.).

these months. In Korea the fifth, fifteenth, and twenty-fifth days of each month are called "broken days." At such times the people avoid any new undertakings.[1] The old Japanese are said to have had five yearly festivals or holidays, "purposely laid on those days which, by reason of their impurity, are judged to be the most unfortunate." These were New Year's Day, the third day of the third month, the fifth of the fifth month, the seventh of the seventh month, and the ninth of the ninth month.[2] In modern Japan the cheap popular calendars, circulating among the lower classes, contain indications for every day of a cycle of six days. Of these, the first is described as good during the forenoon for urgent business, such as lawsuits and petitions, but not good after midday. The second is good in the forenoon and in the evening, but not in the afternoon. The first half of the third day is bad, and no urgent business should be undertaken at such a time; the afternoon, however, is lucky. Nothing done on the fourth day will prosper. The fifth day is very lucky for anything, especially removals or journeys. With the exception of the noontide hour the whole of the sixth day is unlucky. This cycle used in divination furnishes side by side with the week of seven days.[3]

The Tibetans are great astrologers. In every monastery there is at least one divining lama whose business it is to determine propitious and unpropitious times. Calendars exist for all the days of the month, some being described as "good," others as "middling," others as "bad," while one is referred to as "not very good," and still another as "the worst." Among the causes of the luck or unluck attaching to certain days the Tibetans are inclined to lay stress on the periodical

[1] E. A. Slen, *A Journey in Korea: Korea as a Sovereign Power* ... *For Lord Stanmore*, 1891, p. 75.

[2] W. E. Griffis, *Corea, the Hermit Nation* (New York, 1882), p. 306.

[3] E. Kaempfer, *History of Japan*, ii. ... (Glasgow reprint, 1906).

[4] A. Levi, "Death and Disposal of the Dead Japanese," Hastings's *Encyclopaedia of Religion and Ethics*, iv. 486 ff.

migrations of the spirits inhabiting the regions above the earth. It seems that the two kinds of spirits, good and evil, shift their abodes, to some extent every day and also contemporaneously with the phases of the moon, the commencement of a new season, and so on. Their migrations are performed with unequal velocity; hence, the combination of spirits varies for every day. If the good spirits are more numerous than the evil spirits on a particular day, the time will be favourable for any undertaking; and *vice versa*. This belief, we are told, offers a wide field of intrigue to the lamas, who alone are able to decide what have been the actual movements of the spirits.[1]

The Toda, who dwell in permanent villages on the plateaus of the Nilgiri Hills in southeastern India, have a remarkable system of rest days deserving to be described at some length. The social organization of this interesting people consists of two endogamous divisions, called Teivaliol and Tartharol. Each of these primary sections is composed of intermarrying clans, and each clan possesses a group of villages in common. At the present time Toda interests, both economic and religious, centre about their buffaloes. The daily life of the Toda men is largely devoted to the care of these animals and to labour in the dairies. The buffalo is a sacred animal; the dairy itself is almost a temple; and the dairyman is only one remove from a priest. Toda religious rites seem to be, in fact, little more than the arrangements which a pastoral and communistic people have made for the provision and care of an article of food. According to Dr. Rivers, whose careful studies are a model of anthropological investigation, nearly every Toda ceremony has its appointed day or days. The choice of these "is often dependent on another Toda institution, the sacred day, either of the village or of the dairy. Every clan has certain days of the week on which people are

[1] E. Schlagintweit, *Buddhism in Tibet*, Leipzig and London, 1863, pp. 243 *sqq.*

restricted from following many of their ordinary occupations, although they are not the occasions of any special ceremonies. These sacred days are the *madnol*, or village day, and the *palinol*, or dairy day." [1]

Each Toda village has its *madnol*, but, in general, where there are several villages of the same clan, the *madnol* is the same for the whole clan. There are at least eight prohibitions characterizing the observance of this sacred day. Feasts may not be given at such a time, funeral ceremonies may not be performed, people may not bathe or cut their nails, and men may not shave. Clothes are not to be washed, the house is not to be cleansed, and, though the ordinary meals may be prepared, rice and milk must not be cooked together. Other regulations forbid the dairyman to leave the village, the buffaloes to be taken from one place to another, or the people to migrate from one village to another.[2] Though not all work is prohibited, the regulations are extensive enough to affect most of the customary occupations. Among the Teivaliol, one of the two endogamous divisions of the Toda people, the *madnol* is the only sacred day of the week. With the other division, called Tartharol, there is also a dairy day, or *palinol*, the regulations for which have much the same character as for the *madnol*.

Toda ingenuity has devised recognized methods of evading the rules for the holy days, and so of avoiding the inconvenience which might otherwise be entailed on the people. The rule that nothing may be taken from the village on the *madnol* would prevent any purchases from outsiders being made on the holy day, since money would have to pass out of the village in payment. The Toda avoid this awkward consequence by the simple device of taking money beyond the village limits on the day before the *madnol* and burying it in some spot where it can be found when wanted. The rule forbidding Toda women to leave the village

[1] W. H. R. Rivers, *The Todas*, London, 1906, p. 405.　　[2] *Ibid.*, pp. 405 *sq.*

v

on the *madnol* is evaded in a curious fashion. A woman will depart from the settlement before daybreak, will remain outside till the sun is up, and will then return to her home, for breakfast and the performance of any necessary work. During this time she is regarded as ceremonially absent from the village, hence her actual departure later in the day for another village is not considered to be a desecration of the *madnol*. With these possibilities of evasion open to the pious Toda, it follows that the regulations are seldom broken, in the letter if not in the spirit. When a breach of them does occur, the culprit may be obliged to perform a propitiatory sacrifice similar to that which follows the commission of various other ceremonial sins. "It seemed quite clear, however, that this only happened if some misfortune should befall the offender, his family, or his buffaloes. It would seem that a man might habitually and notoriously desecrate the *madnol*, but no steps would be taken by himself or the community so long as things went well with the man. If he should become ill or if his buffaloes should suffer in any way, he would consult the diviners and they would then certainly find that his misfortunes were due to his infringement of the laws connected with the sacred days." [1]

There is much variety in the days observed as the *madnol* or the *palinol* of the different villages and clans. The most frequent days appear to be Wednesday and Friday, which are sacred in six clans. Sunday is sacred in five clans, Monday and Tuesday in three, Thursday in two. In no clan does Saturday appear to be kept as a holy day. [2]

The origin of these sacred days among the Toda is very obscure. Dr. Rivers first suggests the possibility of the institution of *madnol* and *palinol* having grown out of the belief in unlucky days. The code of rules prescribing what might and what might not be done would then be only an elaboration of the common supersti-

[1] Rivers, *Todas*, p. 407. [2] *Ibid.*, p. 408.

tion which restricts activity at such unlucky periods. But there are several difficulties in the way of this view. It is extremely doubtful whether the Toda has any such belief in days lucky and unlucky,[1] and if he has, the idea is probably a recent importation from the Hindus, among whom the superstition is very prevalent. Again, the distinction between *madnol* and *palinol* is one which cannot be satisfactorily explained by such a hypothesis. Finally, the different clans of the Toda have different sacred days, whereas one would expect lucky and unlucky days to be the same for the entire community. This seems especially reasonable when it is considered that the sacred days, by restricting intercourse between the different clans, produce much inconvenience, which, of course, is increased by the fact that the different clans have different *madnol*. Whatever be the origin of these Toda rules, there is, writes Dr. Rivers, "little doubt that when at the present time a given act is done or not done on a given day, the action is not based on a belief in lucky or unlucky days, but, as nearly always among the Toda, on custom prescribing that the act shall or shall not be done on that day." [2]

The question may be raised whether the resemblance of the Toda *madnol* to the Hebrew Sabbath is not accounted for by supposing the former institution to have been founded on ideas borrowed from Christians or Jews. If this has been the case, it is certain that the borrowing took place very long ago. In studying the origin and history of the Toda we have no record that reaches back more than three centuries. From various close resemblances between the Toda customs and those of the people of Malabar, Dr. Rivers thinks it probable that the Toda at one time lived in Malabar, migrating thence to the Nilgiri Hills. Both Chris-

---

[1] See *ibid.*, p. 411, for a reference to certain restrictions which may have arisen out of a belief in unlucky days. W. R. King (*Journal of Anthropology*, 1870, i, 33 *sq.*) expressly attributes this superstition to the Toda.

[2] Rivers, *Todas*, pp. 410 *sq.*

tians and Jews were well established in Malabar more than a thousand years ago. If the Toda left Malabar before these settlements of foreigners were made, then Jewish or Christian influences can be excluded; if the migration took place subsequently, then they may have contributed to the development of the Toda institution.[1]

In spite of these considerations, Dr. Rivers is inclined to consider the Toda *madnol* as substantially a native institution, which may help to explain the origin of the Hebrew Sabbath. "In a·busier community than that of the Toda, the existence of different *madnol* for different clans of the community would soon become a serious obstacle to carrying on the business of life, and such a community would probably agree that all clans should have the same holy day. At present the *madnol* is undoubtedly more sacred than the other sacred days, and if the latter were then to be neglected, we should have a community in which various activities were prohibited on one day of the week, and the institution so arising would differ very little from the Hebrew Sabbath. It is possible that the Toda show in an early stage the institution of a Sabbath in which the whole community has not yet settled on a single and joint holy day." [2] The fact that the Toda employ the seven-day week, which must be entirely a borrowed institution with them, suggests, however, that the prohibitions attaching to certain days of that week were ultimately derived from foreign sources.[3]

---

[1] Rivers, *Todas*, pp. 459, 695 *sqq.*, 710 *sq.*

[2] *Ibid.*, pp. 411 *sq.*

[3] These Toda taboos suggest at once the Jewish sabbatarian regulations and the methods of evading or mitigating them devised by the rabbis (above, p. 264). Until the present day the Bene-Israel, a body of Jews domiciled for many centuries in the Bombay Presidency, have preserved the old Hebrew fasts and festivals, though under Indian names and with Indian features superadded. Their habit of observing Saturday as a Sabbath and of giving their oxen rest from the oil-mills on that day has gained for them among their Hindu neighbours the name of "the Saturday oil-men " (J. H. Lord, "Bene-Israel," Hastings's *Encyclopædia of Religion and Ethics*, ii, 470 *sq.*).

Another curious instance of communal rest days is found among the Siah Posh Kafirs, a primitive Aryan people dwelling in the northeastern part of Afghanistan, between Chitral and the Hindu-Kush. They seem formerly to have occupied a more extended area about the headwaters of the Indus. The conversion of the surrounding tribes, first to Buddhism and later to Mohammedanism, has further served to isolate them. With the Afghans on the west their enmity is deadly and unceasing, but their relations with their eastern neighbours admit of friendly intercourse. It is on this side, therefore, that we must look for the introduction into Kafiristan of Indian cultural elements, among which is the seven-day week.[1] On certain weekdays the Siah Posh Kafirs rest from work. Young and old gather in large buildings erected in the centre of the villages and here they dance all night, to the music of flutes and trumpets, and sing songs in honour of the gods.[2] According to a later and fuller account, the Kafir rest days are called *agar;* in some districts they occur every Thursday, in other districts, every Saturday, but only during the months from April to September, when field work is in progress. The *agar* appear to be rigorously observed by the male inhabitants of a village, but the women, who stop their field-work on these days, do not scruple to engage in other coolie labour during their continuance. "I failed," writes our authority, "to discover anything concerning the origin of these *agar*. Their observance may have become a national custom, the origin of which is as difficult to determine as the Sabbaths of other ancient peoples. As the Kám people were averse to starting on a journey on the *agar* days, and as all the women left their field-work altogether on those occasions, it

[1] The week of seven days, with names derived from the Sanskrit, appears to have been introduced by the Shins into Dardistan and western Kashmir. See J. Biddulf, *Tribes of the Hindoo-Koosh*, Calcutta, 1880, p. 93; G. W. Leitner, *The Hunza and Nagyr Handbook*,[2] Woking, 1893, p. 16.

[2] H. Roskoschny, *Afghanistan und seine Nachbarländer*, Leipzig, 1885, i, 174.

is possible that the *agar* was originally considered an unlucky day." [1]

Perhaps no people have subjected themselves to more irksome restrictions on unlucky days than the natives of Madagascar. In this island systems of taboo are widespread and elaborate, even at the present time. The term *fady* (or *tabu*), used for all objects and persons tabooed, is likewise applied by the Malagasy to unfavourable days and months, the quality of such periods as dangerous or unlucky being considered transmissible to beings and actions.[2] By the Hova, a people of remote, perhaps prehistoric, Malay origin, now occupying the central tableland of Madagascar, only twelve days in the month were regarded as lucky. The first days of some months possessed a most disastrous character, and children born on them were usually put to death. The same cruel practice was found among other tribes, such as the Bara and Tanala, leading, in the latter case, to the destruction of at least one-fourth of all the infants born.[3] The Tanala consider one of the months, called *faosa*, extremely unlucky. "No one works in that month, no one changes his place of abode or goes about. If any one happens to be in the fields

---

[1] Sir G. S. Robertson, *The Káfirs of the Hindu-Kush*, London, 1896, pp. 579 *sq.*

[2] A. van Gennep, *Tabou et totémisme à Madagascar*, Paris, 1904, p. 199. The Malagasy belief in lucky and unlucky days, as determined by the moon stations (above, p. 275), appears to be a direct importation from the Arabs superimposed on an earlier and thoroughly native observance of tabooed seasons. The Malagasy have also taken over from Islam the week of seven days (above, p. 197).

[3] J. Sibree, "Malagasy Folklore and Popular Superstitions," *Folk-lore Record*, 1879, ii, 30–33. The custom still exists among the Masikoro, an inland branch of the Sakalava tribe. Many Vezo (coast Sakalava) families continue to expose a child born on an unlucky day, but it is afterwards rescued and brought up by the relatives as their own. "Such a child is, however, looked upon with some suspicion as to what will be its character, because of its having been born on an unlucky day. It is thought that it may bring some calamity upon the family, or may itself be miserable or unfortunate in one way or another, when grown up. It is a very common opinion that bad conduct is only the result of being born on an unlucky day" (A. Walen, in *Antananarivo Annual*, 1883, no. 7, pp. 51 *sq.*).

when the month comes in, there he remains." [1] The Sihanaka keep Tuesday as an unlucky day on which no work is allowed in the fields. Each Sihanaka family, in addition, inherits a special unlucky day in each week, when it is not permissible to go outside the house.[2] The Sakalava likewise abstain from all business and remain strictly in seclusion on their unlucky days, which belong both to families and to individuals.[3] Among the Betsimisaraka each person has his unlucky day when he does not work; in fact, he can do nothing at this time except eat, drink, sleep, and dress his hair. Since the introduction of Christianity the day kept in this strict fashion is Sunday.[4]

These accounts of lucky and unlucky days observed by half-civilized peoples at the present time throw light on the references to the same superstition found in the records of archaic civilizations. For Egypt we have the evidence of several ancient calendars preserved in papyrus manuscripts. The first of these dates from the Twelfth Dynasty (about 2000 B.C.) and includes all the days of the month, eighteen being defined as "good," nine as "bad," and three (the sixteenth, twenty-second, and twenty-third), as "half-good" and "half-bad." The primitive character of this calendar is indicated by the fact that the same prognostics are attached to the same days of the month throughout the year. The second calendar, dating from about 1000 B.C., is more complicated, since the prognostics of the several days are unlike in the different months, while each day is itself divided into three parts, lucky, unlucky, and neutral. Neither calendar contains mention of the five epagomenal days.[5]

[1] J. Sibree, loc. cit.

[2] A. van Gennep, op. cit., p. 203; Antananarivo Annual, 1891, no. 15, pp. 302 sq.

[3] V. Noel, in Bulletin de la société de géographie, 1843, second series, xx, 71.

[4] A. van Gennep, op. cit., pp. 202 sq.

[5] The two manuscripts (both in the British Museum) have been edited, respectively, by F. L. Griffith (Hieratic Papyri from Kahun and Gurob, London, 1898, pl. 25

The third and best-known of these Egyptian calendars is the *Papyrus Sallier IV*, which in its present
form belongs to about 1200 B.C. but is based on much
earlier documents.[1] Parts of the manuscript at the
beginning and end have been lost, so that it now contains prognostics for only two hundred and thirty-
five days of the year. This interesting production
of ancient though misdirected learning divides the hours
between the rising and the setting of the sun into three
periods, each of which is ruled by its particular influence. Some days were good throughout the three
periods, some were wholly bad, others were critical
— *dubium sed in malum vergens* — while others again
presented combinations of these three characteristics.
The following are typical regulations, arranged according to the order of the Egyptian months.[2] 22
Thoth : eat no fish and light no oil lamp. 23 Thoth :
put no incense on the fire ; kill no animals, domestic
or wild ; eat neither a goose nor a goat. A child born
on this day will amount to nothing. 26 Thoth : do
nothing on this day. 4 Paophi : do not go out of the
house. 5 Paophi : do not go out of the house ; do

text, p. 62 ; and E. A. W. Budge, *Facsimiles of Egyptian Hieratic Papyri*, London, 1911, pls. 31-32). See further W. Wreszinski, "Tage-wählerei im alten Ägypten," *Archiv für Religionswissenschaft*, 1913, xvi, 86-100.

[1] The text was published in *Select Papyri in the Hieratic Character*, London, 1844, pt. i, pls. 144-168, and was translated by F. J. Chabas (*Le calendrier des jours fastes et néfastes de l'année égyptienne*, Chalon-s.-S., 1870). The work of Chabas was masterly, but it has now become antiquated by the progress of Egyptology. F. Bohn (*Der Sabbat im Alten Testament*, Gütersloh, 1903, pp. 57-62) gives a revised and corrected ver-sion of numerous passages, based on the studies of Professor Sethe,

and Wreszinski (*loc. cit.*) translates directly from the Egyptian text. For discussions of this important document see Sir G. Maspero, *Études égyptiennes*, Paris, 1886, i, 29 *sq.* ; *idem*, *Les contes populaires de l'Égypte ancienne*,[2] Paris, 1905, pp. xlix-lii ; *idem*, *New Light on Ancient Egypt*,[2] London, 1909, pp. 128-136 ; A. Erman, *Life in Ancient Egypt*, London, 1894, pp. 351 *sq.* ; A. Wiedemann, *The Religion of the Ancient Egyptians*, London, 1897, pp. 263 *sqq.* ; E. A. W. Budge, *Egyptian Magic*,[2] Lon-don, 1901, pp. 224 *sqq.* ; G. Fou-cart, "Calendar (Egyptian)," Hast-ings's *Encyclopædia of Religion and Ethics*, iii, 100 *sq.*

[2] W. Wreszinski, in *Archiv für Religionswissenschaft*, 1913, xvi, 89 *sqq.*

not have intercourse with a woman. 22 Paophi: do not wash and do not approach a stream. 19 Athyr: light no fire. 6 Mechir: do no work. 13 Pharmuthi: do not go anywhere. In the calendar as a whole the most frequent injunctions relate to quitting the house, travelling, sailing, and undertaking any kind of work. Next in number are the prohibitions of loud talking, singing, and sexual intercourse. There are also prohibitions of drinking, bathing, and killing or eating certain animals, besides others directed against the use of fire and lights. It is clear that in this curious treatise we have a systematization of popular taboos relating to the lucky or unlucky character of certain days. The fact that it was used as a boy's schoolbook indicates how priestly influence had erected into a pseudo-science the uncouth and childish superstitions of the multitude. The calendar itself presents evidence that the priests had begun to rationalize the taboos, for the prohibitions are often accompanied by a summary of the motives which justified them, usually legendary episodes of the gods. For instance, the regulation for the twenty-sixth of Thoth — "do absolutely nothing" — is explained by a reference to the terrific combat between Horus and his uncle Set, which occurred on this ill-omened day.[1]

The Babylonian augural calendar for the intercalated month of Elul and for Markheshwan is not the only example of omen literature to be found in the cuneiform records. We possess a document, preserved in great part, which includes every day in the year, either specifying its nature as favourable or unfavourable or adding other indications with regard to its character. A note like "hostility," appended to the twenty-first day of the second month, is a warning that the gods are out of humour on that day; the twenty-third day, described as "heart not good," is explained by the contrast "heart glad" on the following day. Not content with a simple distinction of

[1] Chabas, op. cit., p. 28; Wreszinski in Archiv für Religionswissenschaft, 1913, xvi, 92 sq.

favourableness and unfavourableness, the calendar
also deals with days "wholly favourable" and "half
favourable." Still other days are noted as those por-
tending "distress," "trouble," "tears," "injury,"
"darkness," "moon obscured," and the like. The precautions and prohibitions set forth for unlucky days
include, among many others, the familiar taboos of
eating specified foods, such as swine's flesh, beef, dates,
and fish, sexual intercourse, buying and selling, wearing
bright garments, travelling, holding law courts, and
so on. The calendar contains a number of references
to the king and may, very probably, have served the
priests in their instructions to the monarch. As
Professor Jastrow remarks, the belief in lucky and
unlucky days has a distinctly popular flavour, making
it probable that the priests embodied in their lists
many of the notions that arose among the people, and
gave to these an official sanction.[1]

The Greeks of Hesiod's time possessed an elaborate
calendar of lucky and unlucky days.[2] "Sometimes
a day is a stepmother, sometimes a mother," Hesiod
remarks pithily. What ancient regulations for the
observance of tabooed periods are embodied in the
calendar is problematical. Many of the prohibitions
with which the first part of the poem concludes are,
however, thoroughly primitive taboos.[3] Hesiod does

---

[1] Rawlinson, *Cuneiform Inscriptions of Western Asia*, v, pls. 48, 49;
Jastrow, *Religion of Babylonia and
Assyria*, pp. 379 *sqq.*, Bohn, *Der
Sabbat im Alten Testament*, pp. 55
sqq. A Babylonian tablet (K. 98),
published by Professor Sayce
(*Zeitschrift für Assyriologie*, 1887,
ii, 333–335), gives a list of days on
which it was fortunate to undertake
such operations as "staking the
canal," "thinning the plantation,"
and "sinking the foundations of a
house." Still another text, published by Dr. Stephen Langdon
(*Expositor*, 1909, xxii, 156), contains the injunction that on the
fifth day of Nisan "he who fears
Marduk or Sarpanit shall not go
out to work." On the Babylonian
subattu see above, p. 241 n.[1]

[2] *Opera et dies*, 765–828. On the
Hesiodic calendar see E. E. Sikes,
"Folk-lore in the Works and Days
of Hesiod," *Classical Review*, 1893,
vii, 389–394, and the Addenda to
Professor A. W. Mair's admirable
version of Hesiod, Oxford, 1908, pp.
162–166. For a full analysis of the
calendar see A. Mommsen, *Chronologie*, Leipzig, 1883, pp. 39–46.

[3] *Opera et dies*, 724–764.

not mention any days when labour is to be entirely
abandoned. We may assume, perhaps, that at the
period when the Hesiodic poems were composed the
rationalizing temper of the Greeks had gotten somewhat the better of their superstitious fears. In the
Hesiodic list, as in the Egyptian and Babylonian
calendars, the notion appears that not only whole
days but even parts of days have an individual character, working for good or evil. The middle ninth (the
nineteenth) is said to be "a better day toward afternoon." The "fourth which followeth the twentieth
of the month is the best at dawn, but it is worse toward
afternoon." Hesiod does not distinguish the months
as lucky or unlucky, and the days which possess either
of these attributes are the same for every month. He
gives no explanation for their luckiness or unluckiness,
though traces of a rationalizing process are perhaps
observable in the directions regarding the "fifths"
(presumably the fifth, fifteenth, and twenty-fifth
days), which are specially unlucky "because on the
fifth men say the Erinyes attended the birth of Oath
(Horkos), whom Strife bare to punish perjurers."
The seventh again is lucky, "for on that day Leto bare
Apollo of the Golden Sword." [1] The Hesiodic injunctions did not cease to be observed in the later classical
epoch and exercised great influence on civil and political life. The superstitions relating to unlucky days
only gained a firmer foothold, under the influence of
Babylonian and Egyptian doctrines, in passing from
Greece to Rome and from Rome to western Europe. [2]

During the Middle Ages perhaps the most widespread
observance of unlucky days had to do with those which
went under the significant name of *dies Ægyptiaci*.
The prohibitions marking them — not to build a house,

---

[1] *Ibid.*, 810, 820, 802 *sqq.*, 770.

[2] The Vergilian calendar (*Georgica*, i, 276 *sqq.*) is obviously an
imitation of Hesiod's, but it may
be presumed that Vergil, with his
intimate knowledge of the farmer's
life, incorporated in his catalogue
of lucky and unlucky days some of
the peasant lore of ancient Italy.

not to buy or sell, not to cut hair, beard, and nails,
and so on — possessed, however, no character specifically Egyptian. The mediæval belief was that these
days received their designation because on one of them
the plagues had been sent to devastate the land
of Egypt, and on another Pharaoh and his host had
been swallowed up in the Red Sea. As early as the
fourth century A.D. Christian writers refer to "Egyptian
days" as times feared and avoided by both pagans
and converts to Christianity.[1] About this period the
superstition gained admittance to the state calendars.
In the *fasti Philocali* (354 A.D.), twenty-five *dies Egyp-
tiaci* are reckoned, two in each month except January,
which contains three.[2] A mediæval French manuscript,
dating from the reign of St. Louis, includes twenty-
four such days, but another manuscript, of the fourteenth century, enumerates thirty days of the year
as very dangerous, when it is necessary to abstain
from buying and selling, building, and planting. Still
another manuscript, of the fifteenth century, reckons
thirty-one wholly evil days, while certain hours of
other days also possess dangerous qualities.[3] In the
seventeenth century J. B. Thiers, the learned curé of
Vibraie, notices the "Egyptian days" in his extensive
list of the superstitious beliefs regarding certain times
and seasons, prevalent in his age but condemned by
theologians (St. Thomas Aquinas), popes (Nicholas I),
and Church synods and councils.[4] Anglo-Saxon calen-

[1] Augustine, *In crocem ad Penit. ep.
ad Galatas*, 4; Ambrose, *Epist.* i,
23; compare Marinus, *Vita Procli*, 19.

[2] *Corpus inscriptionum Latinarum*, i, pt. i,² 256, 297, with T.
Mommsen's commentary. The
anonymous author of the *Versus de
diebus Egyptiacis* (*Poetæ latini
minores*, ed. A. Baehrens, v. 354-
356) reduces their number to
twenty-four:

*Bis deni binique dies scribuntur in
anno,*

*In quibus una solet mortalibus hora
timeri.*

[3] L. Moland, "Calendrier français du treizième siècle," *Revue
archéologique*, 1862, n.s. v. 103
sq.

[4] J. B. Thiers, *Traité des superstitions*,⁴ Paris, 1741, i. 311 sq.
See further Karl Meyer, *Der
Aberglaube des Mittelalters*, Basel,
1884, p. 210; Du Cange, *Glos-
sarium mediæ et infimæ Latinitatis*,
ed. Favre, iii, 106 sq.

dars mention about twenty-four "Egyptian days" in
the year, when it is dangerous, if not fatal, to begin an
enterprise or to travel. A manuscript calendar, dating
from the reign of Henry VI, gives a list of thirty-two
such days. After the Reformation the old unlucky
days appear to have abated much of their malevo-
lence, and to have left behind them only a general
superstition against fishermen starting out to fish, or
seamen to take a voyage, or landsmen a journey, or
domestic servants to enter a new place — on a Friday.[1]

[1] Chambers's *Book of Days*, i, 41.
See also O. Cockayne, *Leechdoms,
Wortcunning, and Starcraft of Early
England*, London, 1866, iii, 150-
197, and John Aubrey's quaint
essay on "Day-fatality; or, Some
Observations of Days Lucky and
Unlucky" (*Miscellanies upon Various Subjects*, London, 1784, pp. 3-
36). Some rules concerning "peril-
ous days" are reprinted by Sir
Lawrence Gomme from a fifteenth
century manuscript (*Folk-lore*, 1913,
xxiv, 121-123).

CONCLUSION

It is fairly obvious that the observance of tabooed and unlucky days must be included among the many superstitions which have retarded the progress of mankind. They hinder individual initiative and tend to prevent the undertaking of lengthy enterprises which may be interrupted by the recurrence of an unfavourable period. Their extensive development compels fitful, intermittent labour, rather than a steady and continuous occupation. The Burman, for example, "is so fettered by his horoscope and the lucky and unlucky days for him recorded therein, which are taught him in rhymes from childhood, that the character has been given him by strangers of alternate idleness and energy. But both are enforced by the numerous days and seasons when he may not work without disaster to himself. Unlucky days cause him so much fear that he will resort to all sorts of excuses to avoid business on them. Similarly, on lucky days he will work beyond his strength, because he is assured of success."[1] Again, it is said that Europeans in India usually fail to realize the great influence which ideas of lucky and unlucky days exert on the conduct of the people. Superstitious avoidance of unpropitious occasions will often explain the failure of the natives to obey a court summons or to keep their appointments with government officers.[2] These remarks, by keen

[1] Sir R. C. Temple, "Burma," in Hastings's *Encyclopædia of Religion and Ethics*, iii. 20; compare Shway Yoe [Sir J. G. Scott], *The Burman, his Life and Notions*, London, 1910, pp. 583–586. On the unlucky days observed in Upper Burma see *Gazetteer of Upper Burma and the Shan States*, edited by Scott and Hardiman, Rangoon, 1900, pt. i, vol. ii, 48 sq.

[2] W. Crooke, *Popular Religion and Folk-lore of Northern India*, Westminster, 1896, ii. 52 sq.

observers, are capable of a wide application to various primitive races. The belief in unfavourable seasons may even directly affect political and social progress, where, as in modern Ashanti and in ancient Rome, assemblies could not be held, or courts of justice stand open, or armies engage the enemy, when the unlucky day came round. It is equally obvious that all such beliefs play into the hands of the astrologer and magician, tending further to strengthen the bonds with which superstition enchains its votaries.

From the economic point of view it deserves to be pointed out how the excessive development of unlucky and unlucky days seriously limits production and thus lowers the efficiency of labour. In Hawaii the seasons of strict abstinence regularly observed during eight months of the year reached a total of seventy-two days, while from time to time still other unlucky days were appointed by the priests.[1] In Ashanti an old writer calculated that there were only from one hundred and fifty to one hundred and sixty days in the year during which business of any importance could be safely undertaken.[2] Few peoples have more holidays than the Hopi Indians of Arizona. Their religious festivals occupy more than half the year. It is a noteworthy fact, however, that the Hopi celebrate their longest and most important ceremonies during the months from harvest time to planting, when there is little work to be done. "Although the Pueblo farmer may thoroughly believe in his ceremonial system as efficacious, his human nature is too practical to consume the precious planting time with elaborate ceremonials."[3] In modern China and Korea so many

[1] C. Kato, Hawaiian Antiquities. Honolulu, 1903, p. 20.

[2] J. Dupuis, Journal of a Residence in Ashantee. London, 1824, pt. ii.; compare John Beecham, Ashantee and the Gold Coast. London, 1841, p. 188.

[3] J. W. Fewkes, "Tusayan Ceremonial." Fifteenth Annual Report of the Bureau of American Ethnology, Washington, 1897, p. 273. The Hopi furnish one of the few instances of harvest-rest days to be found among the American Indians. They hold a mid-winter festival, called the soyaluna, at the

festivals in honour of deities are observed as holidays
that they take the place, to a certain extent, of the
Sabbath institution.[1] Among the ancient Egyptians
the unlucky days varied in number according to the
different months, six, for instance, occurring in Paophi,
seven each in Choiak and Phamenoth, and five in
Pharmuthi. It may be reckoned that "popular superstition rendered useless about one-fifth of the year."[2]
The Athenian festivals are estimated to have occupied
from fifty to sixty days of the year. The irregular
distribution of these holidays throughout the months,
and especially their congestion in spring and autumn,
must have caused much interference with the routine
of daily life.[3] In some city-states the festivals were
more numerous: at Tarentum, in the days of its prosperity, the people are said to have had more holidays
than working days.[4]

In the old Roman calendar, out of three hundred
and fifty-five days, nearly one-third (one hundred and
nine) were marked as *nefasti*, that is, as unlawful for
judicial and political business. These days belonged
wholly to the gods, while eleven more days of the year
were shared by the divine and the human inhabitants
of the city.[5] We know on the evidence of Cicero that

time of the winter solstice. "December is regarded as a sacred
month; no work is performed in it,
and few games are allowed. It is
the month of the return of the sun
and the gods, and bears the same
name as July, in which they
depart" (J. W. Fewkes, "The
Winter Solstice Ceremony at
Walpi," *American Anthropologist*,
1898, xi, 69).

[1] J. H. Gray, *China*, London,
1878, i, 249; W. E. Griffis, *Corea,
the Hermit Nation*, New York,
1889, p. 295. According to one
account the shops in China are
shut and all business suspended
only on the first three days of the
year, though these and numerous

other festivals, both general and
local, are common occasions for
relaxation and merry-making (S.
W. Williams, *The Middle Kingdom*,
New York, 1883, i, 809).

[2] Maspero, *New Light on Ancient
Egypt*, p. 135.

[3] G. F. Schoemann, *Griechische
Alterthümer*, edited by J. H.
Lipsius, Berlin, 1897–1902, ii,
458 sq.; compare Plato, *Leges*, ii,
653; Thucydides, ii, 38.

[4] Strabo, *Geographica*, vi, 3, 4.

[5] This calculation assumes 109
dies nefasti, 192 *dies fasti et comitiales*, on which assemblies might
meet, 43 *dies fasti non comitiales*,
available for judicial business but
not for meetings of the assemblies,

in the last century of the republic the numerous days when courts could not sit had become a resource on which a wealthy criminal could speculate as a means of delaying and evading justice; while Suetonius enumerates among the praiseworthy reforms of Augustus the cutting-down of non-judicial days by thirty, "in order that crimes might not escape punishment or business be impeded by delay."[1] Of the *dies nefasti* sixty-one, including the Ides of every month, the Kalends of three months, and the Nones of July, were numbered in the republican calendar among the public festivals — *feriæ publicæ* — on which the state expected the citizens to abstain, as far as possible, from their private business and labour.[2] But the number of rest days observed really reached a larger total, when we remember that, besides the extraordinary *feriæ*, proclaimed from time to time, there was a marked tendency during the last two centuries of the republic to extend over several days festivals to which originally only one day had been allotted. This was for the purpose of giving time for an elaborate programme of public games (*ludi*), consisting of chariot-races, stage plays, and other forms of popular amusement. As the Roman passion for holidays and their attendant spectacles increased, we find the number of days devoted to them rising from sixty-six in the reign of Augustus to eighty-seven in that of Tiberius, and, under Marcus Aurelius, to a hundred and thirty-five. By the middle of the fourth century their number had reached one hundred and seventy-five.[3] For the lower classes at Rome the gladiatorial combats, chariot-

8 *dies intercisi*, or days partly *fasti* and partly *nefasti*, and 3 *dies fissi* (Wissowa, *Religion und Kultus der Römer*, pp. 368 *sq.*).

[1] Cicero, *In Verrem*, i, 10; Suetonius, *Divus Augustus*, 32. It has been already noticed (above, p. 97) that Roman consuls sometimes instituted extraordinary *feriæ* for the purpose of blocking legislation by their rivals, ferial days being included in the *dies nefasti*.

[2] Above, pp. 94 *sqq.*, 170.

[3] L. Friedländer, *Roman Life and Manners under the Early Empire*, London, 1908, ii, 11 *sq.*; W. W. Fowler, *Social Life at Rome in the Age of Cicero*, New York, 1909, pp. 287 *sqq.* Though the ancients were careful to distinguish the

x

races, and dramatic shows formed the chief pleasure of life. The once-sovereign people of Rome became a lazy, worthless rabble, fed by the state and amused with the games. Of them it was well said by an ancient satirist that they wanted only two things to make them happy — "bread and the games of the circus."[1]

Many of the holy days in the religious calendar of Christendom were borrowed, as is well known, from the public festivals of ancient paganism. This must be the chief reason for the observance of so many non-working days during the Middle Ages. Their number was largely reduced in Protestant Europe as the result of the Reformation, which did away with the majority of saints' days. In Catholic countries, however, there is still an excessive amount of time devoted to religious celebrations. Mexico, for instance, is described as "a land of holidays. Counting Sundays, there are one hundred and thirty-one in the Mexican calendar, and it is asserted that more than half of the people observe them all. . . . On certain of these days all Mexico takes to the festival, and it usually requires from one to three days for the *peons* to sober up and get back to regular work again."[2] The Greek Church, as a celebrated traveller and historian once pointed out, requires her followers to observe so many holy days "as practically to shorten the lives of the people very materially. I believe that one-third of the number of days in the year are 'kept holy,' or rather, *kept stupid,* in honour of the saints: no great portion of the time thus set apart is spent in religious exercises and the people don't betake themselves to any animating pastimes, which might serve to strengthen the frame, or invigorate the

---

feriæ from the *ludi* (compare Gellius, *Noctes Atticæ*, ii, 24, 11: *Diebus ludorum et feriis quibusdam*), yet in late republican and imperial times the joyous aspects of the *feriæ* had become so prominent that nearly all of them were converted into *ludi*.

[1] *Panem et circenses* (Juvenal, x, 81).

[2] W. J. Showalter, in *National Geographic Magazine*, 1914, xxv, 493.

mind, or exalt the taste."[1] In Russia commercial and educational progress is hindered by the multitude of saints' days. "The *dies nefas*, when work is tabooed, becomes a serious handicap in the race of modern life. These saints' days, together with the Sundays, rob the Russian of nearly one-third of his time, for they leave him only about two hundred and fifty days for work. He would sooner work on a Sunday than on a saint's day."[2] In eastern Galicia, where a calendar is in use which permits the observance of the religious festivals of both the Roman and the Greek churches, the number of holidays or non-working days is considerably in excess of one hundred, rising in some districts to one hundred and fifty, and in others reaching the amazing total of two hundred.[3] To what extremes the practice of abstaining from labour on holy days may extend is further illustrated in Abyssinia, where the numerous fasts and feasts are so strictly kept as to render about six months of the year prohibited for any secular employments.[4]

Human nature, it has been said, is always ready for the shift from fast to feast, from Sabbath to Saturnalia. To the student of primitive religion and sociology nothing is more interesting than the contemplation of that unconscious though beneficent process which has converted institutions, based partly or wholly on a belief in the imaginary and the supernatural, into institutions resting on the rock of reason and promoting human welfare. Though the origin of tabooed and unlucky days must be sought in gross superstition, sooner or later they acquire a secular character and may then be perpetuated as holidays, long after their earlier significance has disappeared. The transition, with all its subtle and manifold results on the organization

[1] A. W. Kinglake, *Eothen*, chap. v.
[2] W. F. Adeney, *The Greek and Eastern Churches*, New York, 1908, p. 433.
[3] L. Caro, *Auswanderung und Auswanderungspolitik in Osterreich*, Leipzig, 1909, p. 56.
[4] W. C. Harris, *The Highlands of Ethiopia*, New York [1843], p. 280.

of society, may be followed under our own eyes. The
passage of the holy day into the holiday, beginning in
the lower culture, promises to reach its culmination in
the secularizing of all the great festivals of the Christian year. This evolutionary movement, whether for
weal or woe, at least provides a singularly instructive illustration of the close relations between religion
and social progress, which must ever impress the in-
quirer into the early history of mankind.

INDEX

Primitive Secret Societies

A STUDY IN EARLY POLITICS AND RELIGION

By HUTTON WEBSTER, Ph.D.

Professor of Social Anthropology in the University of Nebraska

---

8vo   Cloth, gilt top $2.00

" The value of his work is apparent, and his book is the most satisfactory presentation of its subject so far made in English. It is the most important American contribution to anthropological theory that has appeared for a long time."

— Frederick Starr, in *The Dial*, 1908.

" As a summary and interpretation of a mass of observations made by many scientists on the social relations of youth among the lower races, it is indeed a significant work. Nowhere else, perhaps, in one volume, may a reader obtain so comprehensive a view of this subject. The author has therefore made a distinct contribution to psychological and sociological literature." — *Literary Digest*, 1908.

" The subject is one of great interest for the ethnologist and the sociologist. Professor Webster has brought together the facts clearly, methodically, and in a manner to impress the reader, even if he has given much previous attention to the subject."

— *Boston Evening Transcript*, 1908.

" This is a solid piece of work. The wide range of Professor Webster's researches shows his scholarly industry; better still is the skill with which he has arranged his material. The result is, a book that can be read with interest." — *Harvard Graduates' Magazine*, 1908.

THE MACMILLAN COMPANY

Publishers   64-66 Fifth Avenue   New York

Primitive Secret Societies — (Cont'd)

"The study bears evidence of wide and careful research as well as industry and skill in the arrangement of material."
—*American Political Science Review*, 1908.

"The descriptive part of the work is excellent, the literature has been thoroughly and almost exhaustively digested, the notes and references are admirable, and the work is one which the student of these matters at once pronounces indispensable."
—W. I. Thomas in *American Historical Review*, 1908.

"This monograph is one of the most important studies in historical and descriptive sociology that has appeared in America since the publication of Morgan's 'Ancient Society.' While less pretentious than that work it is, nevertheless, a most satisfying contribution upon a division of early social history that has been either neglected or treated only incidentally. . . . As an example of scholarly research, judicious statement, and careful interpretation, the book leaves little for criticism."
—U. G. Weatherly, in *Economic Bulletin*, 1908.

"This is probably the best general work on the subject that has yet appeared, at least in English. It is not, of course, exhaustive, being intended, apparently, rather as a textbook for the beginner in anthropology, or a convenient summary of our present knowledge of this subject, than as a treatise for the research student. Viewed in this way it fills a need which instructors in anthropology must feel at the present time, and fills it well."
—J. R. Swanton, in *American Anthropologist*, 1908.

THE MACMILLAN COMPANY
Publishers   64-66 Fifth Avenue   New York

"This is an excellent book, which every anthropologist will do well to add to his working library. Dr. Webster evidently puts his faith in the Tylorian method of going straight to the facts, and letting them, as far as possible, tell their own story. . . . As a systematic arrangement of well-chosen evidence it will take a high place amongst contemporary aids to anthropological study."

— *The Athenæum*, 1908.

"La question des sociétés secrètes chez les peuples primitifs y est serrée de plus près qu'on ne l'avait fait jusqu'alors et elle est traitée d'une manière très méthodique."

— J. M. Lahy, in *Revue des Études Ethnographiques et Sociologiques*, 1909.

"Die klar und exakt geschriebene Arbeit stellt sich als eine wertvolle Ergänzung zu dem Buche des deutschen Forschers dar, namentlich dadurch, dass er die Mannbarkeitsweihen, die Schurtz nür flüchtig gestreift hat, in den Mittelpunkt der Untersuchung rückt. Kein Forscher, der sich mit der gleichen Frage beschäftigt, wird an Webster's Werk vorübergehen dürfen."

— Gustav Antze, in *Mitteilungen der Anthropologischen Gesellschaft in Wien*, 1910.

THE MACMILLAN COMPANY

Publishers   64-66 Fifth Avenue   New York

CPSIA information can be obtained
at www.ICGtesting.com
Printed in the USA
LVHW051526140523
746958LV00011B/1036